Rethinking EU Law-making Policy on Confiscation of the Proceeds of Crime

The book provides a critical analysis of EU law-making policy on the confiscation of the proceeds of crime, using a minimalist restorative approach to justice focused on the rights of victims and communities, and more proactive roles for all participants in confiscation procedures.

This book shows how the examined policy has been translated into the EU law standards adopted as its realisation and whether the gaps identified in these standards are reflected in the domestic law of the comparator EU jurisdictions: Poland, Germany, and France. The post-conviction confiscation regime in England and Wales is also explored as an example of an alternative non-EU model of value-based confiscation. Considering the complex juridical nature of confiscation, which challenges the applicability of the civil–criminal dichotomy, this book recommends a twofold approach when shaping EU confiscation mechanisms, focused on linking policy objectives with a restorative approach to justice, and making the appropriate choice of criminal or civil routes for confiscation.

This book will be of key interest to scholars, students, and practitioners in EU policy and law, criminal law, EU and national law on confiscation, EU criminal justice policy, and more broadly to European studies, criminology, and international organisations.

Ariadna H. Ochnio is Assistant Professor at the Institute of Law Studies of the Polish Academy of Sciences, Warsaw, Poland.

Routledge / UACES Contemporary European Studies

The primary objective of the new Contemporary European Studies series is to provide a research outlet for scholars of European Studies from all disciplines. The series publishes important scholarly works and aims to forge for itself an international reputation.

Series editors: **Eleanor Brooks**, *University of Edinburgh, UK*, **Ben Farrand**, *Newcastle University, UK*, **Helena Farrand Carrapico**, *Northumbria University, UK*, **Benjamin Martill**, *University of Edinburgh, UK*, on behalf of the *University Association for Contemporary European Studies.*

The European Universities Initiative and the 'Euro-internationalisation' of European Higher Education
Edited by Alexander Frame and Barbara Curyło

The Development of Energy Policy in the European Union
Continuity, Critical Junctures and Change
Ingmar Versolmann

The Territorial Dimension of EU Knowledge Policies
Higher Education Institutions for Europe
Alina J. Felder-Stindt

Rethinking EU Law-making Policy on Confiscation of the Proceeds of Crime
Ariadna H. Ochnio

For more information about this series, please visit: www.routledge.com/Routledge-UACES-Contemporary-European-Studies/book-series/UACES

Rethinking EU Law-making Policy on Confiscation of the Proceeds of Crime

Ariadna H. Ochnio

UACES

Routledge
Taylor & Francis Group
LONDON AND NEW YORK

First published 2025
by Routledge
4 Park Square, Milton Park, Abingdon, Oxon OX14 4RN

and by Routledge
605 Third Avenue, New York, NY 10158

Routledge is an imprint of the Taylor & Francis Group, an informa business

British Library Cataloguing-in-Publication Data
A catalogue record for this book is available from the British Library

Library of Congress Cataloging-in-Publication Data
Names: Ochnio, Ariadna H., author.
Title: Rethinking EU law-making policy on confiscation of the proceeds of crime / Ariadna H. Ochnio. Other titles: Rethinking European Union law-making policy on confiscation of the proceeds of crime
Description: Abingdon, Oxon [UK]; New York, NY: Routledge, 2025. | Series: Routledge / UACES contemporary European studies | Includes bibliographical references and index.
Identifiers: LCCN 2024061173 (print) | LCCN 2024061174 (ebook) | ISBN 9781032737669 (hardback) | ISBN 9781032737676 (paperback) | ISBN 9781003465829 (ebook)
Subjects: LCSH: Confiscations–Europe. | Confiscations–European Union countries. | Forfeiture–Europe. | Forfeiture–European Union countries. | Criminal procedure–European Union countries. | Criminal law–European Union countries. | Legislation–European Union countries.
Classification: LCC KJC8251.F67 O34 2025 (print) | LCC KJC8251.F67 (ebook) | DDC 345.24/0773–dc23/eng/20250110
LC record available at https://lccn.loc.gov/2024061173
LC ebook record available at https://lccn.loc.gov/2024061174

ISBN: 978-1-032-73766-9 (hbk)
ISBN: 978-1-032-73767-6 (pbk)
ISBN: 978-1-003-46582-9 (ebk)

DOI: 10.4324/9781003465829

Typeset in Times New Roman
by Deanta Global Publishing Services, Chennai, India

To My Wonderful Children

Contents

Acknowledgements

This book has been written largely thanks to a research grant awarded by the National Science Centre, Poland, Project No. 2019/33/B/HS5/01617. I am likewise grateful to my home Institute of Law Studies of the Polish Academy of Sciences for making the implementation of this project possible. I would also like to express my sincere gratitude to the Faculty of Law of the University of Cambridge for the invitation to be a visiting academic and the Cambridge Centre for Criminal Justice for the possibility to present and discuss the research results of this project. Special thanks are also due to the Max Planck Institute for Comparative Public Law and International Law in Heidelberg for making a research visit possible for the purposes of this project. Words of gratitude are also directed to the reviewers and series editors for their constructive comments which have helped to improve this book. My sincere thanks also go to Rob Brooks for his valuable comments on language issues.

Ariadna H. Ochnio
Warsaw, 30 November 2024

Acronyms and abbreviations

ADR	Alternative Dispute Resolution
AFSJ	Area of Freedom, Security and Justice
AGRASC	*Agence de gestion et de recouvrement des avoirs saisis et confisqués* (Agency for the management and recovery of seized and confiscated asset)
AML(D)	Anti-Money Laundering (Directive)
App(s)	Application(s)
ARO	Asset Recovery Office
CARIN (Network)	Camden Asset Recovery Inter-agency Network
CATS	Coordinating Committee in the area of police and judicial cooperation in criminal matters
CC	Criminal Code
CCP	Code of Criminal Procedure
CETS	Council of Europe Treaty Series
CFSP	Common Foreign and Security Policy
Charter	Charter of Fundamental Rights of the European Union (2016), OJ C 202/389
CiFAR	Civil Forum for Asset Recovery
CJEU	Court of Justice of the European Union
CoE	Council of Europe
Council Directive 2004/80/EC	Council Directive 2004/80/EC of 29 April 2004 relating to compensation to crime victims (2004), OJ L 261/15
CPC	Confiscation of the Proceeds of Crime
Decision 2007/845/JHA	Council Decision 2007/845/JHA of 6 December 2007 concerning cooperation between Asset Recovery Offices of the Member States in the field of tracing and identification of proceeds from, or other property related to, crime (2007), OJ L 332/103
Directive 2011/36/EU	Directive 2011/36/EU of the European Parliament and of the Council of 5 April

	2011 on preventing and combating trafficking in human beings and protecting its victims, and replacing Council Framework Decision 2002/629/JHA (2011), OJ L 101/1
Directive 2012/29/EU	Directive 2012/29/EU of the European Parliament and of the Council of 25 October 2012 establishing minimum standards on the rights, support and protection of victims of crime, and replacing Council Framework Decision 2001/220/JHA (2012), OJ L 315/57
Directive 2014/42/EU	Directive 2014/42/EU of the European Parliament and of the Council of 3 April 2014 on the freezing and confiscation of instrumentalities and proceeds of crime in the European Union (2014), OJ L 127/39
Directive 2024/1260	Directive (EU) 2024/1260 of the European Parliament and of the Council of 24 April 2024 on asset recovery and confiscation (2024), OJ L 2024/1260
Directive 2024/1226	Directive (EU) 2024/1226 of the European Parliament and of the Council of 24 April 2024 on the definition of criminal offences and penalties for the violation of Union restrictive measures and amending Directive (EU) 2018/1673 (2024), OJ L 2024/1226
EAW	European Arrest Warrant
ECHR	European Convention on Human Rights
ECJ	European Court of Justice
ECOFIN	Economic and Financial Affairs Council
ECtHR	European Court of Human Rights
EESC	European Economic and Social Committee
EIO	European Investigation Order
EJN	European Judicial Network
EP	European Parliament
EPPO	European Public Prosecutor's Office
ETS	European Treaty Series
EU	European Union
Europol	European Union Agency for Law Enforcement Cooperation
FATF	Financial Action Task Force
FATF Recommendations	International Standards on Combating Money Laundering and the Financing of Terrorism and Proliferation adopted by the Financial Action Task Force Plenary (2012–2023), Paris: FATF, www.fatf-gafi.org

	/en/publications/Fatfrecommendations/Fatf-recommendations.html
FD	Framework Decision
FD 2001/500/JHA	Council Framework Decision of 26 June 2001 on money laundering, the identification, tracing, freezing, seizing and confiscation of instrumentalities and the proceeds of crime (2001), OJ L 182/1
FD 2003/577/JHA	Council Framework Decision 2003/577/JHA of 22 July 2003 on the execution in the European Union of orders freezing property or evidence (2003), OJ L 196/45
FD 2005/212/JHA	Council Framework Decision of 24 February 2005 on Confiscation of Crime-Related Proceeds, Instrumentalities and Property (2005), OJ L 68/49
FD 2006/783/JHA	Council Framework Decision 2006/783/JHA of 6 October 2006 on the application of the principle of mutual recognition to confiscation orders (2006), OJ L 328/59
FRA	European Union Agency for Fundamental Rights
GFAR	Global Forum on Asset Recovery
JHA (Council)	Justice and Home Affairs (Council)
LIBE	Committee on Civil Liberties, Justice and Home Affairs of the European Parliament
MLA	Mutual Legal Assistance
MONEYVAL	Council of Europe Committee of Experts on the Evaluation of Anti-Money Laundering Measures and the Financing of Terrorism
MS	European Union Member States
NCBC	Non-conviction Based Confiscation
New York Convention	United Nations International Convention for the Suppression of the Financing of Terrorism (1999), UNTS 2178, p. 197
OECD	Organisation for Economic Co-operation and Development
OHCHR	Office of the United Nations High Commissioner for Human Rights
Palermo Convention	United Nations Convention against Transnational Organised Crime (2000), UNTS 2225, p. 209
POCA (2002)	Proceeds of Crime Act (2002), UK Public General Acts 2002 c. 29

Proposal for a directive on confiscation (2022)	Proposal for a directive of the European Parliament and of the Council on asset recovery and confiscation (2022), COM(2022) 245 final, 2022/0167(COD)
Regulation 2018/1805	Regulation (EU) 2018/1805 of the European Parliament and of the Council of 14 November 2018 on the mutual recognition of freezing orders and confiscation orders (2018), OJ L 303/1
Strasbourg Convention	Council of Europe Convention on Laundering, Search, Seizure and Confiscation of the Proceeds from Crime (1990), ETS 141
TEU	Treaty on European Union, consolidated version (2016), OJ C 202/13
TFEU	Treaty on the Functioning of the European Union, consolidated version (2016), OJ C 202/47
UN	United Nations
UNCAC	United Nations Convention against Corruption (2003), UNTS 2349, p. 41
UNODC	United Nations Office on Drugs and Crime
UNTS	United Nations Treaty Series
Vienna Convention	United Nations Convention against Illicit Traffic in Narcotic Drugs and Psychotropic Substances (1988), UNTS 1582, p. 95
Warsaw Convention	Council of Europe Convention on Laundering, Search, Seizure and Confiscation of the Proceeds from Crime and on the Financing of Terrorism (2005), CETS 198

1 Introduction

The rationale of the study

The confiscation of the proceeds of crime (CPC) is a legal institution used in EU policy to combat serious and organised crime having a cross-border dimension. However, despite originally being rooted in the fight against serious and organised crime, its use continues to grow as the EU responds to different types of profit-driven crime, including those not having an organised nature or being of the most serious gravity. The CPC also remains a major concept for other standard setters, e.g., the United Nations (UN), Council of Europe (CoE), and Financial Action Task Force (FATF), who in certain areas offer even more advanced solutions than the EU. The institution of confiscation is continuously being developed in EU policy, but there are still many outstanding issues. The main difficulties arise from challenging the traditional rules of the criminal process, while at the same time ensuring human rights protections in confiscation proceedings. In addition, there are areas that to date have been overlooked in EU confiscation policy, such as the social potential of criminal confiscation, which is currently under-exploited.

The institution of criminal confiscation, i.e., belonging to the criminal realm, in both punitive and non-punitive forms, contains many complex issues. Although it is the dominant type of confiscation across the Member States (MS), in addition to being covered by EU law, the literature has not discussed it as widely as civil confiscation (both in the form dynamically developing in European civil law jurisdictions, and that well-established in common law jurisdictions).

The CPC was examined under research project No. 2019/33/B/HS5/01617, funded by the National Science Centre, Poland. The project included analysis of EU confiscation policy, the legal standards adopted in this field, and its impact on the criminal law of selected European jurisdictions. Starting out, a normative analysis at the EU law layer was conducted in a 'mechanical' manner. The turning point in the research process came when comparing the initial research results with the results of a micro-level analysis of the development of EU policy on the CPC over time (in the pre- and post-Lisbon periods). The juxtaposition of the research results revealed that the entire concept of the CPC in EU policy and law is based on ill-defined assumptions centred around the interests of the State. The State plays two dominant roles: a fighter against profit-making cross-border crime and simultaneously the principal beneficiary of the confiscated assets. In the next stage of the

DOI: 10.4324/9781003465829-1

research process, the results of the comparative studies showed that the MS, partly influenced by EU law, had analogously shaped the legal constructs of confiscation in their domestic laws. As in the EU confiscation mechanism, the position of victims of crime was considered secondary to the position of the State or, in some areas, was even excluded from consideration. The research revealed the need for a reconceptualisation of confiscation at the EU policy level, developing it in a direction that would strengthen the position of the victim and other social actors (at least at the disposal phase of confiscation proceedings) while respecting the interests of defendants and third parties. At the same time, EU criminal policy has started making references to restorative justice, so a restorative approach to justice seemed a promising theoretical context and reference point for further research.

The research results showed that there are areas where EU policy has officially declared objectives in pursuit of a restorative approach to justice, but the EU legal standards do not have a corresponding focus. This incongruity between officially declared policy goals and the methods available for achieving them in law, i.e., a comparison of means to ends (solemn declarations but no appropriate action taken), challenges the rationality of the EU lawmakers. This book advocates for adopting a restorative approach to justice when shaping confiscation mechanisms at the EU level. This means, firstly, the determination of the restorative objectives of confiscation. Secondly, giving priority to victims' interests over those of the States. Thirdly, the provision of appropriate safeguards for the rights of all participants in confiscation proceedings (defendants, third parties, victims, communities). It should be emphasised that the perspective of human rights protections is strongly embedded within the restorative approach to justice. Fourthly, this approach implies the involvement of three principal stakeholders (victims, communities, offenders) to the maximum extent possible in confiscation procedures, especially in the disposal of assets phase, which offers the greatest potential for proceeding in a more restorative manner.

It can be assumed that effective changes to EU confiscation mechanisms depend on the political maturity and current stage of development of legal institutions specific to confiscation (evolutionary approach). According to the minimalist restorative approach to justice adopted in the book, related to conventional criminal justice mechanisms (explained in detail later, in a separate subsection), even minimally increasing the restorativeness of EU confiscation policy can enable considerable progress towards enhancing its social impact. However, adopting a bolder position, the restorative approach may serve as the catalyst for significant changes in the way EU criminal justice policy is conducted and may even influence wider EU policy across many areas.

Public policies regarding confiscation mechanisms have their own unique social dimensions, which should be viewed from a broader perspective. For instance, critique of the concept of integration through law has highlighted its lack of philosophical foundations (Williams 2009, 549–552), as well as low sensitivity to social issues and the overlapping problems of imbalances and particularities within the EU (Azoulai 2016, 461; Davies 2014). In view of the above, reorienting EU confiscation policy towards a more restorative path would at a minimum involve greater consideration of three major stakeholders: the victim, the offender, and the community. An emanation of this policy should be higher EU legal standards, aimed at improving national confiscation schemes, i.a., by better integration of social factors. In addition, restorative justice accounts may provide some philosophical underpinnings for the future shaping of EU confiscation policy, which, being deeply intertwined with other EU policies (e.g., anti-corruption, anti-fraud, anti-money laundering (AML) and combating the financing of terrorism (CFT) policies), could advance the entire area of freedom, security and justice (AFSJ).

The ambition of the book is to provide a far-reaching perspective. The considerations presented herein may have universal appeal to all EU criminal justice policy areas, especially by challenging the prioritisation of the interests of MS over the interests of the EU's citizens and residents. They can also serve to inspire national legislatures when shaping their internal confiscation strategies or other strategies in response to crime.

Why is a restorative justice approach desirable in EU law-making policy on the confiscation of the proceeds of crime?

Eventually, one might wonder why a restorative justice approach is desirable in EU law-making policy on the CPC, especially given that a humanistic approach may offer just as many benefits for the participants in conventional confiscation procedures. Moreover, the underpinnings of a humanistic approach are rooted in a well-established legal and jurisprudential *acquis* in the area of human rights protection. An argument may also be made that strengthening only the rights of victims at the EU level would be an easier path and do the same job as implementing more restorative confiscation mechanisms across the EU. However, when considering whether a humanistic or solely victim-oriented approach can positively influence legislatures, a counter-question arises. Can such approaches prompt a critical rethinking of confiscation objectives and a shift in how legislatures view the roles of victims, communities, defendants, and States in confiscation mechanisms? When answering this question, a substantial difference emerges between these alternatives and a restorative approach. A restorative approach may help to base the EU and national confiscation schemes on the principle that confiscated assets are returned to victims and communities affected by or vulnerable to crime. Secondly, it may help to reconsider the position of defendants, moving them away from being passive recipients of confiscation decisions to active participants in shaping their operation. The second counter-question is whether a humanistic or solely victim-oriented approach has the potential to make confiscation procedures more inclusive, balanced, consultative, and open to a dialogue between victims and communities on one side, and defendants and third parties on the other, stepping away from the arbitrary definition of their interests and rights by the State.

The difference is even deeper, because recasting EU law-making policy on the CPC towards restorative justice means addressing policy not to MS but to the EU's citizens and residents, thus matching the policy questions and goals to the people's needs and interests. Accordingly, including a restorative approach in this policy means that the rights of victims and communities are positioned above the rights of MS and that MS play the role of intermediaries in implementing the policy, rather than being its ultimate addressees. Finally, a restorative approach offers more than a humanistic or solely victim-oriented approach, capturing the strengths of both, since guaranteeing human rights is the necessary minimum required when shaping any responses to crime under a restorative approach. In addition, the victims of crime are at the centre of such responses.

The thematic thread that runs through the book is that there is room to increase the restorativeness of conventional confiscation mechanisms (court-ordered) across the EU by implementing at least a minimalist restorative approach to justice in three dimensions: EU law-making policy on the CPC, EU law standards established in this respect, and national law being shaped under the influence of these standards. In this configuration EU law-making policy on the CPC is considered to be the main factor determining the content of both EU and national confiscation law. EU law standards are considered agents of influence on MS, and MS act as intermediaries in shaping national law addressed to EU citizens and residents, in line with the assumptions of EU law-making policy. Importantly, under this approach, the social potential of this policy may be boosted by the EU's citizens and residents at the grassroots level if it is truly addressed to their needs and interests. However, ultimately MS and the EU itself would equally be beneficiaries of such policy reorientation.

Research questions and methodology

As part of the broader EU criminal justice policy, EU confiscation policy has recently begun referencing restorative justice. Provided that the assumptions of this policy regarding the objectives of confiscation are redefined and implemented into concrete legal solutions, this may be a promising paradigm shift for the policy. Notwithstanding future developments, this development raises fundamental questions: what exactly is offered by a restorative approach to justice, how restorative is EU confiscation policy, and how can its restorativeness be increased?

The main benefit of adopting a restorative approach is the opportunity to refresh the very concept of confiscation (see Chapter 2). However, bearing in mind the versatility of this approach, it may have an even broader impact by offering a new vision of development for the AFSJ. One clear advantage of this approach is that, at minimum, it facilitates a critical reassessment of the current EU confiscation policy, enabling an evaluation of its assumptions to determine both its present developmental stage and the desired future direction. Going further, the conclusions may be relevant for the future of the AFSJ as a whole.

Another strength of the restorative justice concept is that it represents a space where retributivist and reductivist approaches can meet, thus many of the current EU confiscation policy assumptions remain relevant within a more restorative course. At the same time, restorative justice offers a new quality in thinking about EU criminal policy and law, transcending the human rights perspective (humanistic approach), and prompting a search for more advanced solutions to engage all the stakeholders of a 'criminal case' and the related 'confiscation case' (victims, offenders, communities). Strengthening the position of these stakeholders is also relevant to the development of civil society. Accordingly, EU confiscation policy taking a more restorative path may lay the groundwork for greater effectiveness of EU policy in many other areas.

A distinguishing element of the restorative approach to justice is that changes introduced into conventional criminal justice mechanisms, including the confiscation mechanism, may gain grassroots support from EU citizens and residents, because this approach is oriented towards making victims and communities the principal beneficiaries of confiscation. Accordingly, through the return of confiscated assets to the population, confiscation may implicitly strengthen civil society and resilience to crime. The acceptance of changes by EU citizens and residents, seeing their interests placed at the centre of EU confiscation policy instead of the interests of the State, could speed up legal integration in the area of confiscation and breathe new life into this process, especially in the face of recent crises of trust that have disrupted cooperation in criminal matters.

The minimalist restorative approach promoted in this book offers a modern look at the conventional confiscation mechanisms. Apart from strengthening the positions of stakeholders in a 'confiscation case' (defendants, third parties, victims, communities), it grants them some element of decisiveness, as it does not arbitrarily define their interests and how they should be best protected. In addition, it offers the opportunity to use the capabilities of confiscation mechanisms for true rehabilitation of offenders, through exposing the extent of harm caused by a crime across the individual and social dimensions (both directly and indirectly) and enabling the co-participation of offenders and victims in the reparation process. Proceeding in this way may shorten the duration of confiscation procedures and enable closing a 'confiscation case' under the fast track, especially when the harm is repaired voluntarily by the culprit.

Ultimately, changing the direction of EU law-making policy on the CPC may translate into redefined EU law standards in this regard, and thus, it may influence the national confiscation mechanisms of MS (through the implementation of the minimum standards into national law, the mutual recognition mechanism, and sincere cooperation in achieving the objectives of the EU confiscation policy). This can also contribute to the external promotion of the EU values and strengthen the EU's position as a standard setter in the area of confiscation.

EU policy is examined in this book from the angle of a minimalist restorative approach to justice, in order to answer the question of how to increase its restorativeness *hic et nunc* (here and now), i.e., without thorough reforms of the existing EU conventional confiscation scheme. The book argues that the restorative approach to justice represents an added value for EU law-making policy on the CPC. However, it does not focus on the assumptions of any concrete restorative account, as there exists a wide range of views on what, in fact, restorative justice is. The existing descriptions conceive it as a 'process' (Marshall 1996), an 'option for doing justice' (Walgrave 2008) or a 'justice mechanism' (Daly 2016). The term 'restorative justice' has also been used in the context of a theory of justice (Van

Ness and Strong 1997) and in the context of informal justice processes, as opposed to those of conventional criminal justice. In addition, sometimes the term is related to a 'social movement', for instance, Johnstone and Van Ness (2007) understand restorative justice as a 'global social movement with huge internal diversity'. This term is also used in reference to different restorative programs and practices like meetings, conferencing, and mediation in the criminal realm and beyond, wherever conflicts may occur. This proves that the term 'restorative justice' is capable of representing a range of different concepts.

In order to answer the question 'How restorative is the EU law-making policy on the CPC?', from the perspective of the minimalist approach taken in the research, the critical consideration is how this policy addresses the following issues:

- determination of the restorative objective of confiscation, involving the restoration of the status *quo ante* (before a crime) and reparation of the harm (this aspect is also connected with the effectiveness of the confiscation mechanism in taking illicit assets out of circulation and making illegal enrichment impossible, as well as fair redistribution of confiscated assets, including to social and public purposes),
- prioritisation of the position of the victims (in a broad sense) and communities over the position of the State,
- identification of the interests of all stakeholders in the confiscation mechanism (victims, communities, defendants, third parties),
- protection of the rights of all participants in the confiscation mechanism (the human rights protection perspective).

These core questions also characterise the essentials of a minimalist restorative approach to justice. Answering them is crucial for identifying the shortcomings of the examined policy and proposing appropriate policy recommendations. Basing the approach on these questions helps to resolve the dilemma facing us as a European community embedded in a culture of liberal democracy, about which priorities we would like to 'invest in': developing the repressiveness of confiscation schemes, or instead the effectiveness of achieving rationalised political objectives through these schemes; supporting State incentivisation schemes and at the same time empowering the law enforcement apparatus, or supporting grassroots initiatives by communities or their representatives (NGOs, associations, local authorities) to increase their resilience to crime (the local justice perspective); supplementing the State budget with confiscated assets, or returning them to the victims and populations harmed by or vulnerable to crime. These questions also allow reconsideration of the justification behind the inward flow of confiscated assets, which mainly directs them to the State coffers. While this approach may be justified in cases of fiscal crime detrimental to the State budget, it becomes more challenging to support when considering crimes detrimental to the interests of individual or collective victims, as well as entire communities.

The book examines the evolution of EU confiscation policy over time (the dynamic perspective) and indicates when the policy began referring to restorative justice in its ideas (cf. 'single policy study', Kronsell and Manners 2015). The EU's confiscation policy is reflected in adopted strategies, action plans, and documents from different institutional actors shaping this policy and influencing legislative processes in the EU, as well as in the explanatory memorandums accompanying proposals for key legal acts implementing confiscation policy objectives. The study took a critical approach focused on problems and solutions, with the auxiliary use of Wróblewski's theory of rational law-making (comparison of means to ends) (Wróblewski 1973, 1979, 1985; Zirk-Sadowski 2015). In addition, the study attempts to analyse the impact of EU standards on the CPC, as an emanation of EU policy, on shaping the confiscation schemes of selected EU jurisdictions.

Assuming the rationality of the EU lawmaker, the adopted legal standards on the CPC should reflect the assumptions and objectives of EU policy in this field, including those which refer to restorative justice. Accordingly, the book examines how this policy, initially analysed from the angle of a restorative approach to justice, is reflected in the EU law standards addressed to the MS, and whether those standards contain gaps that should be closed, along with whether similar gaps are reproduced in the confiscation law of the comparator jurisdictions.

In order to answer the question of the validity of EU law standards on the CPC, as they currently are (*de lege lata*) and what they should become (*de lege ferenda*), the legal dogmatic method was used, i.e., at the normative layer. To this end, the relevant jurisprudence of the CJEU and ECtHR were also referenced. In addition, the comparative law method was used to examine the normative layer of the CPC in the selected EU jurisdictions (Poland, Germany, and France), with reference to the relevant case law of the highest domestic courts and constitutional courts. Chapter 5 provides justification for the selection of comparator jurisdictions (the *tertium comparationis* quality). The focus is on the model features of criminal confiscation schemes of comparator jurisdictions (descriptive approach) with regard to those elements of EU law standards in which certain shortcomings have been identified. Accordingly, the comments concern the relationship of the national confiscation schemes with these elements of the standards.

The initial assumption has been made that EU confiscation law influences national law in MS. This mechanism results from Article 288 TFEU stating that, to exercise the Union's competences, the institutions adopt regulations, directives, decisions, recommendations, and opinions. The legal acts pertaining to confiscation mainly take the form of directives or regulations. A regulation has general application and is binding in its entirety. It is directly applicable to all MS (except for the opt-outs). A directive is binding as to the result to be achieved in the MS to which it is addressed. Accordingly, the MS are obliged to transpose a directive into their national law within the time-limit set therein. However, national authorities are free to choose the appropriate form and methods to achieve the result specified in the directive. Directives pertaining to confiscation require minimum harmonisation, accordingly, they provide for minimum rules (minimum standards), (see Article 82(2) and 83 TFEU). Prior to the Lisbon Treaty, framework decisions (FDs) played a similar role to directives, as they were also binding as to the results to be achieved while giving the MS free choice as regards the means to this end (see *ex* Article 34(2)(b) TEU, as amended by the Treaty of Nice). Recommendations, like opinions, have no binding force (Article 288 TFEU); nevertheless, as soft-law measures, they may also influence national law. Apart from secondary law, primary law may also influence national law, especially bearing in mind the non-exclusive EU competence in the AFSJ, shared with the MS. According to the principle of sincere cooperation:

> the Union and the Member States shall, in full mutual respect, assist each other in carrying out tasks which flow from the Treaties. The Member States shall take any appropriate measure, general or particular, to ensure fulfilment of the obligations arising out of the Treaties or resulting from the acts of the institutions of the Union. The Member States shall facilitate the achievement of the Union's tasks and refrain from any measure which could jeopardise the attainment of the Union's objectives.
>
> (Article 4(3) TEU)

In view of the above, reorienting EU law-making policy on the CPC towards a more restorative course should be reflected in the content of EU hard law and soft law, both affecting the national law of MS (in different ways depending on the type of legal act). Thus, assuming that EU law fulfils its role as defined in the TFEU (Article 288), under its influence, a similar reorientation of policy and law should take place at a national level.

To align national confiscation law to Directive 2014/42/EU, major changes were introduced to the Polish and German criminal codes in 2017 (in Poland, also in 2015 with reference to the Proposal for a Directive on the freezing and confiscation of proceeds of crime in the EU, COM/2012/085 final). In the case of French criminal law, in addition to Directive 2014/42/EU, framework decision (FD) 2005/212/JHA was of crucial importance. Accordingly, major changes to the French legislation aimed at transposing EU confiscation instruments were introduced in 2007 and 2016. More detailed considerations on changes introduced to domestic law of comparator jurisdictions with reference to EU confiscation law are contained in Chapter 5. At the time of writing the book, the new directive 2024/1260 on asset recovery and confiscation has been adopted (24 April 2024), but the deadline for its transposition by the MS is still in the future (23 November 2026).

The objective of the comparative study is to determine how the EU law standards – analysed initially with reference to EU policy and minimalist restorative approach to justice – have influenced the models of criminal CPC in the comparator jurisdictions. Accordingly, the analysis is focused on those elements of the EU standards in which certain shortcomings have been found (see Chapter 5). To identify the model features of the CPC in comparator jurisdictions, relevant for the legal construct of EU law standards, the following research questions were posed:

1) What criteria apply to the triggering offences?
2) What criteria apply to the subject of confiscation?
3) What criteria apply to the object of confiscation?

4) What are the procedural facilitations in proving a link between the property and criminal conduct?
5) What guarantees of victims' rights are provided within confiscation settings?
6) Have the comparator jurisdictions established a specialised system for the redistribution of confiscated assets for non-State purposes, i.e., for public interest and social purposes?

To broaden the research perspective, the criminal confiscation regime in England and Wales was included in the comparative section, providing an example of an alternative non-EU model of confiscation regime. The main reason for this inclusion was that it represents an alternative concept of confiscation as a 'debt to be paid' (value-based confiscation). From the perspective of EU law, this model of post-conviction confiscation can be regarded as more advanced and far-reaching, albeit focused mainly on efficiency issues. Such an approach was reflected, for instance, in the Impact Assessment accompanying the Proposal for a Directive on the freezing and confiscation of proceeds of crime in the EU (2012), which considered the system of asset recovery adopted in the UK to be close to one of the maximal legislative options under discussion.[1]

Research subject

The subject of the research is three-dimensional. Firstly, the research covers EU law-making policy on the CPC as a major determinant of law, and thus legal integration in the area of confiscation. Secondly, it covers the standards in this field laid down in EU law as an expression of this policy and the realisation of its objectives. The analysis in this respect is aimed at identifying gaps in these standards. Thirdly, it covers the normative frameworks of criminal confiscation adopted in comparator jurisdictions. The focus is on the model features of the national criminal confiscation regimes relevant to these elements of EU law standards in which certain shortcomings have been identified. The concept of the book is to examine how EU law-making policy on the CPC has been translated into EU law standards adopted as a realisation of this policy, and after identifying the shortcomings of these standards, to examine how they have been reflected in domestic law of comparator jurisdictions. The analyses are conducted from the angle of a minimalist restorative approach to justice.

This book also uses the simplified term 'EU confiscation policy', interchangeably with the term 'EU law-making policy on the CPC', i.e., the policy, the ultimate aim of which is creating EU legal norms concerning the CPC that best emanate the policy objectives.

It should be noted at the outset that EU law does not provide a comprehensive legal framework regarding all issues relevant to confiscation, whose intricate nature reaches across various domains of the law: criminal, private, and public. The book focuses on the EU's intervention in the domain of criminal law in both aspects, *de lege lata* (as it exists) and *de lege ferenda* (as it should be). However, since the institution of confiscation does not fit the classic divisions of the law, operating instead at their intersections, where necessary the book also refers to non-criminal domains.

The book relates 'law-making policy' to the activity of the EU as a regional lawmaker, creating legal norms addressed to the MS and individuals (directly or indirectly). In the theory of rational law-making proposed by Wróblewski (1985), 'law-making' is part of a more comprehensive 'law policy' (50). The latter public policy is about using the law as a whole (not only legal norms but also decisions) in order to reach desired goals. The overall 'law policy' consists of three specific policies: 'law-making policy', 'law application policy', and 'law realisation policy'. 'Law-making policy' covers creating legal norms of general and abstract character intended to achieve the assumed goals (50). 'Law application policy' covers issuing decisions that implement laws to achieve set goals. 'Law realisation policy' covers exercising the powers and competences conferred; one example being the policy for executing the penalties imposed (51). Referring to Wróblewski's input, it can be said that this work addresses the issue of political planning of general legal norms concerning the CPC at the EU level that are intended to realise the assumed EU policy goals. The ultimate outcome of the process should be EU legal standards on the CPC, part of which are minimum standards aimed at harmonising the confiscation systems of the MS. Harmonisation of law in this field is one element of the broader process of legal integration of MS criminal justice systems.

From the broader perspective of integration, as one of the EU policy objectives, law should be regarded as a politically useful tool. It is worth quoting here an apt insight from Cappelletti, Seccombe, and Weiler (1986) about the interdependence of the legal and politico-economic systems:

> the legal and politico-economic systems are interdependent, with the law being a product of the polity and the polity to some extent the creature of the law. This interdependence is true also of the integration process. Integration is fundamentally a political process: whether to engage in it, its pace, shape, success and failure are largely determined by political actors and political will. But the law has a vital role to play in the process.
>
> (Cappelletti, Seccombe, and Weiler 1986, 4)

Referring to the concept of integration through law, Azoulai (2016) argues that law plays a double role: both an 'object' and an 'agent' of integration. Nevertheless, there is something more to law, 'although law is pragmatically responsive to social and political factors, it remains amenable to a kind of internal rationality different from the political' (Azoulai 2016, 451). It is also worth mentioning Eckes's view that European law is a factor of integration, and therefore, it is an 'accepted topic of political science research' (Eckes 2022, 203).

Wróblewski (1985) developed a general model of rational law-making, which indicated issues that the lawmaker, if acting rationally, should resolve. The concept of the rational lawmaker assumes that law-making is a rational activity aimed at resolving identified problems. Reference to this model may be used in critical analysis of concrete law-making policy in the area of positive law. This model captures the basic tenets of Wróblewski's theory of law-making, which is also considered universal enough to be used in creating any regulation in the system of positive law (Winiarz 2011). The potential of Wróblewski's approach to law-making has already been acknowledged in the literature from the perspective of EU development and the emergence of a 'multi-level law-making structure' associated with this process (Winiarz 2011, 52).

The initial assumption of Wróblewski's model is that law is a means of purposeful influence on the behaviour of individuals in a society. In this sense, law is a specific means of social control (Wróblewski 1979). It should be highlighted that identifying the appropriate legal intervention in a given area depends on gaining a comprehensive knowledge of reality. Nevertheless, despite developing statistical obligations at the EU law level, knowledge regarding confiscation issues is still limited by a lack of sufficient data from MS. This *status quo* poses the risk of incorrect diagnosis of problems and the choice of inappropriate legal solutions.[2] The normative character of Wróblewski's model indicates the areas a lawmaker should address to be rational (Wróblewski 1985, 133–134). This model, in simplified terms, consists of five elements. The first is a determination of the goal of law-making activity (135). The second is a determination of possible measures to achieve the set goal (144). The third is a determination of which of those means can be legal means (148). The fourth is a choice of legal measure to achieve the set goal (151). The fifth is a determination of the form of legal regulation, ending with its inclusion into the form of legal provisions (152). Of course, this is not the only possible concept of law-making activity; however, the simplified model proposed by Wróblewski was identified as the appropriate point of reference for the research objectives, as universal enough to be applied to both national lawmakers and the EU lawmaker.

For the purposes of the book, 'standards' are understood as the set of norms of EU law of general and abstract character and addressed to the MS and individuals (directly or indirectly, see, e.g., C-41/74, *Van Duyn v Home Office*, EU:C:1974:133; C-148/78, *Ratti*, EU:C:1979:110). They have two areas of operation. In the area of harmonisation of national confiscation schemes, these norms constitute a common criterion for the MS, with which the national schemes should comply (the minimum standard). In the area of mutual recognition of confiscation orders, these norms are not of minimum character. This sphere is currently governed by the directly applied Regulation 2018/1805, which laid down the rules under which a Member State recognises and executes in its territory freezing orders and confiscation orders issued by another Member State.

However, a few important caveats need to be mentioned here, due to the complicated EU legal framework concerning confiscation. Ireland and Denmark are not bound by Regulation 2018/1805. Additionally, Denmark is not bound by Directive 2014/42/EU. In the area of cross-border cooperation with those MS in terms of the execution of confiscation orders, a different instrument is applicable, i.e., FD 2006/783/JHA. As far as the execution of freezing orders is concerned, FD 2003/577/JHA is applicable. Further, Directive 2014/42/EU has not completely replaced FD 2005/212/JHA, which is still in force in terms of minimum rules for so-called 'regular' or 'standard' confiscation, i.e., the confiscation of instrumentalities and proceeds from criminal offences punishable by deprivation of liberty for more than one year, or property the value of which corresponds to such proceeds (Article 2 of FD 2005/212/JHA). The new Directive 2024/1260 completely replaces FD 2005/212/JHA, and MS shall transpose this Directive by 23 November 2026 (excluding Denmark and Ireland).

Delimitations

Current EU policy is focused on criminal confiscation in the broader sense, also covering non-punitive confiscation within a criminal track. It should be emphasised that despite the growing attention devoted to various NCBC mechanisms, EU policy still ties them to the criminal realm. Accordingly, EU law has not yet developed legal standards regarding civil or administrative confiscation, operating outside the realm of criminal justice (i.e., outside 'proceedings in criminal matters', which is an autonomous concept of EU law). Nevertheless, it does not preclude the legislation of the MS providing for confiscation based on the outcome of non-criminal proceedings (see more in Wycichowski-Kuchta 2022, 2023). This is confirmed by the position of the CJEU expressed in the cases: C-234/18, *Agro In 2001*, EU:C:2020:221; C-319/19, *Komisia za protivodeystvie na koruptsiyata i za otnemane na nezakonno pridobitoto imushtestvo* EU:C:2021:883; C-393/19, *Criminal proceedings against OM*, EU:C:2021:8; Joined Cases C-845/19 and C-863/19, *Criminal proceedings against DR and TS*, EU:C:2021:864.

The minimum standards laid down in Directive 2014/42/EU are not addressed to pure *in rem* civil proceedings concerning confiscation not based on a criminal conviction. Although Directive 2014/42/EU also covers certain forms of confiscation independent of a conviction for a criminal offence, the standards are still strongly linked to existing criminal proceedings, which must at least be initiated and lead to positive findings regarding the commission of an offence (Article 4(2) of Directive 2014/42/EU). The new Directive 2024/1260 maintains the link between different types of confiscation and the criminal realm (see, e.g., the meaning of the term 'confiscation' adopted in Article 3(6), or the conditions for NCBC determined in Article 15(2)). Even the new type of confiscation envisaged in Directive 2024/1260, the 'confiscation of unexplained wealth linked to criminal conduct', requires that the court is satisfied that confiscable property 'identified in the context of an investigation in relation to a criminal offence' is 'derived from criminal conduct committed within the framework of a criminal organisation, and that conduct is liable to give rise, directly or indirectly, to substantial economic benefit' (Article 16(1), see also Article 16(5) of Directive 2024/1260).

Moreover, Regulation 2018/1805, operating in the area of mutual recognition, only covers confiscation orders issued within the framework of proceedings in criminal matters. It does not apply to confiscation orders issued within the framework of proceedings in civil or administrative matters (Article 1(4) of Regulation 2018/1805).

Bearing in mind the state of the art, i.e., the level of development of EU confiscation policy, the EU legal framework, and the position of the CJEU on the scope of EU law on confiscation, this book deals with the legal institution of the CPC belonging to the criminal realm. Issues of confiscation adjudicated in civil or administrative proceedings fall outside its scope of interest.

In addition, the confiscation of instrumentalities and the confiscation of contraband, as types of criminal confiscation requiring specific public policies, are beyond the scope of consideration. The book focuses on confiscations, the objects of which are the proceeds of crime. Nonetheless, the issue of different public policies depending on the object of confiscation is also partly addressed in the context of the need for a specific public policy dedicated to the CPC.

Terminology notes

Confiscation, proceeds

Since the considerations are conducted in the context of EU policy and law, the terms relevant to confiscation are, in principle, used in the book in a manner consistent with their use in the EU environment. Nevertheless, they are occasionally used with a different meaning when contexts other than the EU are at stake.

The main harmonisation instrument in the area of confiscation is Directive 2014/42/EU (the new Directive 2024/1260 is to be transposed by MS by 23 November 2026). Its subject matter covers, i.a., establishing the minimum rules on the confiscation of property 'in criminal matters'. In this regard, it should be pointed out that, to date, the scope of the targeted harmonisation is narrower than the range of confiscation solutions available in EU jurisdictions.

'Confiscation' and 'freezing' are autonomous concepts of EU law, a fact which is confirmed in Recital 13 of the Preamble to Directive 2014/42/EU:

> Freezing and confiscation under this Directive are autonomous concepts, which should not prevent Member States from implementing this Directive using instruments which, in accordance with national law, would be considered as sanctions or other types of measures (Directive 2024/1260 represents the same approach in this respect, see Recital 21).

The term 'confiscation' is defined in Directive 2014/42/EU as 'a final deprivation of property ordered by a court in relation to a criminal offence' (Article 2(4); a similar definition is contained in Article 6(3) of Directive 2024/1260). Confiscation can be ordered in relation to a criminal offence after a conviction (post-conviction confiscation), or independent of a conviction (NCBC), though, according to EU minimum rules, still within the criminal track (Article 4(2)). The new Directive 2024/1260 maintains the close links between various types of confiscation and the criminal realm (see, e.g., Article 15(2), and Article 16(1) and (5)).

For the purposes of Directive 2014/42/EU, the term 'freezing' is understood as the 'temporary prohibition of the transfer, destruction, conversion, disposal or movement of property or temporarily assuming custody or control of property' (Article 2(5); a similar definition is contained in Article 3(5) of Directive 2024/1260).

Another term relevant for further consideration is 'proceeds'. Directive 2014/42/EU explains this term as follows:

> 'proceeds' means any economic advantage derived directly or indirectly from a criminal offence; it may consist of any form of property and includes any subsequent reinvestment or transformation of direct proceeds and any valuable benefits (Article 2(1); a similar definition is contained in Article 3(1) of Directive 2024/1260).

Proceedings in criminal matters

Moving on to the perspective of mutual recognition, the main instrument is Regulation 2018/1805, which lays down the rules under which a Member State recognises and executes in its territory confiscation orders issued by another Member State within the framework of 'proceedings in criminal matters'. What is important is that it uses an autonomous concept of 'proceedings in criminal matters'. This concept covers confiscation orders issued without a final conviction. However, as these orders follow proceedings concerning a criminal offence, they still belong to the criminal realm. This Regulation *expressis verbis* states that confiscation orders issued within the framework of proceedings in civil or administrative matters are outside its scope (Article 1(1) and (4)). The legal *status quo* is made even more complicated by the fact that the extent of the mutual recognition of confiscation orders is wider than the extent of the harmonisation established in Directive 2014/42/EU. This aspect was raised in the Preamble to Regulation 2018/1805 (Recital 13):

> 'Proceedings in criminal matters' is an autonomous concept of Union law interpreted by the Court of Justice of the European Union, notwithstanding the case law of the European Court of Human Rights. The term therefore covers all types of freezing orders and confiscation orders issued following proceedings in relation to a criminal offence, not only orders covered by Directive 2014/42/EU. It also covers other types of order issued without a final conviction. While such orders might not exist in the legal system of a Member State, the Member State concerned should be able to recognise and execute such an order issued by another Member State. Proceedings in criminal matters could also encompass criminal investigations by the police and other law enforcement authorities.

Restorative justice, restorative approach to justice, restoration, and restorativeness

Some introductory notes are also needed as regards terms from the thematic area of restorative justice (Chapter 2 includes comments concerning the approach to 'punishment' in restorative accounts). To better understand further considerations, the meaning of the following terms should be clarified at this point: 'restorative justice', 'restorative approach to justice', 'restoration', and 'restorativeness'.

It should be noted that many differing definitions of 'restorative justice' have been proposed in the literature. This concept is not considered uniform and clear-cut (see also Daly 2013, 2016). For instance, Gade (2018, 37) observed the 'definitional vagueness' of restorative justice and that its growing popularity has not improved the clarity of the term. Accordingly, this book is not based on a singular concept of restorative justice. It uses the umbrella term 'restorative approach to justice' without contextualising it to any concrete restorative account, programs or practices. For the purposes of the book, the 'restorative approach to justice' is understood as an approach that focuses on repairing the harm resulting from a crime and restoring the *status quo ante* (before a crime). Actions aimed at reparation and restoration should be directed to the victims and communities affected by a crime, with some active participation by stakeholders in the 'confiscation case' related to a 'criminal case'. This approach prioritises the rights of victims and communities over the rights of the State. The ambition is to provide a critical observation of the EU policy on the CPC and its legal standards affecting the legal orders of the MS from the perspective of a restorative approach to justice.

The literature on restorative justice presents a wide variety of views about the possible meaning of 'restorative justice'. Gade's (2013, 2018) investigation showed that the origins of this term reach back to the 19th century, when it was used in a Christian context. One example is found in *The Christian Examiner and Church of Ireland Magazine* ('View of public affairs for the year 1833' 1834, 3). However, the first use of the term 'restorative justice' is often attributed to Eglash (1977), who contrasted restorative justice against retributive and distributive justice (Daly 2013). Eglash's ideas on restorative justice evolved from the concept of 'creative restitution' (Mirsky 2003). Under this conception, restorative justice is considered a 'technique' for restitution. Eglash (1958) saw 'creative restitution' as something more than 'punishment', 'reparations', 'indemnity', or 'atonement', all of which belong to the 'first mile' (620):

> Only a second mile is restitution in its broad meaning of a complete restoration of good will and harmony. Creative restitution requires that a situation be left better than before an offense was committed.
>
> (Eglash 1958, 620)

The relationship between restorative and other approaches to justice is not currently considered entirely distinct. However, the initial descriptions have concentrated on highlighting the differences. For example, Barnett (1977, 279) confronted the 'old paradigm' of criminal justice, which was identified with 'punishment', with the 'new paradigm', which was identified with 'restitution'. Barnett's concept was based on Kuhn's (1970) theory of a change from one paradigm to another being considered a scientific revolution. According to Kuhn (1970), 'the successive transition from one paradigm to another via revolution is the usual developmental pattern of mature science' (24).

Zehr also initially confronted 'retributive justice' with 'restorative justice', seeing the latter as a 'new paradigm' (Zehr 1985, 1990, cf. 2002). Some of the later views adopted a perspective not based on the varying paradigms, considering the relation between punishment and restoration as not purely alternative (e.g., Marshall 1996, 1999; Daly 2000; Ashworth 2002; see also the 'midway position' proposed by Gade 2021).

According to Zehr (2002), 'restorative justice' provides an 'alternative framework for thinking' about 'wrongdoing'. Zehr (2014) explained 'restorative justice' in the following way:

> Restorative justice is a process to involve, to the extent possible, those who have a stake in a specific offense and to collectively identify and address harms, needs, and obligations, in order to heal and put things as right as possible.
>
> (Zehr 2014, Ch. 2)

Among the differing definitions, it is worth quoting the one provided by Marshall (1999), which enjoys broad recognition. According to Marshall:

> Restorative Justice is a process whereby parties with a stake in a specific offence collectively resolve how to deal with the aftermath of the offence and its implications for the future.
>
> (Marshall 1999, 5)

In addition, Marshall (1999) indicated that restorative justice is an approach to crime consisting of 'problem-solving' involving the parties and the community 'in an active relationship with statutory agencies' (5). Under this view, 'restorative justice' is not one 'particular practice', but a 'set of principles' able to guide the general practice in response to crime (Marshall 1999, 5). This theorist also pointed to the 'social context' of restorative justice:

> Restorative Justice may be seen as criminal justice embedded in its social context, with the stress on its relationship to the other components, rather than a closed system in isolation.
>
> (Marshall 1999, 5)

However, some authors indicated the weaknesses of this definition (e.g., Dignan 2005). Dignan (2005) advocated focusing on developing an analytical framework rather than defining restorative justice and exploring the 'relationship between restorative justice approaches and other victim-focused approaches' (5).

Walgrave (2008) pointed out a tendency towards extending this notion to various 'deliberative practices in resolving conflicts and injustices' (16–17) focused not on adjudication but on informal deliberation (cf. Roche 2006). However, considering that restorative justice is not a clear-cut concept, Walgrave (2008) proposed a restricted perspective focused on the 'way the aftermath of offences is to be dealt with' (17, 20). According to Walgrave, restorative justice should be perceived as:

> an option for doing justice after the occurrence of an offence that is primarily oriented towards repairing the individual, relational and social harm caused by that offence.
>
> (Walgrave 2008, 21; cf. Bazemore and Walgrave 1999, 48)

Notably, the conceptualisation of restorative justice proposed by Walgrave (2008, 20) encompasses deliberative- and non-deliberative interventions – 'judicial sanctions with a view to reparation' (see Daly 2013).

A far-reaching approach is also attributed to Braithwaite (Daly 2013), who perceived restorative justice as going beyond the issue of reforming the criminal justice system (Braithwaite 2003, 1):

> Restorative justice, conceived as an intellectual tradition or as an approach to political practice, involves radical transformation. On this radical view restorative justice is not simply a way of reforming the criminal justice system, it is a way of transforming the entire legal system, our family lives, our conduct in the workplace, our practice of politics. Its vision is of a holistic change in the way we do justice in the world.
>
> (Zehr 1995; Van Ness and Strong 1997)

The next approach is represented by Johnstone and Van Ness (2007), who described restorative justice as a 'global social movement with huge internal diversity', aiming to 'transform the way contemporary societies view and respond to crime and related forms of troublesome behaviour'. However, they noted that there is no agreement 'on the actual nature of the transformation sought by the restorative justice movement' (2007, 5) and suggested that 'restorative justice is an appraisive, internally complex and open concept that continues to develop with experience, and that this helps explain why it is so deeply contested' (8).

'Restorative justice' is also presented as theory and practice (Van Ness and Strong 1997, vii, 12, 24). From the perspective adopted by Daly (2016), 'restorative justice' is considered as a '*contemporary justice mechanism* to address crime, disputes, and bounded community conflict'. The mechanism is a '*meeting* (or several meetings) of affected individuals, facilitated by one or more impartial people' (Daly 2016, 21).

The common way of thinking about what exactly 'restorative justice' is has also been highly influenced by the views of Christie (1977), who considered crime from the perspective of conflict. Christie recognised 'conflicts as property':

> It is the *conflict itself* that represents the most interesting property taken away, not the goods originally taken away from the victim, or given back to him. In our types of society, conflicts are more scarce than property. And they are immensely more valuable.
>
> (Christie 1977, 7)

According to Christie (1977), the value of conflicts should be seen from the perspective of a 'potential for activity, for participation', 'opportunities for norm-clarification', and other opportunities for the involved parties, e.g., giving the offender 'the opportunity for participation in a personal confrontation' (7–10).

It is also worth pointing out a separate theory of conflict resolution, adopted in the field of broadly understood criminal law (substantive and procedural), as outlined by Wiliński (2020). This theory naturally has many elements in common with the concept of restorative justice, despite being a distinct concept. Wiliński (2020, 15–20) considered criminal law as a tool for conflict resolution and prevention (conflicts caused by a crime).

Another term used in the book is 'restoration', understood as the expected 'outcome' of adopting a restorative approach to justice. Restoration may be identified as the main focus of restorative justice concerning the victim, the offender, and the community (Marshall 1999). In Marshall's view (1999), restoration is backward- and forward-looking. Nevertheless, the meaning of 'restoration' is not made entirely clear in the restorative accounts. For instance, Brooks (2017) pointed out that '[r]estorative justice approaches lack clarity about what is to be restored and how that restoration should be achieved' (128). In this context, it is also worth referring to the view of Braithwaite (2002), who gave the following response to the question 'What is to be restored?':

> One answer to the 'What is to be restored?' question is whatever dimensions of restoration matter to the victims, offenders, and communities affected by the crime. Stakeholder deliberation determines what restoration means in a specific context. […] I have defined the following dimensions of restoration as important from a republican perspective: restoring property loss, restoring injury, restoring a sense of security, restoring dignity, restoring a sense of empowerment, restoring deliberative democracy, restoring harmony based on a feeling that justice has been done, and restoring social support.
>
> (Braithwaite 1996, 2002, 11–12)

In this book, the term 'restoration' is related to the confiscation mechanism and means restoring the *status quo ante* (the status before a crime), through the use of the capacities of this mechanism, by repairing harm which resulted from a crime (the latter term is broadly understood as an act also disturbing social relations). Financial compensation is an important element of this process. Therefore, the term 'restoration' encompasses the economic aspect, especially from the viewpoint of an appropriate legal response to profit-making crimes. The book presents the view that transferring confiscated assets, or at least some portion of them, directly to the individuals or communities touched by, or vulnerable to a crime, and not merely to the State coffers by default, is an important factor in repairing the harm. However, the meaning of 'restoration' also goes beyond the financial aspect. Reparation of harm, broadly understood, is also a significant factor in restoring the interpersonal and community relationships disturbed by crime.

The initial assumption has been made that the criminal confiscation procedure, as a part of the conventional criminal procedure, has the potential to adopt, to some extent, the main strengths of the restorative approach to justice, i.a., reparation of harm in a broad sense, involving all stakeholders, to some extent, in the process of restoration (victims, communities, offenders), and shifting the State to a non-dominant position. Accordingly, it has also been assumed that there is scope to transform the current EU law confiscation model into a more restorative one, capable of serving as a harmonisation model for MS.

For the purposes of the book, 'restorativeness' is understood as the extent to which the EU law-making policy and legal standards on the CPC reflect the essentials of a restorative approach to justice. In this context, nevertheless, it is worth referring to the pragmatic view expressed by Van Ness and Heetderks Strong (2010) that, in reality, no system can be fully restorative (163):

> it is difficult to answer the question 'Is this restorative or not?' for virtually all systems combine restorative and nonrestorative elements. A more helpful question would be 'How restorative is this?' A fully restorative system would be one in which the principles and values of restorative justice prevail.

A minimalist approach

A preliminary assumption has been made as to the extent to which the restorative approach to justice should first be included in EU law-making policy on the CPC. This book presents the view that adopting a *de minimis* approach would be more appropriate than a maximalist approach. The minimalist approach, aiming only to make this policy, as related to conventional confiscation mechanisms, slightly more 'restorative' than the *status quo*, can make a significant difference *hic et nunc* (here and now, quickly), even at this stage of policy development. This evolutionary approach is more pragmatic than undertaking a fundamental reform of the differentiated EU confiscation mechanisms belonging to the realm of conventional criminal justice. Such comprehensive reform would ultimately require common political will from all the MS to successfully reflect it in their policies and then confiscation systems. In this context, it should also be taken into account that, despite the extensive harmonisation processes regarding confiscation, the differences between national confiscation schemes in the MS have still not been eliminated. Nevertheless, adopting the minimalist approach may be a small step towards possible deeper future reforms in broader EU criminal justice policy, moving it in a restorative justice direction.

Determining the relationship between restorative justice and conventional criminal justice is difficult, and various solutions come into play, from alternatives to unified systems. In this context, it's worth quoting Pavlich's (2002) view on the linkage of restorative justice with 'current criminal justice provisions' (97):

> Very often, restorative justice (even if inadvertently) replicates the very thought systems it was supposed to eschew. That is why, perhaps, its promises do not so much carve out new conceptual horizons of justice but delineate what restorative justice is not (i.e., it is not repressive, not reactive, reparative, distributive, etc.). One might say that the basis for conceiving restorative justice lies in current criminal justice provisions, indicating a mutually

> constitutive relation between restorative justice and state law (Pavlich 1996; Fitzpatrick 1988).
>
> (Pavlich 2002, 97)

Various views on possible relationships between restorative justice and conventional criminal justice, and accordingly, policy strategies in this respect, have been presented in the restorative justice literature. For the purposes of this book, it's worth referring to two analyses addressing this issue, the first conducted by Dignan (2005) and the second conducted by Van Ness, Heetderks Strong, Derby, and Parker (2022), as they may offer an illustration of some possible approaches for legislatures, including the EU.

Those analyses should also be seen in the context of the intellectual basis of restorative justice, i.e., the 'civilian' (or 'civilisation'), 'communitarian', and 'moral discourse' theses (Dignan 2005, 95–104). Those trends emphasise, respectively, more 'enlightened' and 'human' interventions or civil law aspects, including reparation (the 'civilian' thesis); communities' interests (the 'communitarian' thesis); and the offender's conscience as a controlling behaviour factor (the 'moral discourse' thesis) (Dignan 2005; see also Bottoms 2003; Duff 2003; Walgrave 2003; Daly 2013).

Dignan (2005) distinguished three broad policy strands in the restorative justice movement regarding the relationship between restorative justice and conventional criminal justice, collectively referred to as 'abolitionism', 'separatism', and 'reformism'. However, each of these strands involves a broad spectrum of ideas. Accordingly, 'abolitionism' includes various views presented by the early restorative justice advocates inspired by the critique of the conventional criminal justice and penal systems and by those who perceive restorative justice as an 'alternative paradigm' (Dignan 2005, 106). 'Separatism' stands for a more pragmatic approach. As regards 'separatist' views, Dignan indicated:

> Their solution is based on a 'separatist' approach in which restorative justice programmes should operate completely outside the criminal justice system in a supplementary capacity, because their objectives and practices are so different. There is also a concern that the distinctive aims and values of such programmes will be 'contaminated' if they are required to co-exist with and operate within a criminal justice system whose values are inimical to those of restorative justice.
>
> (Dignan 2005, 106)

'Reformism' involves the view that the conventional criminal justice system can be modified in line with restorative justice principles, values, outcomes, or processes (Dignan 2005). However, as noted by Dignan, this approach is broad and covers greatly varied possibilities, ranging from extremely modest to wildly ambitious (2005, 106–107):

> The most modest approaches are associated with some of the early exponents of the 'civilian thesis', such as Marjory Fry, who campaigned for the introduction

> of restitutive or reparative penalties which they favoured as a more constructive and humane way of dealing with offenders. It is clearly possible to incorporate minor concessions of this kind [...] into the criminal justice system though their overall effect on the system as a whole is likely to be limited.
>
> (Dignan 2005, 107)

A more ambitious approach within this trend is referred to as 'mainstreaming' (Dignan 2005), which also has varied ideas in terms of how to integrate restorative justice principles and practises within the criminal justice system:

> One option is to enable criminal justice decision makers to specify restorative justice interventions as an alternative to more conventional ways of dealing with offenders (and their victims) in cases that come before them. [...] Another is to 'prescribe' restorative justice processes such as conferencing as the standard way of dealing with certain categories of offences or offenders, as New Zealand has done with respect to juvenile offenders.
>
> (Dignan 2005, 107)

The most far-reaching 'reformist' approach involves a thorough reform of the criminal justice system in line with 'restorative justice principles and values' (Dignan 2005, 107):

Further analysis by Van Ness et al. (2022) identified five system models to illustrate the possible relationships between 'restorative processes and practices' and those from the area of contemporary criminal justice. These are the 'augmentation' model, 'safety-net' model, 'dual-track' model, 'hybrid' model, and 'unitary' model (Van Ness et al. 2022, 110). In the 'augmentation' model, restorative justice programs may be chosen instead of the contemporary criminal justice processes by the 'gatekeepers' in contemporary criminal justice (e.g., police, prosecutors), the parties or both. However, this model is mainly considered a 'transitional' model (111). In the second model ('safety-net'), all cases are dealt with in a restorative manner, and contemporary criminal justice here plays the specific role of a 'safety net'. Accordingly, criminal justice mechanisms are activated only when those from the area of restorative justice cannot or do not bring about a resolution (111). Under the third model ('dual-track'), the relationship between restorative and contemporary criminal justice is different, as restorative and contemporary criminal justice constitute two options that the parties may choose, however, with opportunities for support from community or governmental representatives (111). In the fourth model ('hybrid'), matters are handled by criminal justice processes up to a certain point and then transferred to restorative processes (always and automatically). Thus, in this model, restorative and contemporary criminal justice processes do not run alternatively but consecutively (111). Under the fifth model ('unitary'), there is only a 'single, restorative process', without resort to contemporary criminal justice mechanisms (112). This model is considered by the quoted analysts to be the most challenging option, viable only if a 'reparative conception' of restorative justice is adopted (Van Ness et al. 2022, 112, cf.; Van Ness and Heetderks Strong 2010, 161).[3]

However, the approach taken in this book does not reproduce the essential characteristics of any of these models. The idea is to task the legal institution of the CPC with restorative goals while retaining the conventional court-based model of its ordering. With this in mind, one can say that the proposed change in EU law-making policy on the CPC is rather one of a victim-oriented policy initiative than a proposition to integrate a more restorative policy approach. However, the policy shift proposed within the minimalist approach involves making confiscation procedures more inclusive, consultative, and balanced, in which the stakeholders, including the defendants, can play more 'proactive' roles. Especially at the stage of disposal of confiscated assets, the roles of stakeholders may be significantly increased. This part of the procedure offers the greatest potential for deliberation on the destinations of transfers of confiscated assets, with the participation of various stakeholders leading it to develop in a more restorative manner. Thus, the policy changes suggested in this book can be considered to be something more than merely a victim-focused policy initiative. In view of the above, especially when it comes to the stage of disposal of confiscated assets, the proposed policy shift may be considered as somewhat closer to the 'hybrid' model identified by Van Ness et al. (2022, 111). However, it is not identical, because even this stage of confiscation proceedings is still considered in terms of conventional criminal justice, i.e., the State is the organiser of the confiscation mechanism, though not its main beneficiary (confiscated assets are mainly returned to victims and communities, not transferred to the State's treasury).

The minimalist approach adopted in the book also does not reproduce any of the policy strands regarding the relationship between restorative justice and conventional criminal justice, as described by Dignan (2005). Yet, again, it leans somewhat towards a modest variant of the 'reformist' view by proposing some minimal 'restorative' improvements to EU law-making policy on the CPC aimed at taking better care of the interests of victims and communities without undertaking a fundamental reform of EU conventional confiscation mechanisms based on a court-ordered confiscation. In addition, as already indicated, the proposed policy changes provide for introducing some restorative justice practices at the stage of disposal of confiscated assets, involving various stakeholders, not excluding the offenders.[4]

The state of the art and the book's contribution to the knowledge on confiscation of illicit assets

The CPC is widely discussed in the literature. However, greater attention is presently being given to issues of civil confiscation not based on a conviction, as different forms of NCBC are now being developed in many EU jurisdictions. As far as EU law is concerned, the focus is also on extended confiscation in the European doctrine. This type of confiscation has been widely discussed, for example, by Boucht (2019) and Schunke (2017).

Criminal confiscations, both post-conviction and non-conviction based, but ordered within a criminal track, raise many problems that to date have not been resolved in EU policy; however, this issue is not central in the academic discourse on tackling illicit assets, which often prioritises other dominant themes. The topic of the EU confiscation mechanism has recently been addressed, though not from a restorative justice perspective, i.a., by Simonato and Fernandez-Bertier (2019), Maugeri (2018), Ligeti and Simonato (2017), Panzavolta (2017), Vettori and Di Nicola (2017), Montaldo (2015), and Borgers (2014). In addition, it is worth mentioning an older comparative study on confiscation by Vettori (2006) conducted under the legal *status quo* prior to Directive 2014/42/EU. Many valuable analyses of national criminal confiscation schemes have also been produced. Discussing the problems concerning EU confiscation policy and law would be impossible without reference to existing scientific advances in the broader area of confiscation of illicit assets. Thus, this book engages in dialogue with the doctrinal input in this area.

The unique differentiator of this book is addressing confiscation issues from the angle of a minimalist restorative approach to justice. By embracing such an approach, it contributes to the development and advancement of knowledge about the EU law-making policy on the CPC (belonging to the criminal realm, punitive or non-punitive in nature), and the standards established in this respect in EU law.

Outline of the book

The book is structured into seven chapters. The introductory chapter explains the rationale for examining EU law-making policy and EU law standards on the CPC from the angle of a minimalist restorative approach to justice. It provides information on the research questions and methodology, as well as the research subject and delimitations. It also clarifies the meaning of the terms used in the book. In addition, it addresses the possible relationships between restorative justice and conventional criminal justice, to explain the minimalist approach taken in the book. The position taken is that adopting a minimalist approach can make a significant difference *hic et nunc*, without requiring thorough reforms in the existing EU conventional confiscation mechanisms. The following subsections outline the state of the art and explain the book's contribution to the knowledge on confiscation of illicit assets.

Chapter 2 discusses what a restorative approach to justice can offer EU law-making policy on the CPC. To understand the added value of this approach for EU policy, this chapter first addresses the issue of the debatable juridical nature of confiscation, challenging the applicability of the civil-criminal dichotomy. This issue is demonstrated in the main thematic streams in the ongoing discussion on its legal character. Considering those controversies, a twofold approach has been recommended, focused on appropriate policy questions and goals consistent with the restorative approach to justice and, equally, the correct choice of criminal or civil routes, depending on the legal construct of the confiscation and its object. Secondly, this chapter outlines a variety of approaches to punishment under retributivist, reductivist, and restorative accounts, in order to better understand the potential input of restorative justice to EU law-making policy on the CPC, and EU law standards being its emanation. Potential concrete benefits from a recast of EU confiscation policy towards a restorative approach to justice are presented in the last section of the chapter.

The next chapter is devoted to the evolution of EU law-making policy on the CPC in the pre- and post-Lisbon periods (Chapter 3). The emphasis is on referencing restorative justice in this policy. Additional attention is paid to non-EU standard setters, such as the CoE, UN, and FATF, as the main international players impacting the confiscation policies of both the EU and its MS. This chapter also touches on other relevant initiatives undertaken in the framework of the OECD, MONEYVAL, the G8 Roma-Lyon Group, the Basel Institute on Governance, the Stolen Asset Recovery (StAR) Initiative, GFAR, and CiFAR.

The EU law standards for the CPC are discussed in Chapter 4. The purpose of this chapter is to explore the deficiencies of these standards from the perspective of the assumptions of EU policy in this respect, analysed first from the angle of a minimalist restorative approach to justice. The problem is twofold. There are areas where EU policy objectives referring to restorative justice were improperly implemented into EU law (inadequacy of means to ends) and other areas where EU law directly replicates the shortcomings of EU policy objectives. Special attention is given to the lack of standards for fair redistribution of recovered assets, an area with considerable restorative potential. This chapter also argues that a minimalist restorative approach implies something more than just human rights protections, as it encourages legislatures to search for more innovative legal solutions aimed at the inclusion of various groups of stakeholders in confiscation procedures, to better address and balance their interests, and give them the opportunity of more 'proactive' procedural participation.

The main objective of the comparative analysis provided for in Chapter 5 is to capture the model features of the national criminal confiscation regimes in the comparator EU jurisdictions (Poland, Germany, and France) and to determine how the EU law standards (analysed in the previous chapter in relation to restorative aspects of EU confiscation policy) have influenced the national models of the CPC. The analysis refers to these elements of the standards in which certain shortcomings have been identified. To broaden a research perspective primarily centred around models adopted in selected civil law EU jurisdictions, the post-conviction model of confiscation adopted in England and Wales has been included in the comparative section as an example of an alternative non-EU model of value-based confiscation.

Chapter 6 indicates the possible implications of rethinking EU confiscation policy towards a more restorative path for other interconnected EU policies (e.g., anti-corruption, anti-fraud, and AML/CFT policies). However, beneficial implications can be identified not only in the area of shared competences between the EU and MS (the AFSJ) but also in other areas in which the EU has supporting competences (protection and improvement of human health, culture, education, vocational training, youth, and sport), as a result of redirecting confiscated assets to support these areas. In addition, changing the course of EU confiscation policy may have an impact on the area of special competences of the EU (the CFSP), especially in the context of enhancing interstate cooperation in returning confiscated assets to 'victim countries'.

The book's ambition is to provoke a rethinking of EU law-making policy on the CPC, moving its centre of gravity towards the interests of victims and communities, and opening communication channels between them and the defendants. Nevertheless, the ideas presented have a more universal appeal. The possible broader implications of the research results for different areas of EU policy are discussed in Chapter 6.

The book concludes with Chapter 7, which summarises the improvements already delivered in the field of EU law-making policy and EU law standards on the CPC, and indicates which areas still require further attention.

Notes

1 Commission, Commission Staff Working Paper, Accompanying document to Impact Assessment (2012), 12.3.2012, COM(2012) 85 final.
2 See also the issue of 'measuring and modelling the potential impact' of legislative measures, raised by Micklitz (2022, 228–231).
3 See also the three conceptions of restorative justice ('reparative', 'transformative', 'encounter'), Van Ness et al. 2022, Ch. 3.
4 In this context, see also Dignan's considerations on 'court-based restitutive and reparative measures' and 'community reparation boards and citizens' panels' (Dignan 2005, 108–111, 121–124).

References

Ashworth, Andrew. 2002. "Responsibilities, Rights and Restorative Justice." *British Journal of Criminology* 42 (3): 578–595.

Azoulai, Loïc. 2016. "Integration through Law and Us." *ICON* 14 (2): 449–463. https://doi.org/10.1093/icon/mow024.

Barnett, Randy E. 1977. "Restitution: A New Paradigm of Criminal Justice." *Ethics* 87: 279–301.

Bazemore, Gordon, and Walgrave Lode. 1999. *Restorative Juvenile Justice: Repairing the Harm of Youth Crime*. Monsey, NY: Criminal Justice Press.

Borgers, J. Matthias. 2014. "Confiscation of the Proceeds of Crime: The European Union Framework." In *Dirty Assets. Emerging Issues in the Regulation of Criminal and Terrorist Assets*, edited by Colin King and Clive Walker, 27–45. Farnham: Ashgate.

Bottoms, E. Anthony. 2003. "Some Sociological Reflections on Restorative Justice." In *Restorative Justice and Criminal Justice: Competing or Reconcilable Paradigms?*, edited by Andrew von Hirsch, Julian Roberts, Anthony E. Bottoms, Kent Roach, and Mara Schiff, 79–113. Oxford: Hart Pub.

Boucht, Johan. 2019. *The Limits of Asset Confiscation. On the Legitimacy of Extended Appropriation of Criminal Proceeds*. Oxford: Hart Pub.

Braithwaite, John. 2002. *Restorative Justice and Responsive Regulation*. Oxford: Oxford University Press.

Braithwaite, John. 2003. "Principles of Restorative Justice." In *Restorative Justice and Criminal Justice: Competing or Reconcilable Paradigms?*, edited by Andrew von Hirsch, Julian Roberts, Anthony E. Bottoms, Kent Roach, and Mara Schiff, 1–20. Oxford: Hart Pub.

Brooks, Thom. 2017. "Punitive Restoration and Restorative Justice." *Criminal Justice Ethics* 36 (2): 122–140. https://doi.org/10.1080/0731129X.2017.1358930.

Cappelletti, Mauro, Monica Seccombe, and Joseph H. Weiler. 1986. "Integration Through Law: Europe and the American Federal Experience A General Introduction." In *Integration Through Law Europe and the American Federal Experience*, edited by Mauro Cappelletti, Monica Seccombe, and Joseph H. Weiler, EUI Series A/Law, Vol. 1, Book 1, 3–68. Berlin and New York: de Gruyter.

Christie, Nils. 1977. "Conflicts as Property." *British Journal of Criminology* 17 (1): 1–15.

Daly, Kathleen. 2000. "Revisiting the Relationship between Retributive and Restorative Justice." In *Restorative Justice: Philosophy to Practice*, edited by Heather Strang and John Braithwaite, 33–54. Aldershot: Ashgate.

Daly, Kathleen. 2013. "The Punishment Debate in Restorative Justice." In *The Sage Handbook of Punishment and Society*, edited by Jonathan Simon and Richard Sparks, 356–373. London: Sage.

Daly, Kathleen. 2016. "What is Restorative Justice? Fresh Answers to a Vexed Question." *Victims & Offenders* 11(1): 9–29.

Davies, Gareth. 2014. "Internal Market Adjudication and the Quality of Life in Europe." *EUI Working Papers*, LAW 2014/07: 1–26.

Dignan, James. 2005. *Understanding Victims and* Restorative Justice. Maidenhead, Berkshire: Open University Press.

Duff, Robin, Anthony. 2003. "Restoration and Retribution." In *Restorative Justice and Criminal Justice: Competing or Reconcilable Paradigms?* edited by Andrew von Hirsch, Julian Roberts, Anthony E. Bottoms, Kent Roach, and Mara Schiff, 43–59. Oxford: Hart Pub.

Eckes, Christina. 2022. "A Timid Defence of Legal Formalism." In *The Politics of European Legal Research. Behind the Method*, edited by Marija Bartl and Jessica C. Lawrence, 192–207. Cheltenham: Edward Elgar Pub.

Eglash, Albert. 1958. "Creative Restitution – A Broader Meaning for an Old Term." *Journal of Criminal Law and Criminology* 48 (6): 619–622.

Eglash, Albert. 1977. "Beyond Restitution: Creative Restitution." In *Restitution in Criminal Justice: A Critical Assessment of Sanctions*, edited by Joe Hudson and Burt Galaway, 91–100. Lexington: Lexington Books.

Fitzpatrick, Peter. 1988. "The Rise and Rise of Informalism." In *Informal Justice?*, edited by Roger Matthews, 178–198. London: Sage.

Gade, B. N. Christian. 2013. "Restorative Justice and the South African Truth and Reconciliation Process." *South African Journal of Philosophy* 32 (1): 10–35.

Gade, B. N. Christian. 2018. "Restorative Justice: History of the Term's International and Danish Use." In *Nordic Mediation Research*, edited by Anna Nylund, Kaijus Ervasti, and Lin Adrian, 27–40. Cham: Springer. https://doi.org/10.1007/978-3-319-73019-6_3.

Gade, B. N. Christian. 2021. "Is Restorative Justice Punishment?" *Conflict Resolution Quarterly* 38: 127–155. https://doi.org/10.1002/crq.21293.

Johnstone, Gerry, and Daniel W. Van Ness. 2007. "The meaning of restorative justice." In *Handbook of Restorative Justice,* edited by Gerry Johnstone and Daniel W. Van Ness, 5–23. Cullompton: Willan Publishing.

Kronsell, Annica, and Ian Manners. 2015. "Single Policy Study: Three Variations in Design." In *Research Methods in European Union Studies*, edited by Kennet Lynggaard, Ian Manners, and Karl Löfgren, 86–101. Basingstoke: Palgrave Macmillan.

Kuhn, S. Thomas. 1970. *The Structure of Scientific Revolutions*. Chicago: University of Chicago Press.

Ligeti, Katalin, and Michele Simonato. 2017. "Asset Recovery in the EU: Towards a Comprehensive Enforcement Model Beyond Confiscation? An Introduction." In *Chasing Criminal Money. Challenges and Perspectives On Asset Recovery in the EU*, edited by Katalin Ligeti and Michele Simonato, 1–21. Oxford: Hart Pub.

Marshall, F. Tony. 1996. "The Evolution of Restorative Justice in Britain." *European Journal on Criminal Policy and Research* 4: 21–43.

Marshall, F. Tony. 1999. *Restorative Justice: An Overview*. A report by the Home Office Research Development and Statistics Directorate. London: Crown copyright.

Maugeri, M. Anna. 2018. "Mutual Recognition and Confiscation of Assets: An EU Perspective." In *The Palgrave Handbook of Criminal and Terrorism Financing Law,* edited by Colin King, Clive Walker, and Jimmy Gurulé, 399–425. Cham: Palgrave Macmillan.

Micklitz, Hans-W. 2022. "The Measuring of the Law through EU Politics." In *The Politics of European Legal Research: Behind the Method*, edited by Marija Bartl and Jessica C. Lawrence, 223–238. Cheltenham: Edward Elgar Pub.

Mirsky, Laura. 2003. "Albert Eglash and Creative Restitution: A Precursor to Restorative Practices." *Restorative Practices EForum* 3 (December). Accessed February 22, 2024. https://www.iirp.edu/images/pdf/eglash.pdf.

Montaldo, Stefano. 2015. "Directive 2014/42/EU and Social Reuse of Confiscated Assets in the EU: Advancing a Culture of Legality." *New Journal of European Criminal Law* 6 (2): 195–212.

Panzavolta, Michele. 2017. "Forfeiture and Fundamental Rights: Open Questions in the Twenty-First Century." In *Chasing Criminal Money. Challenges and Perspectives On Asset Recovery in the EU*, edited by Katalin Ligeti and Michele Simonato, 25–52. Oxford: Hart Pub.

Pavlich, George. 1996. *Justice Fragmented: Mediating Community Disputes under Postmodern Conditions*. London: Routledge.

Pavlich, George. 2002. "Deconstructing restoration: the promise of restorative justice." In *Restorative Justice. Theoretical Foundations,* edited by Elmar G. M. Weitekamp and Hans-Jürgen Kerner, 90–109. Cullompton: Willan Publishing.

Roche, Declan. 2006. "Dimensions of Restorative Justice." *Journal of Social Issues* 62 (2): 217–238. https://doi.org/10.1111/j.1540-4560.2006.00448.x.

Schunke, Malin Thunberg. 2017. *Extended Confiscation in Criminal Law. National, European and International Perspectives*. Cambridge: Intersentia.

Simonato, Michele, and Michael Fernandez-Bertier. 2019. "Confiscation and Fundamental Rights: The Quest for a Consistent European approach." In *Improving Confiscation Procedures in the European Union*, edited by Alessandro Bernardi, coordinated by Francesco Rossi, 3–29. Napoli: Jovene Editore.

Van Ness, Daniel, and Karen Heetderks Strong. 1997. *Restoring Justice*. Cincinnati, OH: Anderson Pub.

Van Ness, Daniel, and Karen Heetderks Strong. 2010. *Restoring Justice: An Introduction to Restorative Justice*. 4th ed. Cincinnati, OH: Anderson Pub.

Van Ness, Daniel, Karen Heetderks Strong, Jonathan Derby, and Lynette L. Parker. 2022. *Restoring Justice: An Introduction to Restorative Justice.* 6th ed. Abingdon, Oxon: Routledge.

Vettori, Barbara. 2006. *Tough on Criminal Wealth. Exploring the Practice of Proceeds from Crime Confiscation in the EU*. Dordrecht: Springer.

Vettori, Barbara, and Andrea Di Nicola. 2017. "The Social Reuse of Confiscated Assets in EU Member States: From Current Experiences to an EU policy for a 'Powered-by-Citizens' Fight Against Crime." In *Chasing Criminal Money: Challenges and Perspectives on Asset Recovery in the EU*, edited by Katalin Ligeti and Michele Simonato, 321–343. Oxford: Hart Pub.

"View of public affairs for the year 1833." 1834. *The Christian Examiner and Church of Ireland Magazine* 3 (27): 1–11.

Walgrave, Lode. 2003. "Imposing Restoration Instead of Inflicting Pain." In *Restorative Justice and Criminal Justice: Competing or Reconcilable Paradigms?*, edited by Andrew von Hirsch, Julian V. Roberts, Anthony Bottoms, Kent Roach, and Mara Schiff, 61–78. Oxford: Hart Pub.

Walgrave, Lode. 2008. *Restorative Justice: Self-interest and Responsible Citizenship.* Cullompton: Willan Pub.

Williams, Andrew T. 2009. "Taking Values Seriously: Towards a Philosophy of EU Law." *Oxford Journal of Legal Studies* 29 (3): 549–577.

Wiliński, Paweł. 2020. *Zarys teorii konfliktu w prawie karnym*. Warszawa: Wolters Kluwer.

Winiarz, Marcin. 2011. "Teoria racjonalnego tworzenia prawa Jerzego Wróblewskiego a współczesne prawodawstwo polskie." In *Wpływ teorii Jerzego Wróblewskiego na współczesne prawodawstwo*, edited by Tomasz Bekrycht and Marek Zirk-Sadowski, 41–52. Warszawa: C.H. Beck.

Wróblewski, Jerzy. 1973. "Model racjonalnego tworzenia prawa." *Państwo i Prawo* 11: 3–17.

Wróblewski, Jerzy. 1979. "A Model of Rational Law-Making." *Archiv für Rechts- und Sozialphilosophie* 65 (2): 187–201.

Wróblewski, Jerzy. 1985. *Teoria racjonalnego tworzenia prawa*. Wrocław: Zakład Narodowy im. Ossolińskich.

Wycichowski-Kuchta, Gniewomir. 2022. "In Rem Confiscation in EU Law after the *Agro in 2001* Judgement. The Polish Perspective." In *Current Issues of EU Criminal Law*, edited by Ariadna H. Ochnio and Hanna Kuczyńska, 161–176. Warsaw: Publishing House of ILS PAS. https://doi.org/10.5281/zenodo.6860757.

Wycichowski-Kuchta, Gniewomir. 2023. "The Discretion of the EU Member States in Shaping the Non-conviction Based Confiscation Regime in the Light of CJEU and ECHR Case Law." *Ruch Prawniczy, Ekonomiczny i Socjologiczny* 85 (4): 27–47. https://doi.org/10.14746/rpeis.2023.85.4.02.

Zehr, Howard. 1985. "Retributive Justice, Restorative Justice." In *New Perspectives on Crime and Justice: Occasional Papers of the MCC Canada Victim Offender Ministries Program and the MCC U.S. Office of Criminal Justice*, September, No. 4. MCC Canada Victim Offender Ministries, MCC U.S. Office of Criminal Justice. Elkhart, IN.

Zehr, Howard. 1990. *Changing Lenses: A New Focus for Crime and Justice*. Scottsdale PA: Herald Press.

Zehr, Howard. 1995. *Changing Lenses: A New Focus for Crime and Justice*. Scottsdale PA: Herald Press.

Zehr, Howard. 2002. *The Little Book of Restorative Justice*. Intercourse: Good Books.

Zehr, Howard. 2014. *The Little Book of Restorative Justice*. New York: Good Books [EPUB].

Zirk-Sadowski, Marek. 2015. "Wstęp." In *Jerzy Wróblewski. Pisma wybrane.* (*Wybór i wstęp*, by Marek Zirk-Sadowski), 5–12. Warszawa: Wolters Kluwer.

2 What can a restorative approach to justice offer to EU law-making policy on the confiscation of the proceeds of crime?

Introductory remarks

Can CPC be considered a restorative measure in EU law-making policy? This book argues that this may be achieved if confiscation policy priorities are changed from State-centred to victim- and community-centred. Much has already been written about the intricate juridical nature of confiscation. This book builds on previous considerations; however, its main purpose is not to resolve the issue of confiscation's nature but to contribute insights into this legal institution as one of the available responses to acquisitive crime from the perspective of the restorative approach to justice, a promising reference point for the future development of EU confiscation policy.

To understand what benefits restorative justice may offer to EU confiscation policy, the challenges of this area of policy should first be explored. These challenges are reflected in the main thematic streams within the ongoing discussion on confiscation, outlined in the first section of this chapter. They revolve around the questionable juridical nature of confiscation, which challenges the civil–criminal dichotomy. Presenting the main arguments of this discourse is intended to highlight the sophisticated and complex legal identity of confiscation, an institution that escapes the classic divisions, operating instead at the intersection of different branches of law. Thus, as an alternative, a 'policy-oriented approach' distinguished in the legal doctrine is presented. Under this approach, confiscation is framed in the context of political questions and goals. Addressing confiscation at the level of policy questions and goals has the merit of formulating arguments for confiscation tailored to specific, identified needs. Simultaneously, it respects the guarantees of the rights of participants in confiscation proceedings and incorporates the social dimension of confiscation policy into its framework.

Regardless of the various arguments on the legal nature and functions of the CPC, formulated on the background of traditional civil–criminal division, it is an indisputable fact that this institution, depending on its legal construct (e.g., the application of the 'net' or 'gross' principle), may involve an element of 'hardship', which is characteristic of criminal punishment. It may also involve an element of 'blame', even if directed at a non-convicted person. Accordingly, the second section considers the approach to punishment in retributive, reductivist, and restorative accounts, with an emphasis on the latter. However, the purpose

DOI: 10.4324/9781003465829-2

of this section is not to review all the accounts, especially in light of their multiplicity and complexity (forward-looking, backward-looking, hybrid), but to provide some representative examples *via* an energetic journey through the most well-established paths of thought, giving legislatures some perspective on what a restorative approach to justice offers when shaping confiscation mechanisms and determining their objectives. The final section focuses on the concrete possible benefits of redirecting EU law-making policy on the CPC towards a more restorative path.

The juridical nature of the confiscation of the proceeds of crime, challenging the civil–criminal dichotomy

Different patterns of regulation adopted in national legal orders have sparked debate among European researchers concerned about the threat to criminal trial guarantees. The specific characteristics which determine whether confiscation has a punitive or non-punitive nature are regularly disputed (i.a., Gallant and King 2013; Bullock 2014; Bullock and Lister 2014; Rui and Sieber 2015; Boucht 2019; Simonato 2017; Burchard 2019; Mazzacuva 2019; King and Hendry 2023).

The doctrinal perception of how the features of the concrete type of confiscation determine its punitive or non-punitive nature was significantly influenced by the optics of the ECtHR when testing its different forms through the *Engel* criteria[1] concerning a criminal charge. The starting criterion, but not the decisive one, is the classification of an offence in domestic law as criminal. The second criterion, of greater importance, is the nature of the offence. The third criterion is the severity of the maximum penalty that the person risks. The last two criteria are, in principle, alternative. However, if analysis of each criterion does not lead to a clear conclusion on the existence of a criminal charge, they can be assessed cumulatively.[2] The ECtHR considered confiscation to be a penalty, i.a., in *Varvara*[3] and in *Welch.*[4] In the latter case, the ECtHR considered that the 'combination of punitive elements' in a confiscation order amounted to a penalty (see also Zedner 2016).

Being one of the legal responses to acquisitive crime, the CPC can be viewed through different lenses, especially by lawyers rooted in those civil law systems where confiscation has been traditionally treated as a criminal punishment and by lawyers rooted in common law systems for whom it is natural to treat confiscation as a restitutive measure. For example, Bowles, Faure, and Garoupa (2005) indicate that for certain types of offences (committed sequentially or victimless), the removal of illegal gain (net benefit) through the use of confiscation is treated as a 'restitutive measure' (not a 'criminal sanction') and may be a complement to traditional monetary sanctions having a punitive goal, like fines. The latter are limited by proportionality issues (cf. Summers 2022, 91–156; and Boucht's observations on 'retrospective' and 'prospective' proportionality, 2019, 168–185). The literature indicates the development of two approaches to confiscation: 'punitive' and 'deprivatory' (Fisher and Bong-Kwan 2018). In a non-punitive approach, confiscation performs a similar function to civil restitution. Deprivation of the illicit profits is treated as restoration of the previous financial conditions (*restitutio in integrum*).

Confiscation, when formally classified in a legal system as a criminal sanction, is naturally associated with punitive goals like retribution or deterrence (see, e.g., Simonato and Fernandez-Bertier 2019; Fernandez-Bertier 2016). Nevertheless, the process of successive detachment of confiscation from a punitive function can also be observed in civil law jurisdictions, where it traditionally belonged to the code system of penal measures. Confiscation, when formally classified in a legal system as a civil measure, operates *in rem*. In principle, it should not involve the elements of 'hardship' or 'blame' inherent in criminal punishment, which operates *in personam*. However, depriving a person of illicit assets without a conviction may involve an element of apportioning 'blame'. Moreover, confiscation based on the 'gross' principle may involve an element of 'hardship'. As indicated by Levy (1996), 'The trouble is that civil law also may punish, making the distinction between the civil and criminal law somewhat bewildering' (22).

It is worth noting that even civil confiscation is linked with crime control purposes (Naylor 1999, 2003; Simser 2009), and its goals are not perceived as merely non-punitive (reparative) but also punitive (Gallant and King 2013). In addition, the view has been presented that civil and criminal forfeitures do indeed have similar goals (Cassella 2013a). The issue is also complex from the perspective of EU law, which recognises both punitive and non-punitive confiscations ordered within the criminal track.

Another thematic area in the discourse on confiscation pertains to how it is justified, both in the criminal and civil realms (e.g., Fried 1988; Levy 1996). An oft-repeated slogan is: 'crime does not pay'. Alldridge (2002) pointed out that confiscation is justified by the principle 'that people, in general, should not profit from unlawful activity and from crime' (284) and explained:

> It follows from the requirement that, if law is to impact upon people's behavior, it should deliver coherent messages. It is not coherent, on the one hand, to try to create disincentives to a particular form of behaviour but, on the other, to permit someone who does it to benefit.
>
> (Alldridge 2002, 284)

In the same vein, Simser (2009) argued that one of the policy rationales for civil forfeiture is that 'gains from unlawful activity ought not to accrue and accumulate in the hands of those who commit unlawful activity' (13). Fried (1988) contended that the forfeiture of the profits of crime 'is the minimum just penalty, because it ensures that the offender shall not benefit by his wrongdoing' (333) and at the same time observed:

> criminal forfeiture has more in common with civil restitution than with traditional punishments. Like restitution, it merely restores the *status quo ante* and, thus lacks the expressive quality of traditional punishments which have the capacity to express the moral opprobrium of the community.
>
> (Fried 1988, 333)

There are also other voices, such as Levy's (1996), who noted that the 'law neatly divides the legal universe into two words: civil and criminal', but, nonetheless, 'both civil and criminal law inflict forfeitures' (22–23). In this context, Levy raised the non-existence of any 'principled or realistic way (…) to distinguish civil and criminal cases, especially concerning penalties' and indicated that civil forfeitures 'have nothing to do with private rights and remedies' (22).

Depending on the decision of a national lawmaker, confiscation can formally function in the realm of criminal or civil justice (either in parallel or not). Nonetheless, taking into account the ECtHR's approach, the decision of a national legislator to locate a legal institution within a given branch of law is not conclusive. Due to the fact that the civil standard of proof based on the balance of probabilities is less demanding than the criminal one (the latter refers to 'proof beyond a reasonable doubt'), there may be a natural temptation for lawmakers to transfer a legal institution from the criminal to civil realm, while at the same time not eliminating the element of hardship that determines its penal character. In this situation, the action is better described as a re-labelling, not a substantive change. Indeed, making clear demarcations in confiscation issues can be confusing, as it is a multidimensional and, after years of practical application, a legally sophisticated institution that transcends traditional approaches. One obvious consequence of this confusion may be the weakening of guarantees of the rights of individuals, especially if a State only transfers the labelling from the criminal to the civil sphere without also changing the applicable remedies. From the perspective of continental law systems, however, it is important that such a non-criminal procedure (civil) is vertically oriented (between the State and individual) and is not characterised by the equality of the parties inherent in horizontally oriented civil proceedings designed to settle claims of a civil nature.[5] In this context, this procedure has more in common with an 'administrative' procedure. For example, the ambiguous character of civil recovery procedures is reflected in their description as 'hybrid' (civil/criminal) actions (King and Hendry 2023, 21).

In the subject literature, Rui and Sieber (2015) shed light on the possible different natures of confiscation depending on the mechanism adopted in a legal system. These authors also systematised the possible areas of discussion on confiscation issues, thus preparing the ground for developing further considerations. Their achievements in this area offer a stable starting point for EU and national legislatures when rethinking confiscation policy. By adopting the policy-oriented approach proposed by these authors, the varying forms of confiscation may be viewed from the perspective of certain simplified output models available to legislatures.

At this point, an important caveat is that the distinctions made at the level of output models do not contradict the complexity of the goals of criminal punishment, some of which are indisputably forward-looking.

The first model proposed for consideration by these authors is the 'criminal law model', in which confiscation is a penal measure of a retrospective and retributive nature, looking backwards and causing a certain amount of hardship to the offender (Rui and Sieber 2015, 250, 255).

Secondly, a legislature may consider the 'civil law model', in which confiscation is a retrospective measure, limited to restoring the state prior to the commission of the unlawful act (*status quo ante*) without creating additional hardship for the offender. In this option, a 'hardship' is understood as the 'surplus' that determines the penal nature of the measure (Rui and Sieber 2015, 250, 255).

The third option is the 'police law model', in which confiscation is a preventive measure targeting a future 'supposed' unlawful act. Its juridical nature is non-retrospective and non-retributive. The justification for a preventive confiscation refers to the potential danger (posed by a person or property) of committing an unlawful act in the future. As noted by these authors, when used correctly, this measure should not amount to a penalty (Rui and Sieber 2015, 254–255).[6]

The preventive functions of the CPC are derived from the concept of danger emanating from the perpetrator, or more specifically for this legal institution, from property deemed to be illicit (as a result of the use of various legal constructions, including those not based on demonstrating a connection between assets and criminal activity). The well-established justifications for non-conviction based and forward-looking confiscation mechanisms refer, firstly, to the danger emanating from the offender, as in the mechanism adopted in the 'Anti-mafia Code' (2011) in Italy.[7] Specific Italian legal solutions concerning confiscation used in the fight against organised crime are often given as an example of the preventive function of confiscation (Kilchling 1977; Maugeri 2001; Vettori 2006; Simonato 2017). There have also been in-depth analyses that have tended towards the hybrid nature of the Italian 'anti-mafia' solutions, based mainly on the danger coming from the offender and partly on the danger generated by the property (Panzavolta and Flor 2015). It's worth noting that the nature of this measure is described by the Italian Supreme Court as administrative, not civil, which is a more understandable description for a lawyer familiar with continental law (Panzavolta and Flor 2015).[8] At the same time, these analysts remind us that there is a fine line between punitive administrative law and criminal law (Panzavolta and Flor 2015, 140).

In addition, the justifications refer to the danger emanating from the property in question, as in civil recovery proceedings (*in rem*). A challenging area for lawmakers is properly safeguarding the rights of third parties in non-criminal proceedings. It is not without reason that many arguments have already been made around the need for adequate protection of the rights of all individuals involved in civil procedures (not just the *bona fide* ones). In this regard, extensive US experience with civil asset recovery is valuable (e.g., Berman 1999; Cassella 2013b). It is particularly difficult for legislatures to justify a confiscation by reference to the danger posed by property, as any measures taken may ultimately affect and 'blame' the individual who possesses the property, someone who may not have any connection to criminal activity. In this context, it is worth recalling the specific historical roots of civil forfeitures (Finkelstein 1973; Gordon 1995), reaching the law of the deodand, under which an 'inanimate object that caused a death was deemed to be "guilty" of a crime and therefore was offered to God through forfeiture to the King' (Berman 1999, 2). The legal fiction of transferring 'guilt' to inanimate objects or animals served purposes rather disconnected from those of modern civil forfeitures. However, the concept of harm emanating from property has merit if illicit property is considered an initial economic generator for a future crime.

The question arises of whether it is possible for EU law-making policy to refer to the concept of property that 'can do harm' (Vogel 2015, 225), using it as justification for a criminal CPC. From the point of view of civil jurisdictions, such references only in cases of criminal confiscation of contraband do not seem to raise any major doubts. The application of the harm principle is less obvious when it comes to instrumentalities, especially regarding objects whose nature is not usually closely related to criminal activity and not owned by the perpetrator (e.g., real estate). However, assuming that a crime creates a broadly understood social harm by disturbing the functioning of social groups, it seems that the harm principle relating to the danger of property could also be a rationale for a criminal CPC if juxtaposed with the basic tenets of restorative justice. All the more so, given that harm, broadly defined, is the core rationale for criminalisation processes.

Regarding the legal construction of the 'harm principle', Vogel (2015) clarified that it involves 'criminal' harm and perfectly captured its essence, which lies in the statement: 'property which can be (ab-) used to do criminal harm' (226). This approach falls within the broader 'harm prevention principle' (Vogel 2015, 231). A shift to a restorative justice perspective in EU law-making policy on the CPC would theoretically allow it to be partially based on the harm principle pertaining to both elements, the offender and the property, i.e., the danger of causing broadly understood criminal harm (in the social dimension) posed by the person or property. The challenge, of course, is to determine the acceptable limits of interference motivated by the danger emanating from the property. However, the use of this legal structure, placing the burden of 'guilt' on property, seems feasible, at least when shaping the phase of disposing of confiscated property in the EU legal arena. This process should prioritise restorative goals by allocating confiscated assets to social and public purposes that address the needs of communities affected by or vulnerable to crime.

Conversely, relying on concepts such as 'danger' and 'harm prevention' can be a risky proposition, with the potential for unrestrained application exceeding the limits of imperative interference determined by the appropriate level of protection of human rights and the proportionality of the legal response to a crime. At this point, it is worth referring to Boucht's (2019) observation, who noted the 'boundlessness' inherent in preventive measures (132–133).

In this context, a further observation is relevant against the backdrop of the rich American history of civil forfeiture. A noticeable feature of the US legal doctrine concerning forfeiture (equivalent to 'confiscation' in the nomenclature of EU law) is a reduced focus on the dichotomous division between the criminal and civil features of forfeiture. Instead, the focus is on the categories of property subject to forfeiture, i.e., 'forfeiture of contraband', 'forfeiture of proceeds', 'facilitation forfeiture', and 'enterprise forfeiture' (e.g., Worrall 2008, 5–6; Fried 1988, 331–333).

Following this trend of thought, Pimentel (2012) proposed a reconceptualisation of forfeiture procedures, abandoning the criminal-civil distinction in favour of 'new distinctions based on the nature of the forfeiture' (determined by the object of forfeiture): 'contraband forfeitures', 'proceeds forfeitures', 'facilitating-property forfeitures' (34–42). Accordingly, public policy should be redefined in accordance with this new approach (observing these new distinctions). Pimentel's concept was expanded on by Vogel (2015), who determined that the object of confiscation should be the decisive factor for public policies when it comes to appropriately locating the type of confiscation in the legal system.

Vogel (2015) elaborated on this view by indicating appropriate procedures following the distinctions of Pimentel and proposed the following paths for confiscation policies. As far as 'forfeiture of contraband' is concerned, an administrative or police procedure should be appropriate with the guarantee of a judicial review. For 'forfeiture of proceeds', civil procedure should be appropriate, but only on the basis of the 'net profit' principle, which would limit the purpose of this measure to restoring the pre-enrichment *status quo*. Accordingly, Vogel aptly pointed out that if this measure is based on the principle of gross revenues, it may amount to a criminal penalty (or even become 'harshly punitive'), and the standards of criminal procedure should apply (Vogel 2015, 238). Under this view, making the right policy choice is even more complicated when it comes to 'forfeiture of instrumentalities', as relying on the prevention principle is justified only regarding instrumentalities linked to criminal conduct (as in the given example of the equipment in a drug laboratory). This principle cannot serve as a reliable basis for depriving possessors of objects that are instrumentalities of crime but which, by their very nature, are not usually related to criminal activity (e.g., real estate or means of payment) unless the likelihood of its future illegal use is proven. Even more so given that the State does not remove such things from economic circulation and can reinvest them. Accordingly, in Vogel's view, if forfeiture of instrumentalities constitutes 'extra' punishment for a perpetrator, the criminal route is appropriate, and reducing the protection of 'innocent' or 'guilty third parties', whose property was abused, would be 'highly questionable' (Vogel 2015, 242). However, it is common practice in EU jurisdictions to base the CPC on the 'gross principle', which implies that the calculation of assets covers the costs. Bearing in mind the cited considerations of Vogel concerning the punitive route for the type of the CPC based on the 'gross principle', one might conclude that we are dealing with a punitive measure, for which criminal procedure is appropriate.

Undoubtedly, the ECtHR has set the tone for scientific debate on the CPC in the context of EU law. Nevertheless, a narrative focused on the dichotomous civil–criminal division involves a rigid conceptual grid of confiscation issues, largely referring to ECHR guarantees targeted at the criminal or civil spheres (the criminal or civil limbs of Article 6 of the ECHR). The ECtHR's case-law revolves around the necessary elements of punitiveness of the examined legal measures, whereas it is noticeable that confiscation issues have nonetheless evaded such a narrative. On the other hand, it should not be forgotten that the ECtHR's approach to confiscation, although formally based on an apparently meticulous division into criminal and civil spheres, has faced criticism in the literature as unsafe, given the impact of the ECtHR's jurisprudence. For example, Panzavolta and Flor (2015) described the ECtHR's approach as tolerant (142). With regard to the Italian legal solutions on confiscation, Mazzacuva (2019) enquired if it would be reasonable to recommend that the ECtHR follow a 'safer approach' (114). In the opinion of Maugeri (2018), expressed in the context of the case *Gogitidze v Georgia*,[9] the ECtHR presented a 'favourable disposition towards civil forfeiture as a strategy against serious crime' (412). Moreover, Trechsel (2005) raised some objections to the ECtHR's jurisprudence in the context of human rights protections (34–35). Also, Boucht (2019) pointed to the problematic tendency of the ECtHR to treat preventive measures 'fairly generously' and notes that this approach 'does not seem to provide very far-reaching tools for challenging extensive confiscation powers of the member states' (132). While Boucht noted the safety of the civil–criminal division due to the accompanying safeguards, similarly to Steiker (1997) (whose considerations, though relevant, concerned American law), at the same time found this division to be very challenging in cases of asset confiscation. Boucht argued, therefore, in support of a slightly different 'meta-approach', focused not on a rigid civil–criminal division but on building a safeguarding regime, both substantive and procedural. This regime should be based on the nature of the allegation, the interests involved, and the onerous effects on the individual (Boucht 2019, 135).

For critical thinking about EU confiscation policy, observations made against the background of well-established American solutions may to some extent also be relevant. One example is the approach of converging the objectives of civil and criminal forfeitures. Cassella (2013b, 837) and Vogel (2015, 226, 228) share the view that, in principle, civil and criminal forfeitures do not differ in terms of nature, as both have repressive and preventive goals. What distinguishes them is the type of procedure through which they are imposed. Cassella (2015) even refers to civil forfeiture as a 'procedural device' (14). Taking this view into account, it can be concluded that it is mainly procedural issues that differentiate the positions of the individuals affected by these measures. An example of a comprehensive approach towards the goals assigned to criminal forfeitures is the position of the US Supreme Court in *Kaley v United States*:[10]

> Forfeitures help to ensure that crime does not pay: They at once punish wrongdoing, deter future illegality, and 'lessen the economic power' of criminal enterprises. [...] The Government also uses forfeited property to recompense victims of crime, improve conditions in crime-damaged communities, and support law enforcement activities like police training.

In addition, in *Caplin & Drysdale, Chartered v United States*, the US Supreme Court pointed out:[11]

> there is a strong governmental interest in obtaining full recovery of the assets, since the assets are deposited in a fund that supports law-enforcement efforts, since the statute allows property to be recovered by its rightful owners, and since a major purpose behind forfeiture provisions [...] is to lessen the economic power of organized crime and drug enterprises.

The position of the US Supreme Court is also far-reaching in terms of civil forfeitures, as reflected in *Austin v United States*. The Court emphasised in that case that the Eighth Amendment to the US Constitution (concerning protection from excessive bail, excessive fines, and cruel and unusual punishments) is not limited to criminal cases and determined that forfeiture falls within its scope. According to the Court, the question of the civil or criminal character of a forfeiture is not determinative, as civil forfeiture may also constitute a punishment (see also Bowles, Faure, and Garoupa 2005, 281):[12]

> sanctions frequently serve more than one purpose, the fact that a forfeiture serves remedial goals will not exclude it from the Clause's purview [the Excessive Fines Clause], so long as it can only be explained as serving in part to punish.

In sum, the ongoing discussion on confiscation issues, viewed through the prism of political questions and goals, runs parallel to the discussion through the prism of the civil–criminal division. After all, in examining this multi-form legal measure, it cannot be denied that Simonato (2017, 369) is right to state that the question of whether a confiscation is a criminal sanction is crucial. However, in this context, it is also worth quoting the complementary question posed by Burchard (2019) in the title of the article pertaining to the European and German confiscation regimes: 'Confiscation as criminal law (or what)? On how the ill-advised discussion about "the" legal "nature" of confiscation obfuscates what really needs to be discussed' (see also Burchard 2023). Burchard's position focuses on political questions concerning confiscation instead of its legal nature, as confiscation 'operates on the indeterminacy of its many rationalities'. Accordingly, this author introduced the concept of 'normative openness' of the confiscation and its 'possibility of embracing the justificatory pluralism', which referred to the Nietzschean concept of 'fluidity' (Burchard 2019, 213). For Nietzsche (2007, 52), this was one of the two aspects of punishment:

> one is its relative permanence, the custom, the act, the 'drama', a certain strict sequence of procedures, the other is its fluidity, its meaning [Sinn], purpose and expectation, which is linked to the carrying out of such procedures.

The purpose of this book is not to decide which approach is correct, as there are persuasive arguments for and against each position. The focus is on improving EU law-making policy on the CPC, by redirecting it to a more restorative path. However, such a position does not exclude drawing on both of these approaches to address policy questions. Taking all elements into account, there is certainly one major lesson for EU policy to learn from the American approach to forfeiture. The EU legislator should focus as much as possible on strong procedural safeguards, selected depending on the appropriate assignment of the measure to the branch of law, civil (administrative) or criminal. In addition, given that the legal institution of confiscation has a sophisticated juridical nature, the criminal and non-criminal procedures of its adjudication should also be sufficiently sophisticated (especially the *quasi*-criminal ones) in order to effectively guarantee the rights of all participants.

Ultimately, it will be the European judiciary and doctrine that will test the EU's legal solutions concerning confiscation, with reference first to the ECHR and the ECtHR *acquis*, although their views may also evolve towards a 'meta-approach' (see Boucht 2019), and seeking hard guarantees in highly specialised *sui generis* non-criminal procedures dedicated to confiscation. An argument in favour of the development of this trend is the growing experience of applying confiscation measures in EU jurisdictions outside the realm of criminal justice. It should not be forgotten, though, that such an approach brings forth many unresolved questions of human rights protections (see, e.g., the criticism of 'procedural hybrids', as applied in the sphere of civil recovery, and 'middleground processes', expressed by King and Hendry 2023, 21–39).

However, it should be noted that the current EU policy is oriented around developing non-conviction based confiscation mechanisms.[13] It may be expected that EU law will evolve towards developing *sui generis* non-criminal confiscation procedures (*quasi*-criminal). In constructing such procedures, legal safeguards (embedded in procedural and substantive law) should be the most important aspect. The side effect of taking such a policy direction may result in a shift away from the traditional narrative on the criminal-civil division and, consequently, a departure from difficult human rights issues connected with confiscation operating beyond the criminal realm.

Taking into account the doctrinal output on confiscation issues, the most reasonable policy option to safeguard the rights of individuals involved in confiscation proceedings appears to be the adoption of a twofold approach focused on policy questions and goals (consistent with the restorative approach to justice) and, equally, the appropriate choice of criminal or civil routes for confiscation. However, progress in this respect ultimately depends on the inextricably linked issues of 'law-making policy' and 'law', i.e., the objectives of confiscation are determined by the legislature, and its legal construct follows from that.

Approach to punishment in retributivist, reductivist, and restorative accounts

Restorative accounts involve specific views on the appropriate response to crime. However, it should be emphasised at the outset that the advocates of restorative justice express a fairly wide range of views on punishment. The initial analyses have concentrated on highlighting the differences between the 'restorative' and 'retributive' approaches; however, over time, this relationship has come to be perceived as not a choice between alternatives but as a pair of complementary perspectives (see, e.g., Marshall 1996, 1999; Daly 2000; Ashworth 2002; Duff 2011). To better understand various positions on punishment in restorative accounts, considerations should begin with an outline of examples of various justifications of punishment. However, a thorough description in this regard would exceed the thematic framework of the book. Therefore, attention has been paid to the representative examples of the well-established justifications.

If we take a forward-looking utilitarian approach, which focuses on the future consequences of actions, the response to crime should seek to balance the 'good' that has been harmed by an unlawful act (by increasing happiness and reducing pain). Sandel indicates that from a utilitarian view, the principle of 'maximising utility', where 'utility' is understood by Bentham as 'whatever produces pleasure or happiness and whatever prevents pain and suffering', should be guided not only by individuals but also by legislators (Sandel 2009, 34). According to Bentham, the core purpose of law is to increase the 'total happiness':

> The general object that all laws have or ought to have in common is to increase the total happiness of the community; and therefore in the first place to exclude as far as possible everything that tends to reduce that happiness, i.e. to exclude mischief. [...] But all punishment is mischief; all punishment in itself is bad. On the principle of utility it ought to be allowed only insofar as it promises to exclude some greater evil.
>
> [Bentham 2007, 170, (1780) (1789)]

Based on this assumption, Bentham also recognised the problem of the unprofitability of punishment when 'the evil of the punishment exceeds that of the offence' [Bentham 2007, 350, (1780) (1789)].

Utilitarian future-oriented reasoning is associated with the reductivist views, which treat punishment as an element of 'crime control'. In this context, Cavadino et al. (2020) indicated:

> Reductivism is a *forward-looking* (or 'consequentialist') theory: it seeks to justify punishment by its alleged *future consequences*. Punishment is justified, it is claimed, because it helps to control crime. If punishment is inflicted, there will be less crime committed thereafter than there would be if no penalty were imposed.
>
> (Cavadino et al. 2020, Ch. 2.2)

Simplifying, according to the reductivist approach, crime reduction may be achieved through the effects of punishment, which can be identified in various dimensions: deterrence (individual and general), incapacitation of an offender from returning to wrongdoing, rehabilitation (or reform) of an offender, the desistance of an offender from wrongdoing (see also Altman 2023; Carr 2021; Cavadino et al. 2020). In the context of the deterrent effect on crime, which has often been questioned by researchers, it is worth referring to Braithwaite's theory of 'reintegrative shaming', which has also influenced restorative accounts (see also the 'labelling theories', Burke 2014). According to Braithwaite,

> the consequence of reintegrative shaming is that criminal subcultures appear less attractive to the offender. Shaming is the most potent weapon of social control unless it shades into stigmatization. Formal criminal punishment is an ineffective weapon of social control partly because it is a degradation ceremony with maximum prospects for stigmatization.
>
> (Braithwaite 1989, 14)

If we take a backward-looking retributivist approach, the response to a crime is based on the guilt of the perpetrator and the search for an appropriate and proportional reaction to the crime (see also Duff's observations on retributivism 2001, 19–26). Retributivist thoughts have ancient roots and see the essence of punishment differently from the utilitarian mindset. For example, in Kant's theory, 'deserving punishment' was the central concern. Kant equated the 'right to punish' with the right to 'inflict pain' (Kant 2017, 114–115; see also Murphy 1979, 82). In 'Doctrine of Right' Kant argued:

> The right to punish is the right a ruler has against a subject to inflict pain upon him because of his having committed a crime. [...] Punishment by a court (poena forensis) – this is distinct from natural punishment (poena naturalis), in which vice punishes itself and which the legislator does not take into account – can never be inflicted merely as a means to promote some other good for the criminal himself or for civil society. It must always be inflicted upon him only because he has committed a crime. For a human being can never be treated merely as a means to the purposes of another or be put among the objects of rights to things: his innate personality protects him from this, even though he can be condemned to lose his civil personality.
>
> [Kant 2017, 114–115, (1797)]

Notably, Cavadino et al. (2020) observed that retributivism is in some way linked with the rights of offenders and victims:

> there is a natural connection between the retributive approach and the idea that both offenders and victims have *rights*. Reductivist theory (at least in its utilitarian form) has always found it difficult to encompass the notion of rights, even when it comes to asserting that entirely innocent people have a right not to be punished.
>
> (Cavadino et al. 2020, Ch. 2.3)

The same authors advocate for a human rights approach to punishment, seeing a 'basis for a principled compromise between reductivism and retributivism' in rights theory (Cavadino et al. 2020, Ch. 2.7, Ch. 10.3). In addition, they favour the restorative justice approach, seeing the virtue of reparation schemes in how an influence on 'the nature of the offender's punishment' is afforded to the offender and victim, increasing their positive freedom (Ch. 2.7). Another proponent of the human rights perspective is Summers (2022), who sees the virtue of human rights principles in 'clear restrictions on the power of the state to punish':

> Punishment [...] will only be compatible with human rights if it is imposed on a culpable individual for the commission of an act or omission, which is clearly and prospectively defined as criminal. In addition, it must be free from arbitrariness, must not constitute a disproportionate interference with — or fundamentally violate — certain human rights, and must be imposed by a judge in the context of criminal proceedings.
>
> (Summers 2022, 228)

Between the backward- and forward-looking positions exists a broad spectrum of mixed accounts. For the purposes of the book, it is worth referring to two examples of hybrid descriptions, one from Hart with strong forward-looking elements and the second proposed by Duff with strong backward-looking elements (see also Wood 2002; Rawls 1971).

If we take a compromise approach to build on traditional thoughts as proposed by Hart, we should strive to answer a variety of questions, because the 'different principles (each of which may in a sense be called a "justification") are relevant at different points in any morally acceptable account of punishment' (Hart 2008, 3; see also Gardner 2010). Hart posed the following essential questions about punishment:[14]

> What justifies the general practice of punishment? To whom may punishment be applied? How severely may we punish? In dealing with these and other questions concerning punishment we should bear in mind that in this, as in most other social institutions, the pursuit of one aim may be qualified by or provide an opportunity, not to be missed, for the pursuit of others. Till we have developed this sense of the complexity of punishment [...] we shall be in no fit state to assess the extent to which the whole institution has been eroded by, or needs to be adapted to, new beliefs about the human mind.
>
> (Hart 2008, 3)

In addition, Hart (2008) defined the 'standard' or 'central case' of punishment by alluding to Benn (1958) and Flew (1954), the so-called 'Benn-Flew-Hart' definition of punishment (McPherson 1967). Hart's definition consists of five elements:

(i) it must involve pain or other consequences normally considered unpleasant,
(ii) it must be for an offence against legal rules,
(iii) it must be of an actual or supposed offender for his offence,
(iv) it must be intentionally administrated by human beings other than the offender, and
(v) it must be imposed and administrated by an authority constituted by a legal system against which the offence is committed (Hart 2008, 4–5).

Duff's (1986) perception of punishment is different; a punishment emanates from moral criticism directed towards the perpetrator for his past act, i.e., for the wrong that was done (a backward-looking position). Nonetheless, in this view, the true purpose of the punishment is not merely retributive (see also Nozick's (1981) views on 'teleological' retributivism; Cragg 2005). Considering the purpose of law in terms of serving the 'common good', it also involves a forward-looking component (Duff 1986, 91–92):

> Blame, like punishment, is intended to induce suffering in an alleged offender for an alleged offence. [...] This conceptual connection between blame and wrong-doing may be emphasised by a retributivist account of blame as a proper response to wrong-doing: but it can also figure in a consequentialist view of blame as a technique for achieving certain further

> ends, thus distinguishing blame, as a mechanism which operates through the purported condemnation of an offender, from other kinds of social mechanism.
>
> (Duff 1986, 41)

According to Duff (2011), the purposes of the criminal process concern both 'reform of future conduct' and 'reparation for past wrongdoing' (Duff 2011, 78). The view of a complementary, rather than mutually exclusive, relationship between 'restoration' and 'retribution' was explained by Duff (2003, 43) as follows:

> restorative theorists are right to insist that our responses to crime should seek 'restoration', whilst retributive theorists are right to argue that we should seek to bring offenders to suffer the punishments they deserve; but that both sides to the controversy are wrong to suppose that these aims are incompatible. Restoration is not only compatible with retribution: it *requires* retribution, in that the kind of restoration that crime makes necessary can (given certain deep features of our social lives) be brought about only through retributive punishment (see also Daly 2000).

In the study 'Alternatives to Punishment – or Alternative Punishments?' Duff (1992) perceived a conflict (i.e., the idea of crime as a conflict) not as a purely private 'property', but rather as a 'public wrong' (cf. Christie 1977):

> a crime (especially if we think of the central kinds of *mala in se*) attacks not just its direct victim, but the values of the whole community, and the community owes it to its members to protect them against such wrongs.
>
> (Duff 1992, 63)

In addition, Duff (2001) characteristically considered criminal punishment in terms of communication (cf. Nozick's observations on communication theories 1981, 371):

> criminal punishment should be conceived of as a communicative enterprise that aims to communicate to offenders the censure they deserve for their crimes, and thus to bring them to repent their crimes, to reform themselves, and to reconcile themselves with those they have wronged.
>
> (Duff 2001, 129)

It should be noted that various arguments have been formulated to support the ideas of 'restorative punishment' (e.g., Duff 2003; Levanon 2015), 'punitive restoration' (Brooks 2017) or restorative justice as an 'alternative form of punishment' (e.g., Johnstone 2011). Johnstone presented the following view:

> Restorative justice, as Daly (2000) and others suggest, might be more accurately presented as an alternative form of punishment, rather than an alternative to punishment.
>
> (Johnstone 2011, 91)

Next, Levanon (2015), inspired by Hegel, pointed out the restorative aspects of punishment. In Levanon's view, 'crime disrupts the subject-subject relation between the victim and the offender, and that punishment works to restore this relation' (2015, 537). Another example may be found in the ideas of Brooks (2017). In the article 'Punitive Restoration and Restorative Justice', Brooks argued:

> Punitive restoration is *restorative* insofar as it aims to achieve the restoration of rights infringed, or threatened, by criminal offences. [...] This aim is accomplished through recognition of the crime as a public wrong leading to a contractual arrangement agreed upon by stakeholders. Punitive restoration is *punitive* because it extends the available options for a restorative contract to achieve restoration and this may include forms of hard treatment.
>
> (Brooks 2017, 128)

It's also worth referring to Cragg's (2005) theory of punishment, which modifies the purpose of punishment while at the same time retaining the strengths of the traditional concepts (see Brunk 1996). In Cragg's view, the purpose of sentencing is to achieve restorative justice and the imposition of 'hard treatment' is not the purpose but the result of sentencing. Cragg stated:

> The function of enforcement is [...] essentially restorative. And the goal of sentencing is restorative justice. As we shall see, what results is a theory of punishment that captures the essential features of the traditional accounts, accepts the inevitability of punishment as a feature of criminal justice, but goes beyond the traditional accounts by suggesting that, while punishment is unavoidable, imposing hard treatment is not the purpose of sentencing but rather its result. The purpose of sentencing is, and ought to be, restorative justice.
>
> (Cragg 2005, 7)

In addition, Cragg noted three important functions of sentencing:

> sentencing, like enforcement generally, has three functions: to demonstrate widespread willingness to obey the law, conjoined with commitment to conscientious enforcement; to persuade those who might otherwise not obey the law to do so; and to enable those who might not otherwise obey the law to do so.
>
> (Cragg 2005, 138)

An analysis of traditional philosophical accounts of punishment, and the assumption that legal systems arose in response to the 'human need for cooperation' and the 'human vulnerability to violence', led Cragg (2005) to the conclusion that the function of law is to reduce the use of violence in settling disputes and the function of the sentence is to sustain individual and public confidence in the law as capable of fulfilling its role (7). Public confidence, specifically the loss of such as the result of the conflict caused by an offence, and then its restoration through the resolution of the conflict play an important role in Cragg's approach to sentencing:

> The function of a sentence [...] is the resolution of disputes to which criminal offences give rise in ways designed to sustain confidence in the capacity of the law to fulfil its legitimate functions on the part of victims of crime and the public at large. To do this effectively, the sentencing process must demonstrate commitment on the part of authorities to law enforcement, while seeking to persuade and enable offenders to live within the law.
>
> (Cragg 2005, 153)

In this context, it is also worth mentioning Barton's view on the complexity of restorative justice responses:

> In practice, restorative justice responses incorporate both punitive and retributive measures. Typically, they are mixed with other measures such as increased social and community support to eliminate the underlying causes of the offending, and where indicated, further education and treatment.
>
> (Barton 2003, 21)

Nevertheless, there is another strong trend in the discussion on punishment between restorative theorists, involving the opinion that criminal punishment is not in line with restorative justice. The early restorative justice proponents presented such a way of thinking, later expanded upon, i.a., by Braithwaite (1999) or Walgrave (2008).

In the restorative justice literature, attempts have been made to identify some common and distinctive elements in restorative theorists' positions on punishment. For the purposes of this book, it's worth referring to two analyses, one conducted by Daly (2013) and a second by Gade (2021), as they give an overview of the parallel discussions in the punishment debate.

Daly (2013) compared three analysts, London, Duff, and Walgrave. The analysis by Daly (2013) shows that the element common between London, Duff, and Walgrave is the approach to the aim of criminal sentencing identified as 'restoration', while the differences concern their approaches to punishment (understood as intentional infliction of pain or suffering for wrongdoing). Daly (2013) pointed out that such an idea of punishment is seen as 'compatible' with restorative justice in the views of London (2011) and Duff (2003), and 'incompatible' in the view of Walgrave (2008). This argument is advanced by Walgrave's (2008) position that 'suffering, is not at all an appropriate tool in the pursuit of restoration' (49). It should also be noted that in one of the works, Walgrave (2003) stated:

> Punishment is a means which can be used to enforce any legal system. It is an act of power to express disapproval, possibly to enforce compliance, but it is neutral about the value system it enforces. Restoration, on the contrary, is not a means, but an outcome. Restorative justice is indisputably a consequentionalist approach to offending. It is characterised by the aim of doing justice through restoration. The broad scope of restoration inherently demonstrates its orientation to the quality of social life, as a normative beacon.
>
> (Walgrave 2003, 64)

London (2011), the next theorist compared by Daly, saw crime through the prism of a 'breach of trust'. Drawing inspiration from Dimock (1997), London considered trust in two dimensions: 'personal' and 'societal'. Accordingly, 'the restoration of trust also must operate on *both* an individual and a societal level' (London 2011, 9):

> What distinguishes crime from other types of injuries, it seemed to me, is that it represents a fundamental breach of trust. For the victim, the experience of crime results in a loss of trust in the offender and in the society that failed to provide basic security. The offender, now having been labeled as being 'untrustworthy,' is an outsider to the law-abiding community. [...] Is it really possible to restore trust? Is there anything an offender can do to regain trust, or must he remain a permanent outsider? Is there anything the criminal justice system can do to promote the restoration of trust?
>
> (London 2011, 7)

The next analysis, conducted by Gade (2021), distinguished two 'trajectories' of approaching punishment in restorative justice. Gade (2021) indicated that a 'difference trajectory' started in the 1970s with the distinguishing of restorative justice from retributive justice (Eglash 1977)[15] and is represented, i.a., by the views of Zehr (1985, 1990), Umbreit (1998), Braithwaite (1999), and Walgrave (2008). The second trajectory distinguished by Gade (2021) is the 'similarity trajectory'. It involves the arguments that restorative justice does not constitute an alternative to punishment (or an alternative paradigm). This trajectory is represented, i.a., by Marshall (1996), Daly (2000),[16] Duff (2002), Johnstone (2011), and Brooks (2017).

In addition, Gade (2021) proposed a 'midway position', which – depending on how a punishment is determined – either supports the 'similarity trajectory' or the 'difference trajectory'. According to this theorist, conceptualisations of punishment may vary under a 'nine-dimensional punishment framework', involving the following categories: 'guilt', 'type of offence', 'experience', 'voluntariness', 'authority', 'perception of guilt', 'blame', 'intention', and 'self-punishment' (Gade 2021, 131–142, 149).

In sum, the general outline of various positions on punishment expressed by the proponents of restorative justice portrays a picture of the restorative justice 'movement' which is far from homogeneity. Nevertheless, as shown by the analyses of Daly (2013) and Gade (2021), the predominant views regarding punishment can be assigned to the main trends in the restorative justice debate, which collates opinions on whether the traditional concepts of criminal punishment comply with restorative justice, or not.

The areas of possible benefits from recasting EU law-making policy on the confiscation of the proceeds of crime towards a minimalist restorative approach to justice

The main policy challenges concerning the CPC may be identified as falling into three areas. The first challenge is enhancing the effectiveness of confiscation schemes in MS. The second is ensuring an adequate level of protection for the rights of potential participants in confiscation procedures (defendants, third parties, victims, and communities). Finally, developing compatible and transparent systems of fair redistribution of recovered assets across the EU, involving social and public purposes.

The question arises of whether recasting policy towards a restorative approach to justice may help meet those challenges. This book argues that a restorative approach corresponds to the identified challenges and may contribute to addressing them at the level of EU law-making policy. I would identify three main areas in which a restorative approach to justice may foster the development of solutions to the identified challenges.

The first area of possible benefits is found in rethinking the very objective of the CPC. Challenging current assumptions about the objective of the CPC should be seen as the starting point for further changes. Incorporating the restorative objective of the CPC into EU policy implies it being tasked mainly with restoring the *status quo ante* (before a crime) and repairing the harm caused by a crime. This also involves adopting a broad concept of 'victim' and 'crime' connected with the concept of 'harm', including both the individual and societal dimensions. Further analysis will show that there are other specific objectives it can also serve. Achieving those aims is strictly connected with the effectiveness of confiscation schemes in taking illicit assets out of circulation and making illegal enrichment impossible.

The second area of possible benefits from recasting EU law-making policy towards a restorative approach to justice is to better safeguard the interests of all stakeholders (victims, communities, defendants, third parties). Adopting such an approach may contribute to the proper identification of the interests of those stakeholders and, consequently, maximising these interests, i.a., through improved protection for their rights in confiscation procedures. In this respect, it should be emphasised that restorative justice writers have addressed the issue of human rights in different ways. For example, Braithwaite (2003) pointed out that respect for fundamental human rights is one of the 'constraining values' of restorative justice (9). Here, it is also worth mentioning an observation by Skelton and Sekhonyane (2007), who noted that the methods of ensuring human rights protection in fact depend on the link between restorative justice processes and the formal criminal justice process:

> It is likely that those restorative justice processes that are interlinked with the formal criminal justice process will be under particular pressure to conform to due process standards commonly found in the criminal justice system. Restorative justice processes that are less closely linked to the criminal justice system may be able to find informal and individual ways of ensuring rights protection.
>
> (Skelton and Sekhonyane 2007, 593)

The next critical issue in restorative accounts is identifying 'stakeholders'. Zehr (2015) formulated six 'Guiding Questions of Restorative Justice':

1. Who has been hurt?
2. What are their needs?
3. Whose obligation are these?
4. What are the causes?
5. Who has a stake in this situation?
6. What is the appropriate process to involve stakeholders in an effort to address causes and put things right? (see also Zehr 1990, 2002, 2014).

When considering who 'those who have a stake in justice' are, Zehr (2015) identified victims, offenders, and communities as the primary stakeholders. Nevertheless, the issue of how 'stakeholders' are understood in the restorative justice context is a complex one. The term 'stakeholders' can be interpreted narrowly, i.e., limited to direct victims of crime and offenders, or broadly, to a different extent, involving communities (see, e.g., Christie 1986; Walklate 2006; Lewis, Hamilton, and Elmore 2021). In addition, there are different ideas around the definition of which 'communities' may have an interest in the case (Dignan 2005, 99–100). Dignan (2005) identified several strands concerning the issue of stakeholders within the restorative justice movement. According to the so-called 'civilian tendency', 'only the parties who are most directly affected by an offence — offenders and victims — are counted as stakeholders' (Dignan 2005, 4; see also Dignan 2002, 176; Cantor 1976; Wright 1991). However, Dignan noted that there are also voices within 'the civilian camp' for extending the term 'stakeholders' to those less directly affected by the offence (e.g., the families and friends of offenders or victims), the so-called 'offence community' (Dignan 2005, 4). Yet, broader interpretations of this term are possible, such as related to the 'community of interest' or the 'communitarian tendency' (Dignan 2005, 4; Young and Morris 1998, 10). And furthermore, the State – 'its authorised agents and institutions comprising the criminal justice system' – may constitute another group of stakeholders (Dignan 2005, 4).

The third area of potential benefits from recasting EU law-making policy on the CPC towards a restorative approach to justice is by prioritising the position of victims and communities over the position of the State. A transition from the current State-centred confiscation policy towards a victim-centred one may positively influence the establishment of compatible systems of fair redistribution of recovered assets across the EU, where States would not be the principal beneficiaries of confiscated assets. Since at least part of the recovered amount would be transferred to social and public purposes through a fair and transparent system of redistribution.

As far as the extent of the role of the State and its representatives is concerned, it should be noted that there are also differences in the views of restorative justice proponents. The most daring ideas on limiting the role of the State are linked with the position that restorative processes are informal processes. For example, when considering the role of the State, Christie (1981) recommended a bold approach: 'so little State as we dare' (113–114). According to this analyst, '[t]he victim has lost the case to the state' (Christie 1977, 3). Another example is Cragg's (2005) observation about some positive outcomes from the State's dominant position in criminal law, which at the same time includes negative side effects that require mitigation:

> The criminal law places the state between the offender, his victim, and the public. By acting as a buffer, the state can impose procedural safeguards designed to ensure that those accused of offences are fairly treated. The effect of the state's formal intervention, however, is to isolate offenders, making it more difficult for them to repair the harm their actions have caused and win back the confidence of those whose trust has been shaken.
>
> (Cragg 2005, 141)

It should be noted that, given the continuous development of criminal law institutions (substantive and procedural), it is puzzling that the rights of victims and communities are still not fully recognised and secured in EU policy and, hence, in EU law. In contrast, protection for the State's position has become more prominent. This observation is also valid when considering the EU confiscation scheme. However, the position of the State is more complicated when it comes to incorporating a restorative approach to justice into conventional criminal procedures. This book deals with the issue of making EU confiscation policy, and accordingly the EU confiscation scheme, more restorative, but without demanding extensive reform. Following the evolutionary approach, this book suggests that, when introducing changes, the position of the State should be adapted to the current stage of development of both policy and law. It should be taken into account that in conventional confiscation mechanisms, the State is not only the beneficiary of confiscated assets but also the organiser of the complicated confiscation procedures, including in transnational and cross-border contexts, and as such bears their costs. Therefore, realistically, the State currently cannot be completely eliminated from the EU confiscation scheme. This may justify its participation as a beneficiary of confiscated assets, at least to a certain extent, and encourage the effective execution of confiscation procedures by State authorities through various incentive schemes. However, the State's share should be significantly reduced, with preference being given to victims and communities. The stage of disposal of confiscated assets offers a space to integrate, at least to some extent, the informal restorative procedures involving various stakeholders (defendants, victims, communities). At this stage, introducing a deliberation procedure to enable constructive dialogue on the destinations of transfers of confiscated assets, including reuse for social and public purposes, seems to be a viable option.

EU policy is still evolving, increasingly recognising the restorative function of legal instruments, including those belonging to the criminal realm. A new approach is starting to emerge, as evidenced by the Impact Assessment Report which accompanied the recent Proposal for a directive on confiscation (2022).[17] An important aspect raised there is that the confiscation of crime-related assets goes beyond the punitive function and enters into the restorative area:

> confiscation does not necessarily have a punitive character: confiscation aims at taking away criminal profits, and thereby limiting the incentives for and

> capacity of criminals to continue their activities. It also has the **restorative goal** [bolded by A.H.O] of ensuring that victims of crime are compensated and that the money taken away from organised crime can be used for public interest and social purposes.
>
> (Impact Assessment Report 2022, 48)[18]

Nevertheless, much remains to be done in this field. For instance, the European Economic and Social Committee (EESC) pointed to the failure to include modern restorative solutions in that Proposal, such as increasing the transparency of asset recovery systems, and thus, strengthening public trust.[19] The EESC's position should be seen as one of the factors influencing a growing emphasis on the social dimension of EU confiscation policy, recognised in the subject literature as having significant potential for development (in this vein, see, e.g., Montaldo 2015; Vettori, Kolarov, and Rusev 2014; Vettori and Di Nicola 2017; Vettori 2018; Ochnio 2022). The EESC opinion contained conclusions, suggestions, and recommendations regarding the need to undertake additional actions at the EU level. According to the EESC, action by the Commission is needed, i.a., in the following areas of EU asset recovery mechanisms: public access to information on asset recovery (without prejudice to pending proceedings); regular publication of comprehensive statistics; adoption of transparent and accessible national strategies on asset recovery; inclusion of civil society organisations in the mechanisms of social reuse of assets (especially in the management and disposition of confiscated assets); establishing a required minimum percentage for the social reuse of confiscated assets; broadening the meaning of the 'public interest' beyond the context of the activities of public entities; clarifying the rights of victims to compensation and their priority; introducing specific cooperation mechanisms with third countries (including ensuring the rights of victims from third countries); and establishing monitoring mechanisms involving civil society groups.

In light of all these considerations, a minimalist restorative approach to justice may help with the search for appropriate solutions to EU policy challenges in various areas. First of all, this approach implies tasking confiscation with restorative goals. Secondly, by adopting a broad understanding of 'victim', 'crime', and 'harm', involving individual and societal dimensions, better chances of restoration are offered. A minimalist restorative approach also implies strengthening the procedural position of all the stakeholders in a 'confiscation case' (victims, communities, defendants, and third parties), i.a., through opening a dialogue between them on the possibilities of repairing the harm through the reuse of the 'proceeds of crime'. It should be emphasised that one of the strengths of a restorative approach is the respect for the human rights of all participants in confiscation procedures (humanistic perspective).

Moreover, under this approach, the disposal of confiscated assets should be based on the principle of returning confiscated assets to the populations, and at least partly, *via* direct transfers. This would require introducing legal guarantees and structures for such reuse of confiscated assets across the EU. Accordingly, the State's share would have to be reduced. A possible benefit of transferring confiscated assets to support grassroots initiatives (local justice perspective) is the strengthening of civil society, the condition of which determines the effectiveness of many EU policies. Under this approach, the decision-making process on the disposal of confiscated assets should to some extent involve the stakeholders and their representatives in a 'confiscation case', including social groups and local authorities. Another aspect of recasting EU confiscation policy to be more in line with a restorative approach to justice is the enabling of social control over asset recovery mechanisms operating in MS, i.a., through collecting data on confiscated assets and publishing comprehensive statistics. Taking such a policy course may serve to make confiscation procedures more inclusive, consultative, balanced, and transparent.

Taking a broader view, by increasing the added value of EU confiscation law through redirecting national confiscation schemes towards more restorative paths, its positive impact may translate into fostering public confidence in the EU criminal justice system (see also Forsaith et al. 2012). This is one of the most difficult challenges facing the EU during the recent crisis of trust regarding mutual cooperation in criminal matters. Finally, improvement of the quality of the EU *acquis*, and, through its influence, national confiscation laws, can have a positive effect on developing European legal culture (in this context, see Montaldo 2015).

Conclusions

The ambiguous juridical identity of confiscation eludes the civil–criminal division. Therefore, the procedures dedicated to this legal institution should also be sufficiently sophisticated, especially the non-criminal ones, so as to effectively guarantee the rights of all individuals involved. However, the problematic legal nature of confiscation translates into difficulty in constructing balanced procedures suited to a given type of confiscation, including the CPC. These procedures must, on the one hand, ensure the effectiveness of the confiscation process and, on the other hand, include an appropriate level of guarantees of rights.

The institution of confiscation can be viewed from many perspectives. The dominant perspective in European doctrine is the civil–criminal division, supported by the case-law of the ECtHR. However, this division is neither as simple nor as clear-cut as it initially appears. The next perspective is that of political questions and goals. Finally, the perspective focused on the objects of confiscation (proceeds, contraband, instrumentalities, etc.) which may serve to determine the appropriate type of public policy and procedure to apply.

None of these perspectives should be excluded *a priori*, since each implies a direction of consideration that is relevant to resolving the political and legal issues concerning confiscation. From the viewpoint of EU confiscation policy, an important aspect is to specify the criteria for determining which route, criminal or civil, should be appropriate for the concrete type of confiscation to be followed by the national legislatures. Bearing in mind doctrinal input, the concrete public policy should be determined by both the object of confiscation and its legal construct. As far as public policy dedicated to the CPC is concerned, the primary determinants should be the specific object (i.e., proceeds of crime) and whether the legal construct is based on the 'net' or 'gross' principle. The latter decision may predetermine its punitive or non-punitive character and, accordingly, whether it should follow the civil or criminal route.

However, the most important matter for EU law-making policy on the CPC is to properly define the political questions and goals. This book argues for the potential legal and societal gains from linking confiscation with restorative objectives. Accordingly, it recommends a twofold approach focused on developing policy questions and goals consistent with the restorative approach to justice and, equally, the appropriate choice of criminal or civil routes for confiscation. This choice is determined by the inextricably linked issues of 'law-making policy' (the objectives of confiscation determined by the legislature) and 'law' (the legal construct of confiscation).

Moving towards a restorative approach to justice seems to be a promising qualitative change for this policy, and accordingly, for EU law. Adopting the *de minimis* approach towards integrating some elements of restorative values into the EU confiscation scheme presents the opportunity for significant changes in this *milieu* of EU action, without requiring politically challenging fundamental reforms of the conventional schemes.

The main benefit of increasing the 'restorativeness' of EU law-making policy on the CPC should be a reformulation of the very purpose of confiscation, serving primarily to repair the harm caused by a crime (in both dimensions, individual and societal) and restore the *status quo ante* (before the crime). One of the results of the proposed policy recasting may be better recognition of the interests of all stakeholders affected by a crime (victims, communities, defendants, and third parties), which implies a reconsideration of the dominant position of the State in confiscation settings. A further potential benefit of introducing 'restorative' changes at the EU policy level should be an increase in the transparency of confiscation mechanisms and enabling their social control. Improving the quality of EU criminal law through the implementation of an appropriate confiscation policy may, in turn, positively affect the value it offers to national legal orders, thus contributing to the development of European legal culture (in this context, see, e.g., Montaldo 2015).[20] Looking at the broader horizon, moving towards a 'restorative' position offers an opportunity to strengthen civil society and promote public confidence in the EU criminal justice system. Both these aspects are crucial for the effectiveness of EU policy in many areas.

Notes

1 *Engel and others v the Netherlands*, Apps nos 5100/71, 5101/71, 5102/71, 5354/72 and 5370/72 (ECtHR, 8 June 1976). See also *Campbell and Fell v the United Kingdom*, Apps nos 7819/77; 7878/77 (ECtHR, 28 June1984); *Lutz v Germany*, App no 9912/82 (ECtHR, 25 August 1987); *Demicoli v. Malta*, App no 13057/87 (ECtHR 27 August 1991); *Bendenoun v France*, App no 12547/86 (ECtHR, 24 February 1994); *Öztrük v Germany*, App no 8544/79 (ECtHR, 21 February 1984); *Benham v United Kingdom* App no 19380/92 (ECtHR, 10 June 1996); *Jussila v Finland*, App no 73053/01, (ECtHR,

23 November 2006); *Nicoleta Gheorghe v Romania*, App no 23470/05 (ECtHR, 3 April 2012); *Produkcija Plus Storitveno podjetje d.o.o. v Slovenia*, App no 47072/15 (ECtHR, 23 October 2018); *Gestur Jónsson and Ragnar Halldór Hall v Iceland*, Apps nos 68273/14, 68271/14 (ECtHR, 22 December 2020).

2 CoE, ECtHR, 'Guide on Article 6 of the European Convention on Human Rights. Right to a fair trial (criminal limb)', 31 August 2022. https://www.echr.coe.int/documents/d/echr/guide_art_6_criminal_eng (21.03.2024).

3 *Varvara v Italy*, App no 17475/09 (ECtHR 29 October 2013), 72–73.

4 *Welch v the UK*, App no 17440/90 (ECtHR 9 February 1995), 35.

5 In the US legal system, an 'administrative forfeiture' is additionally distinguished from civil and criminal forfeitures (Cassella 2022, 191–246).

6 As regards harm prevention referring to danger posed by a person, see also Duff (2013).

7 Legislative decree No. 159/2011, *Codice delle leggi antimafia e delle misure di prevenzione, nonche' nuove disposizioni in materia di documentazione antimafia, a norma degli articoli 1 e 2 della legge 13 agosto 2010, n. 136.* (11G0201), the so-called 'Anti-mafia Code'.

8 See, e.g., Corte Suprema di Cassazione, Sezioni unite, *Simonelli ed altri*, 3609 (3 July 1996).

9 *Gogitidze v Georgia*, App no 36862/05 (ECtHR 12 May 2015).

10 *Kaley v United States*, 571 U. S. 320 (2014). In the opinion of Cassella (2022), the US Supreme Court in this case 'summarised the goals of the federal asset forfeiture program' (3).

11 *Caplin & Drysdale, Chartered v United States*, 491 U. S. 617 (1989). See also the US Supreme Court position on forfeiture, expressed in the following cases: *Timbs v Indiana*, 586 U. S.___ (2019), *United States v Bajakajian*, 524 U. S. 321 (1998), *Bennis v Michigan, Bennis v Michigan*, 516 U.S. 442 (1996), *United States v Ursery*, 518 U. S. 267 (1996), *Austin v United States*, 509 U. S. 602 (1993).

12 *Austin v United States*, 509 U.S. 602 (1993).

13 See Proposal for a directive on confiscation (2022), and Directive 2024/1260.

14 See also Boucht's (2019) adaptation of these questions to the confiscation settings (96–97).

15 See also Barnett's (1977) ideas on restitution as a 'new paradigm', and Christie's (1977) ideas on 'conflict as property'.

16 See also Ashworth (2002).

17 Commisssion, Commission Staff Working Document. Impact Assessment Report Accompanying the document Proposal for a directive on confiscation (2022), 25.5.2022, SWD(2022) 245 final.

18 See footnote no 17.

19 Opinion of the EESC. 'Asset recovery and confiscation', EESC-2022-03642-AC. https://eur-lex.europa.eu/legal-content/EN/TXT/DOC/?uri=PI_EESC:EESC-2022-03642-AC (03.05.2024).

20 See also Leiss (2023); and EP, LIBE, Report on the proposal for a directive of the European Parliament and of the Council on the freezing and confiscation of proceeds of crime in the European Union, 20.5.2013, Document A7-0178/2013.

References

Alldridge, Peter. 2002. "The Moral Limits of the Crime of Money Laundering." *Buffalo Criminal Law Review* 5: 279–319.

Altman, C. Matthew. 2023. "Introduction: Punishment, Its Meaning and Justification." In *The Palgrave Handbook on the Philosophy of Punishment*, edited by Matthew C. Altman, 1–20. Cham: Palgrave Macmillan.

Ashworth, Andrew. 2002. "Responsibilities, Rights and Restorative Justice." *British Journal of Criminology* 42 (3): 578–595.
Barnett, Randy E. 1977. "Restitution: A New Paradigm of Criminal Justice." *Ethics* 87: 279–301.
Barton, K. B. Charles. 2003. *Restorative Justice. The Empowerment Model*. Leichhardt: Hawkins Press.
Benn, S. I. 1958. "An Approach to the Problems of Punishment." *Philosophy* 33 (127): 325–341.
Bentham, Jeremy. 2007. *An Introduction to the Principles of Morals and Legislation*. Mineola, NY: Dover Publications, republication of the edition published by Oxford at the Clarendon Press in 1907.
Berman, Schiff Paul. 1999. "An Anthropological Approach to Modern Forfeiture Law: The Symbolic Function of Legal Actions Against Objects." *Yale Journal of Law & the Humanities Yale* 11: 1–45.
Boucht, Johan. 2019. *The Limits of Asset Confiscation. On the Legitimacy of Extended Appropriation of Criminal Proceeds*. Oxford: Hart Publishing.
Bowles, Roger, and Michael Faure, and Nuno Garoupa. 2005. "Forfeiture of Illegal Gain: An Economic Perspective." *Oxford Journal of Legal Studies* 25 (2): 275–295. https://doi.org/10.1093/ojls/gqi014.
Braithwaite, John. 1989. *Crime, Shame and Reintegration*. Cambridge: Cambridge University Press.
Braithwaite, John. 1999. "A Future Where Punishment Is Marginalized: Realistic or Utopian?" *UCLA Law Review* 46 (6): 1727–1750.
Braithwaite, John. 2003. "Principles of Restorative Justice." In *Restorative Justice and Criminal Justice: Competing or Reconcilable Paradigms?*, edited by Andrew von Hirsch, Julian Roberts, Anthony E. Bottoms, Kent Roach, and Mara Schiff, 1–20. Oxford: Hart Publishing.
Brooks, Thom. 2017. "Punitive Restoration and Restorative Justice." *Criminal Justice Ethics* 36 (2): 122–140. https://doi.org/10.1080/0731129X.2017.1358930.
Brunk, G. Conrad. 1996. "Restorative Justice and Punishment." *Dialogue* 35 (3): 593–598.
Bullock, Caren. 2014. "Criminal Benefit, the Confiscation Order and the Post-conviction Confiscation Regime." *Crime, Law and Social Change* 62 (1): 45–64.
Bullock, Caren, and Lister Stuart. 2014. "Post-Conviction Confiscation of Assets in England and Wales: Rhetoric and Reality." In *Dirty Assets. Emerging Issues in the Regulation of Criminal and Terrorist Assets*, edited by Colin King and Clive Walker, 47–69. Farnham, Surrey: Ashgate.
Burchard, Christoph. 2019. "Confiscation as Criminal Law (or What)? On How the Ill-Advised Discussion about "the" Legal "Nature" of Confiscation Obfuscates What Really Needs To Be Discussed." *Latin American Legal Studies* 4: 211–242.
Burchard, Christoph. 2023. "Criminal Law Exceptionalism as an Affirmative Ideology, and its Expansionist Discontents." *Criminal Law and Philosophy* 17: 17–27. https://doi.org/10.1007/s11572-021-09614-4.
Burke, Roger Hopkins. 2014. *An Introduction to Criminological Theory*. Abingdon: Routledge.
Cantor, Gilbert. 1976. "An End to Crime and Punishment." *The Shingle* (Philadelphia Bar Association) 39 (4): 99–114.
Carr, Nicola. 2021. "Critical Perspectives on Desistance." *Probation Journal* 68 (2): 141–145. https://doi.org/10.1177/02645505211020980.
Cassella, D Stefan. 2013a. *Asset Forfeiture Law in the United States*. New York: Juris Publishing.
Cassella, D. Stefan. 2013b. "Civil Asset Recovery: The American Experience." *Eucrim* 3: 98–104.

Cassella, D. Stefan. 2015. "Civil Asset Recovery – The American Experience." In *Non Conviction-Based Confiscation in Europe*, edited by Jon Petter Rui and Ulrich Sieber, 13–30. Berlin: Duncker & Humblot.

Cassella, D. Stefan. 2022. *Asset Forfeiture Law in the United States*. New York: Juris Publishing.

Cavadino, Michael, James Dignan, George Mair, and Jamie Bennett. 2020. *The Penal System. An Introduction*. 6th ed. London: Sage Publications. [EPUB].

Christie, Nils. 1977. "Conflicts as Property." *British Journal of Criminology* 17 (1): 1–15.

Christie, Nils. 1981. *Limits to Pain*. Oslo: Universitetsforlaget.

Christie, Nils. 1986. "The Ideal Victim." In *From Crime Policy to Victim Policy. Reorienting the Justice System*, edited by Ezzat A. Fattah, 17–30. Basingstoke: Macmillan Press.

Cragg, Wesley. 2005. *The Practice of Punishment. Towards a Theory of Restorative Justice*. London, NY: Taylor & Francis e-Library (first published by Routledge, London, 1992).

Daly, Kathleen. 2000. "Revisiting the Relationship between Retributive and Restorative Justice." In *Restorative Justice: Philosophy to Practice*, edited by Heather Strang and John Braithwaite, 33–54. Aldershot: Ashgate.

Daly, Kathleen. 2013. "The Punishment Debate in Restorative Justice." In *The Sage Handbook of Punishment and Society*, edited by Jonathan Simon and Richard Sparks, 356–373. London: Sage.

Dignan, James. 1994. "Reintegration through Reparation: A Way Forward for Restorative Justice?" In *Penal Theory and Penal Practice: Tradition and Innovation in Criminal Justice*, edited by Anthony Duff, Sandra Marshall, Rebecca E. Dobash and Russel P. Dobash, 231–244. Manchester: Manchester University Press.

Dignan, James. 2002. "Restorative Justice and the Law: The Case for an Integrated, Systemic Approach." In *Restorative Justice and the Law*, edited by Lode Walgrave, 168–190. Cullompton: Willan.

Dignan, James. 2005. *Understanding Victims and Restorative Justice*. Maidenhead, Berkshire: Open University Press.

Dimock Susan. 1997. "Retributivism and Trust." *Law and Philosophy* 16 (1): 37–62.

Duff, Robin, Antony. 1986. *Trials and Punishments*. Cambridge: Cambridge University Press.

Duff, Robin, Antony. 1992. "Alternatives to Punishment — or Alternative Punishments?" In *Retributivism and its Critics: Papers of the Special Nordic Conference University of Toronto,* 25–27, June 1990, edited by Wesley Cragg, 43–68. Stuttgart: Franz Steiner Verlag.

Duff, Robin, Antony. 2001. *Punishment, Communication and Community*. Oxford: Oxford University Press.

Duff, Robin, Antony. 2002. "Restorative Punishment and Punitive Restoration." In *Restorative Justice and the Law*, edited by Lode Walgrave, 82–100. Cullompton: Willan Publishing.

Duff, Robin, Antony. 2003. "Restoration and Retribution." In *Restorative Justice and Criminal Justice: Competing or Reconcilable Paradigms?*, edited by Andrew von Hirsch, Julian Roberts, Anthony E. Bottoms, Kent Roach, and Mara Schiff, 43–59. Oxford: Hart Publishing.

Duff, Robin, Antony. 2011. "Responsibility, Restoration, and Retribution." In *Retributivism Has a Past: Has It a Future?*, edited by Michael Tonry, 63–85. Oxford: Oxford University Press.

Duff, Robin, Antony. 2013. "Who Must Presume Whom to be Innocent of What?." *Netherlands Journal of Legal Philosoph*y 42 (3): 170–192. https://doi.org/10.5553/NJLP/221307132013042003002.

Eglash, Albert. 1977. "Beyond Restitution: Creative Restitution." In *Restitution in Criminal Justice: A Critical Assessment of Sanctions*, edited by Joe Hudson and Burt Galaway, 91–100. Lexington: Lexington Books.

Fernandez-Bertier, Michaël. 2016. "The Confiscation and Recovery of Criminal Property: A European Union State of the Art." *ERA Forum* 17 (3): 323–342. https://doi.org/10.1007/s12027-016-0436-1.
Finkelstein, Jacob. 1973. "The Goring Ox: Some Historical Perspectives on Deodands, Forfeitures, Wrongful Death and the Western Notion of Sovereignty." *Temple Law Quarterly* 46 (2): 169–290.
Fisher, Jonathan, and Justin Bong-Kwan. 2018. "Confiscation: Deprivatory and Not Punitive — Back to the Way We Were." *Criminal Law Review* 3: 192–201.
Flew, Antony. 1954. "The Justification of Punishment." *Philosophy* 29 (111): 291–307.
Forsaith, James, Barrie Irving, Eva Nanopoulos, and Mihaly Fazekas. 2012. *Study for an Impact Assessment on a Proposal for a New Legal Framework on the Confiscation and Recovery of Criminal Assets*. RAND Europe, EU. Accessed July 4, 2024. https://home-affairs.ec.europa.eu/system/files/2020-09/external_study_used_as_a_basis_for_the_commission_ia_october_2012_en.pdf.
Fried, J. David. 1988. "Rationalizing Criminal Forfeiture." *The Journal of Criminal Law & Criminology* 79 (2): 328–436.
Gade, B. N. Christian. 2021. "Is Restorative Justice Punishment?." *Conflict Resolution Quarterly* 38: 127–155. https://doi.org/10.1002/crq.21293.
Gallant, M. Michelle, and Colin King. 2013. "The Seizure of Illicit Assets: Patterns of Civil Forfeiture in Canada and Ireland." *Common Law World Review* 42(1): 91–109. https://doi.org/10.1350/clwr.2013.42.1.0.
Gardner, John. 2010. "Hart on Legality, Justice, and Morality." *Oxford Legal Studies Research Paper* 44: 1–22. http://dx.doi.org/10.2139/ssrn.1606463.
Gordon, E. Jon. 1995. "Prosecutors Who Seize Too Much and the Theories They Love: Money Laundering, Facilitation, and Forfeiture." *Duke Law Journal* 44: 744– 776.
Hart, H. L. A. 2008. "Prolegomenon to the Principles of Punishment." In *Punishment and Responsibility: Essays in the Philosophy of Law*, with an Introduction by John Gardner, 1–27. Oxford: Oxford University Press.
Johnstone, Gerry. 2011. *Restorative Justice: Ideas, Values, Debates*. Abingdon: Routledge.
Kant, Immanuel. 2017. *The Metaphysics of Morals*. Edited by Lara Denis and translated by Mary Gregor. Cambridge: Cambridge University Press.
Kilchling, Michael. 1977. "Comparative Perspectives on Forfeiture Legislation in Europe and the United States." *European Journal of Crime, Criminal Law and Criminal Justice* 5 (3): 342–361.
King, Colin, and Jennifer Hendry. 2023. *Civil Recovery of Criminal Property*. Oxford: Oxford University Press.
Leiss, Johann Ruben. 2023. "An Introduction to EU Legal Culture." In *Handbook on Legal Cultures*, edited by Sören Koch and Marius Mikkel Kjølstad, 463–524. Cham: Springer.
Levanon, Liat. 2015. "Criminal Punishment As a Restorative Practice." *New Criminal Law Review* 18 (4): 537–574. https://doi.org/10.1525/nclr.2015.18.4.537.
Levy, W. Leonard. 1996. *A License to Steal. The Forfeiture of Property*. Chapel Hill and London: The University of North Carolina Press.
Lewis, Jerome A., James C. Hamilton, and J. Dean Elmore. 2021. "Describing the Ideal Victim: A Linguistic Analysis of Victim Descriptions." *Current Psychology* 40 (1): 4324–4332.
London, Ross. 2011. *Crime, Punishment, and Restorative Justice: From the Margins to the Mainstream*. Boulder: Lynne Rienner Publishers.
Mamak, Kamil, Agnieszka Barczak-Oplustil, Daniel Kwiatkowski, Mikołaj Małecki, and Dominik Zając. 2021. "Should Gains from Criminal Knowledge Be Forfeited?." *Crime, Law and Social Change* 77: 305–320.
Marshall, F. Tony. 1996. "The Evolution of Restorative Justice in Britain." *European Journal on Criminal Policy and Research* 4: 21–43.

Marshall, F. Tony. 1999. *Restorative Justice: An Overview*. A Report by the Home Office Research Development and Statistics Directorate. London: Crown copyright.

Maugeri, M. Anna. 2001. *Le moderne sanzioni patrimoniali tra funzionalità e garantismo*. Università di Catania: Giuffrè.

Maugeri, M. Anna. 2018. "Mutual Recognition and Confiscation of Assets: An EU Perspective." In *The Palgrave Handbook of Criminal and Terrorism Financing Law*, edited by Colin King, Clive Walker, and Jimmy Gurulé, 399–425. Cham: Palgrave Macmillan.

Mazzacuva, Francesco. 2019. "The Problematic Nature of Asset Recovery Measures: Recent Developments of the Italian Preventive Confiscation." In *Chasing Criminal Money*, edited by Katalin Ligeti and Michele Simonato, 101–115. Oxford: Hart Publishing.

McPherson, Thomas. 1967. "Punishment: Definition and Justification Analysis." *Philosophy* 28 (1): 21–27.

Montaldo, Stefano. 2015. "Directive 2014/42/EU and Social Reuse of Confiscated Assets in the EU: Advancing a Culture of Legality." *New Journal of European Criminal Law* 6 (2): 195–212.

Murphy, G. Jeffrie. 1979. *Retribution, Justice, and Therapy. Essays in the Philosophy of Law*. Dordrecht: D. Reidel Publishing Company.

Naylor, R. 1999. "Wash-out: A Critique of Follow-the-Money Methods in Crime Control Policy." *Crime, Law and Social Change* 32: 1–58. https://doi.org/10.1023/A:1008386203362.

Naylor, R. 2003. "Follow-the-Money Methods in Crime Control Policy." In *Critical Reflections on Transnational Organized Crime, Money Laundering, and Corruption*, edited by Margaret E. Beare, 256–290. Toronto: University of Toronto Press. https://doi.org/10.3138/9781442670242-013.

Nietzsche, Friedrich. 2007. *On the Genealogy of Morality*. Edited by Keith Ansell-Pearson and translated by Carol Diethe. Cambridge: Cambridge University Press.

Nozick, Robert. 1981. *Philosophical Explanations*. Cambridge, MA: Harvard University Press.

Ochnio, H. Ariadna. 2022. "Addressing Barriers to Victims' Rights to Recovered Assets in the Mechanism for Mutual Recognition of Freezing and Confiscation Orders." In *Current Issues of EU Criminal Law*, edited by Ariadna H. Ochnio and Hanna Kuczyńska, 137–158. Warsaw: Publishing House of ILS PAS. https://doi.org/10.5281/zenodo.6860700.

Panzavolta, Michele, and Roberto Flor. 2015. "A Necessary Evil? The Italian 'Non-Criminal System' of Asset Forfeiture." In *Non Conviction-Based Confiscation in Europe*, edited by Jon Petter Rui and Ulrich Sieber, 111–149. Berlin: Duncker & Humblot.

Pavlich, George. 2002. "Deconstructing Restoration: The Promise of Restorative Justice." In *Restorative Justice. Theoretical Foundations*, edited by Elmar G. M. Weitekamp and Hans-Jürgen Kerner, 90–109. Cullompton: Willan Publishing.

Pimentel, David. 2012. "Forfeitures Revisited: Bringing Principle to Practice in Federal Court." *Nevada Law Journal* 13 (1): 1–59.

Rawls, John. 1971. *A Theory of Justice*. Cambridge, MA: Belknap Press of Harvard University Press.

Rees, Edward, Richard Fisher, and Richard Thomas. 2015. *Blackstone's Guide to the Proceeds of Crime Act 2002*. Oxford: Oxford University Press.

Rui, Petter Jon, and Ulrich Sieber. 2015. "NCBC in Europe – Bringing the Picture Together." In *Non Conviction-Based Confiscation in Europe*, edited by Jon Petter Rui and Ulrich Sieber, 245–302. Berlin: Duncker & Humblot.

Sandel, J. Michael. 2009. *Justice. What's the Right Thing to Do?* New York: Ferrar, Straus and Giroux.

Simser, Jeffrey. 2009. "Perspectives on Civil Forfeiture." In *Civil Forfeiture of Criminal Property*, edited by Simon N. M. Young, 13–20. Cheltenham: Edward Elgar Pub.

Simonato, Michele. 2017. "Confiscation and Fundamental Rights Across Criminal and Non-criminal Domains." *ERA Forum* 18: 365–379.

Simonato, Michele, and Michaël Fernandez-Bertier. 2019. "Confiscation and Fundamental Rights: The Quest for a Consistent European Approach." In *Improving Confiscation Procedures in the European Union*, edited by Alessandro Bernardi, 3–29: Napoli: Jovene Editore.

Skelton, Ann, and Makubetse Sekhonyane. 2007. "Human Rights and Restorative Justice." In *Handbook of Restorative Justice*, edited by Gerry Johnstone and Daniel W. Van Ness, 580–597. Cullompton: Willan Publishing.

Steiker, S. Carol. 1997. "Punishment and Procedure: Punishment Theory and the Criminal-Civil Procedural Divide." *Georgetown Law Journal* 85(4): 775–819.

Summers, J. Sarah. 2022. *Sentencing and Human Rights: The Limits on Punishment*. Oxford: Oxford University Press. https://doi.org/10.1093/oso/9780192870384.001.0001.

Trechsel, Stefan. 2005. *Human Rights in Criminal Proceedings*. Oxford: Oxford University Press.

Umbreit, S. Mark. 1998. "Restorative Justice Through Victim-Offender Mediation: A Multi-Site Assessment." *Western Criminology Review* 1 (1). Accessed April 24, 2008. https://westerncriminology.org/documents/WCR/v01n1/Umbreit/Umbreit.html.

Walgrave, Lode. 2003. "Imposing Restoration Instead of Inflicting Pain." In *Restorative Justice and Criminal Justice: Competing or Reconcilable Paradigms?*, edited by Andrew von Hirsch, Julian V. Roberts, Anthony Bottoms, Kent Roach, and Mara Schiff, 61–78. Oxford: Hart Publishing.

Walgrave, Lode. 2008. *Restorative Justice, Self-interest and Responsible Citizenship*. Cullompton: Willan Publishing.

Walgrave, Lode, and Ivo Aertsen. 1996. "Reintegrative Shaming and Restorative Justice: Interchangeable, Complementary or Different?." *European Journal on Criminal Policy and Research* 4: 67–85.

Walklate, Sandra. 2006. "Changing Boundaries of the «Victim» in Restorative Justice. So Who Is the Victim Now?" In *Handbook of Restorative Justice: A Global Perspective*, edited by Dennis Sullivan and Larry Tifft, 273–285. Abingdon: Routledge.

Wood, David. 2002. "Retribution, Crime Reduction and the Justification of Punishment." *Oxford Journal of Legal Studies* 22 (2): 301–321.

Worrall, L. John. 2008. "Asset Forfeiture. Problem-Oriented Guides for Police." Response Guides Series 7, The U.S. Department of Justice, Office of Community Oriented Policing Services. Accessed February 6, 2008. https://popcenter.asu.edu/sites/default/files/asset_forfeiture.pdf.

Wright, Martin. 1991. *Justice for Victims and Offenders*. Milton Keynes: Open University Press.

Vettori, Barbara. 2006. *Tough on Criminal Wealth: Exploring the Practice of Proceeds from Crime Confiscation in the EU*. Dordrecht: Springer.

Vettori, Barbara. 2018. "The Disposal of Confiscated Assets in the EU Member States: What Works, What Does Not Work and What Is Promising." In *The Palgrave Handbook of Criminal and Terrorism Financing Law*, edited by Colin King, Clive Walker, and Jimmy Gurulé, 705–733. Cham: Palgrave Macmillan.

Vettori, Barbara, Todor Kolarov, and Atanas Rusev. 2014. *Disposal of Confiscated Assets in the EU Member States Laws and Practices*. Sofia: Center for the Study of Democracy.

Vettori, Barbara, and Andrea Di Nicola. 2017. "The Social Reuse of Confiscated Assets in EU Member States: From Current Experiences to an EU Policy for a «Powered-by-Citizens» Fight Against Crime." In *Chasing Criminal Money: Challenges and Perspectives on Asset Recovery in the EU*, edited by Katalin Ligeti and Michele Simonato, 321–343. Oxford: Hart Publishing.

Vogel, Joachim. 2015. "The Legal Construction that Property Can Do Harm." In *Non Conviction-Based Confiscation in Europe*, edited by Jon Petter Rui and Ulrich Sieber, 225–243. Berlin: Duncker & Humblot.

Young, Warren, and Allison Morris. 1998. "Reforming Criminal Justice: Reflecting on the Present and Imagining the Future." Inaugural lecture presented at the International Youth Conference, New Zealand, October 1998.

Zedner, Lucia. 2016. "Penal Subversions: When Is a Punishment not Punishment, Who Decides and on What Grounds?." *Theoretical Criminology* 20: 20–23.

Zehr, Howard. 1985. "Retributive Justice, Restorative Justice." In *New Perspectives on Crime and Justice*: *Occasional Papers of the MCC Canada Victim Offender Ministries Program and the MCC U.S. Office of Criminal Justice*, September 1985, No. 4., MCC Canada Victim Offender Ministries, MCC U.S. Office of Criminal Justice.

Zehr, Howard. 1990. *Changing Lenses: A New Focus for Crime and Justice.* Scottsdale, PA.: Herald Press. [EPUB].

Zehr, Howard. 2002. *The Little Book of Restorative Justice*. Intercourse, PA: Good Books.

Zehr, Howard. 2014. *The Little Book of Restorative Justice*. New York: Good Books. [EPUB].

Zehr, Howard. 2015. *Changing Lenses. Restorative Justice for Our Times*. Harrisonburg: Herald Press.

3 The evolution of EU law-making policy on the confiscation of the proceeds of crime

Introductory remarks

The purpose of this chapter is to identify the restorative elements of EU law-making policy on the CPC which emerged throughout its development over time (dynamic approach). The argument is that this policy is a major determinant of law and thus legal integration in the area of confiscation. Accordingly, if it contains some restorative elements and the EU lawmaker acts rationally, those restorative elements should be reflected, at least to some extent, in EU law standards on the CPC, and then, bearing in mind the role of the EU legal acts (see Article 288 TFEU), under their influence, in the domestic legislation of MS. The similar expectations may apply to the shortcomings identified in this policy.

However, the restorative elements of EU law-making policy on the CPC need not necessarily take the form of explicit references to restorative justice but may also be implicitly reflected by concrete policy assumptions being in line with a minimalist restorative approach to justice. Insight into these assumptions can provide a broader picture of the evolution of the EU's approach to confiscation and also to the fight against serious and organised crime.

The development of EU law-making policy on the CPC can be divided into two key stages: the periods before and after the Treaty of Lisbon. Accordingly, the aspects characterising each of these periods are discussed in the separate sections of this chapter. In the pre-Lisbon period, policy considerations were mainly determined by two factors. First of all, cooperation in criminal matters, covered by the so-called 'third pillar', in existence from the Maastricht Treaty (1993) to the Lisbon Treaty (2009), was based on the intergovernmental method. Secondly, the first EU political guidelines concerning confiscation were established against the reality of highly differentiated national confiscation schemes, which had the effect of making mutual cooperation in this area difficult. The Treaty of Lisbon opened new possibilities in the AFSJ by departing from the pillar structure, unifying the system of legal acts, extending the competences of the ECJ, and notably, allowing the Community method (the ordinary legislative procedure).[1]

Seen historically, the changes introduced by the Treaty of Lisbon paved the way for undertaking the difficult venture of approximation of confiscation legislation aimed at enhancing judicial cooperation in criminal matters based on the principle of mutual recognition of judgments and judicial decisions (Article 82(1) TFEU).

DOI: 10.4324/9781003465829-3

It is noteworthy that the Treaty of Lisbon changed the hierarchy of the Union's objectives. It put promoting peace, EU values, and the well-being of its citizens in the highest place and prioritised offering its citizens an area of freedom security and justice above establishing an internal market (Article 3 TEU, *ex* Article 2 TEU). Yet ultimately, despite the advancement of harmonisation processes and the mechanism of mutual recognition of confiscation orders and freezing orders over time, which reaches a broader scope than just the harmonisation level, the problem of differentiations between national confiscation schemes is still current (see, e.g., Ochnio 2018; Silva 2022; Hryniewicz-Lach 2023; Maugeri 2024).

When analysing the evolution of EU law-making policy on the CPC over time, attention was drawn to the elements reflecting a restorative approach to justice, and from when and in what context references to restorative justice started to emerge in this policy (directly or indirectly). It should be noted that although this policy did not directly refer to restorative justice in the pre-Lisbon period, it contained some elements that were in line with the restorative approach to justice.

Given that the EU is not the only standard setter in the field of confiscation and not the only one making reference to restorative justice, the third section of this chapter extends the considerations by reference to other international players in this field affecting the policies of the EU and the MS.

The pre-Lisbon period: a focus on effectiveness

Pre-Tampere policy orientations

Initial political guidelines linked the CPC with the fight against serious and organised crime, especially drug trafficking, terrorism, and the related offence of money laundering. Actions targeted at such types of crime, though taken at the European level, were part of intensifying global efforts in the 1980s to find an appropriate response to the international circulation of significant financial resources originating from drug offences and laundered with the use of various services offered by financial institutions (see, e.g., Levi and Osofsky 1995; Jensen and Gerber 1996; Gallant 1999; Vettori 2006; Muller 2007; Ochnio 2018). Following this trend, in 1989, the EU signed the UN Vienna Convention against Illicit Traffic in Narcotic Drugs and Psychotropic Substances (1988) (see also Mitsilegas 2022, 2). In the 1990s, issues related to organised crime were widely discussed in various fora, including scientific communities (Paoli and Fijnaut 2006). Although the EU began looking for solutions in the 1980s, one cannot forget that in the USA, major steps towards employing CPC in the fight against drug trafficking and organised crime were taken a decade earlier, in the 1970s (see, e.g., Block 1980; Levy 1996; Fernandez-Bertier 2019; Gfroerer 2018). Over time, the scope of triggering offences for the legal construct of CPC in EU law has been extended by adding other offences which do not necessarily have an organised nature or cross-border dimension (on the latter element justifying EU interventions, see, e.g., Wieczorek 2021; Öberg 2023). Undoubtedly, the focus of the pre-Lisbon policy concerning the area of justice was on the effectiveness of measures adopted in the fight against serious and organised crime, neither on the rights of individuals involved in criminal procedures nor the social implications of criminal policy in general. At that time, EU policy addressing confiscation issues did not explicitly refer to restorative justice, but some of its aspects, such as concern for victims' rights, dialogue with civil society, or the possibility of the reuse of confiscated assets for the victims or for social purposes, can be considered as corresponding to a minimalist restorative approach to justice.

The problems related to serious and organised crime were addressed in the European Council's conclusions and recommendations, exerting influence on EU law-making processes in the area of justice (on soft-law legal effects, see, e.g., Meijers Committee 2018; Biernat 2012). As currently determined in Article 15(1) TEU, the role of the European Council is to provide the Union with the 'necessary impetus for its development' and to define the 'general political directions and priorities'. It is noteworthy that the topic of confiscation of criminal proceeds made no clear appearances in European Council activities prior to the landmark meeting in Tampere (15–16 October 1999). Nevertheless, some problems related to the proceeds of crime had emerged, albeit in a piecemeal way, in the European Council activities before Tampere.

The analysis of the European Council Conclusions issued in the years 1975–1992 (before the entry into force of the Maastricht Treaty on 1 November 1993) shows that even though the challenges were centred around the economic and social situation in the Community,[2] from the very beginning the issue of combating terrorism was perceived in terms of the common interests of all governments.[3] Another problem that emerged early in the European Council's activities was drug abuse, associated with the phenomenon of drug trafficking.[4] Accordingly, the CPC was initially employed as an element of the strategy to fight drug offences, terrorism, and the related offence of money laundering. Developing a common approach to combating those offences was important from the perspective of the Union as a territory without internal borders. For instance, in the Conclusions of the Brussels European Council of 29 and 30 March 1985, the view was presented that achieving the objective of abolishing frontier formalities 'must remain compatible with the need to combat terrorism and drug-trafficking'.[5] These issues were also present in the Political Declaration by the Governments of the MS (1985), which acknowledged the necessity of cooperation between the MS in the 'combating of terrorism, crime, the traffic in drugs and illicit trading in works of art and antiques'.[6]

The problem of drug trafficking has been raised repeatedly at European Council meetings, for example, at The Hague European Council of 26 and 27 June 1986,[7] and again at the London European Council of 6 December 1986.[8] The issue of ensuring effective measures to combat terrorism, drug abuse, and organised crime was then expanded at the Hannover European Council of 27 and 28 June 1988[9] and the Rhodes European Council of 2 and 3 December 1988. The latter linked the Community's objective of the area without internal frontiers with the progress in 'intergovernmental co-operation to combat terrorism, international crime, drug trafficking and trafficking of all kinds'.[10] Likewise, the Dublin European Council of 28 April 1990 expressed its concern over the threat posed by drug abuse and related drug offences linked with international organised crime.[11] It should be pointed out that the Dublin Council recognised the serious problem posed by the considerable resources (financial and other) available to drug traffickers.

The discussions about the problems related to drugs and organised crime were continued during the second meeting of the European Council held in Dublin on 24 and 25 June 1990. The Dublin European Council welcomed the Commission's proposal to combat money laundering. Adoption of appropriate measures in this respect was expected before July 1991. Importantly, the Dublin European Council invited the MS to adopt legislation providing for 'seizure of the assets of persons involved in drug trafficking'.[12] Then, the Rome European Council of 14 and 15 December 1990 expressed the need to consider 'whether and how activities currently conducted in an intergovernmental framework could be brought into the ambit of the Union' in the key areas of home affairs and justice, with the fight against drugs and organised crime deemed to be a key element.[13]

The issue of money laundering, as closely related to drug trafficking, further emerged in the Conclusions of the Luxembourg European Council of 28 and 29 June 1991.[14] This was on the occasion of the first report by the European Committee to Combat Drugs (CELAD) on the implementation of the European Plan to Combat Drugs (1990) prepared for the Rome European Council of 13 and 14 December 1990.[15] This Plan emphasised the importance of the adoption of the Proposal for the first AML Directive. It also expressed the need for implementing various international instruments, such as the UN Vienna Convention (1988), the CoE Strasbourg Convention (1990), or the FATF Recommendations (established in 1989).

As expected, the first AML Directive (AMLD) on prevention of the use of the financial system for the purpose of money laundering (91/308/EEC) was adopted in 1991.[16] According to its Preamble, money laundering should in the first place be fought by penal measures and with international cooperation among judicial and law enforcement authorities. In this context, reference was made to the Vienna Convention (1988), and the Strasbourg Convention (1990). The AMLD required the MS to ensure that money laundering is prohibited (Article 2); however, at the same time it indicated that the penal approach was not the only possible option. For instance, this directive provided for the MS to adopt specific measures targeted at 'suspicious' assets placed in credit or financial institutions. It required the MS to ensure that, under certain conditions, credit and financial institutions refrain from carrying out suspicious transactions related to money laundering (Article 7). This could then serve as the first step towards subsequent securing of the assets, for example, if criminal proceedings are launched as a result of the data gathered by credit or financial institutions at the prevention phase.

After the entry into force of the Treaty of Maastricht, the Brussels European Council of 10 and 11 December 1993 expressed its determination to make full use of the possibilities the Treaty offered in the area of cooperation in justice and home affairs (JHA), including cooperation against international organised crime.[17] The Treaty on European Union signed in Maastricht introduced a three-pillar structure, where cooperation in the area of JHA was covered by the 'third pillar', the so-called 'intergovernmental pillar' (see also Kaunert, Occhipinti, and Léonard 2014).

Initially, the 'third pillar' related to 'areas of justice and home affairs' and then to the 'area of freedom security and justice' (Klip 2009, 17).

Confiscation of the proceeds of crime was one of the issues addressed in the 'Action Plan to combat organised crime' drawn up by the High-Level Group on Organised Crime and endorsed by the Amsterdam European Council of 16 and 17 June 1997 (hereinafter the 1997 Action Plan).[18] The 1997 Action Plan stressed the importance of well-developed domestic legislation concerning the CPC and the laundering of the proceeds of crime (Political guideline No. 11). It also requested that the Council and the Commission develop proposals allowing the further enhancement of legislation in various areas, including confiscation and money laundering, i.e.:

- introducing special procedures for tracing, seizure and confiscation of proceeds from crime,
- preventing an excessive use of cash payments and cash currency exchanges by natural and legal persons from serving to cover up the conversion of the proceeds from crime into other property,
- extending the scope of the laundering provisions to the proceeds from all forms of serious crime, and making a failure to comply with the obligation to report suspicious financial transactions liable to dissuasive sanctions,
- addressing the issue of money laundering on the Internet and via electronic money products (The 1997 Action Plan, Political guideline No 11).

The 1997 Action Plan recommended ratification by the MS of, i.a., the Strasbourg Convention (1990) and the Vienna Convention (1988), both covering confiscation issues. Additional recommendations on money laundering and the CPC provided for introducing rules enabling confiscation regardless of the presence of the offender (namely when the offender has died or absconded) (26(c)). In that regard, it is worth noting that non-conviction based confiscation was only introduced to EU law many years later by Directive 2014/42/EU and later developed by Directive 2024/1260.

In addition, the 1997 Action Plan recommended carrying out a study on the possibility of sharing assets confiscated following international cooperation at the MS level (Recommendation 26(d)). It also advocated for the broad criminalisation of money laundering. With reference to Political guideline No 11 mentioned above, it recommended undertaking a study 'with a view to strengthening the tracing and seizure of illegal assets and of the enforcement of court decisions on the confiscation of assets of organised crime' (Recommendation 26(b)). This latter recommendation and the Strasbourg Convention (1990) were referred to in the Preamble to Joint Action of 3 December 1998 on money laundering, the identification, tracing, freezing, seizing and confiscation of instrumentalities and the proceeds from crime (98/699/JHA).[19] The 1998 Joint Action placed an emphasis on procedures related to confiscation launched at the request of other MS. For example, it provided for ensuring similar rules in domestic proceedings and those instituted at the request of another MS in respect of 'value confiscation', identification and tracing of suspected proceeds from crime (Article 1(2) and (3)), or minimising the risk of dissipation of assets (Article 5(1)). According to Article 3 of Joint Action 98/699/JHA,

> Member States shall give the same priority to all requests from other Member States which relate to asset identification, tracing, freezing or seizing, and confiscation as is given to such measures in domestic proceedings.

Value confiscation was then addressed in FD 2001/500/JHA; however, the MS had the right to exclude this type of confiscation in cases where the value would be less than EUR 4000 (Article 3). As regards the differences between the 1998 Joint Action 98/699/JHA and the 2001 FD 2001/500/JHA, it is worth quoting the arguments presented in the explanatory statement accompanying the European Parliament (EP) Draft Legislative Resolution on the initiative of the Danish Presidency (consultation procedure 2002/0818/CNS):

> the joint action went no further than to call for cooperation between Member States, in the form of complying with requests for legal assistance, and did not bring forward any practical proposals to improve the legal provisions of the Member States with regard to confiscation, nor any proposals to introduce special procedures for confiscation. It therefore failed to fulfil any of the requirements of the action plan. [...] On 26 June 2001 the Council adopted Framework Decision 2001/500/JHA [...] on an initiative of the French Republic, which abrogated certain articles of the joint action of 1998. The framework decision took further steps forward by introducing the principle of the mutual recognition of national provisions on the seizure and confiscation of the instrumentalities and proceeds of crime.[20]

However, the 2002 EP Report on the initiative of the Kingdom of Denmark with a view to the adoption of a Council FD on confiscation of crime-related proceeds, instrumentalities, and property, A5-0383/2002 (hereinafter the 2002 Report) critically assessed FD 2001/500/JHA as being insufficient towards the demands and opted for further development of common rules concerning confiscation.

Indicative policy orientations concerning the area of justice, including confiscation issues, were also contained in an Action Plan 'on how best to implement the provisions of the Treaty of Amsterdam on the creation of an area of freedom, security and justice' endorsed at the Vienna European Council of 11 and 12 December 1998 (hereinafter the 1998 Vienna Action Plan).[21] The Communication from the Commission 'Towards an area of freedom, security and justice' (1998) proposed the action plan in response to the call of the Cardiff European Council (15–16 June 1998).[22] One of its conclusions related to the Commission's further activities was to 'strike a balance in all areas of action between freedom on the one hand and security and justice on the other' (10). Notably, the proposed action plan highlighted both substantive and procedural aspects of criminal law. It is also worth paying attention to the EU's high ambitions concerning the area of justice at that time, as reflected in the Communication:

> The new impetus and instruments introduced by Amsterdam provide the opportunity to examine what the area of 'justice' should seek to achieve. The ambition is to give citizens a common sense of justice throughout the Union. Justice must be seen as facilitating the day-to-day life of people and bringing to justice those who threaten the freedom and security of individuals and society. This includes both access to justice and full judicial cooperation among Members States (8).

While EU confiscation policy before Lisbon did not refer directly to restorative justice in the context of confiscation, it contained some elements consistent with a restorative approach to justice. For instance, the cited Communication from the Commission (1998) addressed the issue of victims' rights, as persons involved in various procedures, including those concerning enforcement of confiscation:

> Procedural rules should respond to broadly the same guarantees, ensuring that people will not be treated unevenly according to the jurisdiction dealing with their ease. The rules may be different provided that they are equivalent. This would in particular cover matters relevant to the rights of defence, where common principles and codes of good practice should be developed (i.e. interpretation, taking of evidence, …), but could also extend to persons involved in procedures in any other capacity (witness, victim, expert, …). Moreover, in criminal areas, it should not be limited to the proceedings leading to a possible conviction, but should also be applicable to the enforcement of a decision, including, for instance, confiscation of assets, early or conditional releases and reintegration (9–10).

The quoted Communication recognised that judicial cooperation in criminal matters in the difficult area of organised crime was dependent on the 'approximation of legislation and facilitation of procedures' (9):

> In concrete terms this means first of all that criminal behaviours should be approached in the same way throughout the Union: terrorism, corruption, traffic in human beings, organised crime, should be the subject of minimum common rules relating to the constituent elements of criminal acts, and should be pursued with the same vigour wherever they take place. If serious criminal conduct receives an equivalent response and procedural guarantees are comparable throughout the Union, the possibilities of improving co-ordination of prosecution, whenever greater efficiency can be reconciled with respect for individual rights, must be examined.

The 1998 Vienna Action Plan addressed the issue of confiscation in the context of the procedural guarantees enshrined in the ECHR and interpreted by the ECtHR. It should be noted that this plan linked the procedural guarantees with the aspects of 'offender reintegration' and 'victim support', both important from the perspective of a restorative approach to justice (19). In addition, the 1998 Vienna Action Plan provided for the improvement and approximation of national provisions on seizures and the CPC while respecting the rights of *bona fide* third parties (50) (b). It envisaged taking measures in this respect within five years of the entry into force of the Treaty of Amsterdam. During the same period, it envisaged taking measures addressing the 'question of victim support by making a comparative survey of victim compensation schemes and assess the feasibility of taking action within the Union' (51)(c). The Treaty of Amsterdam acknowledged that providing 'citizens with a high level of safety within an area of freedom, security and justice' led through approximation of rules on criminal matters, i.e., 'minimum rules relating to the constituent elements of criminal acts and to penalties in the fields of organised crime, terrorism and illicit drug trafficking' (Article K.1 and Article K.3(e), Title VI TEU, as amended by Treaty of Amsterdam). This approach was then continued in the Treaty of Nice, which entered into force on 1 February 2003 (Article 31(1)(e) TEU, as amended).[23] Pursuant to Article 31(1)(c) TEU, common action on judicial cooperation in criminal matters shall include 'ensuring compatibility in rules applicable in the Member States, as may be necessary to improve such cooperation'. Given the context of improving cooperation in criminal matters, this provision reflected the 'supportive' function of harmonisation (see, e.g., Borgers 2010). Borgers (2010) raised doubts about whether the provision pertained to procedural or substantial criminal law as well while also taking into account its broad interpretation by the MS. In this regard, it should be mentioned that this book uses the notion of 'harmonisation' interchangeably with 'approximation'. One cannot forget, however, that certain divergences and interpretation nuances between these two terms have been raised in the literature (see, e.g., Tadić 2002; Klip 2009, 2016).

Tampere Milestones

The crucial policy orientations and priorities for the creation of an area of freedom, security, and justice were established during a special meeting of the European Council held on 15 and 16 October 1999 in Tampere.[24] The Tampere Conclusions sought to exploit the full legal potential of the Treaty of Amsterdam. The 'Tampere Milestones' towards a Union of freedom, security, and justice addressed the issue of the proceeds of crime in the context of protecting freedom and legal rights from the threat posed by serious crime (Milestone 6 of the Tampere Conclusions). These conclusions produce a broader picture of European integration by identifying its roots in freedom, namely in a 'shared commitment to freedom based on human rights, democratic institutions and the rule of law' (Milestone 1). At the same time, they consider the enjoyment of freedom to have an indissoluble connection with the genuine area of justice characterised by the following features:

> The enjoyment of freedom requires a genuine area of justice, where people can approach courts and authorities in any Member State as easily as in their own. Criminals must find no ways of exploiting differences in the judicial systems of Member States. Judgements and decisions should be respected and enforced throughout the Union, while safeguarding the basic legal certainty of people and economic operators. Better compatibility and more

> convergence between the legal systems of Member States must be achieved (Milestone 5 of the Tampere Conclusions).

In the area of justice, the incompatibility or complexity of legal and administrative systems across the MS should not adversely affect the exercise of the rights of individuals and businesses (28). Accordingly, the Tampere Conclusions expressed an expectation that the Union would protect people's freedom, i.a., by ensuring that there are no 'safe havens' not only for criminals but also for the proceeds of crime. As illustrated by Milestone 6, the problem of hiding the proceeds of crime within the Union was considered one of the most important from the perspective of the threat to freedom and legal rights posed by serious crime:

> People have the right to expect the Union to address the threat to their freedom and legal rights posed by serious crime. To counter these threats a common effort is needed to prevent and fight crime and criminal organisations throughout the Union. The joint mobilisation of police and judicial resources is needed to guarantee that there is no hiding place for criminals or the proceeds of crime within the Union (Milestone 6 of the Tampere Conclusions).

The Tampere Conclusions indicated two principles on which the AFSJ should be based: transparency and democratic control. Even though there was no explicit reference to restorative justice, some statements were included which correspond with a restorative approach to justice (broadly understood). One example of this is stressing the need for the development of an 'open dialogue with civil society on the aims and principles of this area in order to strengthen citizens' acceptance and support' (7). Moreover, some political guidelines were included for protecting the victims of crime by establishing minimum standards in this respect:

> minimum standards should be drawn up on the protection of the victims of crime, in particular on crime victims' access to justice and on their rights to compensation for damages, including legal costs. In addition, national programmes should be set up to finance measures, public and non-governmental, for assistance to and protection of victims (32).

Importantly, the Tampere Conclusions saw the judicial protection of individual rights through the perspectives of, on the one hand, enhanced mutual recognition of judicial decisions and judgments, and on the other hand, the approximation of legislation. A clear view was presented that the 'principle of mutual recognition [...] should become the cornerstone of judicial co-operation in both civil and criminal matters within the Union' (33) (see also Buono 2009). Notably, the principle of mutual recognition should also apply to pre-trial orders, such as those enabling competent authorities to secure evidence and to seize assets which are easily movable (36).

The issue of confiscation was also strongly heard in the Tampere Conclusions in the context of money laundering recognised as being 'at the very heart of organised crime'. Accordingly, the European Council expressed its determination to 'ensure that concrete steps are taken to trace, freeze, seize and confiscate the proceeds of crime' (51). The special attention to combating financial crime, including money laundering, was additionally reflected in the priorities set out in respect of national criminal law:

> efforts to agree on common definitions, incriminations and sanctions should be focused in the first instance on a limited number of sectors of particular relevance, such as financial crime (money laundering, corruption, Euro counterfeiting), drugs trafficking, trafficking in human beings, particularly exploitation of women, sexual exploitation of children, high tech crime and environmental crime (48).

The Tampere European Council called for the approximation of criminal law and procedures on money laundering, including those concerning tracing, freezing, and confiscating funds. Their conclusions envisaged the development of common standards to prevent the 'use of corporations and entities registered outside the jurisdiction of the Union in the hiding of criminal proceeds and in money laundering'. This should also imply making 'arrangements with third country offshore-centres to ensure efficient and transparent co-operation in mutual legal assistance' – in line with the FATF Recommendations (57). Furthermore, the Tampere Conclusions urged the MS to fully implement the first AML Directive (1991), the Strasbourg Convention (1990), and the FATF Recommendations (52).

However, despite the official narrative of the Tampere Conclusions being centred around the protection of freedom, and legal rights, when adopting concrete EU instruments concerning confiscation referring to these conclusions, in fact, the focus was on the effectiveness of the fight against serious and organised crime, not the rights.

Post-Tampere policy orientations

The 2000 EU Strategy for the beginning of the new millennium (hereinafter the 2000 Strategy) addressed the issue of the proceeds of crime with relevance to the political guidelines enshrined in the Tampere Conclusions, as well as recommendations of the 1997 Action Plan and the 1998 Vienna Action Plan, as mentioned previously.[25] The 2000 Strategy noted the need for comprehensive data on organised crime in planning the EU and the MS responses to this type of crime (4). In order to 'detect and interrupt organised criminal activities, apprehend the offenders, demolish the criminal networks, and seize and confiscate the proceeds of crime', it advocated for a 'more proactive, intelligence-led approach' (5). It also stated that improved data could help the MS and the Council in the 'planning of crime prevention and, through this, in best protecting the potential victims of crime' (5).

Notably, the 2000 Strategy saw the CPC as the core element of the fight against profit-driven organised crime:

> The primary motive of much organised crime is financial gain. Effective prevention and control of organised crime, therefore, would focus on tracing, freezing, seizing and confiscating the proceeds of crime. However, this has

> been hampered for example by the slowness of the exchange of information, the differences in legislation and the cumbersome nature of bureaucratic procedures (20).

In addition, the 2000 Strategy expressed the need to accelerate the cross-border enforcement of freezing orders concerning bank accounts and judicial decisions on assistance in tracing illegal assets (20). It also advocated for a broader examination of the complex issue of reversing the burden of proof concerning the origin of assets:

> The possibility of the mitigation of the burden of proof, after the conviction of the offender for a serious offence, concerning the origin of assets held by the offender should be considered. Such mitigation would require that the sentenced person proves that he or she has acquired the assets in question in a legal manner. If this is not done to the satisfaction of the court, the assets can be held to be the illegal proceeds of crime, and confiscated (20).

The issue of the *onus probandi* was also addressed in Recommendation 19 of the 2000 Strategy:

> An examination should be made of the possible need for an instrument which, taking into account best practices operating in the Member States and with due respect to fundamental legal principles, introduces the possibility of mitigating, under criminal, civil or fiscal law, as appropriate, the onus of proof regarding the source of assets held by a person convicted of an offence related to organised crime.

With reference to the Tampere Conclusions, the 2000 Strategy recommended examining the 'possible need for an instrument on confiscation regardless of the presence of the offender' (Recommendation 20) and an instrument on the sharing of confiscated assets among MS (Recommendation 21).

Another important issue related to confiscation procedures which emerged in that Strategy was the protection of the rights of third parties acting in good faith (Recommendation 16):

> the Council should adopt an instrument calling on the Member States to review their legislation and its application in respect of decisions on the tracing, freezing, seizure and confiscation of assets from crime and, where necessary, subsequently establish minimum standards with a view to allowing mutual recognition and execution of such decisions at as early a stage as possible in the investigation and criminal proceedings, taking into account the rights of third parties in bona fide.

The Tampere Conclusions pertaining to money laundering and the proceeds of crime were also the point of reference for the EU Drugs Strategy (2000–2004).[26] However, after Tampere, crucial policy targets for the AFSJ were set in the five-year Hague Programme adopted at the European Council of 4 and 5 November 2004.[27] It should be noted that the way this area was perceived significantly changed after the terrorist attacks on 11 September 2001 in New York City ('9/11'), on 11 March 2004 in Madrid, and on 7 July 2005 in London. The problem of the financing of terrorism was then intensively discussed in international fora, including the EU (see, e.g., Wouters and Naert 2003; Biersteker, Eckert, and Romaniuk 2008; Brent 2008). The policy to combat terrorism was outlined at an extraordinary meeting of the European Council held on 21 September 2001 in Brussels. The European Council called upon the ECOFIN and JHA Councils to take the necessary measures to combat the financing of terrorist activities, in particular through the extension of the first AML Directive and the FD on freezing assets.

Accordingly, confiscation-related issues (i.e., the 'monitoring of suspicious financial flows', the freezing of assets, and developing new tools targeted at cash transactions) emerged in the Hague Programme within the context of fighting the financing of terrorism (2.2).[28] The first AML Directive (1991) was amended in 2001 (the second AML Directive 2001/97/EC).[29] Additionally, in 2003, an instrument was adopted concerning the execution of orders freezing assets or evidence (FD 2003/577/JHA).[30]

It should be pointed out here that the issue of the possible reuse of confiscated assets for compensation of identifiable victims or for social purposes has been recognised since at least 2005 at the EU level, but concrete legal solutions in this respect were not provided in the pre-Lisbon legal framework. This is reflected in the Council and Commission Action Plan implementing the Hague Programme on strengthening freedom, security and justice in the European Union (2005), which provided for i.a. (3.3):

- Examination of standards for the return of confiscated or forfeited assets as compensation or restitution to identifiable victims of crime or charitable organisations [...]
- Review and, if necessary, strengthening of present legislation on confiscation of criminal assets.[31]

However, the reports on the implementation of the Hague Programme did not specifically address this issue.[32] The most extensive observations concerning confiscation were presented in the 2009 Communication from the Commission 'Justice, freedom and security in Europe since 2005: An evaluation of the Hague Programme and Action Plan'. However, once again, that concrete issue was not addressed therein.[33]

Another strategy which employed confiscation in the fight against serious crime was the EU Drugs Strategy for the period 2005–2012, endorsed at the European Council of 16–17 December 2004.[34] Confiscation of assets was indicated in this strategy as one of the important elements required to realise the EU's ambitions regarding drug policy:

> Law enforcement with regard to money laundering in relation to illicit drug trafficking, drug trafficking and the financing of terrorism and confiscation of assets should be given particular attention. The involvement of Eurojust in this regard must be further explored (27(1)).

This strategy involved the use of confiscation measures 'to their full potential' by both the EU and the MS:

> The Union and Member States should learn more about their effectiveness, impact and full potential before introducing new EU-wide measures and regulations. Duplication and overlap should be avoided and resources used to best effect (27(2)).

Accordingly, the issues of money laundering and seizure of accumulated assets in relation to drug crime were addressed in two consecutive action plans: the EU Drugs Action Plan (2005–2008) adopted for the first period of the aforementioned EU Drugs Strategy (23)[35] and in the EU Drugs Action Plan (2009–2012) adopted for its second period.[36] The latter envisaged, i.a., strengthening the cooperation between the MS 'in order to achieve the full application of the legal instruments relating to mutual recognition of confiscation orders' (33), supporting the establishment of effective Asset Recovery Offices (AROs) in the MS in accordance with Decision 2007/845/JHA, as well as supporting the MS involved through the CARIN network and investigations through Europol (34). One of the objectives of Decision 2007/845/JHA (to be replaced by Directive 2024/1260) was to complete the Camden Assets Recovery Inter-Agency Network (CARIN) established in 2004 with the legal framework for the exchange of information between AROs (Recital 5 of the Preamble to Council Decision 2007/845/JHA).

Nevertheless, the nature of the competences of AROs raised some doubts. Should they be focused on collecting information about assets alleged to be obtained from criminal conduct, or should AROs additionally be granted decisive powers to, for instance, temporarily freeze such assets? Alternatively, the latter competence may be attributed only to judicial authorities acting in the course of criminal or civil proceedings. Despite the adoption of Decision 2007/845/JHA, these questions are still vital.[37] For example, Borgers (2014) pointed out that international cooperation in the field of confiscation takes place predominantly at a judicial level, whereas the competences of AROs under this Decision consist of exchanging information at a police level (37–38).[38] The issue of the competences of AROs was addressed in the Communication from the Commission to the EP and the Council: 'Proceeds of organised crime. Ensuring that "crime does not pay"':

> AROs should have access to all relevant databases [...] to identify and trace assets, including financial information (ideally to a central bank account registry at national level), and should have coercive powers to obtain such information. They should have the powers to provisionally freeze assets (e.g. for at least 72 hours) in order to prevent dissipation of the proceeds of crime between the moment when assets are identified and the execution of a freezing or confiscation court order. They should also be able to conduct joint investigations with other authorities (4.2.3).

Shortcomings of policy regarding extended confiscation and asset sharing

EU instruments concerning the CPC operate within two dimensions: internal and external. The former is aimed to approximate national legislation on confiscation, and the latter is aimed to improve the enforcement of confiscation orders in cross-border cases (as indicated previously, this book uses the notions of 'approximation' and 'harmonisation' synonymously). Accordingly, in 2002, the Danish Presidency presented two draft FDs intended to operate in the areas of approximation of national legislation and execution of confiscation orders in cross-border cases. The first legislative proposal was the draft FD on confiscation.[39] The second was the draft FD on the execution of confiscation orders.[40]

The aforementioned 2002 Report concerning initiatives by the Danish Presidency pointed out that FD 2001/500/JHA had proved insufficient, and there was indeed room for a new harmonising instrument in the area of confiscation of crime-related proceeds.[41] The departure point for the concept of harmonisation of legislation on the CPC was strengthening the fight against cross-border organised crime, considered to be motivated by financial gain. This can be read in the Preamble to the draft FD on confiscation:

> The main motive for cross-border organised crime is financial gain. In order to be effective, therefore, any attempt to prevent and combat such crime must focus on tracing, freezing, seizing and confiscating the proceeds from crime. However, this is made difficult inter alia as a result of differences between Member States' legislation in this area (Recital 1).

The draft FD on confiscation aimed to ensure that all MS had effective rules on the CPC, especially those rules governing the burden of proof concerning the origin of assets of a person convicted of an offence related to organised crime (Recital 10). Its Preamble referred to the 1990 Strasbourg Convention, the 1998 Vienna Action Plan, the 1999 Tampere Conclusions, the 2000 Action Plan, the 2000 Palermo Convention, and FD 2001/500/JHA. The legislative proposal of the Danish Presidency provided for two types of confiscation: regular (standard) confiscation (Article 2) and extended confiscation (broadly understood) covering the confiscation from a third party (Article 3). For the first time, rules on confiscation from a third party were introduced by FD 2005/212/JHA, albeit initially envisaged as a non-mandatory type of confiscation. According to the draft FD on confiscation, the objects of regular confiscation were 'instrumentalities and proceeds from criminal offences punishable by deprivation of liberty for more than one year, or property of corresponding value to such proceeds' (Article 2). Unlike 'extended powers of confiscation', regular confiscation did not raise major legal issues during the legislative process. It should also not be forgotten that in relation to tax offences, the final provisions of FD 2005/212/JHA left the possibility open for the MS to use non-criminal procedures to deprive the perpetrator of the proceeds of the offence.[42]

Characteristically for the pre-Lisbon policy on confiscation, there was no political agreement on the definition of a coherent concept of extended confiscation. Consequently, the MS were offered an alternative set of rules governing the 'extended powers of confiscation' (Article 3 of FD 2005/212/JHA). Nevertheless, bearing in mind the legal environment at that time, which consisted of the diversity of national confiscation schemes and intergovernmental methods of decision-making, the rules extending the scope of confiscation in fact loosened the link between confiscated property and specific criminal conduct, which should be seen a significant step forward in EU's approach to tackling the proceeds of crime.

The extension of the scope of confiscation proposed in the draft FD depended on the substantial value of the proceeds, where the act was of such a nature that it could generate substantial proceeds (Article 3(1)(a) of the draft FD), and the severity of penalty (the act being punishable by at least a maximum sentence of up to six years in prison, Article 3(1)(b) of the draft FD). According to the explanatory note accompanying the draft FD, the 'extended powers of confiscation' were targeted at assets of considerable value; in addition, they were designed as non-obligatory.[43]

Confiscation from a third party concerned property acquired by the spouse or cohabitee of the person targeted (under the same conditions as applied to extended confiscation), with the possibility for the MS to disregard cases where the acquisition of the property was made more than three years prior to the commission of the offence or where the marriage or cohabitation did not exist at the time of acquisition (Article 3(2) of the draft FD). This type of confiscation also covered the property transferred to a legal person (under certain conditions relating to relationships between the person concerned and the legal person, Article 3(3) of the draft FD). Similarly, the MS had the right to disregard cases where the transfer of the property to the legal person was made more than three years prior to the commission of the offence (Article 3(3) of the draft FD). In addition, the draft FD on confiscation provided for 'value confiscation', the object of which was an amount equivalent to the value of the property (Article 3(5)). Importantly, extended confiscation and confiscation from a third party were excluded if the person concerned rendered it probable that the 'property was acquired in a legitimate manner or by legitimately acquired means' (Article 3(4) of the draft FD). Accordingly, the MS were required to ensure such persons had the opportunity to present information on the origin of property during the criminal prosecution (Article 3(4) of the draft FD).

As can be seen from the explanatory note accompanying the draft FD on confiscation, the concept of confiscation from a third party was focused mainly on effectiveness, with too little emphasis on rights.[44] Not without reason, the aforementioned 2002 EP Report (consultation procedure 2002/0818/CNS) suggested that the 'extended powers of confiscation' in the form proposed by the Danish Presidency should be limited. First of all, with reference to Article 31 of the Treaty on European Union pertaining to the minimum harmonisation in the field of organised crime, these powers should be limited to organised crime offences (14–15). In addition, this report argued for limiting the reversal of the burden of proof in the legal construct of extended confiscation:

> it would be more appropriate to tone down these provisions, with the prosecution having to prove that the property possessed is disproportionate to

> declared income or the activity pursued, and the person convicted having the onus to prove the lawful origin of the property (15).

The same report argued for mitigating the inversion of the burden of proof in respect of confiscation from a third party:

> it should have to be proven that the property of the partner or cohabitee belongs to the person convicted and that the partner or cohabitee or the representatives of the legal person have only fictitious title or access to it. [...] it is unacceptable that the above-mentioned third parties should – without having committed any crime – be required to prove the lawful origin of the property when there is no proof that such property belongs to the person convicted or that the third parties have fictitious title or access to it (15).

The EP's legislative resolution on the draft FD on confiscation proposed other important changes.[45] For example, the introduction of the notion of proportionality (namely the 'proportion to the criminal offence established'), in order to avoid ordering confiscation disproportionate to the offence committed (6). Secondly, it presented the view that the provisions on confiscation should refer to 'proceeds already ascertained' and not to potential proceeds (7). Moreover, it proposed introducing a new provision ensuring that the *onus probandi* regarding the origin of the property would be on the part of the prosecution, not the defence (8), giving the following justification:

> Otherwise, the unlawful origins of the property could only be argued on the basis of mere suppositions or suspicions. [...] Rules which have mere suspicion as their basis are incompatible with every modern system of criminal law, which draw on the principles of an offence having had to be committed, safeguards and the assumption of innocence (9).

The Council reached a political agreement on the draft FD on confiscation in 2005. However, this agreement did not result in a clear-cut concept of extended confiscation which could be adopted in EU law.[46] It should be noted that the final provisions of FD 2005/212/JHA differed significantly from the legislative proposal of the Danish Presidency in terms of 'extended powers of confiscation'.[47] Pursuant to Article 3(1) of FD 2005/212/JHA, a minimum requirement was for the MS to adopt the necessary measures enabling extended confiscation of the property belonging to a person convicted of one of serious offences related to organised crime and covered by one of the six FDs (2000/383/JHA, 2001/500/JHA, 2002/629/JHA, 2002/946/JHA, 2004/68/JHA, 2004/757/JHA), or offence related to terrorism covered by FD 2002/475/JHA. Additional conditions regarding triggering offences were connected with the severity of the penalty and the possible financial gain (Article 3(1)(b)).

The non-homogenous concept of 'extended powers of confiscation' as finally adopted in FD 2005/212/JHA stemmed mainly from two circumstances: the diversity of national confiscation systems and intergovernmental decision-making procedures at the EU level. Such a legal environment was not conducive to developing a single minimum standard on extended confiscation. Instead, the MS were offered three alternative options of extended confiscation (Article 3(2) of FD 2005/212/JHA).

In the first option, extended confiscation was based on the conviction of the court that the property in question originated from the 'criminal activities' of the convicted person prior to conviction. According to Article 3(2)(a) of FD 2005/212/JHA:

> Each Member State shall take the necessary measures to enable confiscation [...] at least: a) where a national court based on specific facts is fully convinced that the property in question has been derived from criminal activities of the convicted person during a period prior to conviction for the offence referred to in paragraph 1 which is deemed reasonable by the court in the circumstances of the particular case.

In the second option, extended confiscation was based on the conviction of the court that the property in question originated from 'similar criminal activities' of the convicted person prior to conviction. According to Article 3(2)(b) of FD 2005/212/JHA:

> Each Member State shall take the necessary measures to enable confiscation [...] at least: b) where a national court based on specific facts is fully convinced that the property in question has been derived from **similar** [bolded by A.H.O] criminal activities of the convicted person during a period prior to conviction for the offence referred to in paragraph 1 which is deemed reasonable by the court in the circumstances of the particular case.

In the third option, extended confiscation was based on establishing that the value of the property was disproportionate to the lawful income, together with the conviction of the court of the illegal origin of the property of the convicted person. According to Article 3(2)(c) of FD 2005/212/JHA:

> Each Member State shall take the necessary measures to enable confiscation [...] at least: c) where it is established that the value of the property is disproportionate to the lawful income of the convicted person and a national court based on specific facts is fully convinced that the property in question has been derived from the criminal activity of that convicted person.

This indecisive policy on extended confiscation translated into flawed rules being adopted in EU instruments operating in both harmonisation of legislation and execution of confiscation orders in cross-border criminal cases. For example, the problems that occurred in the area of harmonisation were illustrated in the 2007 Commission Report on the implementation of FD 2005/212/JHA. First of all, this Report stated that it was difficult to determine which of the alternatives had, in fact, been adopted by each MS, when taking into account the differing legal systems and concepts of confiscation. In addition, it pointed to the difficulties in the smooth implementation of provisions regarding 'extended powers of confiscation'. According to this Report:

> Article 3(2) appears to have posed the most problems with respect to its implementation. These problems relate primarily to legal traditions and fundamental principles, in particular as regards the administration of the burden of proof, the link usually required between the offence for which an individual has been convicted and the property confiscated, the right to a fair trial and the need for the penalty to be proportional to the facts of the case. At the same time, some Member States have gone further by allowing the courts to impose confiscation of all or part of the property of a convicted person without having to show that such property was derived from criminal activities.[48]

Further problems with extended confiscation resulted from the rules on execution of confiscation orders in cross-border cases. The draft FD on the execution of confiscation orders proposed by the Danish Presidency referred to the Tampere Conclusions, which stressed the significance of the principle of mutual recognition in judicial cooperation in criminal matters and expressed the determination to 'root out' money laundering being at the heart of organised crime. Following the concept adopted in ENA, the draft FD in question provided that in the case of serious offences (listed in Article 5), the execution of a confiscation order was independent of the verification of the double criminality of the act. The draft FD aimed to facilitate and speed up the execution of confiscation orders with the use of standardised certificates. However, ultimately this objective has not been achieved. The first point of failure arose as a consequence of the lack of a single standard on extended confiscation, which translated into an unsatisfactory level of harmonisation of national confiscation regimes. The second issue arose as a consequence of the rules allowing non-execution of orders imposing extended confiscation in cross-border cases. For example, if it appeared that the confiscation order was issued under the 'extended powers of confiscation' and at the same time such an order fell outside the scope of the option adopted by the executing MS (i.e., selected from the options offered by FD 2005/212/JHA), the order should be executed 'at least to the extent provided for in similar domestic cases under national law' (Article 8(3) of FD 2006/783/JHA), however, with the proviso that similar domestic cases existed in the executing MS, given the differing legal concepts regarding extended confiscation. Moreover, if the confiscation order was issued under the 'extended powers of confiscation' resulting from other national provisions (not resulting from the application of the 'extended powers of confiscation' specified in Article 3 of FD 2005/212/JHA), the competent judicial authority of the executing MS was entitled to refuse to recognise and execute such confiscation orders (Article 8(2)(g) of FD 2006/783/JHA). The problems encountered in the execution of orders imposing extended confiscation were illustrated, for example, in the 2010 Commission Report on the implementation of FD 2006/783/JHA. This report listed the MS which had made declarations based on Article 7(5) on non-recognition and execution of extended confiscation orders (Article 2(d)(iv)).[49] In view of the above, it should be reiterated that FD

2006/783/JHA on the application of the principle of mutual recognition to confiscation orders is still applicable to Denmark and Ireland, as well as FD 2003/577/JHA regarding freezing orders. The other MS are currently bound by Regulation 2018/1805, operating in the areas of mutual recognition of confiscation orders and freezing orders.

EU legislative interventions in the area of CPC were initially justified primarily in terms of the effective fight against serious and organised crime; however, it should be considered that efforts to enhance the effectiveness of this fight through the use of CPC have partially failed due to deficiencies of policy regarding extended confiscation, being a type of confiscation which plays a crucial role in combating serious and organised crime. In this context, it is worth recalling a pertinent question posed by Simonato (2016), on whether the mutual recognition regime in the pre-Lisbon period was, in fact, in operation in cases of extended confiscation (729). One can say that the legal confusion that occurred in the area of executing confiscation orders in cross-border criminal cases represents an example of the questionable added value EU law offers to national legal orders rooted in different legal traditions of dealing with the proceeds of crime. However, given the diversity of the national legal orders, questions about the value and coherence of EU legislative interventions repeatedly appear in the literature concerning EU criminal policy (see, e.g., Delmas-Marty 1996; Weyembergh and Wieczorek 2016).

Another important issue which emerged in EU policy in the pre-Lisbon period, which is also essential in a restorative approach to justice, was asset sharing. The draft FD on the execution of confiscation orders proposed by the Danish Presidency did not contain provisions on sharing confiscated assets between MS, which was negatively assessed in the aforementioned 2002 EP Report. In this context, this Report reminded the legislative proposition of the Austrian Republic, which was put forward in the 1990s but not taken forward (15–16). The issue of asset sharing was viewed from a narrow perspective, under which the MS were considered the main beneficiaries of confiscated assets. The possibility of involving other stakeholders in this process, such as victims or social organisations, was initially beyond the scope of interest. However, it should not be overlooked that the draft Joint Action on asset sharing (the Austrian initiative of 1998) provided for the discretion of the MS in terms of expenditure of the assets or the value received by way of asset sharing. Pursuant to Article 4(3) of this draft Joint Action: 'The payment of any funds shall not be made conditional on transferring them to any State, government, organisation, or individual'.[50] This idea, however, was not pursued (see also Vande Reyde and Van Daele 2017, 309). As stated above, the possibility of the reuse of confiscated assets for non-State purposes was more clearly addressed in the Action Plan implementing the Hague Programme on strengthening freedom, security, and justice in the European Union (2005), OJ C 198/1, (3(3)(s)). Nonetheless, there were no concrete legislative steps taken in this respect in the pre-Lisbon period.

The legal solutions finally adopted in FD 2006/783/JHA only considered States in the disposal of confiscated money and other property, i.e., the executing MS and the issuing MS (Article 16). There were no rules aimed at ensuring the return of confiscated assets to identified victims of crime. Such rules only emerged in EU law many years after the Treaty of Lisbon, in Regulation 2018/1805 (Articles 27, 29, and 30).

Data on the performance of confiscation systems

When considering EU legal interventions regarding confiscation in the pre-Lisbon period, the problem of the lack of sufficient data from MS on the scale of proceeds of serious and organised crime and on the effectiveness of confiscation of such proceeds should be addressed. This lack of data should be viewed in the context of the diversity of national confiscation regimes, which the EU itself encouraged by offering the MS three alternatives of extended confiscation. It is worth remembering that neither FD 2005/212/JHA, FD 2003/577/JHA, nor FD 2006/783/JHA contained any provisions on the periodic collection of statistical data on the execution of confiscation orders. The problem of scant data on the implementation of confiscation provisions was identified early on in the subject literature. Vettori (2006, 13–17) raised this issue after investigating practices around the proceeds of crime in 15 MS. Nevertheless, insufficient data on the execution of confiscation orders in MS still remains a current issue despite the introduction of rules on the collection of statistical data by the MS (Article 11 of Directive 2014/42/EU, Article 35 of Regulation 2018/1805, see also Article 28 of Directive 2024/1260). At this point, it is worth mentioning that a better mechanism of collecting statistical data has been developed within the EU AML regime, which engages for this purpose Financial Intelligence Units (FIU); however, some questions have also been raised as regards the comparability of such data (see, e.g., Ferwerda 2014).[51]

Referring to Wróblewski's (1985) model of rational law-making, which indicates issues that a lawmaker, if acting rationally, should resolve, the starting point for identifying appropriate legal intervention in a given area is gaining a comprehensive knowledge of reality to be changed (see Chapter 1). The lack of comparable and relevant data from all MS on the execution of confiscation orders poses the risk of inappropriate legal interventions on the part of the EU (the incorrect diagnosis of problems and the choice of legal solutions to resolve them). Such interventions are intended to be applied across the whole EU territory in which operate various national confiscation schemes. In this context, it should be recalled that the aforementioned 2000 Strategy for the beginning of the new millennium expressed the need for comprehensive data on organised crime in planning the EU and in the responses of the MS to this type of crime (4). The need for data on the performance of the asset recovery systems in the MS was also indicated by Europol (2016) in 'Survey of statistical information 2010–2014':

> At a European level, it is impossible to monitor the performance of the asset recovery systems, and of investigative techniques used during organised crime investigations across Europe, without data on the number and value of assets seized, frozen or confiscated (5).

In addition, Europol (2016) pointed out the difficulties faced in obtaining relevant data on the amount of proceeds of organised crime resulting from the various paths of reinvesting such proceeds by criminals:

> not all the money gained from criminal activities is then invested in the legal economy or laundered through it. On the contrary, criminals reinvest money in other criminal activities and then may invest a share of their ill-gotten gains in the legal economy (5).

Similar observations were presented in the 'European Financial and Economic Crime Threat Assessment 2023' (Europol).[52] According to this assessment, 'no fully reliable data is available on illicit proceeds generated by serious and organised crime in the EU' (Europol 2023, 19). In this context, it is worth quoting the observation of Calderoni (2014), that the field of organised crime is 'vulnerable to mythical numbers, i.e. exaggerated estimates lacking empirical support, but acquiring acceptance through repetition' (138), see also Levi 2015. The Europol survey (2016) also raised the question of 'mythical numbers' referring in this respect to an observation made by Reuter (1984) (Reuter was inspired by Singer (1971)):

> Many scholars and international institutions have tried to estimate the amount of criminal proceeds generated by organised crime groups. Most of these studies provide enormous figures based on many assumptions and estimates. Although these figures are crucial to understanding recovered values in the context of criminal profits, many of them are 'mythical numbers' (Reuter, 1984), i.e. estimates created using unclear data and methodologies.
>
> (Europol 2016, 5)

This problem was also recognised by Forsaith et al. (2012) in the 'Study for an impact assessment on a proposal for a new legal framework on the confiscation and recovery of criminal assets', commissioned by the Commission Directorate-General Home Affairs. This Study pointed out:

> the most common justification for asset confiscation – that it will help to combat organised crime – is unsupported by empirical evidence and subject to plausible macro-level counterarguments. On the other hand, it is relatively clear that asset confiscation has the potential to benefit victims whilst helping to build public confidence in criminal justice. On these bases we may conclude that a low proportion of criminal assets recovered (i.e. a gap between the amount recovered and the amount which could be recovered) would represent a problem.
>
> (Forsaith et al. 2012, 23)

Accordingly, when resolving the problem of insufficient recovery of criminal proceeds, the EU lawmaker bases its vision of the magnitude of criminal proceeds in the EU on limited data. For example, when planning the legal solutions finally adopted in Directive 2014/42/EU (legislative procedure 2012/0036 (COD)), most of the data came from two MS, Italy and the UK. Such data were referenced in the

Impact Assessment accompanying the 2012 Proposal for a Directive on the freezing and confiscation of proceeds of crime in the EU, which stated:

> The problem addressed by this impact assessment is the insufficient recovery of criminal assets in the EU. To date, estimates of money lost to organised crime in the Member States, as well as data on success in asset recovery, remain patchy. Some recent reports and unofficial sources estimate the annual proceeds from organised crime in some Member States as very high (12).[53]

The Explanatory Memorandum to the 2012 Proposal of Directive on the freezing and confiscation of proceeds of crime in the EU also referenced estimates from the United Nations Office on Drugs and Crime (UNODC):[54]

> At global level, according to United Nations estimates, the total amount of criminal proceeds in 2009 was approximately USD 2.1 trillion, or 3.6% of global GDP [UNODC 2011[55]]. There are no reliable estimates of the size of criminal profits in the European Union […], but in Italy the proceeds of organised crime laundered in 2011 have been estimated by the Bank of Italy at € 150 billion. In the United Kingdom in 2006 organised criminal revenue was estimated at £15 billion (2).

As regards the lack of data concerning the scale of criminal assets in the EU, the Explanatory Memorandum indicates that the situation is better when it comes to estimating the value of criminal markets:

> More estimates exist on the value of criminal markets. The global drug trade generated USD 321 billion in 2005 according to the United Nations. Trafficking in human beings is globally worth USD 42.5 billion per year according to the Council of Europe. The global market in counterfeit goods was estimated at up to USD 250 billion per year by the OECD. Corruption in the EU has been estimated to cost as much as 1 % of EU GDP per year.

When designing rules on mutual recognition of confiscation orders and freezing orders (legislative procedure 2016/0412 (COD) preceding the adoption of Regulation 2018/1805), the EU lawmaker referred to estimates presented in Europol's Survey of Statistical Information 2010–2014 (2016),[56] and in the Final Report of project OCP – Organised Crime Portfolio (Savona and Riccardi 2015). The Explanatory Memorandum contained in the 2016 Proposal for Regulation on the mutual recognition of freezing and confiscation orders stated:[57]

> Recent research [Europol 2016] estimates that illicit markets in the European Union generate about 110 billion EUR, i.e. approximately 1% of the EU's GDP in 2010. However, and although existing statistics are limited, the amount of money currently being recovered from proceeds of crime within the EU is only a small proportion: 98.9% of estimated criminal profits are not confiscated and remain at the disposal of criminals (2).

Similarly, when designing new harmonising rules on confiscation, the EU law-maker had limited knowledge of the reality it wanted to change, due to a reliance on estimated and aggregate data on the size of criminal assets in the EU. The draft Directive on asset recovery and confiscation proposed in 2022 (legislative procedure 2022/0167 (COD) preceding the adoption of Directive 2024/1260) stated in the Preamble:

> Europol's 2021 Serious and Organised Crime Threat Assessment (SOCTA)[58] highlighted the rising threat from organised crime and criminal infiltration. Driven by the large revenues generated by organised crime, which amount to at least EUR 139 billion every year, and which are increasingly laundered through a parallel underground financial system, the availability of such proceeds from criminal activities poses a significant threat to the integrity of the economy and society, eroding the rule of law and fundamental rights (Recital 1, the same issue was raised in Recital 1 of the Preamble to Directive 2024/1260).

It seems more feasible to create a common mechanism for collecting data on confiscated assets recognised in national confiscation procedures as being linked to criminal activity. To this end, the relevant data on the operation of national confiscation systems in the MS (collected periodically at the central level in both, national and cross-border cases) should include at least the following categories:

- the number of confiscation orders (issued, executed, not executed, with information about the reasons of non-execution),
- the types of criminal cases in which confiscation orders have been issued (with information on the legal qualification of the offence in the issuing MS),
- the types of confiscation imposed (regular, extended, from a third party, NCBC),
- the type and value (or estimated value) of confiscated assets (with information on the type of confiscation which was applied to capture the assets), (cf. Article 28(h) of Directive 2024/1260),
- the method of disposal of confiscated assets, with information on the directions of transfer of assets and the division into State and non-State purposes (the value and portion of assets transferred to victims, social and public purposes), (cf. Article 28(j)(k) of Directive 2024/1260),
- the participation of non-State actors in the disposal of confiscated assets, and
- the measures ensuring transparency of the operation of national confiscation schemes.

Accordingly, similar data collection rules should be put in place as regards freezing orders, which secure assets for future confiscation (cf. the scope of Article 28 of Directive 2024/1260). Nevertheless, the issue of obtaining relevant and comparable data on the proceeds of crime, which means data suitable for use in EU confiscation policy and its evaluation, is complex. In addition, it is largely dependent on the level of harmonisation achieved within national legislation on confiscation, a challenge still ahead for the EU.

As a final point, there is also a lack of reliable data confirming that confiscation of criminal assets eventually translates into reducing the scale of acquisitive crime or truly contributes to the fight against serious and organised crime (see, e.g., Naylor 1999; Bullock and Lister 2014). Accordingly, these aspects, eagerly used in the rhetoric of confiscation policies at the EU level, may play the function of 'political slogans' underpinning the introduction of more far-reaching confiscation measures. Therefore, in principle, references to combating serious and organised crime should be observed with some reserve and distance when they are made to justify controversial confiscation solutions, those departing from criminal standards of procedure. Conversely, the rationale behind introducing changes aimed at prioritising the position of the victim over the position of the State or enabling the reuse of a larger share of confiscated assets for public interest or social purposes should not raise major controversies, especially when adopting a broad definition of 'crime' and 'victim'.

The post-Lisbon period: a promising paradigm shift in EU criminal justice policy?

Towards a more comprehensive approach

Between the adoption of the Treaty of Lisbon by the EP on 19 February 2008 and its entry into force on 1 December 2009, the Commission presented the Communication defining the strategic priorities in tackling proceeds of crime in the EU: 'Proceeds of organised crime. Ensuring that "crime does not pay"' (20 November 2008).[59] However, its context was limited to the fight against organised crime in the EU. The Communication stated:

> In order to disrupt organised crime activities it is essential to deprive criminals of the proceeds of crime. Organised crime groups are building large-scale international networks and amass substantial profits from various criminal activities. The proceeds of crime are laundered and re-injected into the legal economy (2).

The vision presented by the Commission implied the development of a more comprehensive EU legal framework covering criminal and civil confiscation orders and broadening the scope of mutual recognition. Nevertheless, their overall focus was still directed to effectiveness considerations. Thus, issues such as the social aspect of confiscation, reconsidering its objective, or strengthening the position of victims or communities in confiscation mechanisms, were not considered. The Commission determined the role of confiscation in the following terms:

> To fight crime effectively means to hit criminals where it hurts them most. The confiscation and recovery of the proceeds of crime targets their resources and is an essential part of the wider EU financial crime strategy. More should

> be done to highlight confiscation as one of the most effective ways to fight organised crime (7).

The Communication in question criticised the existing confiscation-related EU legal framework and pointed to the flawed implementation of FD 2003/577/JHA, FD 2005/212/JHA, and Decision 2007/845/JHA. In addition to this, the implementation of FD 2006/783/JHA had also proved insufficient over time. Accordingly, the Commission suggested recasting the EU legal framework (3.2) and expressed its willingness to explore the extension of some legal concepts and introduce new rules, increasing the confiscation possibilities (3.3). Importantly, the Commission beginning to advocate a more balanced approach, where fundamental rights protections accompany effectiveness considerations, although this approach primarily involved the rights of persons subjected to confiscation, not victims or communities:

> as confiscation measures (e.g. the reversal of the burden of proof) may affect fundamental rights (such as the right to property and the right to adequate means for recourse) a balanced approach is necessary and appropriate safeguards need to be provided for (3.3).

Bearing in mind that some MS had developed broader possibilities of confiscation than that provided for by EU law, the Commission suggested developing the discussions on confiscation in the following directions: civil confiscation (3.3.1), introducing the criminal offence of owning 'unjustified' assets (3.3.2), ensuring mutual recognition of freezing orders and confiscation orders (3.3.3), extending the scope of mandatory confiscation in cases of serious criminal offences linked with organised crime (3.3.4), enforcing the obligation to provide information on bank accounts; in this respect the Communication referred to the 2001 Protocol to the Convention on Mutual Assistance in Criminal Matters (3.3.5).[60]

Notably, the Commission considered CPC as a global issue requiring coordinated action at the EU level and within the international cooperation with third countries, especially in the context of flaws of incorporating into Community legislation confiscation-related provisions of the Palermo Convention, the UNCAC and the Strasbourg Convention (5).

It should be noted that the Commission pointed also to 'non-legislative flanking measures' (6). For example, enabling AROs to access centralised national registers. To increase the effectiveness of confiscation, the Commission advocated for exploring the opportunities for improving the 'availability of information on outstanding freezing and confiscation orders' in the EU and creating a relevant list of such orders (6.1). Moreover, the non-legislative measures recommended by the Commission involved the promotion of a wider use of financial investigations and financial criminal analysis (6.2). Finally, the use of non-legislative measures was considered regarding collecting statistics on confiscation; the Communication acknowledged the limited amount of such data, sourced mainly from national databases and reports on AML compliance published by the FATF, the International Monetary Fund and MONEYVAL (6.3). Indeed, as previously noted, most of the data regarding confiscation orders was obtained under the framework of Money

Laundering data collection systematically developed under EU AML rules, the EU Action Plan 2006–2010 on Crime Statistics[61] and the EU Statistics Action Plan 2011–2015.[62]

Despite the unsatisfactory level of harmonisation of national confiscation regimes, after the lecture provided by the Communication, one can form the impression that the EU territory had come to be considered as a unified zone where the execution of confiscation and freezing orders takes place, and the rights of targeted persons are exercised. This perspective justified efforts to further lessen national differences, as well as towards establishing a common standard for the protection of fundamental rights.

The Stockholm Programme

The Stockholm Programme provided for a new agenda for the AFSJ for the years 2010–2014.[63] In the post-Lisbon reality, decision-making processes based on the qualified majority opened new opportunities for creating EU instruments on confiscation in the challenging environment of differing national confiscation schemes. In addition, shaping new harmonising rules with directives binding as to the result (Article 288 TFEU), but also having direct effects if not transposed within the prescribed period, offered EU legislators broader possibilities than FDs to affect national legal orders in line with EU policies (see, e.g., C 41/74, *Van Duyn v Home Office*, EU:C:1974:133; Case 148/78, *Ratti*, EU:C:1979:110).

Nevertheless, non-exclusive EU competence in the AFSJ is shared with the MS. The scope of EU interventions regarding substantive criminal law has been limited to the so-called Euro-crimes. The EU's role in this respect is establishing 'minimum rules concerning the definition of criminal offences and sanctions in the areas of particularly serious crime with a cross-border dimension resulting from the nature or impact of such offences or from a special need to combat them on a common basis' (Article 83(1) TFEU). There is also the so-called criminal 'annex competence' related to the effective implementation of EU policy (Article 83(2) TFEU). In this context, Csonka and Landwehr (2019) indicated that Article 83(2) TFEU excludes references to 'unwritten "implied powers"' (262).

As far as procedural criminal law is concerned, pursuant to Article 82(1) TFEU, judicial cooperation in criminal matters is based on the principle of mutual recognition and includes the approximation of the laws and regulations of the MS, however, to a limited extent. In addition, the EP and the Council may establish minimum rules 'to the extent necessary to facilitate mutual recognition of judgments and judicial decisions and police and judicial cooperation in criminal matters having a cross-border dimension'. When creating such rules consideration shall also be given to the differences between the legal traditions and systems of the MS (Article 82(2) TFEU). Due to the limited extent to which minimum rules may be established, their role is recognised as 'supportive' ('auxiliary') (Zoumpoulakis 2020; see also Weyembergh 2005). Similarly, the condition of necessity is contained in Article 67(3) TFEU (see Schroeder 2020), and the idea of respecting 'national identities' is expressed in Article 4(2) TEU (see also Satzger 2019). However, the question of the functions of harmonisation under the Lisbon Treaty is complex. For example, as Borgers (2010) indicated, under Article 82(1) TFEU, mutual recognition is unconditional, and harmonisation is conditional. Article 82(2) TFEU expresses the 'support' function of harmonisation of the law of criminal procedure, while Article 83 TFEU expresses an autonomous function of harmonisation of substantive criminal law in its paragraph 1 (in the limited field) and paragraph 2 (in a 'weakened form', Borgers 2010, 353).

Pursuant to Article 82(2) TFEU, minimum rules are envisaged in the areas of mutual admissibility of evidence between MS, the rights of individuals in criminal procedure and the rights of victims of crime. However, a 'general clause' contained in Article 82(2)(d) (see, e.g., Herlin-Karnell 2010) allows establishing minimum rules in any other specific aspects of criminal procedure identified by the Council. Furthermore, notwithstanding the EU's competence to establish minimum procedural rules, the MS have the competence to maintain or introduce a higher level of protection for individuals (Article 82(2) TFEU *in fine*).

The Stockholm Programme addressed confiscation-related issues in the context of economic crime and corruption. By focusing on improving the effectiveness of confiscation, it pursued the same approach taken in the Tampere and Hague Programmes. However, it also raised a new aspect: strengthening cooperation between AROs.[64] This issue was then addressed by the 2010 Council Conclusions on Confiscation and Asset Recovery. Their adoption was preceded by discussions on the recommendations of the Alicante Seminar on AROs at the Multidisciplinary Group on Organised Crime (MDG) meetings held in March, April, and May 2010, as well as at the CATS meeting in May 2010.[65]

Based on the Lisbon Treaty, the Stockholm Programme linked the facilitation of mutual recognition with the approximation of substantive and procedural law, where necessary (3.1.1.). This linkage was vital from the perspective of the failure to agree on a single standard of extended confiscation in the pre-Lisbon period, which translated into further problems in executing confiscation orders in cross-border cases. A single standard of extended confiscation was agreed in the post-Lisbon harmonising instrument, i.e., Directive 2014/42/EU, and developed by Directive 2024/1260. In the Stockholm Programme, the European Council called upon the MS and the Commission (where relevant) to take various actions concerning confiscation, such as enhancing financial investigations, improving identification and seizure of the assets of criminals, giving consideration to reusing them 'wherever they are found in the Union', enabling and coordinating sources of information to identify suspicious cash transactions, and confiscating the proceeds of crime according to the 1990 Strasbourg Convention (4.4.5).[66] Nonetheless, the issue of possible reuse of the confiscated assets for non-State purposes took in EU law the form of a soft recommendation, not a strict requirement addressed to the MS (see Article 10(3) of Directive 2014/42/EU). Moreover, this policy position is still upheld, as reflected in current EU law (see Article 19(1) of Directive 2024/1260).

Despite focusing on the effectiveness of measures targeted at combating serious and organised crime, the Stockholm Programme expressed a more balanced approach to developing the AFSJ than the Tampere and Hague Programmes. For instance, it tried to give priority to the interests and needs of citizens. Secondly, respecting fundamental rights and freedoms was considered one of the main challenges. Special attention was paid to the rights of the child, vulnerable groups, and the victims of crime. Moreover, the Commission was called upon to propose measures for developing compensation schemes. Additional emphasis was put on the rights of suspected and accused persons. Finally, the Stockholm Programme saw mutual trust as a central factor determining the operation of the principle of mutual recognition; it referred to the Hague Programme in this respect.

As stated earlier, appropriate legal intervention depends on the legislator's comprehensive knowledge of a given reality (Wróblewski 1985). In view of the above, it should be highlighted that the Stockholm Programme recognised the increased need for reliable statistics in the decision-making process:

> Adequate, reliable and comparable statistics (both over time and between Member States and regions) are a necessary prerequisite, *inter alia*, for evidence-based decisions on the need for action, on the implementation of decisions and on the effectiveness of action (4.3.3).

Accordingly, the European Council invited the Commission to continue the actions indicated in the EU plan for 2006–2010 on developing a comprehensive and coherent EU strategy to measure crime and criminal justice.[67] As far as data on the execution of confiscation orders are concerned, concrete legal solutions for collecting such data were introduced by Directive 2014/42/EU (Article 11), Regulation 2018/1805 (Article 35), and Directive 2024/1260 (Article 28).

In November 2010, with reference to the Stockholm Programme, the Commission presented the Communication 'The EU Internal Security Strategy in Action — Five steps towards a more secure Europe'.[68] It defined five strategic objectives: 'disrupt international crime networks' (1), 'prevent terrorism and address radicalisation and recruitment' (2), 'raise levels of security for citizens and businesses in cyberspace' (3), 'strengthen security through border management' (4), and 'increase Europe's resilience to crises and disasters' (5). Confiscation was mentioned as a means to achieve the first objective:

> To combat the financial incentive of criminal networks Member States must do all they can to seize, freeze, manage and confiscate criminal assets, and ensure that they do not return to criminal hands (6).

The actions envisaged in the strategy included, i.a., proposing legislation to broaden the possibilities of extended confiscation and third-party confiscation, facilitation of mutual recognition of NCBC, enhancing the performance of the AROs and its evaluation, making institutional arrangements for asset management to prevent the loss of value of frozen assets before confiscation, and developing guidance on preventing reacquisition of confiscated assets by criminals (6, 18).

The EP Resolution of 25 October 2011 on organised crime in the EU also raised the problematic EU legal framework for extended confiscation and third-party confiscation.[69] Importantly, this Resolution addressed the issue of the social reuse of confiscated assets and its possible double impact, on the prevention of organised crime, on the one hand, and economic and social development on the other. Recognising the linkage between these two different spheres, the EP presented a further-reaching approach to confiscation than that adopted in the Stockholm Programme. The social dimension of confiscation noticed by the EP broadened the way of thinking about confiscation, centred around combating organised crime and ensuring the rights of targeted persons in confiscation procedures (accused or suspected persons, third parties). The EP Resolution stated:

> the re-use of confiscated assets for social purposes fosters a positive attitude to strategies aimed at tackling organised crime, since confiscating an asset is no longer regarded solely as a means of depriving a criminal organisation of resources but is doubly constructive in that it both helps to prevent organised crime and has the effect of boosting economic and social development (D).

Notably, the EP called on the Commission to take steps regarding European legislation on the reuse of criminal assets for social purposes by indicating an urgent need in this respect:

> the urgent need for European legislation on the re-use of crime proceeds for social purposes, including court witness protection, so that the capital of criminal organisations or their associates can be reinjected into legal, clean, transparent and virtuous economic circuits (9).

References to confiscation issues and the Stockholm Programme can also be found in the EU Anti-Fraud Strategy (2011),[70] which stated:

> In addition to adequate sanctions, convicted and administratively sanctioned persons must be effectively deprived of the proceeds of their offence and defrauded resources must be recovered (2.1).

A (partial) step forward in harmonising confiscation rules

Drawing on the Stockholm Programme and the JHA Council Conclusions on confiscation and asset recovery (2010), the Commission submitted the Proposal for a directive on the freezing and confiscation of proceeds of crime in the EU (2012).[71] The proposal of new harmonising rules in this regard had previously been announced by the Commission, i.a., in the Communication on Fighting Corruption in the EU (2011),[72] which alluded to four reports pointing to the flaws in implementing the existing confiscation measures (4.1.2).[73]

It should be stressed from the outset that various actors delivered valuable comments to EU legislators on restorative aspects of confiscation previously unrecognised in EU policy, which, regrettably, were not incorporated in the text of the directive agreed in the trilogues between the Council, the EP, and the Commission (legislative procedure 2012/0036/COD preceding the adoption of Directive 2014/42/EU). Instead, the existing approach, developing the confiscation policy towards increasing the effectiveness of confiscation and strengthening the position of targeted persons (suspected or accused persons, and third parties), but primarily in terms of the right of defence, was maintained. One can say that the very objective of confiscation, as a multi-faceted legal institution, was not duly recognised by EU legislators. Accordingly, the drive towards harmonising confiscation rules, which concluded with the adoption of Directive 2014/42/EU, should be assessed as only a partial success because of the missed opportunity to increase the restorativeness of EU confiscation law.

Nevertheless, the harmonising rules proposed in 2012 and adopted in 2014 represented a significant step forward in improving many other areas relating to confiscation. The solutions proposed by the Commission in 2012 involved establishing minimum rules for various forms of confiscation and unifying, to some extent, EU legislation on confiscation. The 2012 Proposal provided for the replacement of Joint Action 98/699/JHA, and, in part, FD 2001/500/JHA (point (a) of Article 1 and Articles 3 and 4), and FD 2005/212/JHA (Articles 1 and 3). The idea was to maintain the obligation of the MS to enable ordinary post-conviction confiscation of instrumentalities and proceeds (also in the form of 'value confiscation') for criminal offences not covered by the Proposal (see Article 2 of FD 2005/212/JHA). The scope of the Proposal was limited to the harmonised offences in the areas of crime listed in Article 83(1) TFEU. It also covered other offences if committed in the framework of a 'criminal organisation' in the meaning adopted in FD 2008/841/JHA on the fight against organised crime (2008), OJ L 300/42.[74] Apart from that, the Proposal broadened the concept of 'proceeds' to indirect profits, including 'any subsequent reinvestment or transformation of direct proceeds by a suspected or accused person and any valuable benefits' (Article 2(1) of the 2012 Proposal, cf. Article 1 of FD 2005/212/JHA).

For the first time in EU confiscation policy, harmonising rules on confiscation of proceeds and instrumentalities not based on a criminal conviction were proposed, albeit to a limited extent (Article 5 of the Proposal). The inspiration in this respect was drawn from the UNCAC (Article 54(1)(c)), the output of the FATF (Recommendation No 3), and the G8 Roma-Lyon Group (see more in Rui 2012).[75] In addition, the creation of the rules on NCBC was supported by CARIN and the ARO Platform (the 2012 Proposal, 2.6).

Confiscation without conviction in the proposed form was limited to cases where the further prosecution of the suspected or accused person was prevented by death, illness, or flight from prosecution or sentencing (Article 5 of the Proposal). However, the prerequisite of death was not incorporated into the final version of the Directive. Additionally, under Article 4(2) of Directive 2014/42/EU, the NCBC is subsidiary to post-conviction confiscation. It also provides for the conditions regarding criminal proceedings, which had to be at least initiated relating to a profitable criminal offence 'liable to give rise, directly or indirectly, to economic benefit', and lastly, 'such proceedings could have led to a criminal conviction if the suspected or accused person had been able to stand trial'. Given these points, scholars have raised the pertinent argument that, in reality, the proposed concept of NCBC had little in common with civil confiscation in its traditional meaning, the core of which is independence from a criminal conviction (see, e.g., Rui 2012;

Arcifa 2014; Alagna 2015). Similar reservations concerning the need for a mutual recognition mechanism also covering measures adopted in a 'non-criminal context' were raised by the Italian Senate.[76] After six trilogues between the Council, the EP, and the Commission, and additional informal meetings, a compromise was reached, i.a., regarding the concept of NCBC. However, this compromise was less than perfect (though according to the Council, it was a 'well-balanced compromise').[77] Significantly, in conjunction with the provisional agreement on NCBC (the rules on NCBC were not changed in the final version of Directive 2014/42/EU), the parties agreed to a 'Declaration on an analysis to be carried out by the Commission' regarding national solutions concerning civil confiscation in its traditional meaning with the view of introducing common rules in this respect. An additional declaration concerned submitting a legislative proposal by the Commission on mutual recognition of freezing and confiscation orders.[78] The Commission submitted the Proposal for a Regulation on the mutual recognition of freezing and confiscation orders in 2016 (legislative procedure 2016/0412(COD) was completed in 2018 by adopting Regulation 2018/1805).[79]

The 2012 Proposal also provided for minimum rules on third-party confiscation, this time in a mandatory form (Article 6 of the proposed directive), since it should be remembered that this type of confiscation had so far been optional in EU law (cf. Article 3(3) of FD 2005/212/JHA).

Nevertheless, the most important novelty of the 2012 Proposal was the definition of a single standard of extended confiscation in place of the problematic alternative set of minimum rules contained in FD 2005/212/JHA. In this aspect, the Proposal represented a significant step forward in harmonising legislation concerning confiscation. According to the proposed rules, extended powers of confiscation covered property of a person convicted of a criminal offence, however, not directly originating from that offence. Extending the scope of confiscation to other property was based on a finding of the court that 'it substantially more probable that the property in question has been derived by the convicted person from similar criminal activities than from other activities' (Article 4(1) of the proposed directive). In addition, pursuant to Article 4(2) of the proposed directive:

> Confiscation shall be excluded where the similar criminal activities referred to in paragraph 1 (a) could not be the subject of criminal proceedings due to prescription under national criminal law; or (b) have already been subject to criminal proceedings which resulted in the final acquittal of the person or in other cases where the ne bis in idem principle applies.

The concept of extended confiscation was modified in the compromise text and finally adopted in this form. Importantly, contrary to FD 2005/212/JHA (Article 3), Directive 2014/42/EU severed the link between extended confiscation and organised crime, as the minimum rules on this type of confiscation also relate to offences outside the context of organised crime. However, the explanatory memorandum of the Proposal still emphasised the problems of organised crime.

Under Directive 2014/42/EU, extended confiscation is related to the property of a person convicted of a criminal offence which is 'liable to give rise, directly or indirectly, to economic benefit' (Article 5(1)). Secondly, this type of confiscation requires that a court is satisfied, based on the circumstances of the case (facts and evidence), that the property in question is derived from 'criminal conduct', especially when the value of the property and the lawful income are disproportionate. As can be seen, Directive 2014/42/EU does not base extended confiscation on a court finding about the linkage of assets with 'similar criminal activities' (cf. Article 4 of the 2012 Proposal).

The 2012 Proposal and subsequently adopted harmonising rules significantly developed EU confiscation law, especially concerning the concept of proceeds of crime, extended confiscation, and third-party confiscation. But despite this, specific issues remained unresolved. In addition to the failure to establish minimum rules on civil confiscation (in its traditional meaning), the true objective of confiscation was not thoroughly considered in the legislative process. Criticisms should be expressed regarding the main directions in which EU confiscation policy has systematically evolved. Looking back to the initial considerations on CPC made by the European Council in the 1990s, there are two aspects between which it alternates: exploring opportunities to further extend the scope of confiscation and increase its effectiveness. However, one can say that these aspects represent only one side of the coin, while there is another side – the social aspect of confiscation policy, not merely limited to the goals of the fight against crime, but encompassing wider, more restorative purposes. Properly defining the objective of confiscation should translate into a more harmonious approach to creating EU rules on confiscation, especially as regards strengthening the position of all stakeholders, not only the targeted persons (suspected or accused persons and third parties) but also victims, communities, and their representatives. Secondly, adopting a more balanced approach should translate into a reconsideration of the position of the State, which is currently over-prioritised in EU and national confiscation policies. For instance, the 2012 Proposal, in the opening part of the explanatory memorandum, stressed the position of public authorities while it defined the aims of the proposed directive:

> This proposal for a Directive aims to make it easier for Member States' authorities to confiscate and recover the profits that criminals make from cross-border serious and organised crime. It seeks to attack the financial incentive which drives crime, to protect the licit economy against criminal infiltration and corruption, and to return criminal profits to public authorities providing services for citizens (2).

Thus, the possibility of direct transfer of confiscated assets to other actors, like communities, NGOs, etc., was not considered (2). On the other hand, the 2012 Proposal provided for the collection of statistics by the MS on 'the value of the property destined to be reused for law enforcement, prevention or social purposes' (Article 11(h)). Similarly, the 2012 Proposal did not deal with the rights of victims in confiscation proceedings, even though the explanatory memorandum pointed to contacts established when creating new harmonising rules 'with civil society, notably with organisations promoting legality, the fight against organised crime and the protection of the victims of crime' (e.g., with representatives of the FLARE Network – Freedom, Legality and Rights in Europe, and associated networks).[80]

Various actors in the legislative process have pointed out deficiencies in the proposed harmonising rules concerning the social dimension of confiscation. Particular attention should be paid to the Opinion of the EESC on the Proposal (2012).[81] Apart from the need to strengthen the powers of the AROs and Eurojust in identifying and tracing the proceeds of crime (1.3), the crucial observations of the EESC concerned the social aspect of confiscation. One example of this was the reference to the possible 'double benefit' of social reuse of confiscated assets, firstly, in preventing organised crime and, secondly, in promoting economic and social development (the Opinion of the EESC, 4.9.1). The two-pronged impact had been previously noted also by the EP in the Resolution on organised crime (2011) and Report on organised crime in the EU (2011). Moreover, the ESSC recommended a 'holistic approach' prioritising 'socially beneficial purposes' and, at the same time, mitigating the risk of reacquisition of the assets by criminals:

> If measures to freeze and confiscate the proceeds of crime are to be effective, a holistic approach is needed that governs every dimension of the instrument and, when it comes to the confiscated goods being reused, takes care to give priority to socially beneficial purposes (1.4, see also 3.5.2).

Another aspect highlighted in the EESC Opinion was the need to balance effectiveness issues connected with the fight against organised crime with fundamental rights issues, particularly the rights of the defence (1.5). Finally, the EESC reasserted the 'need to link the fight against organised crime to the Europe 2020 strategy', which did not directly address crime-related questions.[82]

Additional attention should be drawn to the Opinion of the Committee of the Regions on the 'Package on protection of the licit economy' (2012).[83] The Committee of the Regions welcomed the draft directive. However, new harmonising rules concerning the CPC were seen in the broader perspective of protection of the global economy. Notably, the Opinion observed that organised crime threatens 'public order, public health and social cohesion' (I.7). In the context of enhancing the role of local authorities in combating corruption and organised crime, and with reference to Italian solutions regarding the reuse of criminal assets, the Committee called on MS to include the transfer of assets for local and regional purposes in asset sharing. Namely, the MS were called on to:

> provide for a share of the criminal assets seized to be returned to local and/or regional authorities (once legal claims for recovery have been met) as they are the first victims of criminal organisations that destabilise the social order at local level. They are also best placed to take local-level measures to eradicate the deep-rooted causes of crime. This is one way of showing the work of public authorities in a positive light and creating a virtuous cycle involving elected representatives, civil society and families.
>
> (Opinion of the Committee of the Regions, 46)

Next, the LIBE Report (2013) proposed significant amendments to the 2012 Proposal.[84] It is important to emphasise that some of them were related to the restorative aspects of confiscation. For instance, the LIBE Report proposed a new Recital 12c of the Preamble confirming that confiscation 'should not hinder or prevent justified claims by victims' (Amendment 11, cf. Article 8(10) of Directive 2014/42/EU). Secondly, it proposed amendments encouraging the social reuse of confiscated assets. Apart from that, the idea was presented to establish a Union fund dedicated to supporting grass-roots social initiatives, as well as a revolving fund serving to maintain the value of frozen property until confiscation (Amendment 57):

> Property frozen with a view to later confiscation should be managed adequately in order not to lose its economic value, to encourage its social reuse and to avoid the risk of further criminal infiltration. To that end, it would be useful to consider the formation of a Union fund that would collect a part of the confiscated assets from Member States. Such a fund should be open to pilot projects by the citizens of the Union, associations, coalitions of NGOs and any other civil society organisation, to encourage the effective social reuse of the confiscated assets and to expand the democratic functions of the Union (Amendment 16).

In addition, one of the amendments proposed in the LIBE Report stated that confiscated property should be used 'for projects aimed to contrast and prevent crime, and for other institutional or public purposes or social use' (Amendment 17). The social reuse of confiscated assets was considered in the LIBE Report in a broader perspective involving supporting a culture of legality, protection of victims, and combating organised crime (proposed Recital 16b of the Preamble):

> The practice of using confiscated assets for social purposes fosters and sustains the dissemination of a culture of legality, assistance to crime victims and action against organised crime, hence creating 'virtuous' mechanisms, which may also be implemented through non-governmental organisations, that benefit society and the socio-economic development of an area, using objective criteria (Amendment 18, see also Amendment 20).

Lastly, the LIBE Report was in favour of obliging MS to ensure the possibility of the social reuse of confiscated property. Pursuant to Amendment 53, MS 'shall provide for the possibility of confiscated property being used for social purposes' (cf. the soft law recommendation contained in Article 10(3) of Directive 2014/42/EU to use confiscated property for 'public interest' or 'social purposes'). Accordingly, it called on the MS to provide measures for the disposal and the destination of confiscated property, including for law enforcement, public, and social purposes (Amendment 56). Regarding statistics, it proposed collecting data on the 'type of use to which the confiscated property has been put, and the contribution it has made to the social and economic development of the area and local communities concerned' (Amendment 59). However, the solutions agreed upon and finally adopted in Directive 2014/42/EU did not reflect all the valuable amendments proposed by the LIBE. Pursuant to Article 10c of Directive 2014/42/EU, there is no strict obligation on the part of the MS to provide the reuse of confiscated property for public or social purposes. Instead, the MS 'shall consider taking measures' in this respect. Additionally, the meaning of the 'obligation to consider' was developed in Recital 35 of the Preamble to Directive 2014/42/EU in the following way:

> That obligation to consider taking measures entails a procedural obligation for Member States, such as conducting a legal analysis or discussing the advantages and disadvantages of introducing measures. When managing frozen property and when taking measures concerning the use of confiscated property, Member States should take appropriate action to prevent criminal or illegal infiltration (Recital 35).

Embedding these statements in the Preamble gives the impression that EU legislators were willing to enforce changes in domestic legal orders regarding the reuse of confiscated property for non-State purposes. Nevertheless, this remains just an enhanced recommendation, not hard EU law.

The issue of social reuse was also thoroughly analysed by the Basel Institute on Governance in the Note prepared at the request of LIBE (2012).[85] The observation was made that the academic literature did not devote much attention to the destination of confiscated assets (the Basel Note, 21). Nonetheless, the study referred to the output of the G8 Roma-Lyon Group,[86] the Stolen Asset Recovery (StAR) Initiative,[87] the Italian experience as presented by the network LIBERA,[88] as well as the reflections of Golobinek 2006; Olaya, Attisso, and Roth 2011; Brun et al. 2011. This should also be seen in the context that the social reuse of confiscated assets was not common practice in MS legal orders (see, e.g., Rui 2012; Alagna 2015). Given the above, the Basel Institute on Governance presented several options for a 'more coherent European-wide approach in using confiscated assets for civil society and in particular for social purposes', which should be duly considered by EU legislators (the Basel Note, 54).

In this context, special attention should also be paid to the observations indicated in the external study commissioned by the Commission Directorate-General Home Affairs (authored by Forsaith et al. 2012). This study presented clearly defined confiscation-related problems and promoted a balanced approach to confiscation. The problems to resolve were identified in two areas, i.e., increasing the level of recovery and improving the redistribution of criminal assets; such an approach corresponded with the aim of confiscation, which combines these two aspects (Forsaith et al. 2012, 23–24). The study in question indicated the following reasons behind confiscation and asset recovery: combating organised crime, restorative justice for victims, and promoting confidence in the justice system (19–22).[89] However, it associated the restorative aspect mainly with the position of the victim of organised crime (broadly understood, corporate, community or societal) and not with the active role of the defendant. The view was presented that seeking restitution is more challenging in the case of unidentified victims, such as victimised subgroups or communities, when State action may be required (22). The considerations concerning the position of the victim in confiscation procedures involved the context of the Treaty of Lisbon, which emphasised the significance of the rights of victims by including them in the AFSJ in which the EU has a mandate for establishing minimum rules (Article 82(2) TFEU). Regarding confidence in justice systems, the study in question indicated that returning assets to victims and communities may contribute to the promotion of such confidence, and it saw the important role of media in this respect (22–23).

All these observations made an important contribution to the legislative process; however, not all of them were incorporated into the new harmonising rules concerning confiscation. EU legislators did not fully recognise the ambitious approach to confiscation issues adopted by the actors supporting the legislative process. Admittedly, the Impact Assessment accompanying the 2012 Proposal for a directive on the freezing and confiscation of proceeds of crime in the EU addressed the issue of redistribution of confiscated assets for social purposes; however, the approach taken was not ambitious enough.[90] Ultimately, claims that EU legislators were unaware of problems relating to the restorative aspect of confiscation cannot be justified. Applying Wróblewski's (1985) model of rational law-making to this state of affair (see Chapter 1), one can formulate an allegation that the EU lawmaker did not act rationally in this respect, as despite being made aware of the situation, through knowledge provided from many sources, it ignored the very objective of confiscation which combines two aspects – the effectiveness of depriving criminals of the proceeds of crime and their redistribution, involving the interests of victims and communities.

Important concerns about fundamental rights protections were raised in the EU Agency for Fundamental Rights (FRA) Opinion on the Confiscation of proceeds of crime (2012).[91] This Opinion expressed reservations in several areas. Firstly, regarding the proposed non-conviction based confiscation mechanism, there was a need to better integrate the output of the ECtHR, mitigate the serious risk of injustice, and clarify the 'legitimate aim' in relation to the scope of triggering offences (4, 11). Secondly, the FRA Opinion argued for narrowing the scope of triggering offences covered by extended confiscation with the view of the condition of 'necessity' connected with admissible interference with the right to property (12–14). It argued for 'more detailed guidance for the courts' regarding the level of proof (16). In addition, it pointed to access to justice with a focus on the fair trial rights of victims, with reference to ECtHR case-law on Article 6 of ECHR, connecting procedural guarantees with claiming reparation for damage by victims of crime (*Perez v France*, App. no. 47287/99, ECtHR, 12 February 2004, paras. 70–72) (16). Moreover, the FRA Opinion referred to the Palermo Convention, the New York Convention, and the UNCAC, when recommending the use of confiscated assets mainly to compensate the victims of offences (16–17). Accordingly, it suggested including provisions in EU law promoting the reuse of assets for social purposes and to benefit victims (17). Finally, the FRA Opinion advocated for a more balanced approach to the protection of fair trial rights of defendants and victims (17). Notably, it also made references to EU law itself, i.e., Directive 2012/29/EU, which considers crime from a restorative perspective, that is, as a 'wrong against society as well as a violation of the individual rights of victims' (Recital 9).

Additionally, Directive 2011/36/EU (the 'Trafficking Directive') promoted the use of confiscated instrumentalities and proceeds of trafficking offences to compensate victims (Article 7, Recital 13) (the FRA Opinion, 17). The legal solutions in this respect were modified by Directive (EU) 2024/1712, amending the 'Trafficking Directive' (Article 7 of Directive 2011/36/EU was deleted, cf. Article 18(1) of Directive 2024/1260).[92]

It should be noted that the solutions regarding the social reuse of confiscated assets, agreed in trilogues, and finally adopted in Directive 2014/42/EU, faced criticism in the subject literature (see, e.g., Arcifa 2014; Montaldo 2015; Vettori 2018; Ochnio 2022). However, most arguments raised by scholars concerned deficiencies of the EU NCBC regime as not corresponding with the rules on 'civil' confiscation existing in some MS (e.g., Arcifa 2014; Alagna 2015, cf. concerns about protections of rights in NCBC mechanisms, e.g., Hendry and King 2015; Meyer 2020).

Strategic guidelines for the years 2015–2020

After the Stockholm Programme, the strategic guidelines for the AFSJ for the next five years (2015–2020) were defined in the European Council Conclusions of 26–27 June 2014.[93] Nevertheless, confiscation issues were not addressed therein or in their mid-term revision of 2017.[94] Abandoning multiannual programming for the AFSJ faced criticism in the literature, and the added value of the 2014 Conclusions was called into question (e.g., Léonard and Kaunert 2016). On the other hand, the argument was raised that the 'time for big new policy initiatives and multiannual programmes on AFSJ has passed' (Carrera and Guild 2012, 15), and efforts should be made to follow already established directions. After all, some statements contained in the 2014 Conclusions are worth mentioning as being important to the whole AFSJ, of which confiscation is a part. The 2014 Conclusions stated:

> All the dimensions of a Europe that protects its citizens and offers effective rights to people inside and outside the Union are interlinked. Success or failure in one field depends on performance in other fields as well as on synergies with related policy areas (I.2).

The European Council emphasises the importance of ensuring fundamental rights protections in developing the AFSJ (the 2014 Conclusions, I.4). Still, the rights of accused and suspected persons in criminal proceedings were prioritised compared to victim rights. Despite the 2014 Conclusions recognising the need for further action to 'reinforce the protection of victims', in fact they did not deal with the rights of victims in criminal proceedings, in the sense of the active exercise of such rights by their holders. Regarding fundamental rights protections, it is also worth noting the direct reference to restorative justice, made in the EU Action Plan on Human Rights and Democracy 2020–2024, albeit narrowed to ADR mechanisms.[95] It envisaged, i.a., supporting 'human rights-compliant alternative dispute resolution mechanisms' and reducing barriers to justice for victims of human rights violations (1.5.c).

Finally, the 2014 Conclusions expressed respect for national differences (in legal systems and traditions) and the need to enhance mutual trust (I.11). For example, the 'Strategic agenda for the Union in times of change' (2014) annexed to the Conclusions associated the improvement of inter-State judicial cooperation with 'building bridges between the different justice systems and traditions' (Annex 1, (4)). This agenda reinforces the EU's strong mandate to take action against terrorism and organised crime, both characterised by substantial cross-border dimensions, framed by the principles of subsidiarity and proportionality (Article 5 TEU).

New challenges posed by Russia's aggression against Ukraine: linking confiscation issues with international security

In reaction to the illegal annexation of Crimea and Sevastopol by Russia, in 2014, the EU adopted their first package of restrictive measures, later repeatedly amended, based on Article 29 TEU and Article 215 TFEU. They involved the freezing of 'funds and economic resources belonging to, owned, held or controlled by persons having been identified as responsible for the misappropriation of Ukrainian State funds and persons responsible for human rights violations in Ukraine, and natural or legal persons, entities or bodies associated with them', listed in the Annex to Decision 2014/119/CFSP of 5 March 2014 concerning restrictive measures directed against certain persons, entities, and bodies in view of the situation in Ukraine (2014), OJ L 66/26 (Article 1(1)). Asset freezes were also addressed in Regulation (EU) No 208/2014 of 5 March 2014 concerning restrictive measures directed against certain persons, entities, and bodies in view of the situation in Ukraine (2014), OJ L 66/1, and Regulation (EU) No 269/2014 of 17 March 2014 concerning restrictive measures in respect of actions undermining or threatening the territorial integrity, sovereignty, and independence of Ukraine (2014) OJ L 78/6.[96]

'A new strategic agenda 2019–2024' defined by the European Council in 2019 focused i.a. on combating terrorism and cross-border crime and thus continued to develop EU criminal policy in this already well-established direction.[97] However, given the tensions in the international arena, it also tried to face new cybersecurity challenges and protect societies from 'malicious cyber activities, hybrid threats and disinformation originating from hostile State and non-State actors' (3).[98] In accordance with this agenda, 'internal and external challenges' were to be addressed by the EU in an 'integrated manner' (7). One of the emanations of such an approach was linking confiscation-related issues to international security.

In further response to the challenging international situation, the Council adopted Decision (CFSP) 2020/1999 concerning restrictive measures against serious human rights violations and abuses, (2020), OJ L 410 I/13, and Regulation (EU) 2020/1998 concerning such restrictive measures (2020), OJ L 410 I/1. In reaction to the recognition of the non-government-controlled areas of the Donetsk and Luhansk oblasts of Ukraine and the ordering of Russian armed forces into those areas, in 2022, the Council adopted further packages of restrictive measures

(Decision (CFSP) 2022/266 (2022), OJ L 42 I/109; Regulation (EU) 2022/263 (2022), OJ L 42 I/77).

The threat to global security posed by Russia's aggression against Ukraine has undoubtedly affected EU policies in recent years (see, e.g., European Council Conclusions of 22 March 2024,[99] and of 18 April 2024).[100] Aiming to mitigate the risk of violation of Union restrictive measures, and having regard to Article 83(1) third subparagraph TFEU, in 2022, the Council adopted Decision (EU) 2022/2332 on identifying the violation of Union restrictive measures as an area of crime that meets the criteria specified in Article 83(1) TFEU.[101] It was considered that the EU faces exceptional circumstances justifying the extension of areas of crime specified in Article 83(1) TFEU. This is confirmed in Recital 7 of the Preamble to Decision 2022/2332:

> Article 83(1) third subparagraph TFEU allows for a special procedure whereby the Council may identify new areas of crime. This may only be done after a careful assessment of the criteria set out in the Treaty, which reflect the exceptional nature of the procedure. The developments in crime witnessed following Russia's war of aggression against Ukraine constitute exceptional circumstances (Recital 7).

Broadening the scope of Article 83(1) TFEU opened the door for the use of directives to secure the effectiveness of Union restrictive measures. In 2024, the EP and the Council adopted Directive (EU) 2024/1226 on the definition of criminal offences and penalties for the violation of Union restrictive measures and amending Directive (EU) 2018/1673, (2024), OJ L 2024/1226 (see also Csonka and Zoli 2024). Directive 2024/1226 required MS to take the necessary measures to enable the freezing and confiscation of instrumentalities and proceeds from violations of Union restrictive measures constituting criminal offences determined in Articles 3 and 4 of this Directive. MS bound by Directive 2014/42/EU were required to take those necessary measures in accordance with that Directive (Article 10(1) of Directive 2024/1226). In addition, Directive 2024/1226 required MS to take the necessary measures, in accordance with Directive 2014/42/EU, enabling the freezing and confiscation of funds or economic resources covered by restrictive measures in respect of which the designated natural person, or the representative of a designated entity or body, commits or participates in certain offences concerning the circumvention of a Union restrictive measure (Article 10(2) of Directive 2024/1226). As initially conceived, funds or economic resources subjected to restrictive measures were to be considered 'proceeds' of crime (Article 10 of the Proposal for a Directive on the definition of criminal offences and penalties for the violation of Union restrictive measures, 2.12.2022, COM(2022) 684 final). Eventually, however, a different solution was adopted in this respect (see Article 10 of Directive 2024/1226). This issue was also addressed in Recital 29 of the Preamble to Directive (EU) 2024/1226:

> specifically in situations in which the designated person, or the representative of a designated entity or body, commits or participates in certain offences

> concerning the circumvention of a Union restrictive measure, there is a need to enable the freezing and confiscation of funds and economic resources subject to Union restrictive measures, even where they might not constitute instrumentalities or proceeds under Directive 2014/42/EU. [...] Such funds or economic resources should therefore be subject to freezing and confiscation, in accordance with Directive 2014/42/EU. The rights of bona fide third parties should not be prejudiced (Recital 29).

It should be stressed that asset freezes, when adopted as targeted financial sanctions (restrictive measures), are of an administrative nature, not criminal, whereas Directive 2014/42/EU operates in the criminal sphere. The legal consequences of such a situation were clarified in Recital 29 of the Preamble to Directive (EU) 2024/1226:

> The freezing of funds and of economic resources imposed by Union restrictive measures is of an administrative nature. As such, it should be distinguished from freezing measures of a criminal nature, as referred to in Directive 2014/42/EU [...]. Member States should enable the freezing and confiscation of instrumentalities and proceeds from the offences referred to in this Directive. Member States bound by Directive 2014/42/EU should do so in accordance with that Directive.

As can be seen, the threat to global security necessitated revising the EU's approach to tackling illicit assets (see also Moiseienko 2024). Confiscation-related issues once again began to be linked with international security and, thus, to be considered in the CFSP. This link developed in the 2000s in response to a rise in terrorist attacks. External security factors necessitated seeking possibilities for connecting the criminal and administrative domains in EU law, as measures restricting the use of property may operate in either of them. The chosen solution to link these two domains was the introduction of criminal penalties for violating administrative measures.

In 2022, the Commission presented new harmonising rules concerning confiscation, i.e., a Proposal for a new directive on asset recovery and confiscation.[102] This legislative procedure (2022/0167(COD) was completed in 2024 with the adoption of Directive (EU) 2024/1260 on asset recovery and confiscation.[103] Being one of the EU responses to international tensions, this legislative initiative simultaneously fell within the EU's efforts to combat organised and serious crime.[104] The Explanatory Memorandum confirmed that the proposed Directive was 'embedded in the global fight against organised crime, corruption and money laundering' and aimed at implementing the Palermo Convention and the Protocols thereto, the UNCAC, the Warsaw Convention, and Recommendation 4 of the FATF.

Among the reasons behind introducing new harmonising rules were also international operations conducted in several jurisdictions by law enforcement agencies in the years 2018–2021, targeted at capturing data from encrypted digital communications (EncroChat, Sky ECC and ANOM), and subsequent investigations launched by MS, Europol, and Eurojust (the Explanatory Memorandum, 1).[105]

The proposed Directive referred to the EU Strategy to tackle Organised Crime 2021–2025, which announced a revision of Directive 2014/42/EU and Decision 2007/845/JHA towards expanding the scope of criminal offences covered, introducing new rules on NCBC (analysis on NCBC was conducted by the Commission in 2019),[106] and ensuring 'effective management and social reuse of confiscated assets and compensation of victims of crime' (19). These directions were consistent with those indicated in the Commission's Report 'Asset recovery and confiscation, ensuring that crime does not pay' (2020). On the one hand, this Report confirmed the positive impact of Directive 2014/42/EU on developing national asset recovery frameworks. On the other hand, it pointed out the need for further progress.[107] The Report in question indicated the following actions were needed at the EU level, including strengthening the position of victims and supporting the social reuse of confiscated assets:

> (i) extending the scope of criminal offences, to which the Directive is applicable; (ii) introducing more effective rules on non-conviction based confiscation; (iii) being more precise as regards the management of frozen assets; (iv) introducing provisions on the disposal of assets, including the social reuse of confiscated assets; (v) laying down rules on the compensation of victims of crime and (vi) reinforcing the capacity of the Asset Recovery Offices to trace and identify illicit assets (17–18).

Another objective of the proposed Directive was to improve the operational capacities of AROs, i.a., by granting them the competence to impose temporary urgent freezing (Article 11(2) of the Proposal, cf. Article 11(3) of Directive 2024/1260).[108] In the meantime, Directive (EU) 2019/1153 established rules to facilitate access to and the use of financial information and bank account information by competent authorities, including AROs, i.a., for the 'timely identification, tracing and freezing of related assets in view of their confiscation' (Recital 8, Article 1).[109]

The proposed Directive represented a more holistic approach to the multidimensional confiscation mechanism, defined in the Explanatory Memorandum as a 'more strategic approach to asset recovery'. This was reflected in the wide range of issues addressed by the proposed Directive, starting with tracing and identification of assets, through freezing, confiscation, management of assets, and ending with the disposal of assets (see also Sakellaraki 2022). However, all those aspects were still related to the criminal realm (Article 1(1) of the proposed directive). Even if, according to the finally adopted provisions of the new Directive, it 'applies without prejudice to freezing and confiscation measures within the framework of proceedings in civil or administrative matters' (Article 1 of Directive 2024/1260), its subject matter has been narrowed to the criminal realm. The Preamble to Directive 2024/1260 sheds light on its actual scope, which excludes pure 'civil' confiscation:

> This Directive does not prevent Member States from adopting measures that enable the confiscation of unexplained wealth for other crimes or circumstances. The subject matter of this Directive is limited to proceedings in criminal matters, and therefore this Directive does not apply to confiscation

measures in proceedings in civil matters that Member States might have implemented (Recital 35).

It should be noted that initially the subject matter of the proposed Directive explicitly pertained to facilitating the 'effective implementation of Union restrictive measures and the subsequent recovery of related property where necessary to prevent, detect or investigate criminal offences related to the violation of Union restrictive measures' (Article 1(1) of the proposed directive). Finally, this aspect was included in the Preamble to Directive 2024/1260 (Recitals 11, 15, and 39, see also Articles 5(4) and 19(2) of Directive 2024/1260). Furthermore, the scope of the proposed Directive covered criminal offences consisting in the violation of Union restrictive measures (Article 2(3) of the proposed directive). Accordingly, the offences covered by Directive (EU) 2024/1226 were included in the scope of Directive 2024/1260 (Article 2(1)(p)).

The proposed Directive provided for rules concerning various types of confiscation already well-known in EU law: post-conviction confiscation in the form of standard and value confiscation, third-party confiscation, extended confiscation, and NCBC, albeit to a limited extent. Besides, it contained innovative solutions, such as 'confiscation of unexplained wealth linked to criminal activities' (Article 16 of the proposed directive). The latter type of confiscation was also linked with the criminal realm; however, this link was, in fact, relaxed by the 'context of an investigation in relation to a criminal offence' (Article 16 of Directive 2024/1260). This should also be seen from the perspective of the subject matter of Directive 2024/1260 determined in its Article 1, which raises some doubts when juxtaposed with the legal construct of the new type of confiscation determined in Article 16 (see Sakellaraki 2022). Moreover, the 2022 Proposal contained rules on post-conviction tracing and identification of assets (Article 17(1) of the proposed directive) and interlocutory sales aimed at maintaining the value of frozen property (Article 20 of the proposed directive). Lastly, the proposed directive contained rules on cooperation between various actors in asset recovery processes, AROs with EU bodies and agencies (EPPO, Europol, and Eurojust) (Article 28 of the proposed directive). Regarding criminal offences related to the violation of restrictive measures, it contained rules on the cooperation of AROs with their counterparts in third countries (Article 29 of the proposed directive).

Nevertheless, when it comes to increasing the restorativeness of the EU confiscation scheme, both the 2022 Proposal and the finally adopted Directive 2024/1260 represent missed opportunities. This is because, once again, the EU lawmaker did not recognise the social potential of confiscation and its very objective. Even if the considerations on 'social impacts' contained in the Impact Assessment Report raised the need to ensure the availability of confiscated assets for victim compensation or other public interest and social uses (43),[110] EU law has still not used its full potential to ensure such availability in MS legal orders. Given the flawed rules of Directive 2014/42/EU in this respect, it is hard to understand the reasoning behind the repeated failures of the EU lawmaker in the same field. In this situation, the EU lawmaker has acted contrary to the critical opinions of scholars and various actors supporting legislative procedures for adopting Directive 2014/42/EU and Directive 2024/1260. Regrettably, once again, the option of a soft law recommendation prevailed over requiring MS to use a portion of confiscated property for public interest or social purposes (see Article 17(2) of the proposed directive). Ultimately, EU law only encourages MS to 'take the necessary measures to allow the possibility of using confiscated property, where appropriate, for public interest or social purposes' (Article 19(2) of Directive 2024/1260). The position taken by the EU lawmaker is all the more incomprehensible given the references to restorative justice made in the aforementioned Impact Assessment Report. This Report stated:

> it is recalled that confiscation does not necessarily have a punitive character: confiscation aims at taking away criminal profits, and thereby limiting the incentives for and capacity of criminals to continue their activities. It also has **the restorative goal** [bolded by A.H.O.] of ensuring that victims of crime are compensated and that the money taken away from organised crime can be used for public interest and social purposes (48).

The Report in question also referenced restorative justice in the context of evaluation findings concerning the effects of Directive 2014/42/EU (based on information gathered at the ARO Platform and Confiscation Directive meetings held in June and July 2021):

> Besides the benefits of economic returns to the public budget, recovered criminal property further leads to indirect benefits that are not directly quantifiable, such as increased social cohesion and **the long-term impacts of restorative justice on victims and communities** [bolded by A.H.O.] benefitting from returns from social reuse and from lower rates of crime (142).

Notably, some deficiencies of the proposed solutions regarding the social reuse of confiscated assets were pointed out in the EESC Opinion on the 2022 Proposal:[111]

> EESC urges the Commission to reconsider the provision on social reuse in the proposed Directive and to encourage the Member States to devise mechanisms that would include civil society organisations as a priority in managing and disposing of confiscated assets. The Commission should set targets by including a minimum percentage for the social reuse of confiscated assets. Public interest should not be understood to mean only actions under the remit of public entities (1.8).

The EESC's observations put the confiscation mechanism in a broader perspective, containing a restorative justice context:

> Asset recovery is part of the larger EU legislative ecosystem that is intended to contribute to the **restorative justice** [bolded by A.H.O.] that communities need in order to reduce the harm caused by criminal offences (2.3).

Accordingly, the EESC recommended a more ambitious approach to the reuse of confiscated assets than was adopted in the proposed Directive:

> The EESC asks the European Commission to be more ambitious in its efforts to make the social reuse of confiscated assets effective and set a minimum percentage for social reuse for Member States. It is of paramount importance for social cohesion that affected communities get **restorative damages** [bolded by A.H.O.] directly and benefit from the returns from these damages. Moreover, communities need better assistance to help enhance their resilience to organised crime and civil society has to be involved in managing and disposing of confiscated assets (3.8).

Further critique was presented in the LIBE Report, which proposed several amendments to the proposed directive, accentuating the importance of how confiscated assets are reused.[112] For instance, the LIBE Report proposed complementing the Preamble on Recital pertaining to social and public reuse of confiscated assets and, significantly, direct transfers (Amendment 22). Notably, the LIBE Report also justified using such assets for State-related purposes, given the overall costs of confiscation procedures:

> Considering the significant costs associated with tracing and identification, freezing and confiscation, such property can be kept as State property for justice, law enforcement, public service or economic purposes or be transferred to the local or regional authorities responsible for the area in which the property is located for institutional, social or economic purposes, including for assignment to organisations carrying out work of social interest (Amendment 22, cf. Recital 38 of the Preamble to Directive 2024/1260, emphasising respect for the budgetary autonomy of MS).

Importantly, the LIBE Report proposed establishing an obligation for MS to take the necessary measures to reuse confiscated assets for public interest or social purposes, in place of a soft law recommendation. The LIBE Report stated:

> Member States **shall take** [bolded by A.H.O.] the necessary measures to allow confiscated property to be used for public interest or social purposes. Such property may be kept as public property for justice, law enforcement, public service or economic purposes or be transferred to the local or regional authorities responsible for the area in which the property is located, for institutional, social or economic purposes, including for assignment to organisations carrying out work of social interest (Amendment 101).

The LIBE Report proposed amendments regarding the aspects of using frozen or confiscated assets for 'public interest or social purposes and for compensation, restitution and reparations towards States' (Amendment 124), as well as using confiscated assets to compensate the victims (Amendment 125), all to be included in national strategies on asset recovery. According to the LIBE Report, the 'value of the property destined to be reused for law enforcement, prevention or social purposes' should be included in the statistics collected by MS (Amendment 142, cf. Article 28(k) of Directive 2024/1260 as amended). Noteworthy in this context is the negative opinion delivered in the legislative procedure by the Czech Senate pointing out the administrative burden connected with the proposed solutions on national strategy on asset recovery and collecting statistics.[113] However, in view of State-centred national confiscation mechanisms operating across the EU, in which confiscated assets are primarily transferred to State coffers, such a position does not appear to be reasonably justified.

It should be remembered that when the 2022 Proposal for a new directive on confiscation was submitted, there were no appropriate solutions in EU law for returning assets to third countries. This deficiency was raised, i.a., in the external 'Study on freezing, confiscation and asset recovery — what works, what does not work' prepared for the Commission, Directorate-General for Migration and Home Affairs[114] (see also Ochnio 2024). The LIBE Report proposed rules on the returns of assets, which would partially fill this gap in EU law (Amendment 23). According to that Report, such returns should be based on 'publicly available' 'return agreements' determining how to reinvest the funds, for instance, as victim's compensation or for projects of 'high social impact'. The selection of such projects should be transparent and consider the 'needs of the affected populations' (Amendment 23).

Furthermore, some ideas on embedding the issue of the reuse of confiscated assets for public interest or social purposes were contained in the Opinion of the Committee on Legal Affairs for the LIBE (Amendment 2).[115] Similarly, this Opinion was in favour of requiring MS to take measures to allow confiscated property to be used for public interest or social purposes (Amendment 45). Likewise, such a position was expressed in the Opinion of the Committee on Budget (Amendment 31, see also Amendments 32 and 33).[116]

A significant step forward was made regarding strengthening the position of victims in confiscation mechanisms. It should be recognised that EU law has evolved away from approaching victims' rights from the negative side, i.e., that the 'confiscation measure should not affect victims' rights to obtain compensation for their claims' (Article 18 of the proposed directive; Article 8(10) of Directive 2014/42/EU), to a point where victims' claims 'are taken into account within the relevant asset-tracing, freezing and confiscation proceedings' (Article 18(1) of Directive 2024/1260). Nevertheless, it would be desirable for EU law to clearly require MS to enable using confiscated assets directly to satisfy victims' right to compensation. Such a move would be a clear sign for national legislatures of a significant change to the concept of embedding the rights of victims in the EU confiscation scheme.

The input of the EESC was of particular significance to improving the position of victims in EU confiscation law.[117] The EESC Opinion (2022) delivered in this legislative procedure acknowledged that victims' rights to compensation were not sufficiently prioritised in the proposed directive (3.9). The view was presented therein that the Commission should be 'more precise in laying down victims' right to compensation and giving victims priority in the ranking of creditors' (1.9). Secondly, the interlocutory sale 'should remain the last resort with respect to social reuse, considering that the confiscated funds can be allocated to the compensation of the victims' (1.11). The EESC Opinion also highlighted the right to compensation of victims in third countries (1.13, 3.9). In addition, it raised the need to ensure public access to information on asset recovery proceedings. Thus, national authorities should be obliged to publish statistics on confiscation measures (1.4). The EESC called on the Commission to ensure the adoption of national strategies on asset recovery with respect to transparency and accessibility (1.5). Finally, the EESC recommended establishing 'transparent monitoring mechanisms' based on a comparative data collection instrument and involving civil society (1.15).

However, while the compromise text agreed after interinstitutional negotiations somewhat improved the position of victims in the confiscation mechanism, it disregarded the most crucial comments regarding the reuse of assets for public interest or social purposes given the contributions made by the EESC, the LIBE, the Committee on Legal Affairs, and the Committee on Budget.[118] What was ultimately achieved was embedding the issue of the reuse of assets for non-State purposes in the Preamble of the proposed Directive (Recital 29(j) of the compromise text; Recital 38 of Directive 2024/1260). In addition, MS were encouraged, but not obliged, to 'take the necessary measures to allow the possibility of using confiscated property, where appropriate, for public interest or social purposes' (Article 18a of the compromise text; Article 19(1) of Directive 2024/1260). This aspect was also included in national strategies on asset recovery (Article 24 of the compromise text; Article 25 of Directive 2024/1260) and in the statistics to be collected, however, limited to covering only 'social reuse', not for the public interest or to compensate victims (Article 27(k) of the compromise text; Article 28(k) of Directive 2024/1260). Lastly, it should be welcomed that the compromise text and finally adopted provisions of Directive 2014/1260 addressed the interests of third countries in confiscated property, even if this was only a small step towards meeting the growing needs in this complex area (Recital 28(m) of the Preamble and Article 18(a)(2) of the compromise text; Recital 39 of the Preamble and Article 19(2) of Directive 2024/1260; see also Ochnio 2024).

Strengthening the position of victims

Aside from the achievements in supporting the position of victims in the EU confiscation mechanism (see, e.g., Article 18 of Directive 2024/1260), another positive example is found in the first EU Strategy on victims' rights (2020–2025).[119] Adopting this Strategy was in line with Article 82(2)(c) TFEU, which prioritised the rights of victims by including them within the area where the EU has the mandate to establish minimum rules. The Strategy in question represents a 'two-strand approach: empowering victims of crime and working together for victims' rights'. The rights of victims relate to: reporting crime, participating in criminal proceedings, claiming compensation, and as stated in the Strategy, recovering – 'as much as possible – from consequences of crime' (3). Per the Strategy, empowering victims of crime involves using restorative justice services, providing 'victims with a safe environment to make their voice heard and support their healing process'

(6). Nonetheless, it should also be noted that as far as the right to compensation is concerned, this Strategy received some critique in the EESC Opinion (2020).[120] For example, this Opinion pointed out that the international dimension of victims' rights should be strengthened (4.5) and that access to compensation 'should be independent from (or regardless of) the status of the victim' in an EU Member State, with a focus on the weakened position of asylum-seekers, refugees, and migrants in seeking compensation (3.19).

Directive 2012/29/EU established minimum standards on the rights, support, and protection of victims of crime. It should be reiterated that it defined 'crime' in a broad manner, as a 'wrong against society' and a 'violation of the individual rights of victims' (Recital 9 of the Preamble). Given the above, MS were obliged to:

> ensure that victims are recognised and treated in a respectful, sensitive, tailored, professional and non-discriminatory manner, in all contacts with victim support or restorative justice services or a competent authority, operating within the context of criminal proceedings (Article 1).

It also proposed the following definition of 'restorative justice':

> 'restorative justice' means any process whereby the victim and the offender are enabled, if they freely consent, to participate actively in the resolution of matters arising from the criminal offence through the help of an impartial third party (Article 2(1)(d)).

Notably, the previous FD 2001/220/JHA on the standing of victims in criminal proceedings (2001) OJ L 82/1 did not refer to the concept of restorative justice at all. It is also noteworthy that there is no reference to restorative justice in Council Directive 2004/80/EC of 29 April 2004 relating to compensation to crime victims.[121]

Criticism should be expressed regarding the definition of 'victim' applied both in Directive 2012/29/EU – inconsistent with the more restorative definition of 'crime' applied therein, and in Directive 2024/1260 – improperly extended. According to Article 2(1) of Directive 2012/29/EU:

> 'victim' means: (i) a natural person who has suffered harm, including physical, mental or emotional harm or economic loss which was directly caused by a criminal offence;
>
> (ii) family members of a person whose death was directly caused by a criminal offence and who have suffered harm as a result of that person's death.

Firstly, the excessively narrow definition of 'victim' applied in Directive 2012/29/EU affects other EU instruments addressing victims' rights and national legal orders. Admittedly, Directive 2024/1260 expanded the meaning of 'victim' to cover legal persons (Article 3(8)). However, this meaning still does not cover others, such as collected victims, corporate, community, or societal victims. Furthermore, countries can also be considered as victims of crime, e.g., when they are victimised by corruption or war crimes.

Thus, the meaning of a 'victim' based on the definition applied in Directive 2012/29/EU, and then insufficiently extended in Directive 2024/1260, disrupts the achievement of the objectives of the EU confiscation mechanism, the recent revision of which was aimed i.a. at improving the position of victims. To stay in line with current policy objectives, it would be expected that the EU lawmaker discards the narrow meaning of 'victim' by adopting a new directive on the rights of victims, replacing Directive 2012/29/EU, or at least by its revision to introduce a more ambitious definition of 'victim'. The substantive change in understanding the term 'victim' should also influence the future position of the CJEU, which acknowledged the narrow meaning of 'victim' established under Directive 2012/29/EU, not covering legal persons or countries. This position is significant when interpreting national provisions regarding victims in line with EU law. In 2020, the CJEU in *TG and UF* (C-603/19, EU:C:2020:774) expressed the following view:

> 1. Article 2(1) of Directive 2012/29/EU […] must be interpreted as meaning that that directive does not apply to legal persons or to the State, even if national law confers on them the status of injured party in criminal proceedings. 2. Article 325 TFEU must be interpreted as not precluding provisions of national law, as interpreted in national case-law, under which, in criminal proceedings, the State may not claim compensation for damage caused to it by fraudulent conduct on the part of the accused person resulting in the misappropriation of funds from the budget of the European Union, and under which the State does not have, in those proceedings, any other type of action available to it by which it may assert its right as against the accused, provided that, which it is for the referring court to verify, the national legislation provides for effective proceedings for the recovery of assistance wrongly received from the budget of the European Union.

The 2020 Commission Report stated that the implementation of Directive 2012/29/EU was unsatisfactory.[122] Moreover, a recent Evaluation of Directive 2012/29/EU (2022) recognised victims' needs for 'compensation and restoration'.[123] The Evaluation revealed obstacles in exercising the right to compensation from the offender, such as 'cumbersome and lengthy procedures', 'general lack of awareness of this right', and the need to go through two sets of proceedings to receive criminal and civil compensation (19).[124] In addition, the Evaluation in question pointed to NGOs' opinions on the limited access of victims to compensation:

> EU-level NGOs said that effective access to compensation remains an important part of effective access to justice. They also said that victims generally do not have a comprehensive understanding or full awareness of the possibilities the justice system affords them, beyond prosecution and including other aspects such as restorative justice. The length and costs of criminal proceedings are also likely to discourage victims (69).

In 2023, the Commission proposed a revision of Directive 2012/29/EU to facilitate access of victims to compensation.[125] Bearing in mind that the actual position of victims in criminal proceedings depends, i.a., on the efficiency of MS compensation mechanisms, there are many challenges ahead for the EU. One of the solutions available to EU lawmaker is to better integrate victims' rights to compensation into the EU confiscation scheme. Considerable progress has been achieved in this field by the adoption of Directive 2024/1260, which strengthened the position of victims in this scheme.

Facilitating victims' access to compensation is also one of the objectives of the aforementioned EU Strategy on victims' rights (2020–2025). Importantly, it implies improving victims' rights in the EU confiscation mechanism established by Directive 2014/42/EU and Regulation 2018/1805 (the EU Strategy, 17–18). At this point, it is worth considering the Report of the Special Adviser, Jöelle Milquet, to the former President of the European Commission, Jean-Claude Juncker, titled 'Strengthening victims' rights: from compensation to reparation. For a new EU Victims' rights strategy 2020–2025' (2019).[126] This Report saw the confiscation mechanism as a 'more generalised mechanism to help the victims to be compensated' (57). In addition, it pointed out that in the case of specific crimes (trafficking offences) the Commission already promoted the use of seized and confiscated assets originating from trafficking offences for purposes related to victims, including compensation:

> In specific crime areas, such as trafficking in human beings, the European Commission continues to promote the use of available legal instruments and to consider the use of seized and confiscated instrumentalities and the proceeds from the trafficking offences to support victims' assistance and protection, including compensation of victims (57).

As already indicated, the 'Trafficking Directive' promoted the use of confiscated instrumentalities and proceeds of trafficking offences to compensate victims (Article 7 of Directive 2011/36/EU, deleted by Directive (EU) 2024/1712). However, such use of confiscated assets should also be promoted in other areas of crime, as there are no reasons for only linking victims' rights to compensation with the confiscation mechanism in cases of trafficking offences. It seems that the new harmonising instrument in the area of confiscation is more akin to such an approach, as it reflects the promotion of asset use for victims in general (see Article 18(1) of Directive 2024/1260).

According to Article 8(10) of Directive 2014/42/EU, MS 'shall take the necessary measures to ensure that the confiscation measure does not prevent those victims from seeking compensation for their claims'. Regulation 2018/1805 secures victims' rights to compensation and restitution in cross-border cases (Recitals 45, 46, and 48, Articles 26(2), 29 and 30). In addition, the new Directive 2024/1260 provides for significant solutions to strengthen the position of victims in confiscation procedures (discussed above), solutions which MS should transpose by 23 November 2026.

Considering the recent efforts to improve the position of victims in confiscation mechanisms, one can say that the perception of confiscation in EU policy has started to change. Undoubtedly, at least at a policy level, the confiscation of crime-related assets has already gone beyond the punitive function and has entered into the restorative area; thus, the next step is for this revised approach to be reflected in EU law. There remains an open question of whether the observed shift – from perceiving confiscation in terms of effectively combating serious and organised crime to using this legal institution to also restore justice with due account to the interests of all stakeholders – is promising enough to become a consistent course of development for EU confiscation policy, or if it instead constitutes only an additional rhetorical element, which will not be followed up with concrete legal solutions.

The EU as one of the standard setters: the international players affecting European and national confiscation policies

It is apparent that serious and organised crime has more than just a cross-border dimension; it has transnational impacts. Thus, confiscation of the proceeds of such crime is also a matter that needs to be approached by the EU from a global perspective. From this standpoint, the EU's role as one of the global standard setters is of great importance, and its efforts should be coordinated with other international actors. Especially in a time when freezing and confiscation have become legal instruments involved in supporting the effectiveness of the EU's joint foreign and security policy, which faces primarily global challenges, all standard setters should play together. The input of the following actors is particularly relevant for developing international standards on confiscation: the CoE (the Strasbourg Convention, the Warsaw Convention, the Criminal Law Convention on Corruption),[127] MONEYVAL's monitoring programme,[128] the UN (the Vienna Convention, the Palermo Convention, the UNCAC, the UNCAC Coalition),[129] the Office of the United Nations High Commissioner for Human Rights (OHCHR Recommended Principles on Human Rights and Asset Recovery),[130] the FATF (40 Recommendations), the OECD (Convention on Combating Bribery of Foreign Public Officials in International Business Transactions, 1997, and related documents, including Anti-Bribery Recommendation of the Council for Further Combating Bribery, 2021),[131] the G8 Roma-Lyon Group (G8 Best Practices for the Administration of Seized Assets),[132] the Basel Institute on Governance (Basel AML Index),[133] the International Centre for Asset Recovery (ICAR), the Stolen Asset Recovery (StAR) Initiative (a partnership between the World Bank Group and the UNODC), the Global Forum on Asset Recovery (GFAR Principles for Disposition and Transfer of Confiscated Stolen Assets in Corruption Cases),[134] and the Civil Forum for Asset Recovery (CiFAR, Civil Society Principles for Accountable Asset Return).[135]

Considering that tackling illicit assets is a worldwide issue, it is crucial that the EU engages in continual dialogue with other standard setters. The EU should not only eliminate the differences between national confiscation schemes that create 'safe havens' for criminals within EU territory but should also closely monitor and pursue innovative elements that have been progressively introduced in international standards of confiscation. This means that wherever EU law is lagging behind, it should be brought up to these standards, and *vice versa*, other international standard setters should consider the Union *acquis* in the area of confiscation. However, the EU's capacity to influence the European legal landscape, together with the potential to boost the external effects of EU confiscation policy, should be seen as an opportunity for the EU to go beyond a supporting role when setting standards on confiscation. For example, a good opportunity to take the lead would be to propose a bolder definition of 'victim' to be used internationally. This would require working especially on deepening the concept of 'collective' victims. A strong starting point could be, i.a., the output of the StAR initiative (see, e.g., observations of Falconi et al. (2023, 34) regarding 'collective' victims). These authors pointed out:

> Notwithstanding, concepts such as that of the "victim," when integrated into anti-corruption treaties, do require a shift in perspective from the default objective of ensuring accountability by averting impunity to the objective of ensuring the reparation of the harms caused to victims–whether these are individuals, particular groups within societies, or entire states.
>
> (Falconi et al. 2023, 7)[136]

Another area where the EU needs to gain ground is civil confiscation. So far, the EU rules on NCBC are rooted in the criminal realm through various connections with proceedings in criminal matters or investigations in relation to a criminal offence, whereas 'civil' confiscation, in its traditional meaning, is independent of criminal proceedings. At the same time, under EU law, MS are free to develop civil confiscation measures. Thus, when creating such measures, MS are forced to refer to non-EU standards on civil confiscation, such as the FATF Recommendations (see Recommendation No 4, as amended). As a consequence, the EU is losing its influence on shaping national confiscation schemes in this regard. Aside from ongoing discussions on human rights protections in civil confiscation procedures, the undeniable popularity of civil confiscation among MS is a situation that the EU must not underestimate. Given the above, one of the most urgent challenges for EU confiscation policy is filling this loophole in EU law by introducing advanced harmonising rules on civil confiscation and rules on mutual recognition of civil confiscation orders, especially from the perspective of ensuring appropriate human rights protections. A bolder approach to confiscation, in general, would enhance the external effect of EU policy and its international position. Ultimately, it is in the EU's interest to achieve greater internal and external impact for its policies across various fields.

In this context, the observations contained in the EESC Opinion (2012), delivered in the legislative procedure of adopting Directive 2014/42/EU, are still valid.[137] This Opinion stated that the 'European confiscation strategy can only be fully effective if it forms part of a worldwide approach' (3.5.8). Given that, the EESC regretted that the proposed Directive did not address that 'essential element' (3.5.8). Furthermore, the EESC Opinion (2022), delivered during the legislative procedure of adopting the new Directive 2024/1260, recommended considering instruments that would facilitate cooperation with third countries.[138] It stated:

> As organised crime has become more interconnected, international and digital, it is important to ensure that authorities in third countries are able to cooperate with their peers in the Member States. Various assistance and support instruments should be considered in order to further enforce the proposed Directive (3.17).

It is also worth remembering that one of the Tampere Milestones was to develop the Union's 'capacity to act and be regarded as a significant partner on the international scene'. This implied 'close co-operation with partner countries and international organisations' (Milestone 8).[139] In the same vein, the Hague Programme pointed to the need to ensure coherence between the EU and the international legal order (3.4.5).[140] Moreover, it considered the 'development of a coherent external dimension of the Union policy of freedom, security and justice as a growing priority' (4). Moreover, one of the aspects of the Stockholm Programme indicated the need to increase the 'Union's international presence in the legal field' (3.5).[141] Thus, one can say that law serves the EU not only by increasing the level of integration (through law) but also by influencing non-EU legal orders in line with the EU policy objectives in various areas, including the area of criminal justice (external effect). From today's perspective, coherence between the policies in the AFSJ and CSDP (the Common Security and Defence Policy) to accomplish shared goals, as encouraged by the Stockholm Programme, remains very relevant (7.1). Regarding criminal law, the Stockholm Programme provided for a deep commitment of the Union institutions to ensuring 'coherence between the Union and the international legal order', with particular attention to synergy with the CoE's work (3.5.2). When it comes to human rights protections, it is legitimate to expect a significant step forward to be made after an agreement is reached in the ongoing negotiations on EU accession to the ECHR (see also Callewaert 2014).[142] It is worth recalling here the reflections of Vervaele (2019) on '[c]riminal justice and the regulatory triangle', involving the domestic level, the EU, and the CoE legal order, and on the growing significance of the dialogue between the CJEU and ECtHR based on the interaction between the ECHR and the Charter (9).

The EU itself, in addition to its MS, is a non-State party of crucial international conventions addressing confiscation-related issues. For instance, the EU signed the Vienna Convention in 1989 (confirmed in 1990). Next, the EU signed the Palermo Convention in 2000 (approved in 2004) and the UNCAC in 2005 (approved in 2008). Moreover, the EU signed the Warsaw Convention in 2009; however, it has not yet ratified it. It should be noted that almost all EU MS have signed the Warsaw Convention, apart from Czechia and Ireland.[143] In 2024, the Commission issued a Recommendation for a Council Decision authorising the Commission to participate, on behalf of the EU, in negotiations on an additional protocol to the Warsaw Convention (COM(2024) 177 final).[144] The reasoning for that Recommendation involved the argument that 'asset recovery allows for the compensation of the victims of crime, supporting social cohesion and justice'(1). Pursuant to the Terms of Reference 2024–2025 of the CoE Committee of Experts on Criminal Asset Recovery, the additional draft protocol should include provisions aimed at: enhancing 'certainty and consistency in the sharing of confiscated assets between States Parties in transnational cases'; ensuring 'efficient and effective management of seized, confiscated and repatriated assets, including the execution of confiscation decisions'; facilitating the 'introduction of non-conviction-based confiscation procedures and of extended confiscation in criminal matters, including co-operation regarding and execution of requests in transnational cases'; and 'any other issue which it deems to be of consequence to strengthen co-operation among Parties with respect to asset recovery'.[145]

Approaching confiscation-related issues from a broader perspective than cross-border cooperation within the EU (in this respect, see more Mirandola 2020) implies reconsidering the manner in which foreign confiscation orders are executed under the MLA mechanisms. One of the concepts discussed is the direct enforcement of foreign confiscation orders. Betti, Kozin, and Brun (2022), in their book with the telling title 'Orders without Borders', indicated the 'growing recognition of the value of direct enforcement as an international cooperation tool', which is, however, 'not fully used or understood despite its advantages in speeding up and streamlining asset recovery proceedings' (2). In addition, these authors noted the widespread unawareness of the UNCAC requirement concerning the direct enforcement of confiscation orders (Betti, Kozin, and Brun 2022, 2; see Article 55(1)(b) of the UNCAC). Bearing in mind that the EU itself is a non-State party to the UNCAC, its contribution to the MS developing mechanisms of direct enforcement of confiscation orders issued by the authorities of third countries would be of incredible importance.

However, as already mentioned, the EU has not yet managed to establish harmonising rules on NCBC (in the traditional meaning of this term, i.e., 'civil' confiscation) to meet the demands of cross-border cooperation even within the EU. One can say that, though the EU's own legal programme still needs to develop some fundamental elements, the field of transnational cooperation in confiscation cases is even more neglected. Accordingly, there is a great challenge ahead of the EU in order to create common rules for directly executing civil confiscation orders in transnational cases.

Considering the growing popularity of civil confiscation (see, e.g., Simonato 2015; Boucht 2019; Bright Line Law 2020) and the freedom of MS in establishing their specific rules in this respect, juxtaposed with the lack of rules in the areas of harmonisation and cooperation, hampers not only cross-border cooperation in this area between Member State peers but also transnational cooperation with third countries. This state of affairs raises questions about human rights protections in cross-border and transnational cases concerning the execution of civil confiscation orders. Concerns were also expressed in the subject literature in the context of the discretion of the MS in establishing rules on NCBC (see, e.g., Wycichowski-Kuchta 2023). The lack of legal certainty in this respect is evidenced by several requests for preliminary rulings submitted to the CJEU. For instance, requests were lodged on the background of Bulgarian legislation on civil confiscation: C-234/18 *Agro in 2001*, EU:C:2020:221; C-319/19 *ZV and AX*, EU:C:2021:883; C-393/19, *Plovdiv*, EU:C:2021:8 (see also the request for a preliminary ruling from the Criminal Court of Appeal of the Republic of Croatia: C-8/24, *Županijsko državno odvjetništvo*, Case in progress). In addition, the ECtHR examined the Bulgarian Forfeiture of Proceeds of Crime Act (2005) in *Todorov and Others v Bulgaria* (Applications nos. 50705/11 and 6 others, 13 July 2021).[146]

Lastly, the contributions of the CoE and the UN towards developing a restorative approach to justice should be stressed as valuable points of reference for both the EU and EU jurisdictions when shaping confiscation schemes. Nonetheless, further dialogue would be recommended between these international actors and the EU, towards developing a coherent vision of incorporating the basic tenets of restorative justice into criminal justice mechanisms. In particular, the following contributions of the CoE and the UN may be considered in this respect:

1) CoE, Recommendation No R(85)11 of the Committee of Ministers of the Council of Europe on the position of the victim in the framework of criminal law and procedure (1985),
2) CoE, Recommendation No. R (99) 19 of the Committee of Ministers to member States concerning mediation in penal matters (1999),
3) CoE, Rebuilding community connections – mediation and restorative justice in Europe, Strasbourg: CoE (2004);
4) CoE, Recommendation CM/Rec(2018)8 of the Committee of Ministers to member States concerning restorative justice in criminal matters (2018),
5) CoE, Recommendation CM/Rec(2023)2b of the Committee of Ministers to member States on rights, services and support for victims of crime (2023),
6) UN, Declaration of Basic Principles of Justice for Victims of Crime and Abuse of Power, adopted by General Assembly Resolution 40/34 (1985),
7) UN, Standard Minimum Rules for Non-custodial Measures (The Tokyo Rules), General Assembly resolution 45/110 (1990),
8) UN, The Economic and Social Council, Resolution 1999/26, Development and Implementation of Mediation and Restorative Justice Measures in Criminal Justice (1999),
9) UN, Vienna Declaration on Crime and Justice: Meeting the Challenges of the 21st Century, Resolution adopted by the UN General Assembly A/RES/55/59 (2001),
10) UN, The Economic and Social Council (ECOSOC) Resolution 2002/12, Basic principles on the use of restorative justice programmes in criminal matters (2002),
11) UNODC, Introduction. Criminal Justice Assessment Toolkit, New York: UN (2006),
12) UNODC, Compendium of United Nations standards and norms in crime prevention and criminal justice, New York: UN (2016),
13) UN, The Economic and Social Council resolution 2016/17, Restorative justice in criminal matters (2016),

14) UN, The Commission on Crime Prevention and Criminal Justice (CCPCJ) Resolution 27/6, Restorative justice, (2018),
15) UNODC, Handbook on Restorative Justice Programmes, Second edition, Vienna: UN (2020).

In sum, when shaping the EU confiscation scheme, due regard should be given to international achievements in making criminal justice more restorative in general. Resorting to the international *acquis* in this field would also help to develop overall EU criminal policy, towards increasing the participation of stakeholders in criminal cases, and orienting responses to crime towards repairing harm in a broad sense, encompassing the harm caused to individuals and social bonds. Regrettably, a broader dialogue between international partners is still lacking in this respect. Recommendation CM/Rec(2018)8 of the Committee of Ministers to member States concerning restorative justice in criminal matters recognised the 'need to enhance the participation of stakeholders, including the victim and the offender, other affected parties and the wider community, in addressing and repairing the harm caused by crime'. In addition, among the basic principles of restorative justice, it highlighted two principles that seem particularly important for the development of the EU confiscation scheme: the 'principle of stakeholder participation' and the 'principle of repairing harm':

> The core principles of restorative justice are that the parties should be enabled to participate actively in the resolution of crime (the principle of stakeholder participation), and that these responses should be primarily oriented towards addressing and repairing the harm which crime causes to individuals, relationships and wider society (the principle of repairing harm).
>
> (Recommendation CM/Rec(2018)8, III.13)

Returning to the initial thesis presented on the potential of the EU to become a leading standard setter in the field of tackling illicit assets, the first stage is to identify the appropriate direction for confiscation policy development. In order to become desirable for non-EU jurisdictions to follow, this direction should be, on the one hand, sufficiently ambitious and corresponding to genuine needs, and on the other hand, socially just, which means also including the interests of third countries and respecting the differences between their legal traditions and systems. Adopting a more restorative approach to justice in this policy would help the EU set the right course, leading not only to an increase in the global effectiveness of depriving offenders of the proceeds of crime but also contributing to the higher goal of restoring justice through confiscation mechanisms in which all the stakeholders can actively participate.

Conclusions

Any comprehensive discussion of the CPC should begin with properly identifying the objectives of this legal institution. The analysis of EU confiscation policy in the pre- and post-Lisbon periods has shown that this preliminary question has not yet been given due consideration in this policy. From the very beginning, EU policy has treated confiscation as a useful tool in combating serious and organised crime, at least at the level of the official policy rhetoric. However, it should be remembered that the real impact of confiscation on reducing this type of crime has so far not been underpinned by reliable data.

In the 1980s, the Union started to follow the global trend of actions to combat drug trafficking and organised crime. The Conclusions of the European Council adopted during this decade pointed to the problems of drug abuse and related drug offences, as well as organised crime and terrorism. In the 1990s, confiscation began to be seen in EU policy as a useful weapon targeted at resources driving serious and organised crime (see, e.g., the 'Action Plan to combat organised crime' (1997);[147] Joint Action 98/699/JHA;[148] the Vienna Action Plan (1998)[149]). Depriving criminals of the proceeds of crime was recognised in the Tampere Conclusions (1999) as an important component in the development of the AFSJ (the Tampere Milestone 6). In addition, special attention was drawn to the fight against money laundering, considered to be 'at the very heart of organised crime' (the Tampere Conclusions, 51, 55).

Being concentrated on effectiveness issues, the EU's approach to confiscation evolved over time to become more balanced, with increasing attention given to human rights protections. In addition, integrating, at least to some extent, the interests of non-State stakeholders in the EU confiscation scheme. Initially, the rights of targeted persons in confiscation procedures were at the forefront (suspected or accused persons), and later third parties were also included. On the other side, the EU policy recognised the importance of securing the rights of victims in confiscation procedures. However, policy declarations formulated in this respect were not translated into concrete legal solutions prior to Lisbon (see, e.g., the Vienna Action Plan (1998); the Communication from the Commission (1998);[150] the Tampere Conclusions (1999); the 2000 EU Strategy for the beginning of the new millennium[151]). The real position of victims in the EU confiscation scheme started to be progressively strengthened in the post-Lisbon period (see Directive 2014/42/EU, Regulation 2018/1805, Directive 2024/1260). Nonetheless, EU policy viewed victims' rights in terms of arbitrary protection by public authorities rather than in terms of free exercise by their holders.[152]

In the early 2000s, EU policy around freedom, security, and justice was influenced by the threat to international security raised by the terrorist attacks in New York City ('9/11', 11 September 2001), Madrid (11 March 2004), and London (7 July 2005). For instance, the Hague Programme focused, i.a., on fighting terrorism financing by developing tools targeted at preventing suspicious transactions and freezing of assets. Notably, the possibility of returning confiscated assets to identifiable victims or charitable organisations was explicitly mentioned in the Action Plan implementing the Hague Programme (2005),[153] but this postulate never translated into concrete legislative actions during the pre-Lisbon period.

It is also important to emphasise that the EU legal environment before Lisbon was not conducive to the development of common standards concerning the most controversial forms of confiscation, such as extended confiscation, confiscation from third parties, or NCBC. This legislative environment was a consequence of both the diversity of national confiscation schemes and intergovernmental decision-making processes in cooperation in criminal matters covered by the 'third pillar'. Therefore, the failure to establish a single standard on extended confiscation (MS could choose between three options of extended confiscation), the introduction of very limited rules on non-mandatory confiscation from a third party (FD 2005/212/JHA), and a lack of common rules regarding NCBC should be seen against the challenging legal background before Lisbon, which hindered reaching a compromise acceptable to the whole family of MS.

The Treaty of Lisbon marked a significant turning point in the EU's approach to confiscation. It brought the opportunity to adopt a bolder approach due to decision-making processes based on the qualified majority and the possibility to influence domestic legislation through directives instead of FDs. Even before the Treaty's entry into force, the Commission was considering recasting the EU legal framework towards extending the mutual recognition mechanism on civil confiscation orders and criminalising the possession of 'unjustified' assets.[154] In addition, confiscation has increasingly come to be treated as a global issue, where international standards play an important role.[155] This shift in approach was in line with the Strasbourg Programme, which emphasised the importance of the external dimension of the EU's policy in the areas of freedom, security, and justice. As a result, the role of cooperation with third countries in confiscation-related procedures found a greater appreciation in EU policy. However, concrete legal solutions regarding the cooperation of AROs with their counterparts in third countries and the reuse of confiscated property to support third countries were introduced many years later, in Directive 2024/1260.

The new legal reality following the Treaty of Lisbon enabled agreement to be reached on several difficult areas of confiscation mechanisms, such as extended confiscation, confiscation from a third party or confiscation without conviction, albeit not on pure 'civil' confiscation. In 2012, the Commission proposed new harmonising rules based on Article 82(2) and Article 83(1) TFEU.[156] The novelty of the 2012 Proposal consisted in offering a single standard of extended confiscation, mandatory confiscation from a third party (so far optional in EU law), and for the first time in EU law, rules on NCBC, albeit very limited and strongly rooted in the criminal realm. It should be reiterated that NCBC, in the form provided for in that Proposal, as well as the form finally adopted, is not equivalent to 'civil' confiscation independent from criminal proceedings (traditionally referred to as NCBC). In addition, the 2012 Proposal broadened the concept of 'proceeds' to include indirect profits. In 2014, the legislative procedure (2012/0036 (COD)) was concluded by adopting Directive 2014/42/EU. During this procedure, various actors, such as the EESC, the LIBE, the Committee of the Regions, the FRA, and the Basel Institute on Governance, delivered valuable opinions to EU legislators on the perceived flaws of the proposed directive, which can be summarised as pointing out its poor attention to the social dimension of confiscation. Regrettably, their observations were not reflected in the final version of the directive. Therefore, Directive 2014/42/EU should be regarded as a significant, but only partial, step forward in harmonising confiscation rules. This Directive lacks provisions requiring MS (in place of the soft recommendation contained therein) to ensure that some portion of confiscated assets is reused for the public interest or social purposes, and at least part of this portion in the form of direct transfers, not through special funds, etc. Consequently, under the EU confiscation scheme, the disposal of confiscated assets was not sufficiently removed from the State's remit.

Another missed opportunity when adopting Directive 2014/42/EU was ensuring the right of victims to obtain compensation for criminal harm directly from confiscated assets. This would require the EU lawmaker to depart from the concept of considering the rights of victims as a negative premiss to freeze or confiscate the assets (under Article 8(10) of Directive 2014/42/EU the MS are required to ensure that the 'confiscation measure does not prevent those victims from seeking compensation for their claims'). Indeed, this concept changed in 2018, but only partially, as new rules were introduced in respect of cross-border cases, in which the rights of victims to confiscated assets gained better protection than in similar domestic cases (cf. Recitals 45, 46, and 48; Articles 26(2), 29, and 30 of Regulation 2018/1805). Recently, a more innovative approach in this respect was adopted in Directive 2024/1260, where victims' claims are considered within the relevant asset-tracing, freezing and confiscation proceedings (Article 18(1)) and ceased to be treated as a negative premise to order such measures. However, the wording of Article 18(1–4) of Directive 2024/1260 is not entirely clear and leaves room for different interpretations, especially in the context of Article 18(5) of that Directive. One can say that despite introducing some important changes, the rights of victims to compensation should be further strengthened by embedding them directly in the EU confiscation scheme, which should be acknowledged by EU law in a manner more readable to national legislatures, for example, by requiring MS to enable the possibility of satisfying victims' rights directly from confiscated assets.

EU confiscation policy evolved further as the international situation deteriorated. Confiscation-related issues came to be more strongly linked with the challenges of protecting international security, and thus, were also considered in the context of achieving the objectives of the CFSP. In 2014, in response to the illegal annexation of Crimea and Sevastopol by Russia, the EU adopted an initial package of restrictive measures, including asset freezes. Further restrictive measures were adopted in 2022 in response to the recognition of the non-government-controlled areas of the Donetsk and Luhansk oblasts of Ukraine and the ordering of Russian armed forces into those areas. In the same year, the Council adopted Decision (EU) 2022/2332 on identifying the violation of Union restrictive measures as an area of crime that meets the criteria specified in Article 83(1) TFEU. This enabled the EU lawmaker to apply directives establishing minimum rules defining criminal offences and penalties for the violation of Union restrictive measures. In 2024, the EP and the Council adopted Directive 2024/1226 on the definition of criminal offences and penalties for the violation of Union restrictive measures. Importantly, this move allowed the EU lawmaker to connect the two legal spheres, administrative and criminal, in which the measures restricting the use of property may operate (such as asset freezes when used as targeted financial sanctions of an administrative nature). Accordingly, MS were required to take the necessary measures to enable the freezing and confiscation of instrumentalities and proceeds from the criminal offences constituting a violation of Union restrictive measures (Article 10(1) of Directive 2024/1226), as well as assets subject to Union restrictive measures in respect of which the designated natural person, or the representative of a designated entity or body, commits, or participates in certain offences consisting in circumventing a Union restrictive measure (Article 10(2) of Directive 2024/1226). In 2022, the Commission proposed a new directive on confiscation with an extended scope of triggering offences. Finally, Directive 2024/1260 applies to criminal offences covered by Directive 2024/1226.

It should be added that the approach to confiscation in EU policy has recently changed to a more 'strategic' one. An emanation of this change is treating multiple activities, taken before and after a confiscation order is issued, as a single asset recovery process. Accordingly, Directive 2024/1260 addresses a wide range of confiscation-related issues, from tracing and identification of assets to their disposal after confiscation.

Nevertheless, despite some positive developments, there are still areas for improvement. For instance, similar to the legislative procedure preceding the adoption of Directive 2014/42/EU, the EU lawmaker once again failed to properly respond to the need to develop the social aspect of confiscation. Valuable comments in this respect were delivered by various actors in the legislative procedure (2022/0167(COD)) preceding the adoption of new Directive 2024/1260 (the EESC, the LIBE, the Committee on Legal Affairs, the Committee on Budget). In consequence, the concept of redistribution of confiscated assets, in the form adopted in Directive 2024/1260, leaves a lot to be desired. MS were only encouraged, not required, to 'take the necessary measures to allow the possibility of using confiscated property, where appropriate, for public interest or social purposes' (Article 19(1) of Directive 2024/1260, cf. Article 10(3) of Directive 2014/42/EU). In addition, as stated above, Directive 2024/1260 lacks a strict and clear obligation addressed to MS to ensure the possibility of satisfying victims' claims for compensation or restitution directly from confiscated assets; however, it approaches victims' rights from the positive side, contrary to Directive 2014/42/EU (see Article 18(1) and (5) of Directive 2024/1260). Furthermore, MS were not required to subject their national confiscation mechanisms to any social control, especially relevant to the process of redistributing confiscated assets.

In view of the above, the 'double constructiveness' of confiscation should be recalled, as rightly recognised in the 2011 EP Resolution on organised crime in the EU.[157] Regrettably, EU legislators did not sufficiently appreciate this specificity of confiscation in both legislative procedures (2012/0036 (COD)) and (2022/0167(COD)). Notably, arguments in the same vein, demonstrating that the singular focus on depriving criminals of assets can no longer be supported, can be found in the Impact Assessment Report accompanying the Proposal for a new Directive on confiscation (2022) (SWD(2022) 245 final). This Report explicitly stated that confiscation also has the 'restorative goal of ensuring that victims of crime are compensated and that the money taken away from organised crime can be used for public interest and social purposes' (48).

Regarding the position of victims of crime in EU law, it should be noted that this is predominantly dependent on solutions adopted in Directive 2012/29/EU, as the main harmonising instrument in this area. However, the 2020 Commission Report highlighted its unsatisfactory implementation.[158] Indeed, this Directive expresses a broad concept of 'crime' (Recital 9), while at the same time only including a narrow concept of 'victim' (Article 2(1)(a)), which does not cover legal persons and other collective victims, including communities. In 2022, the Commission announced the revision of the victims' rights *acquis*.[159] It is legitimate to formulate a postulate addressed to the EU lawmaker, to use this occasion also to rethink the current definition of 'victim' applied in that Directive, and better integrate victims' rights to compensation into the EU confiscation scheme. Taking such a policy direction would also be consistent with the first EU strategy on victims' rights (2020–2025).

Bearing in mind that serious and organised crime has a predominantly global dimension, the confiscation of the proceeds from such crime should also be approached globally. From this standpoint, the EU takes the role of an important actor in setting the standards for confiscation. However, to boost the global effects of EU confiscation policy, this policy should duly consider the input of other standard setters, especially the CoE, including the MONEYVAL, the UN, the FATF, the OECD, the G8 Roma-Lyon Group, the Basel Institute on Governance, the International Centre for Asset Recovery (ICAR), the Stolen Asset Recovery (StAR) Initiative, the GFAR, and the CiFAR. For instance, as signalled in the subject literature, there is a lot of work to be done in transnational cooperation with third countries, in order to develop MLA mechanisms enabling the direct execution of foreign confiscation orders in line with the UNCAC. In this context, too, there is a need to complement the existing EU legal framework with rules on civil confiscation, the popularity of which is growing in both EU and non-EU jurisdictions. Another area for improvement is by establishing harmonising rules on transnational returns of assets to third countries victimised, i.a., by corruption or war crimes, as these particulars are absent in EU law. However, a significant step towards reusing confiscated property to support third countries has been made in the new Directive 2024/1260 (Article 19(2)).

Nevertheless, to play a leading role in setting the standards of confiscation, it is not enough for the EU to merely follow international conventions and recommendations. A good opportunity for the EU to take a proactive role would be by introducing an innovative definition of 'victim' in EU law, covering 'collective' victims, from the corporate to community level. Moreover, there is a need to establish minimum standards on civil confiscation that EU MS can follow when introducing or developing this type of confiscation into their national legal orders. Currently, the EU leaves this role to other standard setters, especially the FATF (Recommendation No. 4, as amended). At the same time, EU law leaves its MS free to develop non-criminal confiscation procedures (see Article 1(2) of Directive 2014/42/EU and Article 1(2) of Directive 2024/1260). The interest of MS in introducing (or extending) civil confiscation mechanisms is growing. This fact should not be underestimated in EU policy. Filling this gap in EU law seems to be one of the most urgent challenges, especially in terms of ensuring appropriate human rights protections in civil confiscation procedures.

It should not be forgotten that it is not only the EU which has referred to restorative justice. Other international players, such as the CoE and the UN, have made contributions in this regard. However, further dialogue by all international actors should help to develop a coherent vision (currently lacking) on how to develop a restorative approach to justice. It is worth recalling that achieving a leadership position for setting rules on tackling criminal assets would be consistent with pursuing the ambitions expressed in the Tampere Conclusions about the Union being a 'significant partner on the international scene' (Tampere Milestone 8). Proceeding in this direction would also enhance the external dimension of EU policy in the area of freedom, security, and justice, as envisaged in the Hague Programme, and strengthen the 'international presence' of the Union in the 'legal field', as provided for in the Stockholm Programme.

Considering the legislative procedure of adopting Directive 2024/42/EU (2012/0036 (COD)) and legislative procedure of adopting Directive 2024/1260 (2022/0167(COD)), in the context of Wróblewski's (1985) model of rational law-making (see Chapter 1), one can say that the EU lawmaker did not act rationally when not making use of the social potential of confiscation. This conclusion is justified in light of the fact that the EU lawmaker acquired the relevant knowledge on the need to extend the social aspect of the EU confiscation scheme, especially by better integrating the interests of non-State stakeholders. This missing aspect was signalled by various actors delivering opinions and recommendations in both legislative procedures. Thus, the very objective of confiscation, to combine two different aspects – the effectiveness of depriving criminals of the proceeds of crime, and the redistribution of those assets involving the interests of victims (encompassing various subgroups and communities) – has still not been properly recognised by the EU lawmaker. One can say that this failure pervades the entire EU confiscation policy and is reflected in EU law, which lacks solutions corresponding with social needs.

In view of Wróblewski's (1985) model, the mismatch occurred in identifying which real problems needed to be resolved at the EU law level. These problems remain evident in the state-centred national confiscation models, which can only become more balanced by better integrating the interests of non-State stakeholders (victims, communities, and subjected persons).

The next misstep by EU legislators occurred when deciding on the final shape of minimum rules governing the reuse of confiscated assets. Contrary to comments from various actors supporting the legislative processes, the position was taken that soft law measures were likely to result in national confiscation models changing to be more socially just. Given that confiscation is a 'double constructive' legal tool, helping prevent crime and 'boosting economic and social development' (the 2011 EP Resolution), its social aspect should be treated with the same priority in EU policy as the aspect consisting in its capacity to effectively deprive offenders of the proceeds of crime.

The ultimate answer to the question 'How restorative is EU confiscation policy?' should begin by noting that this policy is a still-evolving process increasingly incorporating restorative elements. From this perspective, the policy has significantly changed since the 1990s, in particular, due to better integration of the rights of defendants and victims, but it still disregards communities. In the post-Lisbon period, EU policy started explicitly referring to restorative justice. However, even prior to Lisbon, the overall vision for EU criminal policy, as presented in various political declarations, contained many restorative elements, such as giving priority to the interests and needs of citizens when developing the AFSJ, recognising the importance of open dialogue with civil society, or appreciating 'mutual trust' as factor conditioning the operation of the principle of mutual recognition. For instance, the Tampere Conclusions viewed the AFSJ as based on transparency and democratic control. They identified the roots of European integration in freedom based on human rights, democratic institutions, and the rule of law (Milestone 1). In addition, they connected the enjoyment of freedom with the genuine area of justice. The 1998 Vienna Action Plan linked the procedural guarantees enshrined in the ECHR with the aspects of 'offender reintegration' and 'victim support', both important from the perspective of a restorative approach to justice.[160]

One can say that the social dimension of confiscation, which constitutes the 'second side' of this legal institution, has already been well recognised by the EU lawmaker, albeit not yet properly included in its legislative activity, and thus not sufficiently reflected in current EU law. Therefore, there is still much work to be done in this field. First of all, the EU lawmaker should rethink who should be at the centre of the EU confiscation scheme, and who the principal beneficiary of this mechanism is. Will the State be in this position, or victims and communities? Accordingly, changes would be desirable not only in harmonising rules concerning specifically confiscation but also for those concerning the position of victims of crime in general. Therefore, the very concept of 'victim' adopted in Directive 2012/29/EU should go far beyond natural persons by covering collective victims in varying degrees of organisation.

Notes

1 See Article 82(1) in connection with Article 294 TFEU.
2 European Council, Conclusions from 1975 to 1992 available online at: https://www.consilium.europa.eu/en/european-council/conclusions/1992-1975/ (20.05.2024), from 1993 to 2003: https://www.consilium.europa.eu/en/european-council/conclusions/1993-2003/ (21.05.2024).
3 See, e.g., European Council, Conclusions: Brussels, 22 July 1976. https://www.consilium.europa.eu/media/20797/bruxelles_july_1976__eng_.pdf (20.05.2024); Brussels, 8 December 1976. https://www.consilium.europa.eu/media/20791/the_hague_november_1976__eng_.pdf (20.05.2024); Copenhagen, 20 April 1978. https://www.consilium.europa.eu/media/20773/copenhagen_april_1978__eng_.pdf (20.05.2024).

4 See European Council, Conclusions, Fontainebleau, 25–26 June 1984, https://www.consilium.europa.eu/media/20673/1984_june_-_fontainebleau__eng_.pdf (20.05.2024).

5 European Council, Conclusions, Brussels, 29 and 30 March 1985, p. 9. https://www.consilium.europa.eu/media/20653/1985_march_-_brussels__eng_.pdf (20.05.2024).

6 European Council, Conclusions, Luxembourg, 2–3 December, 1985, p. 10. https://www.consilium.europa.eu/media/20433/1985_december_-_luxembourg__eng_.pdf (20.05.2024).

7 European Council, Conclusions, The Hague, 26–27 June 1986, p. 12. https://www.consilium.europa.eu/media/20638/1986_june_-_the_hague__eng_.pdf (20.05.2024).

8 European Council, Conclusions, London, 6 December 1986, p. 19. https://www.consilium.europa.eu/media/20630/1986_december_-_london__eng_.pdf (20.05.2024).

9 European Council, Conclusions, Hannover, 27–28 June 1988, p. 5. https://www.consilium.europa.eu/media/20606/1988_june_-_hannover__eng_.pdf (20.05.2024).

10 European Council, Conclusions, Rhodes, 2–3 December 1988, p. 4. https://www.consilium.europa.eu/media/20597/1988_december_-_rhodes__eng_.pdf (20.05.2024). See also European Council, Conclusions, Strasbourg, 8–9 December 1989, pp. 5–6. https://www.consilium.europa.eu/media/20580/1989_december_-_strasbourg__eng_.pdf (20.05.2024).

11 European Council, Conclusions, Dublin, 28 April 1990, p. 7. https://www.consilium.europa.eu/media/20571/1990_april__-_dublin__eng_.pdf (20.05.2024).

12 European Council, Conclusions, Dublin, 25–26 June 1990, p. 10. https://www.consilium.europa.eu/media/20562/1990_june_-_dublin__eng_.pdf (20.05.2024).

13 European Council, Conclusions, Rome, 14–15 December 1990, Part 1, pp. 8, 14. https://www.consilium.europa.eu/media/20537/1990_december_-_rome__eng__part_i.pdf (20.05.2024).

14 European Council, Conclusions, Luxembourg, 28–29 June 1991, p. 11. https://www.consilium.europa.eu/media/20528/1991_june_-_luxembourg__eng_.pdf (20.05.2024). See also the Essen Council Conclusions on combating fraud (a profit-driven offence with strong relevance to the protection of the Communities' financial interests), European Council, Conclusions, Essen, 9–10 December 1994, pp. 6–7. https://www.consilium.europa.eu/media/21198/essen-european-council.pdf (21.05.2024).

15 European Committee to Combat Drugs (CELAD), Report to the European Council meeting in Rome on 13 and 14 December 1990, European Plan to Combat Drugs (1990), pp. 13–14. https://www.emcdda.europa.eu/system/files/media/attachments/documents/5440/1.%20EU%20action%20Plan%201990.pdf (20.05.2024).

16 Directive of 10 June 1991 on prevention of the use of the financial system for the purpose of money laundering, (91/308/EEC), (1991) OJ L 166/77.

17 European Council, Conclusions: Brussels, 10–11 December 1993, pp. 16–17. https://www.consilium.europa.eu/media/21216/82736.pdf (21.05.2024); Corfu, 24–25 June 1994, III.2. https://www.consilium.europa.eu/media/21207/corfu-european-council.pdf (21.05.2024). Essen, 9–10 December 1994, pp. 6–7. https://www.consilium.europa.eu/media/21198/essen-european-council.pdf (21.05.2024).

18 Action plan to combat organised crime (adopted by the Council on 28 April 1997), (1997) OJ C 251/1; European Council, Conclusions, Amsterdam, 16–17 June 1997. https://www.consilium.europa.eu/media/21136/amsterdam-european-council.pdf (21.05.2024).

19 Joint Action of 3 December 1998 adopted by the Council on the basis of Article K.3 of the Treaty on European Union, on money laundering, the identification, tracing, freezing, seizing and confiscation of instrumentalities and the proceeds from crime (98/699/JHA), (1998) OJ L 333/1.

20 EP, Committee on Citizens' Freedoms and Rights, JHA, Report, 7 November 2002, Final A5-0383/2002, p.14. https://www.europarl.europa.eu/doceo/document/A-5-2002-0383_EN.pdf (4.06.2024).
21 Action Plan of the Council and the Commission on how best to implement the provisions of the Treaty of Amsterdam on an area of freedom, security and justice – Text adopted by the JHA Council, 3 December 1998, (1999), OJ C 19/1.
22 Commission, Communication from the Commission 'Towards an area of freedom, security and justice', Brussels, 14.07.1998, COM(1998) 459 final. See also European Council, Conclusions, Cardiff, 15–16 June 1998, p.17. https://www.consilium.europa.eu/media/21103/54315.pdf (29.05.2024).
23 See also CJEU, case C-176/03 *Commission of the European Communities v Council of the European Union*, EU:C:2005:542; case C-440/05 *Commission of the European Communities v Council of the European Union*, EU:C:2007:625.
24 European Council, Conclusions, Tampere, 15–16 October 1999. https://www.consilium.europa.eu/media/21059/tampere-european-council-presidency-conclusions.pdf (21.05.2024).
25 European Council, 'The prevention and control of organised crime: a European Union strategy for the beginning of the new millennium' (2000), OJ C 124/1.
26 Note from COREPER to the Council, EU Drugs Strategy (2000–2004), 1 December 1999, 12555/3/99. https://www.emcdda.europa.eu/system/files/media/attachments/documents/5448/5.%20EU%20Strategy%202000-2004.pdf (29.05.2024).
27 European Council, 'The Hague Programme: strengthening freedom, security and justice in the European Union' (2005), OJ C 53/1.
28 European Council, Conclusions and plan of action, 21 September 2001. https://www.consilium.europa.eu/media/20972/140en.pdf (31.05.2024).
29 Directive 2001/97/EC of the European Parliament and of the Council of 4 December 2001 amending Council Directive 91/308/EEC on prevention of the use of the financial system for the purpose of money laundering, (2001) OJ L 344/76.
30 Communication from the Governments of the French Republic, the Kingdom of Sweden and the Kingdom of Belgium of 22 December 2000. https://data.consilium.europa.eu/doc/document/ST-13986-2000-ADD-1/en/pdf (31.05.2024).
31 The Council and Commission Action Plan implementing the Hague Programme on strengthening freedom, security and justice in the European Union (2005), OJ C 198/1. See also the Communication from the Commission to the Council and the European Parliament 'The Hague Programme: Ten priorities for the next five years. The Partnership for European renewal in the field of Freedom, Security and Justice' COM/2005/0184 final.
32 See Communications from the Commission: 'Justice, freedom and security in Europe since 2005: An evaluation of the Hague Programme' (2009), COM(2009) 263 final; 'Justice, Freedom and Security in Europe since 2005: An Evaluation of the Hague Programme and Action Plan: Follow-up of the implementation of legal instruments in the fields of justice, freedom and security at national level – Implementation Scoreboard' (2009), SEC(2009) 765; 'Justice, Freedom and Security in Europe since 2005: An Evaluation of the Hague Programme and Action Plan: An extended report on the evaluation of the Hague Programme', (2009), SEC(2009) 766; 'Report on the implementation of the Hague programme for 2007', (2008), COM(2008) 373; 'Report on the implementation of the Hague programme for 2006', (2007), COM(2007) 373; 'Report on the implementation of the Hague programme for 2005', (2006), COM(2006) 333; 'Implementing The Hague Programme: the way forward', (2006), COM(2006) 331.
33 Commission, 'An Evaluation of the Hague Programme and Action Plan: An extended report on the evaluation of the Hague Programme', (2009), SEC(2009) 766.
34 Council, 'EU Drugs Strategy' (2005–2012), 22 November 2004. https://data.consilium.europa.eu/doc/document/ST-15074-2004-INIT/en/pdf (31.05.2024).

35 Council, EU Drugs Action Plan (2005–2008), (2005), OJ C 168/1.
36 Council, EU Drugs Action Plan (2009–2012), (2008), OJ C C 326/7.
37 See also the draft decision: Council, Initiative of the Republic of Austria, Belgium and Finland with a view to the adoption of a Council Decision concerning arrangements for cooperation between Asset Recovery Offices of the Member States, 14.12.2005, 15628/05.
38 Cf. Report from the Commission to EP and the Council based on Article 8 of the Council Decision 2007/845/JHA of 6 December 2007 concerning cooperation between Asset Recovery Offices of the Member States in the field of tracing and identification of proceeds from, or other property related to, crime, 12.04.2011, COM(2011) 176 final.
39 Initiative of the Kingdom of Denmark with a view to the adoption of a Council Framework Decision on Confiscation of Crime-Related Proceeds, Instrumentalities and Property, (2002) OJ C 184/3.
40 Initiative of the Kingdom of Denmark with a view to the adoption of a Council Framework Decision on the execution in the European Union of confiscation orders (2002) OJ C 184/8.
41 EP, Committee on Citizens' Freedoms and Rights, JHA, Report, 7 November 2002, Final A5-0383/2002, p.14. https://www.europarl.europa.eu/doceo/document/A-5-2002-0383_EN.pdf (4.06.2024).
42 See Article 2(2) of FD 2005/212/JHA, and explanatory note accompanying the draft FD on confiscation proposed by the Danish Presidency. Council, Communication from the Kingdom of Denmark: Initiative by the Kingdom of Denmark with a view to adoption by the Council of a draft Framework Decision on Confiscation of Crime-Related Proceeds, Instrumentalities and Property (2002), p. 6. https://data.consilium.europa.eu/doc/document/ST-9956-2002-ADD-1/en/pdf (6.06.2024).
43 Council, Communication from the Kingdom of Denmark: Initiative by the Kingdom of Denmark with a view to adoption by the Council of a draft Framework Decision on Confiscation of Crime-Related Proceeds, Instrumentalities and Property (2002) p. 6. https://data.consilium.europa.eu/doc/document/ST-9956-2002-ADD-1/en/pdf (6.06.2024), p. 7.
44 Council, Communication from the Kingdom of Denmark: Initiative by the Kingdom of Denmark with a view to adoption by the Council of a draft Framework Decision on Confiscation of Crime-Related Proceeds, Instrumentalities and Property (2002). https://data.consilium.europa.eu/doc/document/ST-9956-2002-ADD-1/en/pdf (6.06.2024).
45 EP, Legislative resolution on the initiative of the Kingdom of Denmark with a view to the adoption of a Council Framework Decision on confiscation of crime-related proceeds, instrumentalities and property (2004), OJ C 25 E/203.
46 2477th Council meeting (JHA), Brussels, 19 December 2002, 15691/02 (Presse 404). https://ec.europa.eu/commission/presscorner/detail/en/PRES_02_404 (6.06.2024).
47 Council FD on Confiscation of Crime-Related Proceeds, Instrumentalities and Property (2005). https://data.consilium.europa.eu/doc/document/ST-14648-2004-INIT/en/pdf (6.06.2024).
48 Commission, Report from the Commission pursuant to Article 6 of the Council Framework Decision of 24 February 2005 on confiscation of crime-related proceeds, instrumentalities and property (2005/212/JHA), (2007), COM(2007) 805 final, p.5.
49 Report from the Commission to the European Parliament and the Council based on Article 22 of the Council Framework Decision 2006/783/JHA of 6 October 2006 on the application of the principle of mutual recognition to confiscation orders, (2010) COM(2010) 428 final, p. 8. See also notifications concerning extended confiscation orders based on Article 7 (5) of FD 2006/783/JHA indicated in the Note from General Secretariat: 'Implementation of the Framework Decision of the Council of the European Union of 6 October 2006 (2006/783/JHA) on the application of the principle

of mutual recognition to confiscation orders', 9859/1/21, 8 July 2021. https://data.consilium.europa.eu/doc/document/ST-9859-2021-REV-1/en/pdf (7.06.2024).

50 Council, Outcome of proceedings, Multidisciplinary Working Party on Organised Crime, Annex: Draft Joint Action on asset sharing, 8 February 1998. https://data.consilium.europa.eu/doc/document/ST-13007-1998-REV-3/en/pdf (6.06.2024).

51 See also Commission, Developing a comprehensive and coherent EU strategy to measure crime and criminal justice: an EU Action Plan 2006–2010, 7.8.2006, COM/2006/437 final; Article 33 of the Directive 2005/60/EC of the European Parliament and of the Council of 26 October 2005 on the prevention of the use of the financial system for the purpose of money laundering and terrorist financing (2005), OJ L 309/29; Articles 40–44 of Directive (EU) 2015/849 of the European Parliament and of the Council of 20 May 2015 on the prevention of the use of the financial system for the purposes of money laundering or terrorist financing, amending Regulation (EU) No 648/2012 of the European Parliament and of the Council, and repealing Directive 2005/60/EC of the European Parliament and of the Council and Commission Directive 2006/70/EC (Text with EEA relevance), (2015) OJ L 141/73.

52 Europol, 'The Other Side of the Coin', 'European Financial and Economic Crime Threat Assessment 2023' (2023). https://www.europol.europa.eu/cms/sites/default/files/documents/The%20Other%20Side%20of%20the%20Coin%20-%20Analysis%20of%20Financial%20and%20Economic%20Crime%20%28EN%29.pdf (9.10.2024).

53 Commission Staff Working Paper, Impact Assessment, Accompanying document to the Proposal for a Directive of the EP and of the Council on the freezing and confiscation of proceeds of crime in the EU, 12.3.2012, COM(2012) 85 final, SWD(2012) 31 final.

54 Commission, Proposal for a Directive of the EP and of the Council on the freezing and confiscation of proceeds of crime in the EU, 12.3.2012, COM(2012) 85 final, 2012/0036 (COD).

55 UNODC, 'Estimating illicit financial flows resulting from drug trafficking and other transnational organised crime' (2011). https://www.unodc.org/documents/data-and-analysis/Studies/Illicit_financial_flows_2011_web.pdf (31.07.2024).

56 Europol, Criminal asset recovery in the EU, Survey of Statistical Information 2010–2014, 'Does crime still pay?', 4, European Police Office 2016. https://www.europol.europa.eu/sites/default/files/documents/criminal_asset_recovery_in_the_eu_web_version_0.pdf (30.07.2024).

57 Commission, Proposal for a Regulation of the EP and the Council on the mutual recognition of freezing and confiscation orders, 21.12.2016, COM(2016) 819 final, 2016/0412 (COD).

58 Europol, European Union Serious and Organised Crime Threat Assessment, 'A Corrupting Influence: The infiltration and undermining of Europe's economy and society by organised crimes' (2021), the so-called 'SOCTA 2021'. https://www.europol.europa.eu/cms/sites/default/files/documents/socta2021_1.pdf (30.07.2024).

59 Commission, Communication from the Commission to the EP and the Council: Proceeds of organised crime. Ensuring that 'crime does not pay', 20.11.2008, COM(2008) 766 final.

60 Protocol established by the Council in accordance with Article 34 of the Treaty on European Union to the Convention on Mutual Assistance in Criminal Matters between the Member States of the European Union, (2001) OJ C 326/2.

61 Commission, Communication from the Commission to the EP, the Council and the EESC – Developing a comprehensive and coherent EU strategy to measure crime and criminal justice: an EU Action Plan 2006–2010, 7.8.2006, COM(2006) 437 final.

62 Commission, Communication from the Commission to the EP and the Council – Measuring Crime in the EU: Statistics Action Plan 2011–2015, 18.1.2012, COM(2011) 713 final.

63 European Council, 'The Stockholm Programme — An open and secure Europe serving and protecting citizens' (2010), OJ C 115/1.
64 See also the conclusions on implementation of Decision 2007/845/JHA (the implementation was assessed as 'moderately satisfactory') contained in the Report from the Commission to the EP and to the Council based on Article 8 of the Council Decision 2007/845/JHA, 12.4.2011, COM(2011) 176 final.
65 Council Conclusions on Confiscation and Asset Recovery, 28.05.2010, Council document 7769/3/10; Adoption of draft Council Conclusions on Confiscation and Asset Recovery, 28.05.2010, Council document 9657/10.
66 See also Commission, 'Delivering an area of freedom, security and justice: Action plan implementing the Stockholm Programme', 20.04.2010, COM(2010) 171.
67 Communication from the Commission to the European Parliament, the Council and the European Economic and Social Committee – Developing a comprehensive and coherent EU strategy to measure crime and criminal justice: an EU Action Plan 2006–2010, 7.8.2006, COM/2006/437 final.
68 Commission, The EU Internal Security Strategy in Action: Five steps towards a more secure Europe, 22.11.2010, COM(2010) 673 final.
69 EP, Resolution of 25 October 2011 on organised crime in the European Union (2010/2309(INI)), P7_TA(2011)0459. See also EP, Report on organised crime in the European Union, 25.11.2010, Document A7-0333/2011. https://www.europarl.europa.eu/doceo/document/A-7-2011-0333_EN.html (28.06.2024).
70 Commission, Anti-Fraud Strategy, 24.6.2011, COM(2011) 376 final.
71 Commission, Proposal for a Directive of the European Parliament and of the Council on the freezing and confiscation of proceeds of crime in the European Union (2012), COM/2012/085 final.
72 Commission, Fighting Corruption in the EU, 6.6.2011, COM(2011) 308 final.
73 These are the following reports: Report from the Commission to the European Parliament and to the Council based on Article 8 of the Council Decision 2007/845/JHA of 6 December 2007 concerning cooperation between Asset Recovery Offices of the Member States in the field of tracing and identification of proceeds from, or other property related to crime (COM(2011) 176 final); Report from the Commission to the European Parliament and the Council based on Article 22 of the Council Framework Decision 2006/783/JHA of 6 October 2006 on the application of the principle of mutual recognition to confiscation orders (COM(2010) 428); Report from the Commission pursuant to Article 6 of the Council Framework Decision 2005/212/JHA of 24 February 2005 on confiscation of crime-related proceeds, instrumentalities and property (COM(2007) 805 final); Report from the Commission based on Article 14 of the Council Framework Decision 2003/577/JHA of 22 July 2003 on the execution in the European Union of orders freezing property or evidence (COM(2008) 885 final).
74 Commission, Proposal for a Directive of the European Parliament and of the Council on the freezing and confiscation of proceeds of crime in the European Union, 12.3.2012, COM(2012) 85 final (para. 2.3).
75 Final report of the project on 'Confiscation: Legal issues and international cooperation' developed within the Criminal Legal Affairs SubGroup (CLASG) of the G8 Roma-Lyon Group (2009). See also G8 Meeting of the Ministers of Justice and Home Affairs 'G8 Best Practice Principles on Tracing, Freezing and Confiscation of Assets' https://star.worldbank.org/sites/default/files/2023-03/E1_G-8_Best_Practice_Principles_on_Tracing_Freezing_and_Con.pdf (1.04.2024).
76 Risoluzione della 14ª Commissione Permanente (Politiche dell'Unione europea), 13.06.2012, Doc. XVIII-bis
no 70. https://www.europarl.europa.eu/RegData/docs_autres_institutions/parlements_nationaux/com/2012/0085/IT_SENATE_CONT1-COM(2012)0085_IT.pdf (10.07.2024).

77 Council, Approval of the final compromise text, 28.11.2013, Council document 16861/13.
78 Council, Approval of the final compromise text, 28.11.2013, Council document 16861/13 ADD1.
79 Proposal for a Regulation of the European Parliament and of the Council on the mutual recognition of freezing and confiscation orders (2016) COM(2016) 819 final.
80 Commission, Proposal for a Directive of the European Parliament and of the Council on the freezing and confiscation of proceeds of crime in the European Union, Explanatory Memorandum (2.1), 12.3.2012, COM(2012) 85 final.
81 EESC, Opinion of the European Economic and Social Committee on the 'Proposal for a Directive of the European Parliament and of the Council on the freezing and confiscation of proceeds of crime in the European Union', 4.10.2012, COM(2012) 85 final, OJ C 299/128.
82 Commission, Europe 2020 – A strategy for smart, sustainable and inclusive growth, 3.3.2010, COM(2010) 2020 final.
83 Opinion of the Committee of the Regions on 'Package on protection of the licit economy' (2012), OJ C 391/134.
84 EP, LIBE, Report on the proposal for a directive of the European Parliament and of the Council on the freezing and confiscation of proceeds of crime in the European Union, 20.5.2013, Document A7-0178/2013.
85 Basel Institute on Governance, Note requested by the LIBE, 'The need for new EU legislation allowing the assets confiscated from criminal organisations to be used for civil society and in particular for social purposes', (2012), http://www.europarl.europa.eu/RegData/etudes/note/join/2012/462437/IPOL-LIBE_NT(2012)462437_EN.pdf (3.07.2024).
86 G8 Roma-Lyon Group, 'G8 Best Practices for the Administration of Seized Assets' (2005). https://star.worldbank.org/sites/default/files/2023-03/E2_G-8_Best_Practices_for_the_Administration_of_Assets.pdf (4.07.2024).
87 See, e.g., The Stolen Asset Recovery (StAR) Initiative, Management of Returned Assets: Policy Considerations (2009), Washington D.C.: The World Bank. https://www.unodc.org/documents/corruption/Publications/StAR/StAR_Publication_-_ManagementReturnedAssets.pdf (4.07.2024).
88 See LIBERA, 'Uso sociale dei beni confiscati'. https://www.libera.it/schede-4-uso_sociale_dei_beni_confiscati (4.07.2024).
89 See also Matrix Insight, 'Assessing the effectiveness of EU Member States' practices in the identification, tracing, freezing and confiscation of criminal assets. Final Report' (2009), the external study commissioned by the Commission.
90 Commission, Commission Staff Working Paper Accompanying document to the Proposal for a Directive of the European Parliament and the Council on the freezing and confiscation of proceeds of crime in the European Union, Impact Assessment, 12.3.2012, SWD(2012) 31 final, COM(2012) 85 final.
91 FRA, Opinion on the Confiscation of proceeds of crime, No. 03/2012, 4.12.2012. https://fra.europa.eu/sites/default/files/fra-opinion-3-2012_confiscation-of-proceeds-of-crime.pdf. (4.07.2024).
92 Directive (EU) 2024/1712 of the European Parliament and of the Council of 13 June 2024 amending Directive 2011/36/EU on preventing and combating trafficking in human beings and protecting its victims (2024), OJ L, 2024/1712. Cf. Article 7 of the draft directive (Proposal for a Directive of the EP and of the Council amending Directive 2011/36/EU on preventing and combating trafficking in human beings and protecting its victims (2022), COM(2022) 732 final, 2022/0426(COD)).
93 European Council, Conclusions, Brussels, 27 June 2014, EUCO 79/14. https://data.consilium.europa.eu/doc/document/ST-79-2014-INIT/en/pdf (27.06.2024).

94 Council document 15224/1/17, Mid-term review of the JHA strategic guidelines, 1 December 2017.
95 Council document 12848/20, EU Action Plan on Human Rights and Democracy 2020–2024, 18 November 2020.
96 See also Decision 2014/386/CFSP of 23 June 2014 concerning restrictions on goods originating in Crimea or Sevastopol, in response to the illegal annexation of Crimea and Sevastopol (2014), OJ L 183/70; Regulation (EU) No 692/2014 of 23 June 2014 concerning restrictions on the import into the Union of goods originating in Crimea or Sevastopol, in response to the illegal annexation of Crimea and Sevastopol (2014), OJ L 183/9; Decision 2014/512/CFSP of 31 July 2014 concerning restrictive measures in view of Russia's actions destabilising the situation in Ukraine (2014), OJ L 229/13; Regulation (EU) No 833/2014 of 31 July 2014 concerning restrictive measures in view of Russia's actions destabilising the situation in Ukraine (2014), OJ L 229/1.
97 European Council, A new strategic agenda 2019–2024 (2019). https://www.consilium.europa.eu/media/39914/a-new-strategic-agenda-2019-2024.pdf (10.07.2024).
98 See also the European Multidisciplinary Platform Against Criminal Threats (EMPACT), Joint Communication Strategy (2022). https://www.consilium.europa.eu/media/58605/empact-joint-communication-strategy_web.pdf (16.07.2024); Council, Conclusions setting the EU's priorities for the fight against serious and organised crime for EMPACT 2022–2025, 12.05.2021, Council document 8665/21.
99 European Council, Conclusions, 22 March 2024. https://www.consilium.europa.eu/media/70880/euco-conclusions-2122032024.pdf (11.07.2024).
100 European Council, Conclusions, 18 April 2024. https://www.consilium.europa.eu/media/m5jlwe0p/euco-conclusions-20240417-18-en.pdf (11.07.2024).
101 Council Decision (EU) 2022/2332 of 28 November 2022 on identifying the violation of Union restrictive measures as an area of crime that meets the criteria specified in Article 83(1) of the Treaty on the Functioning of the European Union, (2022) OJ L 308/18.
102 Proposal for a Directive of the European Parliament and of the Council on asset recovery and confiscation, 25.5.2022, COM(2022) 245 final.
103 The 2022 Proposal referred to the statements of the EP and the Council made in 2014. See Council, Statements (2014), Council document 7329/1/14/REV 1 ADD 1.
104 See, e.g., Council Conclusions on enhancing financial investigations to fight serious and organised crime, 17 June 2020, Council document 8927/20; EP, Resolution of 15 December 2021 on the impact of organised crime on own resources of the EU and on the misuse of EU funds with a particular focus on shared management from an auditing and control perspective, P9_TA(2021)0501, (2022) OJ C 251/37.
105 See also Europol, Internet Organised Crime Threat Assessment (IOCTA) 2021, Luxembourg: Publications Office of the EU. https://www.europol.europa.eu/cms/sites/default/files/documents/internet_organised_crime_threat_assessment_iocta_2021.pdf (10.07.2024); Europol, Press News, '800 criminals arrested in biggest ever law enforcement operation against encrypted communication', 8.06.2021. https://www.europol.europa.eu/media-press/newsroom/news/800-criminals-arrested-in-biggest-ever-law-enforcement-operation-against-encrypted-communication (10.07.2024).
106 Commission Staff Working Document, Analysis of non-conviction-based confiscation measures in the European Union, 12.4.2019, SWD(2019) 1050 final.
107 Report of the Commission to the European Parliament and to the Council, 'Asset recovery and confiscation, ensuring that crime does not pay', 2.6.2020, COM(2020) 217 final.
108 Commission, EU Strategy to tackle Organised Crime 2021–2025, 14.4.2021, COM(2021) 170 final.
109 Directive (EU) 2019/1153 of the European Parliament and of the Council of 20 June 2019 laying down rules facilitating the use of financial and other information for the

prevention, detection, investigation or prosecution of certain criminal offences, and repealing Council Decision 2000/642/JHA, (2019) OJ L 186/122.

110 Commission Staff Working Document, Impact Assessment Report, 25.5.2022, SWD(2022) 245 final.

111 EESC, Opinion Asset recovery and confiscation, SOC/738, 14.12.2022. https://dm-publicapi.eesc.europa.eu/v1/documents/P6FJPSUHKDC2-1050578159-9846/download (12.07.2024).

112 LIBE, Report on the proposal for a directive of the European Parliament and of the Council on asset recovery and confiscation, 26.5.2023, A9-0199/2023. https://www.europarl.europa.eu/doceo/document/A-9-2023-0199_EN.pdf (12.07.2024).

113 Senate of the Parliament of the Czech Republic, 59th Resolution of the Senate on the Proposal for a Directive of the European Parliament and of the Council on asset recovery and confiscation (Senate Print No N 190/13, COM (2022) 245), 1.12.2022, Courtesy translation. https://www.europarl.europa.eu/RegData/docs_autres_institutions/parlements_nationaux/com/2022/0245/CZ_SENATE_CONT1-COM(2022)0245_EN.pdf (16.07.2024).

114 Commission, Directorate-General for Migration and Home Affairs, Study on freezing, confiscation and asset recovery – What works, what does not work – Final report, Publications Office of the European Union, 2021, p. 122. https://data.europa.eu/doi/10.2837/649661.

115 Opinion of the Committee on Legal Affairs for the LIBE, 24.3.2023, 2022/0167(COD). https://www.europarl.europa.eu/doceo/document/JURI-AD-740764_EN.pdf (12.07.2024).

116 Opinion of the Committee on Budgets for the LIBE, 30.3.2023, 2022/0167(COD). https://www.europarl.europa.eu/doceo/document/BUDG-AD-739737_EN.pdf (12.07.2024).

117 EESC, Opinion Asset recovery and confiscation, SOC/738, 14.12.2022. https://dm-publicapi.eesc.europa.eu/v1/documents/P6FJPSUHKDC2-1050578159-9846/download (12.07.2024).

118 EP, LIBE, Provisional agreement resulting from interinstitutional negotiations, 18.01.2024, PE759.655. https://www.europarl.europa.eu/RegData/commissions/libe/inag/2024/02-23/LIBE_AG(2024)759655_EN.docx (13.07.2024).

119 Commission, EU Strategy on victims' rights (2020–2025), 24.6.2020, COM(2020) 258 final.

120 The EESC Opinion: Victims' Rights Strategy, SOC/652 (2020). https://webapi2016.eesc.europa.eu/v1/documents/EESC-2020-03013-00-00-AC-TRA-EN.docx/content (3.08.2024).

121 In addition to Directive 2012/29/EU and Council Directive 2004/80/EC, the following EU instruments address various victims' rights: FD 2005/214/JHA on the application of the principle of mutual recognition to financial penalties, (2005) OJ L 76/16; Directive 2011/36/EU of 5 April 2011 on preventing and combating trafficking in human beings and protecting its victims, and replacing Council Framework Decision 2002/629/JHA, (2011) OJ L 101/1; Directive 2011/93/EU of 13 December 2011 on combating the sexual abuse and sexual exploitation of children and child pornography, and replacing Council Framework Decision 2004/68/JHA, (2011) OJ L 335/1; Directive 2011/99/EU of 13 December 2011 on the European protection order, (2011) OJ L 338/2; Regulation (EU) No 606/2013 of 12 June 2013 on mutual recognition of protection measures in civil matters, (2013) OJ L 181/4; Directive (EU) 2017/541 of 15 March 2017 on combating terrorism and replacing Council Framework Decision 2002/475/JHA and amending Council Decision 2005/671/JHA, (2017) OJ L 88/6.

122 Commission, Report on the implementation of Directive 2012/29/EU of the European Parliament and of the Council of 25 October 2012 establishing minimum standards

on the rights, support and protection of victims of crime, and replacing Council Framework Decision 2001/220/JHA, 11.5.2020, COM(2020) 188 final.

123 Commission Staff Working Document, Evaluation of Directive 2012/29/EU, 28.6.2022, SWD(2022) 179 final. https://eur-lex.europa.eu/legal-content/EN/TXT/PDF/?uri=CELEX:52022SC0179 (13.07.2024).

124 The 2022 Evaluation referred to the external study carried out for Directorate-General Justice and Consumers, Commission: ICF, Study to support the evaluation of Directive 2012/29/EU establishing minimum standards on the rights, support and protection of victims of crime. Final report, (2022), Luxembourg: Publications Office of the European Union, p. 49. https://data.europa.eu/doi/10.2838/830643 (13.07.2024).

125 Commission, Proposal for a Directive amending Directive 2012/29/EU establishing minimum standards on the rights, support and protection of victims of crime, and replacing Council Framework Decision 2001/220/JHA, 12.7.2023, COM(2023) 424 final.

126 Jöelle Milquet, 'Strengthening victims' rights: from compensation to reparation. For a new EU Victims' rights strategy 2020–2025' (2019), Luxembourg: Publications Office of the EU. https://commission.europa.eu/system/files/2019-03/strengthening_victims_rights_-_from_compensation_to_reparation_rev.pdf (3.08.2024).

127 CoE, Criminal Law Convention on Corruption (1999), ETS No. 173.

128 See MONEYVAL, Strategy on anti-money laundering, combating the financing of terrorism and proliferation financing (2023–2027). https://rm.coe.int/moneyvalstrategy2023-2027-en/1680ab0b06 (19.07.2024).

129 The UNCAC Coalition is a global network of civil society organisations promoting ratification and supporting implementation of the UNCAC (established in 2006). See https://uncaccoalition.org/about-us/about-the-coalition/ (19.07.2024).

130 OHCHR, Recommended Principles on Human Rights and Asset Recovery (2022). https://www.ohchr.org/sites/default/files/2022-03/OHCHR-RecommendedPrinciplesHumanRightsAssetRecovery_0.pdf (19.07.2024).

131 OECD, Convention on Combating Bribery of Foreign Public Officials in International Business Transactions (1997), OECD/LEGAL/0293. This convention contains legal solutions concerning seizure and confiscation of assets linked with corruption offences (Article 3(3)); Commentaries to this convention adopted by the Negotiating Conference on 21 November 1997. See also Recommendation of the Council for Further Combating Bribery of Foreign Public Officials in International Business Transactions (2021). According to the 2021 Recommendation, the member countries should 'ensure that a broad range of investigative measures is available […] such as access to financial, banking and company information, including on beneficial ownership, asset tracing, forensics, and special investigative techniques, where appropriate' (Recommendation X(i)). 'Convention on Combating Bribery of Foreign Public Officials in International Business Transactions. And related documents', https://www.oecd.org/content/dam/oecd/en/publications/reports/2011/03/convention-on-combating-bribery-of-foreign-public-officials-in-international-business-transactions_037f7856/2bfa620e-en.pdf (24.11.2024). In addition, see OECD Anti-Corruption Network for Eastern Europe and Central Asia 'Confiscation of instrumentalities and proceeds of corruption crimes in Eastern Europe and Central Asia' (2018), https://www.oecd.org/content/dam/oecd/en/publications/reports/2018/01/confiscation-of-instrumentalities-and-proceeds-of-corruption-crimes-in-eastern-europe-and-central-asia_5fbf82bf/78637cac-en.pdf (24.11.2024).

132 G8 Roma-Lyon Group, 'G8 Best Practices for the Administration of Seized Assets' (2005). https://star.worldbank.org/sites/default/files/2023-03/E2_G-8_Best_Practices_for_the_Administration_of_Assets.pdf (4.07.2024).

133 Basel Institute on Governance, Basel AML Index 2023: 12th Public Edition – Ranking money laundering and terrorist financing risks around the world (2023). https://

index.baselgovernance.org/api/assets/8ebee704-b518-42ca-8de5-c67dbc71a18a (19.07.2024).

134 StAR, the World Bank, UNODC, GFAR Principles for Disposition and Transfer of Confiscated Stolen Assets in Corruption Cases (2017). https://star.worldbank.org/sites/star/files/thegfar-principles.pdf (19.07.2024).

135 CiFAR, Civil Society Principles for Accountable Asset Return (2019). https://cifar.eu/wpcontent/uploads/2020/10/CSO-Principles_EN.pdf (19.07.2024).

136 See also Serious Fraud Office (SFO), General Principles to compensate overseas victims (including affected States) in bribery, corruption and economic crime cases (2018), agreed by the SFO, the Crown Prosecution Service (CPS) and the National Crime Agency (NCA). https://www.sfo.gov.uk/download/general-principles-to-compensate-overseas-victims-including-affected-states-in-bribery-corruption-and-economic-crime-cases/?ind=1527843781375&filename=General%20Principles%20to%20compensate%20overseas%20victims.pdf&wpdmdl=19594&refresh=669a68b67b92b1721395382 (19.07.2024).

137 EESC, Opinion of the European Economic and Social Committee on the 'Proposal for a Directive of the European Parliament and of the Council on the freezing and confiscation of proceeds of crime in the European Union' (2012), OJ C 299/128.

138 EESC, Opinion – Asset recovery and confiscation, SOC/738. https://dm-publicapi.eesc.europa.eu/v1/documents/P6FJPSUHKDC2-1050578159-9846/download (17.07.2024).

139 European Council, Conclusions, Tampere, 15–16 October 1999. https://www.consilium.europa.eu/media/21059/tampere-european-council-presidency-conclusions.pdf (21.05.2024).

140 European Council, The Hague Programme: strengthening freedom, security and justice in the European Union, (2005), OJ C 53/1.

141 European Council, The Stockholm Programme – An open and secure Europe serving and protecting citizens, (2010), OJ C 115/1.

142 See more CoE, EU accession to the ECHR ('46+1' Group). https://www.coe.int/en/web/human-rights-intergovernmental-cooperation/accession-of-the-european-union-to-the-european-convention-on-human-rights (17.07.2024).

143 See CoE, Treaty Office, Chart of signatures and ratifications of Treaty 198. https://www.coe.int/en/web/conventions/full-list?module=signatures-by-treaty&treatynum=198 (17.07.2024).

144 See Council Decision (EU) 2024/1764 of 13 June 2024 authorising the Commission to participate, on behalf of the European Union, in negotiations on an additional protocol to the Council of Europe Convention on Laundering, Search, Seizure and Confiscation of the Proceeds from Crime and on the Financing of Terrorism, (2024), OJ L, 2024/1764.

145 CoE, Committee of Experts on Criminal Asset Recovery (PC-RAC), Terms of Reference 2024–2025, CM(2023)131-addfinal – excerpt. https://rm.coe.int/cm-2023-131-addfinal-excerpt-tor-pc-rac/1680aea175 (17.07.2024). See also CoE, Meeting report, 15th meeting of the conference of parties of the CoE Convention on Laundering, Search, Seizure and Confiscation of the Proceeds from Crime and on the Financing of Terrorism (CETS No. 198) on 9 and 10 November 2023, 9 December 2023, C198-COP(2023)10. https://rm.coe.int/c198-cop-2023-10-cop-15-plenary-meeting-report-en/1680adf1a5 (17.07.2024).

146 See also ECtHR, *Microintelect OOD v Bulgaria*, Application no. 34129/03, 4 March 2014, paras 41–46.

147 Action plan to combat organised crime (Adopted by the Council on 28 April 1997), (1997) OJ C 251/1; European Council, Conclusions, Amsterdam, 16–17 June 1997. https://www.consilium.europa.eu/media/21136/amsterdam-european-council.pdf (21.05.2024).

148 Joint Action of 3 December 1998 adopted by the Council on the basis of Article K.3 of the Treaty on European Union, on money laundering, the identification, tracing, freezing, seizing and confiscation of instrumentalities and the proceeds from crime (98/699/JHA), (1998) OJ L 333/1.
149 Action Plan of the Council and the Commission on how best to implement the provisions of the Treaty of Amsterdam on an area of freedom, security and justice – Text adopted by the JHA Council, 3 December 1998, (1999), OJ C 19/1.
150 Commission, Communication from the Commission 'Towards an area of freedom, security and justice', Brussels, 14.07.1998, COM(1998) 459 final. See also European Council, Conclusions, Cardiff, 15–16 June 1998, p.17. https://www.consilium.europa.eu/media/21103/54315.pdf (29.05.2024).
151 European Council, 'The prevention and control of organised crime: a European Union strategy for the beginning of the new millennium' (2000), OJ C 124/1.
152 See, e.g., European Council, Conclusions, Brussels, 27 June 2014, EUCO 79/14. https://data.consilium.europa.eu/doc/document/ST-79-2014-INIT/en/pdf (24.07.2024).
153 The Council and Commission Action Plan implementing the Hague Programme on strengthening freedom, security and justice in the European Union (2005), OJ C 198/1.
154 See Commission, Communication from the Commission to the EP and the Council: Proceeds of organised crime. Ensuring that 'crime does not pay', 20.11.2008, COM(2008) 766 final.
155 See, e.g., Council Conclusions on Confiscation and Asset Recovery, 28.05.2010, Council document 7769/3/10, Council document 9657/10.
156 Commission, Proposal for a Directive of the European Parliament and of the Council on the freezing and confiscation of proceeds of crime in the European Union (2012), COM/2012/085 final.
157 EP, Resolution of 25 October 2011 on organised crime in the European Union (2010/2309(INI)), P7_TA(2011)0459, (8). See also EP, Report on organised crime in the European Union, 25.11.2010, Document A7-0333/2011. https://www.europarl.europa.eu/doceo/document/A-7-2011-0333_EN.html (28.06.2024).
158 Commission, Report on the implementation of Directive 2012/29/EU of the European Parliament and of the Council of 25 October 2012 establishing minimum standards on the rights, support and protection of victims of crime, and replacing Council Framework Decision 2001/220/JHA, 11.5.2020, COM(2020) 188 final.
159 Commission work programme 2007–2023, 'Making Europe stronger together', 19.10.2021, COM(2021) 645 final. See Commission, Proposal for a Directive of the EP and of the Council amending Directive 2012/29/EU establishing minimum standards on the rights, support and protection of victims of crime, and replacing Council Framework Decision 2001/220/JHA, 12.7.2023, COM(2023) 424 final, 2023/0250(COD).
160 Action Plan of the Council and the Commission on how best to implement the provisions of the Treaty of Amsterdam on an area of freedom, security and justice – Text adopted by the JHA Council, 3 December 1998, (1999), OJ C 19/1.

References

Alagna, Federico. 2015. "Non-conviction Based Confiscation: Why the EU Directive Is a Missed Opportunity." *European Journal on Criminal Policy and Research* 21: 447–461. https://doi.org/10.1007/S10610-014-9252.

Arcifa, Gabriella. 2014. "The New EU Directive on Confiscation: A Good (Even If Still Prudent) Starting Point for the Post-Lisbon EU Strategy on Tracking and Confiscating Illicit Money." *Università di Catania — Online Working Paper* 64. http://www.cde.unict.it/quadernieuropei/giuridiche/64_2014.pdf.

Betti, Stefano, Vladimir Kozin, and Jean-Pierre Brun. 2022. *Orders without Borders: Direct Enforcement of Foreign Restraint and Confiscation Decisions*. Washington, DC: International Bank for Reconstruction and Development / The World Bank. https://doi:10.1596/978-1-4648-1830-1.

Biernat, Tadeusz. 2012. "*Soft law* a proces tworzenia prawa w Unii Europejskiej. Wpływ *soft law* na konstrukcję i treść uzasadnień aktów normatywnych." *Studia Prawnicze. Rozprawy i Materiały* 2 (11): 27–38.

Biersteker, Thomas J., Sue E. Eckert, and Peter Romaniuk. 2008. "International Initiatives to Combat the Financing of Terrorism." In *Countering the Financing of Terrorism*, edited by Thomas J. Boersteker and Sue E. Eckert, 234–259. Abingdon: Routledge.

Block, Alan A. 1980. "The Organized Crime Control Act, 1970: Historical Issues and Public Policy." *The Public Historian* 2 (2): 39–59.

Borgers, Matthias J. 2010. "Functions and Aims of Harmonisation after the Lisbon Treaty: A European Perspective." In *The Future of Police and Judicial Cooperation in the European Union*, edited by Cyrille Fijnaut and Jannemieke Ouwerkerk, 347–356. Leiden: Martinus Nijhoff Pub.

Borgers, Matthias J. 2014. "Confiscation of the Proceeds of Crime: The European Union Framework." In *Dirty Assets. Emerging Issues in the Regulation of Criminal and Terrorist Assets*, edited by Colin King and Clive Walker, 27–45. Farnham: Ashgate Pub.

Boucht, Johan. 2019. "Asset Confiscation in Europe – Past, Present, and Future Challenges." *Journal of Financial Crime* 26 (2): 526–548. https://doi.org/10.1108/JFC-04-2018-0043.

Brent, Richard. 2008. "International Legal Sources IV – the European Union and the Council of Europe." In *Banks and Financial Crime. The International Law of Tainted Money*, edited by William Blair and Richard Berent, 101–150. Oxford: Oxford University Press.

Bright Line Law. 2020. *The Use of Non-Conviction Based Seizure and Confiscation*. Strasbourg: Council of Europe. Accessed July 18, 2024. https://rm.coe.int/the-use-of-non-conviction-based-seizure-and-confiscation-2020/1680a0b9d3.

Brun, Jean-Pierre, Larissa Gray, Clive Scott, and Kevin M. Stephenson. 2011. *Asset Recovery Handbook: A Guide for Practitioners, StAR Initiative, UNODC*. Washington, DC: The World Bank.

Buono, Laviero. 2009. "From Tampere to The Hague and Beyond: Towards the Stockholm Programme in the Area of Freedom, Security and Justice." *ERA Forum* 10: 333–342. https://doi.org/10.1007/s12027-009-0127-2.

Bullock, Karen, and Stuart Lister. 2014. "Post-Conviction Confiscation of Assets in England and Wales: Rhetoric and Reality." In *Dirty Assets. Emerging Issues in the Regulation of Criminal and Terrorist Assets*, edited by Colin King and Clive Walker, 47–69. Farnham: Ashgate Pub.

Calderoni, Francesco. 2014. "Mythical Numbers and the Proceeds of Organised Crime: Estimating Mafia Proceeds in Italy." *Global Crime* 15 (1–2): 138–163.

Callewaert, Johan. 2014. *The Accession of the European Union to the European Convention on Human Rights*. Strasbourg: The CoE Pub.

Carrera, Sergio, and Elspeth Guild. 2012. "Does the Stockholm Programme matter? The Struggles Over Ownership of AFSJ Multiannual Programming." *CEPS Paper in Liberty and Security in Europe* 51: 1–40.

Csonka, Peter, and Oliver Landwehr. 2019. "10 Years after Lisbon – How 'Lisbonised' is the Substantive Criminal Law in the EU?" *Eucrim* 4: 261–267. https://doi.org/10.30709/eucrim-2019-023.

Csonka, Peter, and Lucia Zoli. 2024. "The New Directive on the Violation of Union Restrictive Measures in the Context of the EPPO." *Eucrim*, Article submitted, June 12, 2024. Accessed July 13, 2024. https://eucrim.eu/articles/the-new-directive-on-the-violation-of-union-restrictive-measures-in-the-context-of-the-eppo/#statement.

Delmas-Marty, Mireille. 1996. "Beter or Worse?" In *What Kind of Criminal Policy for Europe*, edited by Mireille Delmas-Marty (Mark A. Summers, associated editor and translator, Ginette Mongin, assistant editor), 3–6. The Hague: Kluwer Law International.

Europol. 2016. *Does Crime Still Pay? Criminal Asset Recovery in the EU: Survey of Statistical Information 2010–2014*. The Hague: European Police Office.

Europol. 2023. *European Financial and Economic Crime Threat Assessment 2023 – The Other Side of the Coin: An Analysis of Financial and Economic Crime*. Luxembourg: Publications Office of the European Union.

Falconi, Felipe Freitas, José Ugaz, Juanita Olaya Garcia, and Yara Esquivel Soto. 2023. *Victims of Corruption. Back for Payback*. StAR Initiative, the World Bank, UNODC. Washington, DC: The World Bank. Accessed July 19, 2024. https://star.worldbank.org/sites/default/files/2023-11/Victims-report-05_0.pdf.

Ferwerda, Joras. 2014. "Collection of Statistics." In *The Economic and Legal Effectiveness of the European Union's Anti-Money Laundering Policy*, edited by Brigitte Unger, Joras Ferwerda, Melissa van den Broek, and Ioanna Delenanu, 162–186. Cheltenham: Edward Elgar Pub.

Fernandez-Bertier, Michaël. 2019. "The History of Confiscation Laws: From the Book of Exodus to the War on White Collar-Crime." In *Chasing Criminal Money: Challenges and Perspectives on Asset Recovery in the EU*, edited by Katalin Ligeti and Michele Simonato, 53–75. Oxford: Hurt Pub.

Forsaith, James, Barrie Irving, Eva Nanopoulos, and Mihaly Fazekas. 2012. *Study for an Impact Assessment on a Proposal for a New Legal Framework on the Confiscation and Recovery of Criminal Assets*. RAND Europe, EU. Accessed July 4, 2024. https://home-affairs.ec.europa.eu/system/files/2020-09/external_study_used_as_a_basis_for_the_commission_ia_october_2012_en.pdf.

Gallant, Michelle. 1999. "Money Laundering, Criminal Assets and the 1998 Proposed Reforms." *Journal of Financial Crime* 6 (4): 325–332.

Golobinek, Robert. 2006. *Financial Investigations and Confiscation of Proceeds of Crime – Training Manual for Law Enforcement and Judiciary*. Strasbourg: Council of Europe. Accessed July 4, 2024. https://rm.coe.int/CoERMPublicCommonSearchServices/DisplayDCTMContent?documentId=09000016806efd5f.

Gfroerer, Joseph. 2018. *War Stories from the Drug Survey: How Culture, Politics, and Statistics Shaped the National Survey on Drug Use and Health*. Cambridge: Cambridge University Press.

Hendry, Jennifer, and Colin King. 2015. "How Far Is Too Far? Theorising Non-conviction-based Asset Forfeiture." *International Journal of Law in Context* 11 (4): 398–411.

Herlin-Karnell, Ester. 2010. "The Lisbon Treaty: A Critical Analysis of its Impact on EU Criminal Law." *Eucrim* 2: 59–64. https://doi.org/10.30709/eucrim-2010-005.

Hryniewicz-Lach, Elżbieta. 2023. "Expanding Confiscation and its Dimensions in EU Criminal Law." *European Journal of Crime, Criminal Law and Criminal Justice* 31 (3–4): 243–267. https://doi.org/10.1163/15718174-bja10046.

Jensen, Eric L., and Jurg Gerber. 1996. "The Civil Forfeiture of Assets and the War on Drugs: Expanding Criminal Sanctions While Reducing Due Process Protections." *Crime & Delinquency* 42 (3): 421–434.

Kaunert, Christian, John D. Occhipinti, and Sarah Léonard. 2014. "Introduction: Supranational Governance in the Area of Freedom, Security and Justice after the Stockholm Programme." *Cambridge Review of International Affairs* 27 (1): 39–47. doi: 10.1080/09557571.2014.877261.

Klip, André. 2009. *European Criminal Law: An Integrative Approach*. Antwerp, Oxford and Portland: Intersentia.

Klip, André. 2016. *European Criminal Law: An Integrative Approach*. 3rd ed. Antwerp, Oxford and Portland: Intersentia.

Léonard, Sarah, and Christian Kaunert. 2016. "Beyond Stockholm: In Search of a Strategy for the European Union's Area of Freedom, Security, and Justice." *European Politics and Society* 17 (2): 143–149. http://dx.doi.org/10.1080/23745118.2016.1160636.

Levi, Michael. 2015. "The Impacts of Organised Crime in the EU: Some Preliminary Thoughts on Measurement Difficulties." *Contemporary Social Science* 11 (4): 392–402.

Levi, Michael, and Lisa Osofsky. 1995. *Investigating, Seizing and Confiscating the Proceeds of Crime*. London: Home Office Police Department, Police Research Group: Crime Detection and Prevention Series, Paper 61.

Levy, Leonard W. 1996. *A License to Steal: The Forfeiture of Property*. Chapel Hill and London: University of North Carolina Press.

Maugeri, Anna Maria. 2024. "Regulation (EU) 2018/1805: Mutual Recognition of Freezing and Confiscation Orders Between Efficiency and Safeguards. 'Proceedings in Criminal Matters' and Non-conviction Based Confiscation." *New Journal of European Criminal Law* 15 (2): 164–208. https://doi.org/10.1177/20322844241239781.

Meijers Committee (standing committee of experts on international immigration, refugee and criminal law). 2018. "1806 Note on the Use of Soft Law Instruments under EU Law, in Particular in the Area of Freedom, Security and Justice, and Its Impact on Fundamental Rights, Democracy and the Rule of Law." April 9, 2018. Accessed May 27, 2024. https://www.commissie-meijers.nl/wp-content/uploads/2021/09/CM1806_EN.pdf.

Meyer, Frank. 2020. "Recognizing the Unknown – the New Confiscation Regulation." *European Criminal Law Review* 10 (2): 140–170. https://doi.org/10.5771/2193-5505-2020-2-140.

Mirandola, Sofia. 2020. "Borderless Enforcement of Freezing and Confiscation Orders in the EU: The First Regulation on Mutual Recognition in Criminal Matters." *ERA Forum* 20: 405–421. https://doi.org/10.1007/s12027-019-00581-x.

Mitsilegas, Valsamis. 2022. *EU Criminal Law*. Oxford: Hart Pub.

Moiseienko, Anton. 2024. "Crime and Sanctions: Beyond Sanctions as a Foreign Policy Tool." *German Law Journal* 25: 17–47. https://doi.org/10.1017/glj.2023.103.

Montaldo, Stefano. 2015. "Directive 2014/42/EU and Social Reuse of Confiscated Assets in the EU: Advancing a Culture of Legality." *New Journal of European Criminal Law* 6 (2): 195–212.

Muller, Wouter H. 2007. "Anti-Money Laundering – A Short History." In *Anti-Money Laundering: International Law and Practice*, edited by Wouter H. Muller, Christian H. Kälin, and John G. Goldsworth, 1–11. Chichester: John Wiley and Sons, Ltd.

Naylor, R. T. 1999. "Wash-out: A Critique of Follow-the-Money Methods in Crime Control Policy." *Crime, Law and Social Change* 32: 1–58. https://doi.org/10.1023/A:1008386203362.

Öberg, Jacob. 2023. "Normative Justifications of EU Criminal Law: European Public Goods and Transnational Interests." *European Law Journal* 27 (4–6): 408–425. https://doi.org/10.1111/eulj.12451.

Ochnio, Ariadna, H. 2018, "Between the Medium and the Minimum Options to Regulate Mutual Recognition of Confiscation Orders." *New Journal of European Criminal Law* 9 (4): 432–445.

Ochnio, Ariadna, H. 2022. "Addressing Barriers to Victims' Rights to Recovered Assets in the Mechanism for Mutual Recognition of Freezing and Confiscation Orders." In *Current Issues of EU Criminal Law*, edited by Ariadna H. Ochnio and Hanna Kuczyńska, 137–158. Warsaw: Publishing House of ILS PAS. https://doi.org/10.5281/zenodo.6860700.

Ochnio, Ariadna, H. 2024. "Recent Developments in EU Anti-corruption Strategy: The Missing Element of the Return of Corrupt Assets to «Victim Countries»." *Journal of Money Laundering Control* 27 (7): 1–12. https://doi.org/10.1108/JMLC-11-2023-0176.

Olaya, Garcia Juanita, Kodjo Attisso, and Anja Roth. 2011. "Repairing Social Damage Out of Corruption Cases: Opportunities and Challenges as Illustrated in the Alcatel Case in Costa Rica." 6 December 2010. http://dx.doi.org/10.2139/ssrn.1779834.

Paoli, Letizia, and Cyrille Fijnaut. 2006. "Organised Crime and Its Control Policies." *European Journal of Crime, Criminal Law and Criminal Justice* 14 (3): 307–327.

Reuter, Peter. 1984. "The (Continued) Vitality of Mythical Numbers." *The Public Interest* 75: 135–147.

Rui, Jon Petter. 2012. "Non-conviction Based Confiscation in the European Union—an Assessment of Art. 5 of the Proposal for a Directive of the European Parliament and of the Council on the Freezing and Confiscation of Proceeds of Crime in the European Union." *ERA Forum* 13: 349–360.

Sakellaraki, Anna. 2022. "EU Asset Recovery and Confiscation Regime – *Quo Vadis*? A First Assessment of the Commission's Proposal to Further Harmonise the EU Asset Recovery and Confiscation Laws. A Step in the Right Direction?" *New Journal of European Criminal Law* 13 (4): 478–501. https://doi.org/10.1177/20322844221113957.

Satzger, Helmut. 2019. "The Harmonisation of Criminal Sanctions in the European Union - A New Approach." *Eucrim* 2: 115 – 120. https://doi.org/10.30709/eucrim-2019-007.

Savona, Ernesto U., and Michele Riccardi (eds.). 2015. *From Illegal Markets to Legitimate Businesses: The Portfolio of Organised Crime in Europe. Final Report of Project OCP – Organised Crime Portfolio.* Trento: Transcrime – Università degli Studi di Trento. Accessed July 30, 2024. https://www.transcrime.it/wp-content/uploads/2015/12/ocp.pdf.

Schroeder, Werner. 2020. "Limits to European Harmonisation of Criminal Law." *Eucrim* 2: 144–148. https://doi.org/10.30709/eucrim-2020-008.

Silva, Sandra, e Oliveira. 2022. "Regulation (EU) 2018/1805 on the Mutual Recognition of Freezing and Confiscation Orders: A Headlong Rush into Europe-wide Harmonisation?" *New Journal of European Criminal Law* 13 (2): 198–215. https://doi.org/10.1177/20322844221104916.

Simonato, Michele. 2015. "Directive 2014/42/EU and Non-Conviction Based Confiscation: A Step Forward on Asset Recovery?" *New Journal of European Criminal Law* 6 (2): 213–228. https://doi.org/10.1177/203228441500600205.

Simonato, Michele. 2016. "Extended Confiscation of Criminal Assets: Limits and Pitfalls of Minimum Harmonisation in the EU." *European Law Review* 41 (5): 727–740.

Singer, Max. 1971. "The vitality of mythical numbers." *The Public Interest* 23: 1–9.

Tadić, Felicitas M. 2002. "How Harmonious Can Harmonisation Be? A Theoretical Approach towards Harmonisation of (Criminal) Law." In *Harmonisation and Harmonising Measures in Criminal Law*, edited by André Klip and Harmen van der Wilt, 1– 21. Amsterdam: Royal Netherlands Academy of Arts and Sciences.

Vande Reyde, Laura, and Dirk Van Daele. 2017. "Asset Sharing as a Tool for a More Efficient Cross-Border Asset Recovery in the EU? The EU Asset Sharing Model and its Implementation in Belgium and the Netherlands." In *Chasing Criminal Money. Challenges and Perspectives on Asset Recovery in the EU*, edited by Katalin Ligeti and Michele Simonato, 305–319. Oxford: Hurt Pub.

Vervaele, John A. E. 2013. "Harmonised Union Policies and the Harmonisation of Substantive Criminal Law." In *Approximation of Substantive Criminal Law in the EU: The Way Forward*, edited by Francesca Galli and Anne Weyembergh, 43–71. Bruxelles: Editions de l'Université de Bruxelles.

Vervaele, John A. E. 2019. "European Criminal Justice in the European and Global Context." *New Journal of European Criminal Law* 10 (1): 7–16. https://doi.org/10.1177/2032284419840708.

Vettori, Barbara. 2006. *Tough on Criminal Wealth. Exploring the Practice of Proceeds from Crime Confiscation in the EU.* Dordrecht: Springer.

Vettori, Barbara. 2018. "The Disposal of Confiscated Assets in the EU Member States: What Works, What Does Not Work and What Is Promising." In *The Palgrave Handbook of Criminal and Terrorism Financing Law*, edited by Colin King, Clive Walker, and Jimmy Gurulé, 705–733. Cham: Palgrave Macmillan.

Weyembergh, Anne. 2005. "The Functions of Approximation of Penal Legislation within the European Union." *Maastricht Journal of European and Comparative Law* 12 (2): 149–172.

Weyembergh, Anne, and Irene Wieczorek. 2016. "Is There an EU Criminal Policy?" In *EU Criminal Justice and the Challenges of Diversity*, edited by Renaud Colson and Stewart Field, 29–47. Cambridge: Cambridge University Press.

Wieczorek, Irene. 2021. "The Emerging Role of the EU as a Primary Normative Actor in the EU Area of Criminal Justice." *European Law Journal* 27 (4–6): 378–407. https://doi.org/10.1111/eulj.12450.

Wouters, Jan, and Frederik Naert. 2003. "The European Union and 'September 11'." *Indiana International & Comparative Law Review* 13 (3): 719–775.

Wróblewski, Jerzy. 1985. *Teoria racjonalnego tworzenia prawa*. Wrocław: Zakład Narodowy im. Ossolińskich.

Wycichowski-Kuchta, Gniewomir. 2023. "The Discretion of the EU Member States in Shaping the Non-conviction Based Confiscation Regime in the Light of CJEU and ECHR Case Law." *Ruch Prawniczy, Ekonomiczny i Socjologiczny* 85 (4): 27–47. https://doi.org/10.14746/rpeis.2023.85.4.02.

Zoumpoulakis, Konstantinos. 2020. "From the Ground up: The Use of Minimum Rules in EU Procedural Criminal Law and the Question of Member States' Discretion." *European Papers* 5 (3): 1289–1303. https://doi.org/10.15166/2499-8249/426.

4 Gaps in EU law standards for the confiscation of the proceeds of crime

Introductory remarks

After examining the progressive incorporation of restorative elements into EU law-making policy on the CPC being a primary factor determining EU law and legal integration in the area of confiscation, the standards in this field laid down in EU law should be analysed as an expression of this policy and the realisation of its objectives. The analysis in this respect is conducted from the angle of a minimalist restorative approach to justice and aims to identify gaps in the existing standards.

In principle, current EU confiscation law is well-developed and addresses a wide range of issues. However, this does not mean that there are no remaining areas for improvement. It should be recalled that even under a minimalist restorative approach, effectiveness issues cannot be overlooked, as using the confiscation mechanism for compensation purposes (including restitution) depends, i.a., on effectively capturing and seizing criminal assets. As laid out in this book's introduction, the EU 'standards' are understood as the set of norms of EU law of general and abstract character, addressed to the MS and individuals (directly or indirectly) (see, e.g., C 41/74, *Van Duyn v Home Office*, EU:C:1974:133; Case 148/78, *Ratti*, EU:C:1979:110). The EU standards for confiscation are composed of substantive and procedural norms. In the area of harmonisation, these norms constitute a common criterion for the MS, with which the national confiscation schemes should comply (the minimum standard). In the area of mutual recognition of confiscation orders, these norms are not of a minimum character intended to be transposed into national law, as this sphere is currently predominantly governed by the directly applied Regulation 2018/1805, which laid down the rules under which a Member State must recognise and execute in its territory freezing orders and confiscation orders issued by another Member State.

The claim of this book is that the EU should strive for the highest standards possible within the existing constraints that prevent establishing 'gold standards' across the entire EU and with universal potential for adoption also by non-EU jurisdictions. It should be remembered that the EU legal system is complex and multi-layered. It is worth citing the pertinent question posed by Nielsen (2012): 'How many legal systems are there in the European Union?' This question focuses on whether the EU legal system is distinct from MS' legal systems, or whether only MS's legal systems are relevant. Another possibility is that there is only a single EU

DOI: 10.4324/9781003465829-4

legal system comprised of the sub-systems of MS' legal systems and international law. The last option is that there is a single EU legal system; however, this system is a multi-layered and interactive one, which comprises sources of law 'stemming from the EU level and from the international and national levels' (Nielsen 2012, 91–92). Nielsen opted for the latter concept (see also Dickson 2008).

From a Treaty perspective, the approximation of criminal laws is walking behind mutual recognition of judgments and is conditioned by the prerequisite of necessity (Articles 67(3) and 82(1) TFEU). In addition, the mutual recognition mechanism may indirectly influence harmonisation processes by the so-called 'side door' (Ochnio 2018), especially when the mechanism adopted requires one Member State to recognise to some extent judicial decisions in criminal matters from another Member State, which imposes a type of measure not known in domestic law, as in the case of orders imposing a type of confiscation falling outside the minimum scope of harmonisation. In addition, pursuant to Article 82(2) TFUE, when establishing minimum procedural rules, the differences between the legal traditions and systems of the MS should be taken into account, which are highly differentiated in the area of tackling illicit assets. These reasons undermine the pursuit of a 'single path' by all the MS.

Therefore, alongside the harmonisation processes, some diversity of confiscation schemes across the EU may be assumed *a priori*. Nevertheless, the acceptance of this diversity ends at the point where the mutual recognition mechanism is impeded. One can say that through the mutual recognition mechanism, EU law indirectly requires that one MS respect the different legal tradition and system of another MS. When we consider the priority of mutual recognition above the harmonisation of criminal laws, together with the high degree of differentiation of national confiscation schemes, it becomes clear that the scope of mutual recognition of confiscation orders issued in the framework of proceedings in criminal matters may be broader than the scope of harmonisation of legislation on confiscation related to a criminal offence. However, when national confiscation schemes are little compatible, this may translate into a deficit of the mutual trust required for effective cooperation between MS. In a similar way, deeper harmonisation can guide the smooth running of the mutual recognition mechanism.

The characteristics of interstate differences in the area of confiscation mechanisms should be considered together with the differences regarding applicable EU confiscation law (harmonising and mutual recognition instruments). As mentioned in the Introduction, Denmark is not bound by Directive 2014/42/EU (see Articles 1 and 2 of Protocol (No 22) on the position of Denmark annexed to the TEU and to the TFEU). In addition, those MS bound by Directive 2014/42/EU (Article 14) are also bound by FD 2005/212/JHA in respect of regular confiscation (Article 2). The legal landscape is even more complicated, as the new Directive 2024/1260 on asset recovery and confiscation (to be transposed into national legislation by 23 November 2026) replaces both FD 2005/212/JHA and Directive 2014/42/EU. However, Denmark and Ireland are not bound by this new Directive 2024/1260 (Recitals 63 and 64 of its Preamble). Moreover, as far as mutual recognition of confiscation orders and freezing orders is concerned (the area currently governed by

Regulation 2018/1805), FD 2006/783/JHA and FD 2003/577/JHA are still applicable for cooperation with Denmark and Ireland.

The next important point which hinders the creation of 'gold standards' for confiscation at the EU level is that serious and organised crime is a global phenomenon, and accordingly, the issue of tackling illicit assets needs to be approached from a broader perspective than the cross-border one adopted as a rule in EU confiscation law. Accordingly, the EU is not the only player when it comes to modelling confiscation regimes, and international standards developed under the aegis of the CoE, the UN, or the FATF have an influence on both national laws and EU law itself. Currently, in some areas, these standards even offer more advanced solutions than EU law (e.g., the UNCAC). Accordingly, the development of confiscation mechanisms is simultaneously the target of Europeanisation and globalisation processes.

In view of the above, at this stage of development, the EU legal standards for confiscation cannot be expected to be the conclusive 'gold standard'. Taking a realistic approach, it is more reasonable to expect the EU lawmaker to establish standards for confiscation that are as high as possible within existing constraints. These standards should be targeted at increasing convergence between confiscation mechanisms across MS, to reach a level enabling the smooth operation of the mutual recognition mechanism. Nonetheless, this should not hold back the EU's endeavour to strengthen its international position by setting more universal standards for tackling illicit assets.

Given the function of the minimum standards, if they contain gaps, they risk inappropriately influencing national laws, as similar shortcomings and omissions may then be 'duplicated' in national laws as part of the implementation process. One should expect that EU confiscation law reflects the policy objectives as officially declared. However, the analysis revealed there are areas where improvement is needed to meet those objectives, for instance in giving due priority to victims' rights, or securing the fair redistribution of confiscated assets. In addition, some areas were identified where EU confiscation law reflects shortcomings previously identified at the EU policy level, for instance in defining the comprehensive objective of the CPC, or mitigating procedural and excessive legislative reach risks in extended confiscation settings. The question was also posed of whether providing human rights protections is enough from a restorative viewpoint, or whether it implies a further search for innovative solutions for developing the 'proactive' role of stakeholders in confiscation procedures.

Areas for improvement

Defining the objective of the confiscation of the proceeds of crime

According to the legal definition of 'confiscation' contained in Article 2(4) of Directive 2014/42/EU, the term means the 'final deprivation of property ordered by a court in relation to a criminal offence'. Thus, the objective of this legal measure is not a definitional element. Moreover, throughout the entirety of Directive 2014/42/EU, there is no explicit explanation of the complexity of the objectives of confiscation. Instead, its Preamble is focused on highlighting just one aspect, i.e., the prevention of and combating organised crime:

> the effective prevention of and fight against organised crime should be achieved by neutralising the proceeds of crime and should be extended, in certain cases, to any property deriving from activities of a criminal nature (Recital 1). [...] Among the most effective means of combating organised crime is providing for severe legal consequences for committing such crime, as well as effective detection and the freezing and confiscation of the instrumentalities and proceeds of crime (Recital 3).

Nonetheless, in the context of this Preamble, one might level the criticism that Directive 2014/42/EU also applies to other offences not having an organised nature (see Article 3 and Article 5(2)).

As already indicated in Chapter 3, sufficient attention was not paid to the complexity of the objective of confiscation at the EU policy level, and this omission was 'inherited' by EU confiscation law. In connection with this, it is worth quoting an apt observation by Simonato (2015, 216):

> asset recovery, for the EU, is a multi-phase process relying on forfeiture laws, to be launched every time a criminal offence has generated a financial gain, whose primary objective is to deprive criminals of their illegally-obtained profit.

At the same time, Simonato's analysis suggested that recovered assets should be used for compensating victims of crime or social purposes. This aspect, as is well-known at the EU level, should be inherent in a comprehensive asset recovery strategy (Simonato 2015, 216). Many accurate observations in this regard were delivered, for example, by the Basel Institute of Governance in their study requested by the LIBE.[1]

From a different perspective, one can defensibly claim that a statement of purpose is not an essential element of the definition of a legal measure. Indeed, this is so, but as the EU harmonising instrument is a central pillar of the Union's legal system regarding confiscation issues, this instrument should be completely clear about the objective of the measures provided therein. In addition, the opinions delivered in this respect by various actors in legislative processes, as well as scholars, should not be ignored, especially in areas where they speak with one voice. Therefore, some indications regarding the complexity of the objective of confiscation, for example, in the Preamble, would be advisable to influence and guide domestic legal orders in the right direction. Appropriate prominence when indicating the objective of confiscation is even more justified in view of its 'autonomous' concept in EU law (see Chapter 1). It should be emphasised that the same problems discussed above reoccur in the new Directive 2024/1260, to be transposed by MS by 23 November 2026 (see Recitals 2, 3, and 21 of the Preamble; Article 3(6) contains the same legal definition of 'confiscation').

When defining the objective of confiscation, its 'double constructiveness' should be considered the most important characteristic. This implies a departure from exploiting only the aspects focused on its potential capacity to prevent and combat organised crime. For instance, some pertinent insights from the EP Resolution of 25 October 2011 on organised crime in the EU can serve as a starting point for properly identifying the objective of confiscation in EU law.[2] According to this Resolution, confiscation should no longer be regarded 'solely as a means of depriving a criminal organisation of resources', because confiscation is 'doubly constructive' in preventing organised crime and 'boosting economic and social development' (D). The latter aspect is also strongly connected with the social reuse of confiscated assets. The Resolution in question sees the reuse of confiscated assets for social purposes as an action that 'fosters a positive attitude to strategies aimed at tackling organised crime' (D). The EP's position corresponds with a restorative approach to justice, which implies objectives of confiscation such as restoring the *status quo ante* (before a crime) and repairing the harm caused by a crime, while still giving due regard to the effectiveness of taking illicit assets out of circulation and making illegal enrichment impossible.

Prioritising the position of the victim of crime

The narrative adopted at the EU policy level stresses the importance of strengthening the rights of victims to compensation and restitution. This direction is in line with the Treaty of Lisbon giving special attention to the rights of victims of crime (Article 82(2) TFEU). The first-ever EU Strategy on victims' rights (2020–2025) sees the potential to better use EU confiscation mechanism for this purpose, i.e., by improving victims' rights in Directive 2014/42/EU and Regulation 2018/1805.[3] Such a course of action was also indicated in Milquet's Report (2019) preceding the adoption of this Strategy.[4] However, despite some progress made in this respect by adopting new Directive 2024/1260, there are still some areas for improvement.

First of all, to make the EU confiscation scheme more restorative, the position of the victim of crime and the State should be rethought. Contrary to the officially declared policy objectives and the soft law recommendations formulated in this respect, it is still formally in line with hard EU law to cumulate the various roles in the State: the organiser of the confiscation mechanism, the sole decision-maker regarding transfers of confiscated assets, the main beneficiary of confiscated assets, and the sole supervisor of the entire national confiscation mechanism. Bearing in mind that confiscation is a 'doubly constructive' legal measure, the social aspect should have equal importance to its potential capacity to prevent and combat crime. Adopting a restorative approach to justice implies prioritisation of the victim's claims for compensation and restitution over the interest of the State in confiscated assets. Accordingly, victims (including affected communities) should replace the State at the centre of the EU confiscation scheme.

To this end, EU law should also ensure that the voice of victims is heard not only in main criminal proceedings but also in confiscation proceedings, to determine their claims to compensation and restitution and consider the possibilities to respond to them within the confiscation mechanism (e.g., by the use of confiscated assets) with the active participation of the persons subjected to confiscation measures. However, here we come to the question of who exactly should be heard in this respect – in other words, who should be recognised as a victim of crime in the confiscation mechanism? Once again, the objective of confiscation is crucial to answering this question. Considering confiscation as a mechanism serving primarily to help victims and populations, and in the light of the definition of a crime being a 'wrong against society' and a 'violation of the individual rights of victims' (Recital 9 of the Preamble to Directive 2012/29/EU), a broad definition of victim would be recommended, one which encompasses various collective victims, including communities.

Recent developments in EU law have only partly acknowledged the status of collective victims, with Directive 2024/1260 recognising legal persons as victims of crime (Article 3(8)). In addition, for the purpose of Regulation 2018/1805, the notion of 'victim' is rooted in national law with the extension to legal persons (Recital 45). As already indicated in Chapter 3, the definition of victim in Directive 2012/29/EU, the principal EU instrument establishing the standards for their rights, is narrowed to a 'natural person who has suffered harm, including physical, mental or emotional harm or economic loss which was directly caused by a criminal offence', and 'family members of a person whose death was directly caused by a criminal offence and who have suffered harm as a result of that person's death' (Article 2(1) of Directive 2012/29/EU). This state of affairs affects EU confiscation law wherever it relates to victims' rights, therefore the definition of victim has been slightly extended for the purposes of Regulation 2018/1805 and Directive 2024/1260 (Article 3(8)). However, on the occasion of the announced revision of Directive 2012/29/EU, the comprehensive definition of 'victim' should also be addressed by EU legislators.[5] It should be noted that the relevant Proposal submitted by the Commission in 2023 omits the issue of redefining the term 'victim'.[6] The 2020 Commission Report on the implementation of Directive 2012/29/EU indicated several areas for improvement, but the need to rethink the definition of 'victim', a term of relevance to the entire EU legal system, was not considered therein.[7]

If one of the current policy objectives is to facilitate the access of victims to compensation, the procedures should not put victims seeking compensation at risk of secondary victimisation, which may arise from the complexity of procedures, their differentiations or the need to follow a double track (criminal and civil) in respect of claims resulting from a single offence. For instance, the 2022 Evaluation of Directive 2012/29/EU,[8] and the external study to support the evaluation, indicated insufficient awareness of victims about their rights.[9] In the context of secondary victimisation through procedural difficulties, it is worth referring to the CJEU's position in *Gambino and Hyka*, C-38/18, 29 July 2019, EU:C:2019:628. The CJEU ruled:

> the competent national authorities must, under Article 22 of Directive 2012/29, conduct an individual assessment of that victim to identify his specific protection needs and, where appropriate, to afford him the protection measures provided for in Articles 23 and 24 of that directive (57). The

> referring court must therefore ensure that the victim in the main proceedings has no specific protection needs during the criminal proceedings (58).

In view of the above ruling, procedural hurdles should also be eliminated at the practice level, i.e., the competent national authority should ensure that a concrete victim has no specific protection needs when realising their claims to compensation (including restitutions) resulting from a criminal offence within the relevant confiscation proceedings. First of all, however, procedural hurdles should be eliminated at the normative level. Providing the identified victim with comprehensible instructions about their right to compensation (including restitutions) and the relevant procedures within the confiscation mechanism seems a crucial step. Currently, there are no mandatory rules regarding informing the victims of crime about the possibility of executing their right to compensation within confiscation proceedings, i.e., directly from confiscated assets (see Article 8(10) of Directive 2014/42/EU; Article 4(1)(e) of Directive 2012/29/EU). Similarly, Directive 2024/1260 does not require MS to ensure the right of victims to be informed about the possibility of exercising their right to compensation directly from confiscated assets. Further, the new rules in this respect may not be entirely clear for the national legislatures. Article 18(1) of Directive 2024/1260 states that victims' claims against the person who is subject to a confiscation measure 'are taken into account within the relevant asset-tracing, freezing and confiscation proceeding'. In addition, Article 18(5) of that Directive states that the 'execution of confiscation measures provided for under this Directive does not prejudice victims' rights to obtain compensation'. However, there is still no explicit statement that victims' claims can be satisfied directly from the confiscated assets.

Notably, the Explanatory Memorandum of the Proposal for a Directive amending Directive 2012/29/EU establishing minimum standards on victims' rights (2023) does not explore the possibilities of linking compensation schemes with confiscation schemes to benefit the position of victims.[10] Synergies in this regard are to some extent already recognised in various international instruments; however, they touch on different confiscation-related issues, and there is no coherent approach to link these two schemes. This issue is addressed, i.a., in Article 57 of the UNCAC (alongside the concept of 'victim countries'). In addition, Article 14(2) of the Palermo Convention reads:

> States Parties shall, to the extent permitted by domestic law and if so requested, give priority consideration to returning the confiscated proceeds of crime or property to the requesting State Party so that it can give compensation to the victims of the crime or return such proceeds of crime or property to their legitimate owners.

Relevant solutions are also provided for in Article 25(2) of the Warsaw Convention. Furthermore, Resolution 2218 (2018) of the CoE Parliamentary Assembly states:[11]

> Confiscation of illegal assets has multiple benefits: it makes crime less financially rewarding, saps the power criminals derive from their wealth, deprives them of 'seed money' needed for future crimes and generates resources to

> compensate victims and rebuild communities damaged by criminal activities (2).

In this context, it is also worth mentioning the study 'Confiscation of instrumentalities and proceeds of corruption crimes in Eastern Europe and Central Asia', prepared within the framework of the Anti-Corruption Network for Eastern Europe and Central Asia of the OECD.[12] This study indicates:

> At the very least, confiscation of the proceeds of corruption pursues the following purposes: 1. Preventive: deprival of corrupt officials of the gains obtained by criminal means not only prevents them from committing new offences, but also serves as a deterrent for other individuals prone to similar wrongdoing. 2. Reparative/recovery: compensation of damages and restoration of other rights and interests of victims of corruption offences. In some countries, confiscation continues to perform a punitive function, as not only instruments, means used to commit and proceeds derived from corruption offence are subjected to confiscation, but essentially all assets of the convicted person, including those obtained on lawful grounds and from legitimate sources (7).

According to the Explanatory Memorandum of the Proposal for a Directive amending Directive 2012/29/EU (2023):[13]

> in relation to right to receive a decision on compensation from the offender, too large margin of manoeuvre is left to the Member States. These have been damaging for the practical application of victims' rights. These problems hamper victims' ability to rely on their rights under the Directive and undermine the trust in national justice schemes and those in other Member States (2).

However, this Proposal does not clearly acknowledge, in a manner readable by the national legislatures, that the victims of crime have a right to obtain compensation directly from confiscated assets. According to its Preamble:

> All victims should be able to obtain a decision on compensation from the offender within the criminal proceedings to avoid their engagement in multiple cumbersome and lengthy proceedings in separate civil proceedings. All victims should benefit from the schemes on compensation in which, following a decision on compensation from the offender at the end of the criminal proceeding, they receive, without a delay, the compensation from the state. The state afterwards should be able to recuperate the compensation from the offender (Recital 12).

At the same time, this should not affect State compensation systems for victims of violent intentional crimes established under Council Directive 2004/80/EC (Recital 12 of the Proposal, see also Article 10b(2)(2)).[14] In this context, the high differentiation of national compensation schemes (sourced from the State and the offender), including the variety of procedures relevant in domestic and cross-border cases, must also be taken into account. Council Directive 2004/80/EC, which concerns cross-border compensation from the State, has not been amended since its adoption in 2004. It is worth mentioning here that the study 'Criminal procedural laws across the European Union – A comparative analysis of selected main differences and the impact they have over the development of EU legislation' (Sellier and Weyembergh 2018) pointed out the differentiation of national compensation schemes, the need of their approximation, and the need for revision of Directive 2004/80/EC (144).

It should be remembered that Article 29(1) of Regulation 2018/1805 pertains to a decision on restitution of 'frozen property' to the victim, issued by the competent authority in accordance with its national law. Similarly, Article 30(1) of Regulation 2018/1805 pertains to a decision on restitution of 'confiscated property' to the victim or to compensate the victim, issued by the competent authority in accordance with its national law. The issues of compensation from the offender and the right of victims to the return of property fall under Directive 2012/29/EU, and these areas are left to the MS. Thus, decisions on compensation, including restitution, are rooted in national laws, which vary significantly between MS. Rooting compensation decisions in national laws (executed within the mutual recognition mechanism established by Regulation 2018/1805) was acknowledged in Eurojust's Note (2020), which indicated: '[u]nder the Regulation, property claims must be demanded in the issuing State', and '[i]f there is a decision to restitute frozen property to the victim, the issuing authority must inform the executing authority' (4).[15] However, the wide differentiation of national laws in this respect can have a negative effect on cross-border cooperation actions aimed at satisfying victims' claims directly from confiscated or frozen assets.

Some difficulties result from the legal definition of 'freezing order'. Currently, EU law provides for the definition of 'freezing' in the harmonising instrument and the definition of 'freezing order' in the mutual recognition instrument. The first definition is contained in Directive 2014/42/EU:

> 'freezing' means the temporary prohibition of the transfer, destruction, conversion, disposal or movement of property or temporarily assuming custody or control of property.
>
> (Article 2(5) of Directive 2014/42/EU; Directive 2014/1260 provides for the same definition of 'freezing' in Article 3(5))

The second definition is contained in the mutual recognition instrument:

> 'freezing order' means a decision issued or validated by an issuing authority in order to prevent the destruction, transformation, removal, transfer or disposal of property with a view to the confiscation thereof.
>
> (Article 2(1) of Regulation 2018/1805)

The definition of a 'freezing order' narrows the purpose of freezing to confiscation, and therefore there is a valid concern that freezing orders issued to secure a victim's claims to compensation or restitution do not formally fall under the mutual recognition mechanism established in Regulation 2018/1805. This legal uncertainty can cause difficulties for victims seeking compensation (in a broad sense) in cross-border proceedings, especially when national legislations approach the compensation scheme separately from the confiscation scheme. Although Regulation 2018/1805 contains provisions aimed at prioritising victims' right to compensation over the interests of States (Recital 45 of the Preamble, Article 26(2), Article 29, Article 30), a 'freezing order' when issued purely with the view of providing compensation to a victim and without any link to a confiscation may in fact not be executed in another Member State, because such an order, at least under the formal designation, falls outside the scope of the legal definition of 'freezing order' contained in Article 2(1) of Regulation 2018/1805. Of course, bearing in mind the spirit of that Regulation, the issuing authority and the executing authority should reach an agreement on the execution of such a freezing order, for example, based on the information provided in the freezing certificate or communicated at a later stage (see Article 29(1)) pertaining to frozen property, and Article 30(1) pertaining to confiscated property). However, such proceedings can cause unnecessary delays in the mutual recognition mechanism, and thus, in obtaining compensation or restitution. Such challenges may certainly occur, especially when a Member State's national law does not include victims' rights to compensation in the confiscation mechanism. In this configuration, a freezing order issued purely to satisfy victims' claims may not benefit (in domestic cases) from the substantive and procedural facilitations attributed specifically to confiscation proceedings. In addition, it can be at risk of non-execution by the executing State (in cross-border cases).

In view of the above points, it would improve the position of victims, in cases both purely domestic and cross-border, to promote further approximation of national legislation towards ensuring the possibility of executing decisions on compensation and restitution directly from assets captured within the confiscation mechanism, as well as freezing orders securing victims' claims.

However, the overall intention of the EU lawmaker, as expressed in Recital 45 of the Preamble to Regulation 2018/1805, was to give the rights of victims to compensation and restitution their rightful priority within the confiscation mechanism. Accordingly, the current legal *status quo* is that EU law better secures the rights of victims in cross-border cases than in domestic cases. First of all, the wording in Regulation 2018/1805 is more precise than Directive 2024/1260, by stating that '[r]ules for the disposal of frozen or confiscated property should give priority to the compensation of, and restitution of property to, victims' (Recital 45 of the Preamble to Regulation 2018/1805). In the case of multiple orders in respect of the same specific item of property, the 'executing authority shall give priority to the interests of victims where possible' (Article 26 (2)). Further, Article 29(1) specifically refers to the decision 'to restitute frozen property to the victim', and Article 30(1) refers to the decision 'to restitute confiscated property to the victim or to compensate the victim'. It should also be noted that the provisions on collection of statistics by the MS give due attention to the 'number of cases in which a victim was compensated or granted restitution of the property obtained by the execution of a confiscation order' under Regulation 2018/1805 (Article 35(2)(a)).

The crucial benefit for victims of embedding their rights to compensation directly in the confiscation mechanism consists of the substantive and procedural facilitations applied specifically in confiscation proceedings in order to capture criminal assets. Such facilitations concern i.a. determining the criminal origin of assets with the use of a lessened standard of proof, the possibilities to extend the scope of confiscation or address the confiscation order to a third party, and the possibility to identify criminal assets with the help of AROs and their counterparts. The main beneficiary of procedural simplifications is the State, as assets captured with the use of modern confiscation procedures mainly flow into State coffers, as legal solutions enabling attributing assets to non-State actors are not yet equally well-developed across the EU. However, growing attention is being drawn to reusing confiscated assets for non-State purposes. For example, advanced mechanisms in this respect have been introduced by France (the *Agence de gestion et de recouvrement des avoirs saisis et confisqués* – AGRASC) and Italy (the *Agenzia nazionale per l'amministrazione e la destinazione dei beni sequestrati e confiscati alla criminalità organizzata* – ANBSC). Practices in this respect are also being developed by other EU jurisdictions, i.a., Spain, the Netherlands, Belgium, Bulgaria, Hungary, Luxembourg, and Romania (see Vettori and Di Nicola 2017; Baruzzo et al 2021).

Furthermore, some deficiencies may be identified at an early stage of the asset recovery process, starting with the identification of assets and their capturing. The European Investigation Order (EIO) mechanism only applies to freezing orders issued for the purpose of evidence gathering, and does not involve freezing orders issued for the purpose of compensation or restitution, nor freezing orders issued for the purpose of subsequent confiscation. This state of affairs may cause some confusion in cross-border cases at the early stage of securing assets for non-evidence-gathering purposes, as evidenced in the practice of the European Judicial Network (EJN) and Eurojust. For instance, recourse has been made to Article 8 of the Convention on Mutual Assistance in Criminal Matters between the MS of the EU (2000), OJ C 197/3, dealing with mutual assistance in cases concerning restitution (Ochnio 2021).[16]

'Great absentees' – the missing standards for fair redistribution of confiscated assets

The issue of the missing standards for fair redistribution of confiscated assets is closely connected with securing the rights of victims within the confiscation mechanism. First of all, it should be reiterated that EU law does not directly create the victims' rights, and thus, decisions on compensation and restitution must be rooted in national legislation (see Articles 29(1) and 30(1) of Regulation 2018/1805), which is still not harmonised to a satisfactory level. Secondly, rules on the disposal of confiscated assets are absent in the harmonising instruments (see Article 10 of Directive 2014/42/EU; Article 19 of Directive 2024/1260). EU law is also silent on such important issues as the minimum portion of assets that should be reused for public interest and social purposes. It also lacks minimum rules requiring MS to ensure that at least part of that portion of assets attributed to non-State purposes is realised in the form of direct transfers. Moreover, it does not contain harmonising rules on the indirect transfer of assets for non-State purposes, for instance, through specialised aid/competition funds (see also Recital 48 of Regulation 2018/1805). Lastly, it does not require MS to ensure that statistics are publicly available and that the overall mechanism of disposal of confiscated assets is transparent and subject to social control. In the context of these shortcomings, it is worth recalling the Opinion of the EESC on the Proposal for a directive of the EP and of the Council on asset recovery and confiscation (COM(2022) 245 – final), as it provides many pertinent insights on how such mechanisms should be designed (see more in Chapter 2).[17]

There are dual consequences from the assumption that at least a part of confiscated assets should be returned to the populations. First, at the phase of disposal of confiscated assets, the non-State actors considered as potential beneficiaries of asset transfers and their representatives should have the possibility to present (directly or indirectly) their needs and problems resulting from a crime (understood as a 'wrong against society' and a 'violation of the individual rights of victims', Recital 9 of the Preamble to Directive 2012/29/EU), and, if relevant, their capacities to restore the status prior to the crime in a given environment (e.g., local communities, NGOs, etc.). Secondly, the subjected persons should have the procedural possibility to know the stand taken by social actors (the purpose of their intervention) and respond (directly or indirectly, e.g., in written form). However, the possibility to respond should also be seen in a broader perspective, as a possibility to repair the 'conscious harm' done by a crime. Such shaping of the confiscation procedure creates the possibility of closing a 'confiscation case' on a fast track and seems to be an interesting proposition for all the stakeholders, not excluding the State.

Furthermore, as far as the disposal of confiscated assets is concerned, EU law secures the rights of victims to a greater extent in cross-border cases than domestic cases. Even if the new Directive 2024/1260 places more emphasis on strengthening the position of victims in the confiscation mechanism (see subsection above), Regulation 2018/1805 contains more detailed rules in this respect. Its Preamble explicitly prioritises victims' rights to compensation and restitution in cross-border cases (Recital 45). However, in another aspect, the same Preamble raises some doubts over whether the rules encouraging MS to establish a national fund with the purpose of guaranteeing appropriate compensation for special types of victims ('families of police officers and public servants killed or permanently disabled in the line of duty', Recital 48) should be placed in the mutual recognition or harmonising instrument. It appears that this issue should be comprehensively regulated in the main EU harmonising instrument laying down the standards on the rights, support, and protection of victims of crime, i.e., Directive 2012/29/EU, as it is relevant to interpreting all EU legislation wherever it pertains to victims and their rights.

Regulation 2018/1805 provides for the rules on direct or indirect (*via* the issuing State) transfers of assets to the victims for the purpose of compensation or restitution (Article 30(2)(3)(4)). In addition, it contains the rules on refraining from disposing of confiscated assets if proceedings to restitute property to, or compensate, the victim are pending in the issuing State (Article 30(5)). Without prejudice to victims' rights the 'property may be disposed of in various forms, including its use for public interest or social purposes in the executing State in accordance with its law', however, 'subject to the consent of the issuing State' (Article 30(6)(d)). Victims' rights also have priority in asset sharing between the executing State and the issuing State (Article 30(7)).

Lastly, despite some progress in addressing the rights of third countries to confiscated assets (see Article 19(2) of Directive 2024/1260), this area is still a challenge ahead for the EU, especially from the perspective of the UNCAC. Article 51 of the UNCAC reads:

> The return of assets pursuant to this chapter [Chapter V — Asset recovery] is a fundamental principle of this Convention, and States Parties shall afford one another the widest measure of cooperation and assistance in this regard.

Accordingly, future discussions on confiscation-related issues should cover the question of the EU's capacity, as a non-State Party to the UNCAC, to contribute to the protection of the interests of third countries in confiscated assets, touched i.a. by corruption or war crimes (see, e.g., Ivory 2017; Pavlidis 2018; Ochnio 2024). Efforts should be made towards establishing common rules on transnational cooperation on asset recovery between the MS and third countries, in accordance with the provisions of the UNCAC (Articles 51 and 57; see also Betti, Kozin, and Brun 2022). The transnational return of assets placed within the EU should be based on a consistent approach followed by all the EU MS. Establishing common rules in this respect would facilitate concluding bilateral and multilateral agreements and arrangements (Article 59 of the UNCAC). It should be noted that the importance of returning illicit assets to the country of origin 'to foster sustainable development and the full realisation of human rights' was recognised in UN Human Rights Council Resolution 19/38 (2012).[18] This issue was also addressed i.a. in the EP Resolution of 23 May 2013 on asset recovery by Arab Spring countries in transition (2013/ 2612(RSP)).[19]

Human rights protections, or something more?

When adopting a minimalist restorative approach, the criteria for assessing the EU regulatory framework for confiscation go further than necessary human rights protections, as set out in the ECHR, the EU Charter, and complemented by the dialoguing courts – the ECtHR and the CJEU. Aside from ensuring the necessary human rights protections, such an approach implies more inclusive, consultative, sustainable and just confiscation procedures. Thus, it encourages the search for more innovative legal solutions aimed at the inclusion of various groups of stakeholders in confiscation procedures to better address and balance their interests with their active participation. Looking at a broader perspective, developing confiscation procedures towards a restorative direction may be relevant for strengthening the resistance of stakeholders to crime, and thus, boosting the potential effect of confiscation most appreciated by the legislatures, and at the same time widely discussed in the doctrine, the prevention of and combating of crime.

One of the vital questions here is how to ensure participation in confiscation mechanisms, not only by victims (in a broad sense) having legitimate claims resulting from a crime but also by persons subjected to confiscation measures (suspects or accused persons, and third parties). So far, the guarantees attributed by EU law to the latter group of stakeholders are more aimed at challenging confiscation orders and freezing orders, of course, with due account for human rights protections. However, while many elements that constitute the right of defence can be inferred from the general guarantees of a fair trial remaining applicable in confiscation procedures, difficulty arises when going beyond this level of protection, i.e., when seeking appropriate legal solutions to ensure the 'proactive' procedural participation of stakeholders in a 'confiscation case'. 'Proactive' procedural participation here means voluntary (i.e., not requiring resort to coercion), constructive, and responsible participation that contributes to the just resolution of confiscation case through realising the harm done by a crime in individual and societal dimensions.[20]

The procedural isolation of this group of stakeholders (offenders and other subjected persons) from the dialogue on key confiscation issues, as identified in the EU confiscation scheme (a state which may be reproduced in national confiscation schemes under the influence of EU law), could translate into a lack of possibility for these stakeholders to influence the 'substance' of confiscation-related decisions and limited responsibility for actions aimed at restoring the *status quo ante* (before a crime) and repairing harm with the use of assets captured within the confiscation mechanism. This state of affairs may also translate into misunderstanding and non-acceptance of confiscation-related decisions. While the positive contributions of this group of stakeholders should not be discarded *a priori* by legislatures, conversely, the lack of inclusion of the interests of this group of stakeholders in confiscation procedures cannot be considered compatible with a minimalist restorative approach, which promotes inclusive and consultative procedures.

As indicated above, the current EU legal framework is focused on securing the rights of the affected persons to challenge a confiscation order or freezing order (Article 8(1)(4)(6) of Directive 2014/42/EU). At the level of national law, this protection should include, for example, the 'right of access to a lawyer throughout the confiscation proceedings' in order to uphold their rights. However, the minimum rules in this respect explicitly pertain only to proceedings regarding the 'determination of the proceeds and instrumentalities' (Article 8(7) of Directive 2014/42/EU). In addition, in the case of extended confiscation, national law should afford the affected persons the right to 'challenge the circumstances of the case, including specific facts and available evidence' on the basis of which the court forms its view on the criminal origin of the property (Article 8(8) in connection with Article 5 of Directive 2014/42/EU; see also Article 24(5) of Directive 2024/1260). Third parties should be afforded the right to claim titles of ownership or other property rights (Article 8(9) in connection with Article 6 of Directive 2014/42/EU; see also Article 24(7) of Directive 2024/1260).

As far as communication between public authorities and the affected persons is concerned, the minimum procedural standards consist of several components. Firstly, EU law requires MS to secure the right of the affected person to be informed about the freezing order, namely the freezing order must be 'communicated to the affected person as soon as possible after its execution', and '[s]uch communication shall indicate, at least briefly, the reason or reasons for the order concerned' (Article 8(2) of Directive 2014/42/EU). The competent authorities may only postpone communicating the freezing order to 'avoid jeopardising a criminal investigation' (Article 8(2) of Directive 2014/42/EU). Secondly, MS are required to 'ensure that reasons are given for any confiscation order and that the order is communicated to the person affected' (Article 8(6) of Directive 2014/42/EU). Moreover, Regulation 2018/1805 addresses the rights of the affected persons in cross-border cases (see Article 32 on the limited information obligations and Article 33 on the legal remedies).

Nonetheless, the issue of communication between public authorities, affected persons, and also victims has not been comprehensively addressed in the EU confiscation scheme due to the overlooking of the right of affected persons to know the grounds for claims by individual and collective victims. One may say that EU law does not place the proper emphasis on the knowledge of the persons subjected to confiscation measures about the needs and problems encountered by victims or communities in the aftermath of a crime to which confiscation proceedings are related. This observation is valid for both domestic and cross-border cases. Likewise, Directive 2014/42/EU, Directive 2024/1260, and Regulation 2018/1805 are silent about hearing from victims or the representatives of communities in this respect in confiscation proceedings (not only in the main criminal proceedings) or the possibilities for the subjected persons to know the position of these actors and deliver a response during such proceedings (by direct or indirect communication not exposing an avenue for secondary victimisation). Importantly, the possibility of such communication should be specifically ensured not only in the main criminal proceedings but also in confiscation proceedings, in order to properly use the captured assets to restore the status before the crime. Dialogue between the parties may contribute to finding a constructive resolution for the harm suffered (in a broad sense, encompassing material and non-material damage), as well as understanding and acceptance of confiscation decisions by their addressees. Such dialogues may also lead to repairing the harm done without having to resort to any kind of coercion in confiscation proceedings or completing such proceedings on a 'fast track'. In this context, it is worth remembering that EU law requires MS to 'promote measures to encourage offenders to provide adequate compensation to victims' (Article 16(2) of Directive 2012/29/EU).

A further consideration is that Directive 2014/42/EU does not address the participation of stakeholders, including subjected persons, when dealing with the possible transfers of confiscated assets to public interest and social purposes. There are very limited minimum rules concerning this phase of proceedings (see Article 10 of Directive 2014/42/EU and Article 19 of Directive 2024/1260). Even though Directive 2024/1260 contains some advances regarding the management of confiscated property (Articles 20 to 22), they cannot be considered sufficient to ensure the 'proactive' participation of affected persons, victims, and communities. Nevertheless, it should be recognised that the minimum rules on interlocutory sales do involve the right of the affected persons to be informed and heard (Article 21(2) and Recital 43 of the Preamble to Directive 2024/1260).

The most important point is that Directive 2024/1260, similar to Directive 2014/42/EU, is still focused on securing the rights of the affected persons to challenge decisions issued in the course of confiscation-related procedures (i.e., freezing orders, confiscation orders, and sales orders), in order to uphold their rights (Articles 23 and 24 of Directive 2024/1260). Some progress has been made as regards the scope of the right of defence, with the right of the affected persons to be heard 'on issues of law and fact and, where relevant, the right to interpretation and translation' being explicitly indicated in Article 24(2) of Directive 2024/1260. However, the emphasis is still placed on challenging decisions issued in confiscation proceedings, whereas when it comes to contributing to resolving a 'confiscation case', the essence of which seems to lie in repairing the 'conscious harm' done by a crime (to benefit all the stakeholders, including the offenders). EU law assigns the affected persons a rather 'reactive' role, not a 'proactive' one.

In sum, to improve the restorative aspect of conventional confiscation procedures, EU law should go further than just ensuring human rights protections, the latter should be seen as a fundamental requirement. Accordingly, the transition of the EU confiscation scheme to a higher level of development implies beginning to explore legal solutions enabling more 'proactive' participation of stakeholders in 'confiscation cases', including the affected persons.

Extended confiscation: mitigating procedural risk and excessive legislative reach

The FRA Opinion on the Confiscation of proceeds of crime (2012),[21] requested by the EP in the legislative procedure preceding the adoption of Directive 2014/42/EU, indicated that restricting extended confiscation to particularly serious crimes 'would exclude those crimes which *per se* are not particularly serious crimes', in respect of which the proportionality of extended confiscation could be questioned (14). Accordingly, it argued for adopting a 'more restricted approach' than that represented in Article 83(1) TFEU, which specifies 'areas of serious crime', but 'this does not imply that every single crime falling in these areas necessarily forms a particularly serious offence' (14). The concerns expressed in this regard are absolutely justified. It should be noted that the problem of the overly broad scope of triggering offences in the legal construct of extended confiscation concerns both Directive 2014/42/EU and Directive 2024/1260.

The key issue is the vague aim of such a broad legislative reach, which poses the question of whether extended confiscation really serves a 'legitimate aim' prescribed by law and meets the condition of 'necessity' required when interfering with the right to property (Article 1 of the first Protocol to the ECHR; Article 17 of the Charter). Failure to meet these criteria may amount to an inadmissible interference with the right to property, and thus, could expose public authorities to a risk of compensation liability for delivering decisions based on flawed rules on extended confiscation (influenced by EU law). The guarantees of the right to property, including the 'reasonable relationship' of proportionality between the means employed to achieve the 'legitimate aim' (i.e., necessary and provided by law, see ECtHR, *Sunday Times v the UK*, Application No 13166/87, 26 November 1991, paras 49, 50, and 55), determine the extent of legislative reach also in confiscation settings. This relationship has been regularly acknowledged in the jurisprudence of the ECtHR (see, e.g., *Raimondo v Italy*, Application No 12954/87, 22 February 1994, paras 30 and 39; *Phillips v the UK*, Application No 41087/98, 5 July 2001, paras 51 and 52; *Silickienė v Lithuania*, Application No 20496/02, 10 April 2012, para 50; *Paulet v the UK*, Application No 6219/08, 13 May 2014, paras 63–69; *Karapetyan v Georgia*, Application No 61233/12, paras 34, 37 and 40; *Imeri v Croatia*, Application No 77668/14, 24 June 2021, paras 82–85, and 93). This issue was also explored by the CJEU (see, e.g., *Plovdiv*, C-393/19, 14 January 2021, EU:C:2021:8, paras 53 and 55–58; *Adusbef and Federconsumatori*, C-686/18, 16 July 2020, EU:C:2020:567, para 85; *Ledra Advertising v Commission and ECB*, C-8/15 P, 20 September 2016, EU:C:2016:701, paras 69–70; *Bank Melli Iran v Council*, C-548/09 P, 16 November 2011, EU:C:2011:735, para 113; *Bank of Industry and Mine v Council*, C-358/15 P, 12 May 2016, EU:C:2016:338, para 55).

Bearing in mind the scope of offences indicated in Articles 3, 5(2), and 14(3) of Directive 2014/42/EU, as well as in Articles 2 and 16(4) of Directive 2024/1260, extended confiscation (and confiscation of unexplained wealth provided for in the latter Directive) can also be ordered in cases of offences of medium gravity. It should be noted that under FD 2005/2012/JHA, extended confiscation was linked with serious crime having the nature of organised or terrorist crime (Article 3). However, further harmonising instruments, i.e., Directive 2014/42/EU and Directive 2024/1260, severed that link but at the same time without providing a persuasive justification for this move. The explanatory memoranda presented in the legislative processes referred to the fight against serious crime, especially of an organised nature, whereas the draft legal provisions were not strictly related to such types of crime. In this way, EU law deprived extended confiscation of an attribute of extraordinariness, which should be a necessity for the specificity of extended confiscation (Ochnio 2019). Accordingly, under EU law, extended confiscation is not targeted at high-level offenders, and there are no boundaries preventing its use against first-time offenders without any ties to organised crime. This substantive change can negatively affect national legislation, and regrettably, this scenario has already occurred, as indicated in Chapter 5. An example of broad legislative reach can be found in German legislation, where since 2017, extended confiscation is no longer associated with the listed offences (see Section 73a of the German Criminal Code).

Here we come to the next vital question, whether such a normative framework is compatible with the criteria of 'proportionality' and 'necessity' required to make admissible interference with the right to property (in this context, see the ECtHR's case-law, e.g., *Sporrong and Lönnroth v. Sweden*, 23 September 1982, Application Nos 7151/75 and 7152/75, para 61; *Lithgow and Others v the UK*, Application Nos

9006/80; 9262/81; 9263/81; 9265/81; 9266/81; 9313/81; 9405/81, 8 July 1986, paras 106 and 120; *AGOSI v the UK*, Application No 9118/80, 24 October 1986, para 54; *Paulet v the UK*, Application No 6219/08, 13 May 2014, para 65).

Another question is whether EU law properly manages the procedural risk connected with a broad scope of triggering offences in the legal construct of these types of confiscation which do not require the high standard of proof applied in the criminal process when establishing a connection between the property and the offence. And finally, does the public interest plausibly substantiate such risky departures from the traditional route of legal appraisals, in favour of a civil standard of proof in non-heavyweight cases and without links with organised crime? Indeed, the public interest in recourse to the civil standard of proof is clearest in cases concerning organised crime, as this type of crime poses the greatest difficulty in proving the real origin of the resources, through the use of fictitious entities, dependencies or transactions. However, this interest becomes doubtful when such recourse is made in cases of offences of medium or even minor gravity.

The question of whether the public interest reasonably justifies resorting to extended confiscation is all the more important when referring to the ECtHR's position in *Phillips v the UK* (Application No 41087/98, 5 July 2001, para 22), concerning a confiscation ordered under the civil standard of proof (balance of probabilities) on the basis of the Drug Trafficking Act (1994). One can say that the ECtHR perceived this legal measure as closer to a 'procedural device', the latter term was used by Cassella (2015, 14) as regards 'civil forfeiture'. In *Phillips*, the ECtHR held:

> the purpose of this procedure was not the conviction or acquittal of the applicant for any other drug-related offence. […] Instead, the purpose of the procedure under the 1994 Act was **to enable the national court to assess the amount at which the confiscation order should properly be fixed** [bolded by A.H.O.]. The Court considers that this procedure was analogous to the determination by a court of the amount of a fine or the length of a period of imprisonment to be imposed on a properly convicted offender. This, indeed, was the conclusion which it reached in *Welch* […] when, having examined the reality of the situation, it decided that a confiscation order constituted a 'penalty' within the meaning of Article 7.
>
> (*Phillips v the UK*, para 34; see also *Geering v the Netherlands*, Application No 30810/03, 1 March 2007, para 43)

Importantly, the ECtHR observed in *Phillips* that despite the mandatory assumption applied by the sentencing court in assessing the extent the applicant 'had benefited from the proceeds of drug trafficking, the system was not without safeguards' (para 43). Apart from traditional procedural guarantees, there were two crucial elements. Firstly, the assumption 'could have been rebutted if the applicant had shown, again on the balance of probabilities, that he had acquired the property other than through drug trafficking'. Secondly, the 'judge had a discretion not to apply the assumption if he considered that applying it would give rise to a serious risk of injustice' (para 43).

When comparing these two safeguards identified by the ECtHR in *Phillips* to the legal construct of extended confiscation in EU law, two shortcomings can be identified.

The first issue is that EU law does not secure the same standard when rebutting an assumption as to the extent of assets covered by a confiscation order (balance of probabilities). The safeguard of a 'mirror standard' for public authorities and subjected persons would make their positions equal in proceedings concerning extended confiscation. The current *status quo* is that the possibility of using the 'civil standard' of proof is explicitly assigned to the court (Recital 21 and Article 5 of Directive 2014/42/EU; Recital 29 and Article 14 of Directive 2024/1260). Accordingly, EU law is silent about the standard of proof under which the subjected person may rebut the court's assumption. The question which arises is which standard should apply to the subjected persons' attempts to rebut the court's assumption. Must they prove that it is more probable that the assets in question have a licit origin, or do they have to prove a licit origin beyond reasonable doubt? It appears that under a well-balanced procedure, a single standard of proof should apply to the same legal measure for both the public authorities and the defendants. Such an approach should be acknowledged and secured in EU law. There is no need for further justification beyond that the position of the State, being the stronger actor, should not be further privileged by burdening the subjected person with a more demanding standard of proof.

The second issue is that EU law does not properly manage the procedural risk inherent in extended confiscation settings. As indicated by the ECtHR in *Phillips*, despite the mandatory assumption applied when determining the extent of assets to be covered by a confiscation order, the court had an open route to challenge the application of that assumption, by resorting to the clause of 'serious risk of injustice'. It should be pointed out that EU confiscation law does not provide a similar 'brake' which would enable a court to mitigate the procedural risk of an erroneous determination of the scope of confiscation in any specific case.

One can say that the necessary discretion of the court has not been properly secured in the EU standards for extended confiscation, which allow for a mandatory assumption about the illicit origin of assets. It should be noted that these comments are also valid as regards the new Directive 2024/1260, which only provides for the possibility for a court to suspend the execution of an order for an interlocutory sale, e.g., 'where necessary to safeguard the legitimate interests of the affected person, in particular where there is a risk of irreparable harm' (Recital 43, Article 24(6)). Nonetheless, Directive 2024/1260 leaves it up to the MS to regulate the important issue of appropriate procedures for challenging the scope of confiscation orders and freezing orders. There are no requirements regarding applying 'mirror' standards of proof for the State and the subjected person in national procedures, and no procedural brakes (e.g., the clause of 'serious risk of injustice') securing against excessive scope of extended confiscation orders (see Article 24(3) and (5) of Directive 2024/1260). Whereas a general reference to the right to an 'effective remedy and a fair trial' (Article 24(1) of Directive 2024/1260) cannot be regarded as sufficient safeguard for the rights of affected persons in extended confiscation proceedings, even though these formally belong to the framework of proceedings in criminal matters, as approached in Article 1 of Directive 2024/1260 (without entering here into the legal nature of concrete types of confiscation). Therefore, one can conclude that the EU standards regarding extended confiscation do not secure the necessary discretion of the court to enable the departure from applying mandatory assumptions about the origin of assets in case of a 'serious risk of injustice' identified in a specific case.

In connection with this, it is also worth recalling the observation of Boucht (2019), who captured an important feature of 'extended appropriation' in confiscation settings consisting of a 'risk of wrongful confiscation decisions' covering licit property (233). Boucht made a valid point in this respect:

> A certain risk in this respect will always be inherent in extended appropriation proceedings. However, it is important to consider what kind of risk may be acceptable within a liberal criminal law, and to consider adequate mechanism by which a more far-reaching risk may be compensated.
>
> (Boucht 2019, 233)

The next issue which is worth attention is the retroactive effect of extended confiscation, which is possible under EU law. According to the Preamble to Directive 2014/42/EU, MS could 'determine a requirement for a certain period of time during which the property could be deemed to have originated from criminal conduct' (Recital 21). A similar solution is provided for in Directive 2024/1260 (Recital 29). Moreover, the possible retroactive effect also concerns 'confiscation of unexplained wealth', as MS 'can also determine a requirement for a certain period of time during which the property could be deemed to have originated from such criminal conduct' (Recital 33 of the Preamble to Directive 2024/1260). It should be recognised that the Preamble to the latter Directive contains some general indications limiting the use of 'confiscation of unexplained wealth orders'. National authorities can depart from ordering or executing this special type of confiscation where the 'application of the rules set out in this Directive would be manifestly unreasonable or disproportionate' in a concrete case (Recital 33). In addition, MS should ensure the appropriate protection of the procedural rights of the affected person and the rights of *bona fide* third parties (Recital 33).

Nonetheless, EU law does not set reasonable boundaries for public authorities when retrospectively determining assets to be subject to a confiscation order. Bearing in mind that we are dealing with the minimum standards, it would be desirable for EU law to propose some limits for the possible retroactive effect of extended confiscation, for instance by referring to the statutory retention periods in national law for business, tax, and banking documentation. Otherwise, such retroactive reach can be excessive and thus makes exercising the right of defence unrealistic (contrary to the standard of a fair trial). Another aspect is that a wide range of solutions have been adopted across national legal orders in this respect, as national legislatures are free to determine the period of time during which property can be deemed to have criminal origins. Thus, bearing in mind that this aspect determines the scope of confiscation, the position of defendants in confiscation proceedings across the EU cannot be considered sufficiently equal.

For instance, one of the solutions adopted by MS enables public authorities to search assets acquired or taken in possession by the subjected person at a time prior to the commission of a prohibited act. The second solution makes reference to the time prior to the initiation of the criminal proceedings related to such a prohibited act. The difference between these approaches is of great importance for the right of defence. The former solution carries the risk of establishing an erroneous scope for extended confiscation, since criminal proceedings relevant to the prohibited act may be instituted a great many years later, i.e., when the subjected person has very little chance to demonstrate proof to the contrary to rebut the public authority's assumption about the criminal origin of the assets. Another solution is limiting the retrospectivity of confiscation by the statute of limitation applied to confiscation measures. In view of the above, EU law should balance such risk by limiting the scope of retroactive reach when national legislatures shape extended confiscation mechanisms. This risk should be seen together with the separation of the use of extended confiscation from the most serious and organised crime. Though EU policy still maintains a narrative focused on using this type of confiscation to prevent and combat serious and organised crime, this linkage was in fact severed in Directive 2014/42/EU, and Directive 2024/1260 pursues this high-risk direction.

Furthermore, when dealing with the minimum EU confiscation standards, the national legislatures can also realise the objectives of their internal criminal policies, i.e., resolving local problems with crime not having a serious, organised, or cross-border dimension, under the slogan of implementing EU law. In other words, the use of those standards may become 'instrumental' in domestic criminal policies. For example, the use of practices of 'cherry picking' when under-implementing EU law or 'gold-plating' when over-implementing it (on these practices, in different contexts, see, e.g., Král 2021; Ouwerkerk 2017) can negatively affect extended confiscation mechanisms by jeopardising fundamental rights, since the risk of judicial error is an inherent element of this type of confiscation. This is the next argument in favour of the EU having a regulatory framework involving tools for mitigating various risks connected with extended confiscation settings, including the risk of legislative overreach by national legislatures when implementing EU law.

Lastly, EU standards are silent about the consequences of the method of calculation of assets to be applied in confiscation settings for the appropriate choice of criminal or civil routes by national legislatures. Whereas basing extended confiscation on the 'gross' (profit) principle or the 'net' principle may be critical in determining its legal nature, i.e., whether it amounts to a criminal penalty (because of the surplus element of 'hardship') for which the standards of criminal procedure should apply, or whether its function is intended to restoring the previous financial conditions (the status before a crime, see more Vogel 2015) justifying the use of civil route. Accordingly, bearing in mind that the 'gross' principle is widely applied in EU and non-EU jurisdictions, EU law should clarify to national legislatures that the method of calculation of the 'gross profit' in extended confiscation settings may have critical consequences for the choice of the appropriate procedure for its ordering. In this context, it is worth recalling the view presented in *R v May* (2008) UKHL 28 (House of Lords), as an example of one possible legal meaning of confiscation, relating to the 'total value of the property or advantage obtained':

> The legislation is intended to deprive defendants of the benefit they have gained from relevant criminal conduct, whether or not they have retained such benefit, within the limits of their available means. It does not provide for confiscation in the sense understood by schoolchildren and others, but nor does it operate by way of fine. The benefit gained is the total value of the property or advantage obtained, not the defendant's net profit after deduction of expenses or any amounts payable to co-conspirators.
>
> (*R v May* 2008, 48(1))

Bearing in mind the various positions on the judicial nature of confiscation which have been expressed by scholars in the context of the traditional civil/criminal division (see Chapter 2), this book argues for connecting the method of calculation of assets which are subject to the CPC with the appropriate legislative choice of criminal or non-criminal procedures and standard of proof (see also Vogel 2015). Such an approach secures the right to a fair trial when a criminal penalty is at stake, mitigates the risk of judicial errors, and gives national legislatures clear and simple guidance on how to choose the appropriate procedure for each definite variety of the CPC. The 'gross' principle when applied in too extensive a manner may amount to extended confiscation being a criminal penalty, no matter if the provisions are placed in civil or criminal normative acts, therefore the criminal standard of proof should apply. To perform the function of restoring the status *quo ante*, the precautionary approach in the method of calculating the expenses should be applied, i.e., limited to those strictly connected with committing or preparing an offence, and excluding a far-reaching calculation covering for example taxes or the estimated total value of business contracts concluded as a result of an offence (covering the expected and never achieved benefits). In other words, the extent of the 'gross' principle should be rationalised at the EU law level, and not left to MS for unlimited discretion.

However, it should be remembered that the complex nature of confiscation has already raised many doubts among analysts, and different justifications in this respect can also come into play. This book aims to put under discussion the problem of connecting three aspects at the levels of EU policy and law – the restorative objective of the CPC, the method of calculation of criminal proceeds in extended confiscation settings, and the choice by national legislatures of appropriate procedure and standard of proof. Because in the end, it is the method of calculation of the 'gross profit' that makes the most substantial impact on the function and 'criminal surplus' of extended confiscation. Therefore, this conclusive aspect should not be absent in EU law standards for confiscation.

Conclusions

Current EU confiscation law should be seen as an emanation of EU policy assumptions which perceive confiscation mainly in terms of its potential capacity to prevent and fight crime. Therefore, the most developed legal solutions concern the effective capturing of criminal assets. In addition, significant progress has been made in respect of strengthening the position of victims in confiscation mechanisms, especially in cross-border cases. However, this cannot be said regarding the promotion by EU law of 'proactive' participation of the subjected persons (suspects, accused persons, and third parties) in resolving a 'confiscation case'. To this end, EU law should support a 'procedural dialogue' between victims, communities, subjected persons, and public authorities. Adopting at least a minimalist restorative approach to justice may be helpful for legislatures in achieving this goal, as it inspires the search for solutions that deliver more just, inclusive, consultative, and balanced confiscation procedures.

The analysis of EU harmonising and mutual recognition instruments concerning confiscation from the angle of a minimalist restorative approach to justice revealed several areas for improvement. First of all, EU harmonising instruments should provide national legislatures with a clear vision of the complex objectives of confiscation. When defining these objectives, the 'double constructiveness' of confiscation should be taken into account: this measure can contribute not only to the prevention of and combating crime but also to restoring social and economic relationships affected by a crime. It should be noted that this latter aspect of confiscation is still not fully recognised in EU law.

The second area that needs to be rethought is the relationship between the position of the victim and the State. A restorative approach to justice implies the prioritisation of the position of the victim. However, this cannot be achieved without revising the definition of 'victim' in the main harmonising instrument relevant to victims' rights, Directive 2012/29/EU, as it also affects EU confiscation law wherever it deals with victims' rights. The definition of victim should be compatible with the definition of 'crime' contained in this Directive (Recital 9), and thus, it should cover collective victims, including communities. In general, victims' rights to compensation and restitutions are better secured in cross-border than in domestic cases, since Regulation 2018/1805 contains more detailed rules in this respect than the harmonising instrument. However, the definition of 'freezing order' contained therein should be revised, because, at least formally, it limits such orders solely to confiscation purposes. Accordingly, freezing orders issued for purely compensatory purposes are exposed to the risk of non-execution within the mutual recognition mechanism established by Regulation 2018/1805.

Additionally, the procedural hurdles identified at the normative level pose the risk of secondary victimisation in cross-border and domestic cases, especially when national legislation does not recognise the synergies between compensation and confiscation schemes. In this context, the extensive differentiation of these schemes should also be taken into account. Embedding victims' rights directly in the confiscation mechanisms would enable the victims to benefit from the substantive and procedural facilitations attributed specifically to confiscation proceedings with a view to more effectively capturing criminal assets.

Strengthening the position of victims is also closely connected with the rules on the disposal of confiscated assets, which should involve solutions enabling direct and indirect transfers to non-State actors (communities, NGOs, etc.). EU law offers very limited rules in this respect, it neither secures transparency of the disposal of confiscated assets nor social control of this activity. There are also very limited rules on returning confiscated assets to third countries, whereas the UNCAC, of which the EU is a non-State party, treats the returns of assets to 'victim countries' as a general rule.

Significant shortcomings of EU legislation can also be identified as regards the legal construct of extended confiscation. Bearing in mind that this type of confiscation carries serious risk of judicial error, EU law should include some 'brakes' mitigating this risk, for example by requiring the MS to ensure in their national laws that courts may depart from the mandatory assumption about the origin of the assets by resorting to the clause of a 'serious risk of injustice' in a specific case.

Another risk connected with extended confiscation concerns the broad scope of triggering offences adopted in Directive 2014/42/EU (and the new Directive 2024/1260), which also covers offences of medium gravity. Thus, under current EU law extended confiscation is not targeted solely at high-level offenders, as its legal construct does not provide any boundaries limiting the use of this extraordinary legal measure as regards first-time offenders without any ties to organised crime. This state of affairs raises questions about the 'legitimate aim' and proportionality of extended confiscation (Article 1 of the first Protocol to the ECHR; Article 17 of the Charter).

The next area for improvement is securing a 'mirror' standard of proof attributed to the courts when determining the scope of assets to be the subject of extended confiscation (with the use of legal assumptions) and attributed to the subjected persons when rebutting the court's assumptions about the criminal origin of the assets.

Moreover, EU law should contain some tools for managing the risk of the excessive retroactive effect of extended confiscation, for example by limiting the maximum time period of 'stepping back' by public authorities when determining the scope of assets to be the subject of extended confiscation. The maximum time should at least refer to the maximum statutory periods set in national law for retaining business, tax, and banking documentation. Otherwise, such excessive retroactive effect can make the right of defence unrealistic, and hence contrary to the standard of a fair trial.

Legislative overreach may also occur when implementing EU law on extended confiscation into national law. Given the inherent risks of extended confiscation, resulting from the lessened standard of proof adopted in its legal construct, the risk of judicial error can be further increased when EU minimum standards are used 'instrumentally' by national legislatures who resort to 'cherry picking' or 'gold plating' practices to resolve local problems with crime of medium or minor gravity. The German example shows that extended confiscation, in spite of its risky nature, can be converted in national law, in line with EU law, into a non-extraordinary legal measure applied in cases concerning offences of medium or minor gravity (Section 73a of the German Criminal Code, see more Chapter 5).

Finally, given that basing extended confiscation on the 'gross' (profit) principle may be critical for its 'criminal surplus', and legal function (e.g., not limited to the 'pre-enrichment *status quo*', see Vogel 2015), this conclusive aspect should not be avoided in EU law standards for confiscation. An attempt should be made to rationalise the extent of the 'gross' principle, which would require broad discussions at the EU policy level. However, EU law should at minimum recognise the connection between the method of calculation of criminal proceeds in extended confiscation settings and the choice of an appropriate procedure and standard of proof by national legislatures. These conclusive aspects should not be left to MS with unlimited discretion and should be considered at the levels of EU policy and law together with the restorative objective of the CPC.

Notes

1 Basel Institute on Governance, Note requested by the LIBE, 'The need for new EU legislation allowing the assets confiscated from criminal organisations to be used for civil society and in particular for social purposes', (2012). http://www.europarl.europa.eu/RegData/etudes/note/join/2012/462437/IPOL-LIBE_NT(2012)462437_EN.pdf (6.08.2024).

2 EP, Resolution of 25 October 2011 on organised crime in the European Union (2010/2309(INI)), P7_TA(2011)0459. See also EP, Report on organised crime in the European Union, 25.11.2010, Document A7-0333/2011. https://www.europarl.europa.eu/doceo/document/A-7-2011-0333_EN.html (28.06.2024).

3 Commission, EU Strategy on victims' rights (2020–2025), 24.6.2020, COM(2020) 258 final, 17–18.

4 Jöelle Milquet, 'Strengthening victims' rights: from compensation to reparation. For a new EU Victims' rights strategy 2020–2025' (2019), Luxembourg: Publications Office of the EU. https://commission.europa.eu/system/files/2019-03/strengthening_victims_rights_-_from_compensation_to_reparation_rev.pdf (3.08.2024).

5 See Commission work programme 2007–2023, 'Making Europe stronger together', 19.10.2021, COM(2021) 645 final.

6 Commission, Proposal for a Directive of the EP and of the Council amending Directive 2012/29/EU establishing minimum standards on the rights, support and protection of victims of crime, and replacing Council Framework Decision 2001/220/JHA, 12.7.2023, COM(2023) 424 final, 2023/0250(COD).

7 Commission, Report from the Commission to the EP and the Council on the implementation of Directive 2012/29/EU of the European Parliament and of the Council of 25 October 2012 establishing minimum standards on the rights, support and protection of victims of crime, and replacing Council Framework Decision 2001/220/JHA, 11.5.2020, COM/2020/188 final.

8 Commission Staff Working Document, Evaluation of Directive 2012/29/EU, 28.6.2022, SWD(2022) 179 final. https://eur-lex.europa.eu/legal-content/EN/TXT/PDF/?uri=CELEX:52022SC0179 (13.07.2024).

9 ICF, Study to support the evaluation of Directive 2012/29/EU establishing minimum standards on the rights, support and protection of victims of crime. Final report, (2022), Luxembourg: Publications Office of the European Union, p. 49. https://data.europa.eu/doi/10.2838/830643 (13.07.2024).

10 Commission, Proposal for a Directive of the EP and of the Council amending Directive 2012/29/EU establishing minimum standards on the rights, support and protection of

victims of crime, and replacing Council Framework Decision 2001/220/JHA, 12.7.2023, COM(2023) 424 final, 2023/0250(COD).

11 CoE, Parliamentary Assembly, Resolution 2218 (2018) 'Fighting organised crime by facilitating the confiscation of illegal assets'. https://assembly.coe.int/nw/xml/XRef/Xref-XML2HTML-en.asp?fileid=24761 (8.08.2024).

12 OECD, Anti-Corruption Network for Eastern Europe and Central Asia, 'Confiscation of instrumentalities and proceeds of corruption crimes in Eastern Europe and Central Asia' (2018), 7. https://www.oecd.org/content/dam/oecd/en/publications/reports/2018/01/confiscation-of-instrumentalities-and-proceeds-of-corruption-crimes-in-eastern-europe-and-central-asia_5fbf82bf/78637cac-en.pdf (8.08.2024).

13 Commission, Proposal for a Directive of the EP and of the Council amending Directive 2012/29/EU establishing minimum standards on the rights, support and protection of victims of crime, and replacing Council Framework Decision 2001/220/JHA, 12.7.2023, COM(2023) 424 final, 2023/0250(COD).

14 Cf. Commission Decision of 19 April 2006 establishing standard forms for the transmission of applications and decisions pursuant to Council Directive 2004/80/EC relating to compensation to crime victims (2006/337/EC), (2006) OJ L 125/25.

15 Eurojust, Note on the Regulation (EU) 2018/1805 on the mutual recognition of freezing orders and confiscation orders. A new legal framework for judicial cooperation in the field of asset recovery (2020). https://www.eurojust.europa.eu/sites/default/files/assets/20201207_note_on_regulation_eu_2018_1805.pdf (9.08.2024).

16 See, e.g., Eurojust, Report on Eurojust's casework in the field of the European Investigation Order, (2020) 18–19. https://www.eurojust.europa.eu/sites/default/files/2020-11/2020-11_EIO-Casework-Report_CORR_.pdf (8.08.2024); Eurojust, European Judicial Network (EJN), Joint Note of Eurojust and the EJN on the practical application of the European Investigation Order (2019) 5, 16. https://www.eurojust.europa.eu/sites/default/files/assets/eurojust_ejn_joint_note_practical_application_european_investigation_order.pdf (8.08.2024); EJN, Conclusions on the European Investigation Order (2018) 2, 8, Council document 14755/18. https://ejn-crimjust.europa.eu/ejn/libshow-document/EN/3096/EN (8.08.2024).

17 Opinion of the EESC 'Asset recovery and confiscation', EESC-2022-03642-AC. https://eur-lex.europa.eu/legal-content/EN/TXT/DOC/?uri=PI_EESC:EESC-2022-03642-AC (19.08.2024).

18 UN, Human Rights Council Resolution 19/38, The negative impact of the non-repatriation of funds of illicit origin to the countries of origin on the enjoyment of human rights, and the importance of improving international cooperation (2012), A/HRC/RES/19/38. https://www.right-docs.org/download/6413/ (9.08.2024).

19 EP, Resolution of 23 May 2013 on asset recovery by Arab Spring countries in transition (2013/ 2612(RSP)), P7_TA(2013)0224, (2013), OJ C 55/90.

20 Some characteristics of this procedural position resemble the description of 'proactivity' originating from psychology and subsequently adapted by other sciences, see, e.g., Bateman and Crant 1993.

21 FRA, Opinion on the confiscation of proceeds of crime, No. 03/2012, 4.12.2012. https://fra.europa.eu/sites/default/files/fra-opinion-3-2012_confiscation-of-proceeds-of-crime.pdf (4.07.2024).

References

Baruzzo Giulia, Tatiana Giannone, and Giulia Pasinato. 2021. *The Social Re-use of* Confiscated Assets *in Europe: A* First Mapping. Translated by Orsetta Spinola and Denise DeVries. Good(s) Monitoring Europe! Accessed August 8, 2024. https://

www.confiscatibene.it/sites/default/files/blog-upload/The%20social%20re-use%20of%20confiscated%20assets%20in%20Europe_a%20first%20mapping.pdf.

Bateman, Thomas S., and J. Michael Crant. 1993 "The Proactive Component of Organizational Behavior: A Measure and Correlates." *Journal of Organizational Behavior* 14 (2): 103–118. http://www.jstor.org/stable/2488028.

Betti, Stefano, Vladimir Kozin, and Jean-Pierre Brun. 2022. *Orders without Borders: Direct Enforcement of Foreign Restraint and Confiscation Decisions*. Washington, DC: International Bank for Reconstruction and Development / The World Bank. https://doi:10.1596/978-1-4648-1830-1.

Boucht, Johan. 2019. *The Limits of Asset Confiscation. On the Legitimacy of Extended Appropriation of Criminal Proceeds*. Oxford: Hart Publishing.

Cassella, D. Stefan. 2015. "Civil Asset Recovery – The American Experience." In *Non Conviction-Based Confiscation in Europe*, edited by Jon Petter Rui and Ulrich Sieber, 13–30. Berlin: Duncker & Humblot.

Dickson, Julie. 2008. "How Many Legal Systems? Some Puzzles Regarding the Identity Conditions of, and Relations between, Legal Systems in the European Union." *Oxford Legal Studies Research Paper*. Paper No 40/2008 (October 6, 2008): 1–28. https://ssrn.com/abstract=1279612 or http://dx.doi.org/10.2139/ssrn.1279612.

Forsaith, James, Barrie Irving, Eva Nanopoulos, and Mihaly Fazekas. 2012. *Study for an Impact Assessment on a Proposal for a New Legal Framework on the Confiscation and Recovery of Criminal Assets*. RAND Europe, EU. Accessed July 4, 2024. https://home-affairs.ec.europa.eu/system/files/2020-09/external_study_used_as_a_basis_for_the_commission_ia_october_2012_en.pdf.

Ivory, Radha. 2017. "Asset Recovery in Four Dimensions: Returning Wealth to Victim Countries as a Challenge for Global Governance." In *Chasing Criminal Money: Challenges and Perspectives on Asset Recovery in the EU*, edited by Katalin Ligeti and Michele Simonato, 175–210. Oxford: Hart Pub.

Král, Richard. 2021. "National Public Interest Grounds Justifying Gold-Plating of EU Law." In *Public Interest in Law*, edited by Luboš Tichý and Michael Potacs, 109–124. Cambridge: Intersentia.

Nielsen, Ruth. 2012. "Towards an Interactive Comparative Method for Studying the Multi-Layered EU legal order." In *European Legal Method – in a Multi-Level EU Legal Order*, edited by Ulla Neergaard and Ruth Nielsen, 89–116. Copenhagen: DJØF Pub.

Ochnio, Ariadna, H. 2018. "Between the Medium and the Minimum Options to Regulate Mutual Recognition of Confiscation Orders." *New Journal of European Criminal Law* 9 (4): 432–445.

Ochnio, Ariadna, H. 2019. "The Problematic Scope of Extended Confiscation in Comparative Perspective." *Nowa Kodyfikacja Prawa Karnego* 52: 119–133. https://doi.org/10.19195/2084-5065.52.8.

Ochnio, Ariadna, H. 2021. "The Tangled Path from Identifying Financial Assets to Cross-Border Confiscation. Deficiencies in EU Asset Recovery Policy." *European Journal of Crime, Criminal Law and Criminal Justice* 29 (3–4): 218–240. https://doi.org/10.1163/15718174-bja10024.

Ochnio, Ariadna, H. 2024. "Recent Developments in EU Anti-corruption Strategy: The Missing Element of the Return of Corrupt Assets to "Victim Countries." *Journal of Money Laundering Control* 27 (7): 1–12. https://doi.org/10.1108/JMLC-11-2023-0176.

Ouwerkerk, Jannemieke, W. 2017. "Criminalization Powers of the European Union and the Risks of Cherry-Picking between Various Legal Bases: The Case for a Single Legal Framework for EU Level Criminalization." *Columbia Journal of European Law* 23 (3): 503–550.

Pavlidis, George. 2018. "Towards More Responsible International Asset Recovery: The European Union Should Lead the Way." *New Journal of European Criminal Law* 9 (3): 300–307. https://doi.org/10.1177/2032284418802096.

Sellier, Elodie, and Anne Weyembergh. 2018. *Criminal Procedural Laws Across the European Union – A Comparative Analysis of Selected Main Differences and the Impact They Have Over the Development of EU Legislation*. Study requested by the EP, LIBE. Accessed August 8, 2024. https://www.europarl.europa.eu/RegData/etudes/STUD/2018/604977/IPOL_STU(2018)604977_EN.pdf.

Simonato, Michele. 2015. "Directive 2014/42/EU and Non-Conviction Based Confiscation: A Step Forward on Asset Recovery?" *New Journal of European Criminal Law* 6 (2): 213–228. https://doi.org/10.1177/203228441500600205.

Vettori, Barbara, and Andrea Di Nicola. 2017. "The Social Reuse of Confiscated Assets in EU Member States: From Current Experiences to an EU policy for a 'Powered-by-Citizens' Fight Against Crime." In *Chasing Criminal Money. Challenges and Perspectives on Asset Recovery in the EU*, edited by Katalin Ligeti and Michele Simonato, 321–343. Oxford: Hart Pub.

Vogel, Joachim. 2015. "The Legal Construction that Property Can Do Harm." In *Non Conviction-Based Confiscation in Europe*, edited by Jon Petter Rui and Ulrich Sieber, 225–243. Berlin: Duncker & Humblot.

5 The influence of EU law standards on the confiscation of the proceeds of crime on the normative framework of confiscation in Poland, Germany, and France

Introductory remarks

The two previous chapters discussed the evolution of EU confiscation policy from the angle of a restorative approach to justice, and accordingly, the EU law standards addressed to the MS, as an emanation of this policy. This chapter addresses the influence of those standards on the legal framework of confiscation (belonging to a criminal realm) in comparator jurisdictions: Poland, Germany, and France. The focus is on those elements of the standards in which certain shortcomings have been found. The function of the minimum standards is to influence national legal orders in a direction that gives the best chance of reaching the EU's policy objectives in a given field. The ability of EU law to influence the national law of MS results from the legal force of the legal acts of the Union, which varies depending on the type (Article 288 TFEU and Article 34(2)(b) TEU, as amended by the Treaty of Nice, in the case of FDs). Some are binding on MS in their entirety and are directly applicable (regulations), others are binding upon each Member State to which they are addressed as to the result to be achieved, while at the same time leaving the choice of form and methods to the national authorities (directives, and FDs prior to the Lisbon Treaty). Pursuant to Article 288 TFEU, decisions are binding in their entirety; however, if they specify to whom they are addressed, they are binding only on them. Soft law instruments (recommendations and opinions) have no binding force, but they may also influence national legislation, especially if the issuing body enjoys recognition and their content represents added value for national legislation. Accordingly, assuming that the Union's legal acts fulfil the role assigned to them in the Treaty, one can also expect them to have an impact on the national law of MS, at least to some extent. Usually, when introducing changes to national law under the influence of EU law, the official justifications of proposed changes indicate the concrete EU legal act with which the national law should comply. Beyond that, bearing in mind the non-exclusive EU competence in the AFSJ, shared with the MS, primary law may also be an important factor affecting national law, especially in the view of the principle of sincere cooperation (Article 4(3) TEU).

It should be noted that the process of shaping EU law standards, including those concerning the CPC, does not operate in a political and legal vacuum. Inspiration is found in national solutions, and thus, to some extent, the EU standards themselves

DOI: 10.4324/9781003465829-5

follow a variety of national legal patterns. Sometimes the national solutions may be more far-reaching and offer a higher level of procedural guarantees than those provided by EU law. Accordingly, there is interplay between EU and MS policies and laws. For instance, when drafting minimum standards for confiscation in 2012, the Impact Assessment accompanying the Proposal for a Directive on the freezing and confiscation of proceeds of crime extensively discussed the profitability of the system of asset recovery adopted in the UK (58–71).[1] The reason for the focus on the UK was that it was considered the only EU MS 'for which income and costs for all elements of the asset confiscation system' could be estimated (35). In addition, the UK's asset confiscation system was considered a 'reasonable approximation' of one of the far-reaching (maximal) legislative options under discussion (35).

The normative analysis of the CPC in comparator jurisdictions is aimed at capturing the essential (model) features (descriptive approach), which are relevant for the areas of EU standards on the CPC affected by shortcomings. Accordingly, the comments on national confiscation models concern their relation to these areas of EU law standards. To illustrate the main characteristics of the national models of CPC, auxiliary reference was made to the relevant case-law of the highest courts and constitutional courts in the examined jurisdictions.

The legal construct of EU standards for the CPC consists of substantive and procedural norms. The normative analysis revealed the deficiencies in the following elements of these standards: the scope of triggering offences, subject and object of confiscation, procedural facilitations in establishing a link between the property and criminal conduct, guarantees of the victims' rights, rules for redistribution of confiscated assets for non-State purposes. National models of the CPC in selected EU jurisdictions were analysed with reference to these common elements, which justifies the comparability (the *tertium comparationis* quality) in this regard (see observations on the 'comparability' of phenomena by Tokarczyk 1989; Van Hoecke 2015; Bhat 2019).

To identify the model features of the CPC in comparator jurisdictions, relevant from the perspective of the flawed elements of the examined EU law standards, the following research questions were posed:

1) What criteria apply to the triggering offences? (catalogue/listed offences, severity of criminal threat, value of benefit),
2) What criteria apply to the subject of confiscation? (nexus with criminal activity/no requirement to demonstrate such nexus),
3) What criteria apply to the object of confiscation? (value, in specie, net/gross principle),
4) What are the procedural facilitations in proving a link between the property and criminal conduct? (standard of proof, retrospective effect, statutory assumptions, discretion of the court),
5) What guarantees of victims' rights are provided within confiscation settings?
6) Have the comparator jurisdictions established a specialised system for the redistribution of confiscated assets for non-State purposes, i.e., for public interest and social purposes?

The choice for comparative analysis of the confiscation regimes of Germany and France was justified by the historically strong influence of their criminal law systems on the development of other continental systems (see, e.g., von Bar 1916; Mueller and Le Poole-Griffiths 1969; Dubber 2005; Bohlander 2009, (i); cf. Masferrer 2018), including the Polish one. Poland, a country within Central and Eastern Europe, was until 1989 part of the so-called 'Eastern Bloc', a situation which had an impact on the experience of regulating confiscation as an institution of criminal punishment (Ochnio 2016, see also analysis conducted by Rzeplińska 1997).

An additional reason for including the German law on confiscation was the fact that it underwent a major reform in 2017 under the influence of EU law. The choice of French law was also supported by the original solutions regarding the disposal of seized property and the long-term activity of the Agency for the management and recovery of seized and confiscated asset (*Agence de gestion et de recouvrement des avoirs saisis et confisqués* – AGRASC). The initial assumption was made that the adoption of similar solutions at the EU level to harmonise MS legislation in this respect would be easier than, for example, in the case of the Italian solutions, which were introduced under the influence of specific issues with organised crime, a point also taken into account by the ECtHR when testing them.

To broaden the research perspective, additional reference was made to the post-conviction confiscation regime in England and Wales, as an example of an alternative non-EU model of confiscation representing the differing concept of confiscation as a 'debt to be paid' (see, e.g., the Law Commission report on post-conviction confiscation (2022), 32).[2] From the perspective of EU law, this confiscation regime can be regarded as more advanced and far-reaching. This was reflected, for instance, in the previously cited Impact Assessment (2012), which considered the system of asset recovery adopted in the UK to be close to one of the maximal legislative options under discussion. However, in view of the above it should not at the same time be overlooked that one of the characteristics of that regime is its exceptional strictness.

The status of the UK during its membership in the EU differed from that of other countries due to the ability to apply the opt-out clause, which was used, *inter alia*, against a key piece of legislation for the harmonisation of confiscation, i.e., Directive 2014/42/EU (Recital 43). Nevertheless, the UK (as an EU MS at the time) declared its willingness to participate in the mechanism of mutual recognition of confiscation orders regulated by Regulation 2018/1805 (Recital 55). After leaving the EU in 2020, the UK participates in legal exchange for criminal matters with the EU MS under the EU–UK Trade and Cooperation Agreement (see, e.g., Ramos and Pons 2021).

Poland

The core substantive rules determining the model features of the CPC are contained in Chapter Va of the Polish Criminal Code – CC (*Kodeks karny* (1997)).[3] This Code uses the term 'forfeiture' (*przepadek*), the equivalent of 'confiscation' in

EU law. Until 1 July 2015, forfeiture was classified as a penal measure. The Act of 20 February 2015 amending the CC and several other acts (Journal of Laws (2015), item 396), in force from 1 July 2015, has changed the systematics of measures imposed in the framework of criminal proceedings by excluding forfeiture from the catalogue of penal measures (Article 39(4) of the CC). Forfeiture has been transferred to Title Va of the CC as a *sui generis* legal measure. Nevertheless, the same substantive change has not been introduced as regards forfeiture governed by the Fiscal Criminal Code, in which forfeiture has still the status of a penal measure (Article 22(2) of the Fiscal Criminal Code).[4] Therefore, the reform of 2015 may be considered inconsistent with respect to the intended function of forfeiture in the Polish legal order.

Considering the first criterion relevant for EU law standards on the CPC, i.e., the scope of triggering offences, it should be noted that there are different rules in this respect depending on the type of forfeiture. In the case of regular conviction-based forfeiture of objects derived directly from the offence, the CC does not establish any conditions regarding triggering offences. Therefore, this type of forfeiture is applicable to any type of criminal offence and is mandatory (Article 44(1) of the CC). Polish criminal law provides for *in specie* and value confiscation. If ordering the forfeiture of objects is not possible, the court may order forfeiture of equivalent value (Article 44(4) of the CC). In addition, if the perpetrator derived (even indirectly) a material benefit from the offence, which is non-forfeited under the provisions on the forfeiture of objects, the court is obliged to order the forfeiture of such benefit or its equivalent. Proceeds from the objects or rights are also deemed to be elements of material benefit (Article 45 of the CC).

A separate regulation concerns specific offences consisting of violating the prohibition of production, possession, trading, or transporting the objects. In cases provided for by law, the court may, or shall, order the forfeiture of objects (Article 44(6) of the CC). For example, mandatory forfeiture applies to counterfeit money, documents and marks of value, even if they do not constitute the property of the perpetrator (Article 316 of the CC). In addition, in certain drug offences, mandatory forfeiture covers a narcotic drug, a psychotropic substance or a new psychoactive substance, even if they do not constitute the property of the perpetrator (Article 70(2) of the Act of 29 July 2005 on Counteracting Drug Addiction, *Ustawa o przeciwdziałaniu narkomanii*, Journal of Laws 2005, 1485, as amended). Moreover, special provisions govern the forfeiture of objects and instrumentalities serving or intended to commit certain drug offences (Article 70(1) of the Act on Counteracting Drug Addiction). It should be added that one special forfeiture regulation concerns the offence of money laundering. This forfeiture covers the objects and material benefits (or their equivalent), derived directly or indirectly from money laundering or related offences, even if they do not constitute the property of the perpetrator. Forfeiture is excluded in whole or in part if an object, a material benefit or its equivalent is returned to the injured party or another authorised entity (Article 299(7) of the CC).

Mandatory forfeiture also includes motor vehicles and is applicable in cases of certain offences committed in land traffic (Article 44b of the CC). However, safety issues are the motivation behind the latter type of forfeiture, not tackling criminal proceeds (land traffic safety). Under Polish criminal law, forfeiture of an enterprise is also possible, since 27 April 2017.[5] It is applied when the enterprise served to commit an offence or hide the proceeds originating from an offence. Accordingly, an enterprise is treated in this legal construct as a forfeitable instrumentality, not as criminal proceeds (Article 44a of the CC). However, the use of this measure is in fact very limited, as it pertains only to the natural person being the owner of an enterprise; thus, legal persons and other collective entities cannot be subjected to that measure (the reports of criminal courts on the persons judged show that its application is so far marginal).[6] In addition, this type of forfeiture (non-mandatory) is limited to cases of conviction for an offence from which the perpetrator obtained a material benefit of significant value. The intended limitation of its application is also reflected in the Explanatory Memorandum accompanying the draft of the act introducing this type of forfeiture to Polish criminal law.[7] Both forfeiture of motor vehicles and forfeiture of enterprise are outside the scope of minimum harmonisation of national legislation with EU law standards on confiscation.

Unlike regular forfeiture, the legal construct of extended forfeiture limits the scope of triggering offences (Article 45(2) of the CC). Application of extended forfeiture depends on various conditions: obtaining material benefit from an offence (or the possibility of its obtaining), the value of the benefit, the severity of the criminal threat, and ties to organised crime. The legal construct of extended forfeiture underwent a major reform in 2017 aimed at aligning Polish law to Directive 2014/42/EU (Act of 23 March 2017 amending the CC and certain other acts, Journal of Laws 2017, item 768).

Firstly, extended forfeiture (mandatory) is applicable in the event of conviction for an offence, from which a material benefit of significant value has been obtained (even indirectly). The term 'material benefit' covers a benefit for oneself or someone else (Article 115(4) of the CC). The term 'significant value' was considered 'highly evaluative' until the introduction of its legal definition in 2017 (Ochnio 2016). Currently, the meaning of the term 'significant value' is related to the term 'property of significant value' (Article 115(5) and (7) of the CC), which means a property the value of which exceeds 200,000 PLN (Polish Zloty) at the time the offence is committed.[8] The average exchange rate is 4.27 PLN to 1 EUR (as of 23 August 2024).

Secondly, extended forfeiture is applicable in the event of conviction for an offence, from which a material benefit has been or may have been obtained (even indirectly) and additionally, such an offence is punishable by deprivation of liberty for which the upper limit is at least 5 years (cumulative conditions). In this set of conditions, the value of the material benefit is irrelevant. The element of the possibility of obtaining a material benefit is evaluative and should be assessed in relation to the facts and circumstances of the concrete case.

Thirdly, extended forfeiture is applicable in the event of conviction for an offence having an organised nature, namely, if committed within an organised criminal group or association aimed at committing an offence. The criteria of obtaining the material benefit, its value or severity of criminal threat, are irrelevant under this criterion. Nonetheless, under Polish criminal law, the fact of committing an offence within the framework of organised crime (organised criminal group or association) has consequences for the aggravated severity of penalty (e.g., Article 65 of the CC). In addition, participation in such a group or association is punishable by a penalty of deprivation of liberty, the upper limit of which (for the basic type of this offence) is 8 years (Article 258(1) of the CC). Thus, the aspect of severity of penalty is also indirectly involved in this criterion of ordering extended confiscation.

Bearing in mind the risk inherent in the legal construct of extended confiscation, which results from the non-criminal standard of proof being applied (see Chapter 4), the first criterion for its ordering under Polish law poses some doubts, as confiscation based on a mandatory legal assumption about the criminal origin of material benefit may also be applied to a first-time offender with a clean criminal record and without any ties to organised crime. In light of the above, merely adding the criterion of a material benefit of significant value, which under Polish criminal law is not a high bar to meet, further increases the risk of a court ordering extended confiscation of licit property.

Moreover, when we juxtapose the second criterion, composed of the cumulative elements of material benefit of any value and severity of criminal threat, with the internal structure of criminal penalties adopted in the Polish CC, the conclusion is that the court is also obliged to apply extended confiscation in cases of offences of medium gravity. Likewise, such measures can be targeted not only at high-profile offenders but also at low-profile and first-time offenders. For example, in the category of common profit-oriented offences against property (determined in Chapter XXXV of the CC), extended confiscation is applicable to almost all offences, including, in their basic types: burglary (Article 279 of the CC), robbery (Article 280 of the CC), aggravated theft (Article 281 of the CC), racketeering and extortion (Article 282 of the CC), and fraud (Article 286 of the CC). Given the broad scope of triggering offences, extended forfeiture under Polish criminal law lacks the attribute of extraordinariness, desirable to mitigate the risk it carries.

The observations on the scope of triggering offences are also valid in respect of forfeiture from a third party (Article 45(3) of the CC). The condition for ordering this type of forfeiture is the transfer of property constituting a material benefit (derived from the same triggering offences as indicated in Article 45(2) of the CC) to a natural person, legal person, or an organisational unit without legal personality. When those conditions are met, a mandatory legal assumption is applied that the objects in the autonomous possession of those entities, and their property rights, belong to the perpetrator. However, the application of such an assumption is excluded when, under the circumstances of the acquisition of such objects or rights, it would not have been possible to assume that the property originated from a prohibited act (even indirectly). The construct of this legal assumption does not fully reflect the indications given by Directive 2014/42/EU. Pursuant to Article 6 of that Directive, confiscation from a third party should be possible 'at least if [...] third parties knew or ought to have known that the purpose of the transfer or acquisition was to avoid confiscation'. In addition, Directive 2014/42/EU provides some indications helpful for national courts, namely that the assessment of the purpose of transfer or acquisition should be based on the 'concrete facts and circumstances, including that the transfer or acquisition was carried out free of charge or in exchange for an amount significantly lower than the market value' (Article 6).

The legal construct of forfeiture from a third party adopted in Polish criminal law was amended in 2015 (Act of 20 February 2015 amending the CC and certain other acts, Journal of Laws 2015, item 396). One of the rationales given in the draft of this act (submitted on 15 May 2014) was the search for solutions to align Polish law to the Proposal for a Directive on the freezing and confiscation of proceeds of crime in the EU (COM/2012/085 final).[9]

Considering the criteria applied in Polish law to the subject of forfeiture, it should be pointed out that regular forfeiture is applicable to a person convicted for any offence, who obtained the object or the material value from that offence. In the legal construct of extended forfeiture, the nexus of the subjected person with organised crime is only required in one of the alternative set of conditions of its ordering. As stated above, this type of forfeiture is targeted, i.a., towards persons sentenced for an offence committed within an organised criminal group or association aimed at committing an offence, the aspects of obtaining any material benefit or its value are not considered under that criterion, and the severity of criminal threat plays an indirect role here (Article 45(2) of the CC). In the two other sets of conditions for ordering extended forfeiture, there is no requirement to demonstrate a nexus of the subjected person with organised crime or previous involvement in criminal activity in any form. In view of the risky nature of extended confiscation, the most secure criterion for ordering extended forfeiture under Polish criminal law seems to be that related to persons with ties to organised crime.

As far as the criteria relating to the object of forfeiture are concerned, as already indicated, Polish criminal law provides for *in specie* and value confiscation. Notably, the provisions of the CC are silent about the method for determining the scope of criminal proceeds, i.e., whether the 'net' or 'gross' profit principle is applicable. This issue has mainly been considered by the Supreme Court (*Sąd Najwyższy*) in cases concerning drug offences. The Supreme Court expressed the view that the total value of proceeds is relevant. This position has recently been confirmed by the Supreme Court in the judgment of 8 November 2023, IV KK 133/23, in which the court acknowledged that all expenses effected by the perpetrator for obtaining the goods being a subject of further resale in the framework of committed offence fall under the scope of forfeitable material benefit in the meaning of Article 45(1) of the CC. Thus, the legal meaning of 'proceeds' exceeds the amount of 'remuneration' for production of narcotic drugs, as it also covers the costs of obtaining the material benefit. In addition, the Supreme Court held that if it is impossible to determine the amount of material benefit obtained separately by each perpetrator, it should be ordered in equal parts. According to the Supreme Court, the expenses involved in obtaining the object derived from an offence constitute a forfeitable material benefit, even if they had a licit source and exceeded the amount of the ultimate benefit (Decision of the Supreme Court of 26 August 2010, I KZP 12/10). The Supreme Court acknowledged that the total value of the proceeds is relevant in legal appraisals under Article 45(1) of the CC also in the following cases: V KK

154/15;[10] V KK 515/18;[11] V KK 505/21.[12] In addition, in case V KK 515/18, the Supreme Court considered that this method of calculating criminal proceeds gives a ground for adjudicating – as regards each subsequent trading participant – forfeiture of material benefit corresponding to the price obtained by such participant from sold narcotic drugs without excluding the expenses made for their acquisition. The way in which the perpetrator disposed of the obtained material benefit is irrelevant (Judgment of the Supreme Court of 31 October 2017, KK 189/17).[13] The view that the criminal proceeds should represent the totalled revenue, not only the 'net' profit is currently also widespread in the Polish legal literature (see, e.g., Konarska-Wrzosek 2023; Zakrzewski 2024).

Moving to the next area of interest relevant to the explored EU law standards of confiscation, i.e., the procedural facilitations in proving a link between the property and criminal conduct, it should be noted that the legal construct of extended forfeiture adopted in Polish criminal law does not completely reflect the essentials of such facilitations envisaged in Directive 2014/42/EU (as well as in the new Directive 2024/1260). Article 5(1) of Directive 2014/42/EU reads:

> Member States shall adopt the necessary measures to enable the confiscation, either in whole or in part, of property belonging to a person convicted of a criminal offence which is liable to give rise, directly or indirectly, to economic benefit, where a court, on the basis of the circumstances of the case, including the specific facts and available evidence, such as that the value of the property is disproportionate to the lawful income of the convicted person, is satisfied that the property in question is derived from criminal conduct (see also Article 14(1)(2) of Directive 2024/1260).

Directive 2014/42/EU contains some guidance regarding on which grounds the national court should base its assumptions about the criminal origin of assets. The court should take into account all the circumstances of the case, including the specific facts and available evidence. In addition, the special focus should be on the disproportionality of the value of the property to the lawful income of the convicted person. Compared to these indications, Polish provisions on forfeiture do not give guidance for the court on which grounds the specific mandatory assumption on the criminal origin of assets should be based, there is also no reference to the disproportionality issues. The general principle of the free assessment of evidence by the court is applicable here (Article 7 of the CCP), but this should also be seen in the context of a mandatory assumption provided for in the legal construct of extended forfeiture (Article 45(2) of the CC). Thus, on the one hand, the discretion of the national court in this respect is limited, and on the other, the subjected person can be put in a situation of legal uncertainty when attempting to rebut the court's assumption about the criminal origin of property without any statutory indications on which grounds this rebuttal should be based.

It should be pointed out that in some areas Polish criminal law duplicates the flaws identified in the EU law standards. For example, it does not guarantee the subjected person the 'mirror' lessened standard of proof (when rebutting the legal presumption about the criminal origin of property) which is attributed to the court (when determining the link between the property and criminal conduct on the basis of legal presumption). According to Article 45(2) of the CC, the assumption made in this respect may be rebutted if the perpetrator or other interested person provides proof to the contrary (reversed burden of proof). Accordingly, the person subjected to extended forfeiture may in fact be obliged not only to prove (on the balance of probabilities) that this is more likely that the property has a licit origin but to prove this circumstance beyond a reasonable doubt. In addition, as mentioned above, the disproportionality of the value of the property to the lawful income is not conclusive for the application of such legal assumption by the court.

From the other side, this legal uncertainty also concerns the court, obliged to adopt a mandatory presumption without any specific statutory indications in this respect and without statutory 'brakes' mitigating the risk of miscarriages of justice when applying it. For example, by reference to the serious risk of injustice enabling the departure from the application of mandatory application in the concrete case.

Furthermore, Polish criminal law reflects the shortcomings identified in EU law in respect of the retroactive effect of extended confiscation (EU law does not impose any time limits on retroactive effect). It should be noted that the possibility to cover by extended forfeiture the property obtained in the time before the commitment of an offence was introduced to Polish criminal law in 2017 under the influence of Directive 2014/42/EU (Act of 23 March 2017 amending the CC and certain other acts, Journal of Laws 2017, item 798).[14]

Pursuant to Article 45(2) of the CC, the mandatory assumption about the criminal origin of the forfeitable property extends to the property, which the perpetrator has obtained within a period of 5 years prior to committing an offence (until the moment of issuing even a non-final sentence). Whereas the offence may not be detected until many years after its commission, accordingly, criminal proceedings may be instituted many years after the offence. Accordingly, the person subjected to extended confiscation may face a factual situation, in which providing the proof of licit origin of property to rebut mandatory legal assumption is impossible, especially when the statutory periods for retaining tax, accounting or banking documentation, have expired. Thus, the possibility of exercising the real right of defence may actually become a legal fiction. In addition, in view of the protection of the right to property (Article 1 of the first Protocol to the ECHR; Article 17 of the Charter), the lack of reasonable limits applicable in determining the scope of forfeitable property may undermine the existence of legitimate interest required to admissible interference with such right in the concrete case, because conditions of proportionality and necessity may not be fulfilled.

The retrospective effect of provisions on forfeiture results from the aforementioned Act of 23 March 2017 amending the CC and certain other acts (Article 23), which excluded the rules *lex retro non agit* and *lex mitior agit* (see Article 4(1) of the CC). The amended provisions on extended forfeiture and non-conviction-based forfeiture (based on the selected conditions indicated in Article 45a(2) of the CC, see below) are applicable also in cases concerning the unlawful acts committed before the entry into force of the aforementioned Act (27 April 2017). The same rule concerns extended forfeiture and non-conviction-based forfeiture, based on the conditions indicated in Article 43a of the Fiscal Criminal Code. According to the statute of limitations, forfeiture cannot be executed if 10 years passed since the forfeiture order has become final (Articles 103(1) no 3 and 103(2) of the CC). It should also be recalled that, while the above-mentioned Act of 20 February 2015 amending the CC and several other acts changed the systematics of measures imposed in the framework of criminal proceedings by excluding forfeiture from the catalogue of penal measures (Article 39(4) of the CC) and transferring it to Title Va of the CC as a *sui generis* legal measure, it has not introduced the same substantive change as regards forfeiture governed by the Fiscal Criminal Code, in which forfeiture still has the status of a penal measure (Article 22(2) of the Fiscal Criminal Code). Thus, the subsequent reform of 2017 allowed retrospective adjudication of forfeiture being formally a penal measure under the Fiscal Criminal Code, which raises significant concerns in the context of the constitutional principle *nullum crimen sine lege poenali anteriori* (Article 42(1) of the Constitution of the Republic of Poland).

The legal construct of non-conviction-based forfeiture was changed in 2017 under the influence of Directive 2014/42/EU (Explanatory Memorandum of the Draft of the Act amending the CC and several other acts 2016, the Sejm, eighth term of office, print no. 1186). Non-conviction-based forfeiture may be ordered under Polish criminal law in the following situations: negligible social harmfulness of the act, conditional discontinuance of proceedings, establishing that the perpetrator acted in a state of insanity (as determined in Article 31(1) of the CC), establishing circumstances excluding the imposition of penalty (Article 45a(1) of the CC). In addition, if the collected evidence indicates that a forfeiture would have been ordered in the event of conviction, the court may also order forfeiture in case of the death of the perpetrator, discontinuance of the proceedings due to an undetected perpetrator, and suspension of the proceedings when the accused cannot be apprehended or cannot participate in proceedings due to mental illness or another serious illness (Article 45a(2) of the CC).

Moving to the next point of interest, i.e., the protection of victims' rights within confiscation settings, the approach adopted in Polish criminal law is similar to that adopted in Directive 2014/42/EU, which perceives the rights of victims to confiscated assets from the negative side (Article 8(10)). As indicated in Chapters 3 and 4, Directive 2024/1260 represents a more innovative approach in this respect (Article 18(1)(5)). Regular forfeiture of objects is excluded if they are subject to return to the injured party or another authorised entity (Article 44(5) of the CC). A similar rule concerns the forfeiture of a material benefit (Article 45(1) of the CC). These provisions, however, were not influenced by EU law, as similar solutions on victims' rights in domestic regulation of forfeiture of objects were in force since 1 September 1998, when the CC of 1997 became effective.[15] As far as forfeiture of material benefit is concerned, a similar regulation has been in force since 2001.[16] Accordingly, from the beginning of this Code, the rights of victims to compensation and restitution have not been embedded in the national forfeiture scheme and still, victims' claims cannot be directly satisfied with the forfeited assets (at the stage of execution of the forfeiture order). In turn, they constitute a negative premise to order forfeiture.

As to the next question, of whether the examined jurisdiction established a specialised system for the redistribution of confiscated assets for non-State purposes, i.e., for public interest and social purposes, it should first be noted that Polish law represents the traditional approach in this regard, that the principal beneficiary of confiscated assets is the State. According to Article 187(2) of the Executive Criminal Code – ECC of 1997 (*Kodeks karny wykonawczy*),[17] an object, a material benefit, or their equivalents become the property of the State Treasury, as soon as the judgment becomes final (see also Raglewski 2016). And if a third party subjected to confiscation brings a civil action against the State Treasury asking for a determination that the property in question is not forfeitable either in whole or in part, ownership of the property is transferred to the State Treasury as soon as the judgment dismissing a claim becomes final. At the normative level, there are no complex rules on redistributing forfeited assets for public interest and social purposes. Likewise, at the institutional level, there is no specialised central agency established to redistribute forfeited assets to public interest and social purposes. In this context, it should be noted that the legal possibilities of transferring forfeited proceeds to non-State purposes are very limited under Polish executive criminal law. For instance, Article 195aa of the ECC pertains to the execution of forfeiture in the form of transferring an object of scientific, artistic, or historic value to a museum (museums established by private entities are not excluded from these provisions). However, according to Article 188(6) of the ECC, objects of historical, scientific, or artistic value should preferably be transferred free of charge to a State museum, library, or archive, but if no institution wishes to acquire them, they should be sold. In addition, the Regulation of the Minister of Justice of 27 February 2017 (Journal of Laws 2018, item 2139) lists those objects which are not to be handed over to the head of the tax office – who, as a rule, is the enforcement authority – such as weapons and ammunition, counterfeit money and documents, or narcotic drugs; however, these are instead transferred to various State institutions. Some objects of importance for forensic science can be transferred to higher education institutions, without conditions with regard to their private or public status, or to the Central Forensic Laboratory of the Police. In addition, some objects of importance in combating crime may be handed over to the Police Headquarters or other State institutions empowered with investigative powers. It should be noted that, exceptionally, under the provisions on administrative enforcement proceedings (*Ustawa o postępowaniu egzekucyjnym w administracji* 1966), movable assets which have not been sold by the enforcement authority under the regular sale, may be offered to organisational units of health care, educational institutions, culture institutions, or charity organisations to carry out their statutory activities (Article 108(2) of the Act of 17 June 1966 on administrative enforcement proceedings, Journal of Laws 1966, No 24, item 151, as amended).[18]

In view of the Polish normative framework on forfeiture, one might conclude that EU soft law encouraging MS to reuse confiscated assets for the public interest and social purposes (Recital 35 and Article 10(3) of Directive 2014/42/EU) has not been effective in influencing Polish law, as it lacks solutions enabling the broad social reuse of confiscated assets. Such use is rather subsidiary and exceptional.

It should also be remembered that while the EU confiscation policy promotes the social reuse of confiscated assets, regrettably, the new Directive 2024/1260 pursues the route of a soft law recommendation addressed to MS (it provides no hard law stipulations in this respect, Recital 38 and Article 19(1)).

Comments on the Polish model

Polish forfeiture law partly reflects the shortcomings previously identified at the EU law level in the following areas: the broad scope of triggering offences in the legal construct of extended forfeiture including the offences of medium gravity; the possibility to order extended forfeiture against a low-profile and first-time offender without any ties to organised crime or other criminal conduct; a lack of guarantees of the same (lessened) standard of proof for the subjected persons when challenging the extended forfeiture order as that attributed to the court when it applies the legal presumption about the criminal origin of property; a lack of provisions mitigating the excessive retroactive effect of forfeiture which can make exercising the right of defence impossible in practice; perceptions of victims' rights to compensation and restitution within forfeiture settings from the negative side (as a negative premise for imposing confiscation), and a lack of concrete legal solutions allowing satisfying victims' claims at the execution phase of forfeiture orders. Finally, under the Polish legal system, the State is the main beneficiary of confiscated assets, and a complex and centralised system of redistributing confiscated assets to non-State purposes has so far not been established.

In view of the above, Directive 2024/1260 can play a role, as it represents a more complex and strategic approach to confiscation issues than Directive 2014/42/EU. It offers the MS a chance to reform their domestic confiscation mechanisms starting from the strategic level, especially by introducing national strategies on asset recovery (see Recital 54 and Article 25 of Directive 2024/1260). The MS shall adopt such strategies by 24 May 2027 and update it regularly, at least every 5 years. Article 25(2) of Directive 2024/1260 indicates the following compulsory elements of national asset recovery strategies:

a) elements concerning the priorities of national policy in this area, and the objectives and measures to achieve them,
b) the role and responsibilities of the competent authorities, including arrangements for coordination and cooperation among them,
c) resources,
d) training,
e) measures to be taken, where applicable, on the use of confiscated assets for public interest or social purposes,
f) activities to be undertaken on cooperation with third countries,
g) arrangements allowing for regular evaluation of results.

Germany

The basic substantive rules determining the model features of the CPC are contained in the Seventh Title of the German CC (*Strafgesetzbuch*).[19] Although confiscation belongs to the criminal realm, its nature is perceived as non-penal, but restitutive, the influences on its penal nature were against the background of the introduction of the 'gross' principle in the extensive form in 1992 (Böse and Weyer 2019; Eser 1993). In 2017, the Code's provisions concerning forfeiture and confiscation underwent a major reform, introduced to implement Directive 2014/42/EU (the Act to reform criminal confiscation, *Gesetz zur Reform der strafrechtlichen Vermögensabschöpfung*, 13 April 2017, Federal Law Gazette 2017, I, No. 22, 872).[20] The changes entered into force on 1 July 2017 and covered, i.a., the Code's terminology. The term 'confiscation' (*Einziehung*) was recognised as being more comprehensible and suited to the terminology of EU law and prompted a departure from the use of the term 'forfeiture' (*Verfall*) (see the Explanatory Memorandum of the Draft of the Act to reform criminal asset confiscation 2016, German Bundestag Document No 18/9525, 18th term of office; cf. Schunke 2017, 91, as regards the *status quo* before the reform of 2017).[21]

Considering the criteria of triggering offences in the legal construct of confiscation in German criminal law, it should be noted that, similarly to Polish forfeiture law, they differ depending on the type of confiscation. Regular confiscation (post-conviction) concerns 'anything' (*etwas*) obtained through or for an unlawful act, as well as benefits obtained from the proceeds. Regular confiscation (mandatory) applies to all types of offences. In addition, similarly to Polish forfeiture law, the German CC does not contain any requirement as regards the subjected persons, thus, regular post-conviction confiscation is applicable to all offenders, including low-profile and first-time offenders without any criminal record or ties to organised crime (Section 73 of the CC). There is also non-mandatory confiscation of objects (in the meaning of products or instrumentalities of crime). This type of confiscation is limited to intentional offences (Section 74(1) of the CC). In addition, confiscation of the objects of crime may be imposed under specific provisions, for example for security and prevention reasons (Sections 74-74b of the CC). Moreover, confiscation may be targeted at 'tangible content', the distribution of which is a criminal offence (Section 74d of the CC).

Notably, after the reform of 2017, the German CC no longer limits the scope of triggering offences in the legal construct of extended confiscation (mandatory). This type of confiscation covers items obtained through or for other unlawful acts than a 'basic' ('underlying') offence, for which the provisions do not lay down any conditions (Section 73a(1) of the CC). There are also no specific conditions regarding the type of offence, severity of criminal threat, or value of benefit (obtained or possible to obtain). It should be remembered that prior to the reform of 2017, the use of extended confiscation was limited to serious listed offences with a focus on ties with organised crime and terrorism (the former 'extended forfeiture', *Erweiterter Verfall*, Section 73d(1) of the CC in the version before 1 July 2017; see Peters and Bröckers 2019, 74). Thus, under German criminal law, extended confiscation originally emerged from the fight against organised crime (Podolski et al. 2019, 60; Kilchling 2004, 723). It was introduced in 1992 by the Act to Combat Illegal Drug Trafficking and Other Forms of Organised Crime (*Gesetz zur Bekämpfung des illegalen Rauschgifthandels und anderer Erscheinungsformen der Organisierten Kriminalität* – OrgKG, 1992, Federal Law Gazette 1992 I, 1302). Nevertheless, in the area of extended confiscation, German law currently contains far greater legislative reach than the original concept and also the EU minimum standards contained in Directive 2014/42/EU (Article 5(2)), as well as those provided for in the new Directive 2024/1260 (Article 14(3)). Compared to Polish criminal law, which makes some attempts to limit the use of extended confiscation at least to offences of medium gravity, German criminal law does not impose any boundaries in this regard and allows its application in cases concerning any offence from minor to high gravity.

Directive 2014/42/EU and Directive 2024/1260 both include two methods for determining the minimum scope of triggering offences in the legal construct of extended confiscation: catalogue offences ('listed offences') and the severity of criminal threat. Bearing in mind that the harmonising rules in this respect are of minimal character, there may be a natural inclination by national legislators to exceed the *de minimis* threshold of harmonisation to achieve internal policy objectives. However, if such practices (e.g. 'gold plating') are applied when implementing EU law relevant to human rights, they can negatively affect the protection of such rights, an example of this being when the overreach concerns measures susceptible to miscarriages of justice, such as extended confiscation.

As far as confiscation from a third party is concerned, it is targeted at a person other than a perpetrator or participant. It can be imposed when a perpetrator or participant acted on a third party's behalf and such party acquired something through an offence, and when the acquired object was transferred to the third party free of charge, or without legal cause, or when the object was transferred to a third party who recognised or should have recognised that it originated from an unlawful act. In addition, when the object was obtained by a third party as an heir, beneficiary or legatee (Section 73b(1) of the CC). The statutory provisions, as in Poland (cf. Article 45(3) of the Polish CC), do not limit the imposition of this type of confiscation to only natural persons.

Whereas the method of 'listed offences' has been used to limit the scope of triggering offences in the legal construct of non-conviction based confiscation of assets of unknown origin, based on conditions determined in Section 76a(4) of the CC. Depending on the typology adopted, this legal measure can be systematised as a variety of extended confiscation independent from conviction, a specific type of NCBC, or a *sui generis* measure which combines the features of NCBC and extended confiscation. Pursuant to Section 76a(4) of the CC, an asset seized on the basis of suspicion of committing one of the catalogue offences (seizure applied in the course of investigations concerning one of the listed offences) and any benefit obtained from it are covered by confiscation independently, even in cases when the asset comes from an unlawful act and the person touched by the seizure cannot be prosecuted or convicted for an 'underlying' offence. The catalogue covers various offences of serious gravity determined in the CC, including: preparation of a serious act of violence endangering the State, financing of terrorism, formation of criminal or terrorist organisations, pimping, offences concerning child pornographic content, human trafficking, forced prostitution or labour, and money laundering (Section 76a(4) no 1 of the CC). In addition, the catalogue in question covers several serious offences determined in the Tax Code, the Asylum Act, the Resident Act, the Foreign Trade Act, the Consumer Cannabis Act, the Medical Cannabis Act, the War Weapons Control Act, and the Weapons Act (listed in Section 76a(4) no 2 to 8 of the CC). However, despite limiting the use of NCBC to cases concerning serious offences, and the requirement that the court must be convinced about the criminal 'origin' of the assets (Explanatory Memorandum, 73, No 18/9525), from a constitutional viewpoint this type of confiscation has raised some concerns in the German subject literature, especially in respect of the right to property (Article 14(2) of the German Basic Law), and the principle *nullum crimen sine lege poenali anteriori* (Article 103(2) of the German Basic Law), see, e.g., Höft 2018; Heuer 2021.

As far as criteria applied to the object of confiscation are concerned, under German criminal law, confiscation can be imposed in the form of *in specie* or value confiscation. It is worth emphasising here that the CC uses the specific and broad term 'anything' (*etwas*) which covers all that has been obtained (Section 73(1) of the CC).

The provisions also determine the method of calculating the value of what was acquired, allowing for estimation of its extent and value (Section 73d(2) of the CC), including expenses (see Reitemeier 2017). Notably, the reform of 2017 introduced statutory limits on the broad application of the 'gross' principle (*Bruttoprinzip*). This principle was introduced in a broad form in 1992 (the Act amending the Foreign Trade Act, the Criminal Code and other acts, *Gesetz zur Änderung des Außenwirtschaftsgesetzes, des Strafgesetzbuches und anderer Gesetze*, 28 February 1992, Journal of Laws 1992, I, 372; Schmidt 2019, 62; Fischer 2021, 754). After the reform of 2017, expenditures on the part of the perpetrator, participant, or the other person are, as a rule, deductible (Section 73d(1) of the CC). Nonetheless, specific investment costs, i.e., expenditures incurred while committing or preparing an unlawful act, are not deductible, unless the amount spent was used to fulfil an obligation to a victim of an offence (see also Ullenboom 2019, 39). Given that the method of calculating the proceeds of crime is a key factor influencing the severity of confiscation, prior to the reform of 2017, a far-reaching approach in recognition of expenses under the 'gross' principle was widely explored in the jurisprudence of the Federal Court of Justice (FCJ), *Bundesgerichtshof* (BGH), attempting to rationalise the extent of this principle in cases concerning corruption-related offences involving business entities. For instance, the FCJ found that tax is 'deductible' (BGH, 5 StR 138/01, 21 March 2002; see also BGH, 5 StR 119/05, 2 December 2005; BGH, 5 StR 224/09, 27 January 20103; BGH, 3 StR 343/11, 19 January 2012). On the other hand, a far-reaching approach was also presented (e.g., BGH, 2 StR 468/93, 19 November 1993; BGH, 1 StR 115/02, 21 August 2002; BGH, 1 StR 166/07, 30 May 2008). It should be added that the German Federal

Constitutional Court (FCC), *Bundesverfassungsgericht* (BVerfG) made no challenge to the acceptability of the 'gross' principle, in the extensive form existing before the reform of 2017 (BVerfG, 2 BvR 564/95, 14 January 2004). Notably, in the same case, the FCC found that extended forfeiture does not have a punitive nature.

As far as the procedural facilitations in proving a link between the property and criminal conduct are concerned, it should be pointed out that in this respect the legal construct of extended confiscation differs from that adopted in Polish criminal law. On the formal side, the provisions of the German CC do not provide for a legal presumption (*presumption iuris tantum*) about the criminal origin of proceeds (Section 73a(1) of the CC). However, the outcome of the court's reasoning is considered in the doctrine to be similar, as assets without a proven link to the concrete offence (under the criminal standard of proof beyond a reasonable doubt) also fall within the scope of extended confiscation, as a result of a balancing of probabilities or 'weighing up' of evidence (see, e.g., Böse and Weyer 2019; as regards the *status quo* before the reform of 2017, see Esser 2015, 74). This also applies to NCBC, determined in Section 76a(4) of the CC. The legal construct of extended confiscation only requires proving the commission of at least one offence performing the function of an 'underlying' offence (see also Reitemeier 2017; Köhler 2017), accordingly, the provisions do not require the proving of the linkage of the assets with such offence. The conditions for ordering NCBC are even more relaxed, as they are based on the 'suspicion' that an offence has been committed, which is also considered as a condition for seizing the assets. Thus, proving the commission of one of the listed offences is not required.

Notably, the relevant element of the legal construct of extended confiscation (Section 73a of the CC) is to establish that any offence has been committed (this can also be a non-acquisitive offence). The subject literature draws attention to the problem that the court must be satisfied ('convinced') that the assets have criminal origins, which is not an easy task even under the broad discretion that is given to the court under German law (e.g., Esser 2015, 74; BGH 3 StR 529/12, 4 April 2013). The principle of free judicial assessment of evidence is applicable in this respect (Section 261 of the Code of Criminal Procedure – CCP, *Strafprozeßordnung*). In addition, the view presented in the doctrine is that some guidance can be derived from the former provisions on extended forfeiture (the old version of Section 73d of the CC), and Section 437 of the CCP, even if the latter formally pertains to NCBC (Section 76a(4) of the CC) (Reitemeier 2017; Ullenboom 2019, 78). Nevertheless, Section 73a of the CC does not formally give the courts any guidance in this respect and does not reverse the burden of proof. This may pose the question of how the subjected person should rebut court findings on the criminal origin of assets made under a lessened standard of proof. From the formal side, similarly to Polish criminal law, the provisions of the German CC do not guarantee subjected persons a 'mirror' standard of proof matching that attributed to the court when determining the scope of extended confiscation. Referring to possible indications for the courts indicated in the doctrine, if making auxiliary use of the former Section 73d of the CC, the court should take into account all circumstances giving reason to assume that the assets were obtained from or for unlawful acts. When referring to Section 437 of the CCP, the court can take into account the aspect of disproportionality (a disproportional relation between the value of the assets and the lawful income), the results of investigations regarding an 'underlying' offence, the circumstances of finding and securing the assets, and the personal and material conditions of the person. Importantly, the legal *status quo* before the reform of 2017 provided the courts with the possibility to resort to the clause of 'undue hardship', enabling them to avoid imposing confiscation to an extent which would cause undue hardship (the old version of Section 73c of the CC). It should be added that, after the reform of 2017, the aspect of proportionality is relevant for the confiscation of objects (Section 74f of the CC).

Compared to the Polish legal solutions, there are no time limits regarding the acquisition of the assets in the extended form of confiscation; therefore, the retrospective effect of confiscation may be even greater than under Polish law (cf. Article 45(2) of the Polish CC establishing a 5-year period). Confiscation proceedings may take place separately from the main proceedings under Section 422 of the CCP. In addition, the initiation of independent confiscation proceedings takes place from the substantiated application by a public or private prosecutor based on the results of investigations (Section 435 of the CCP). Pursuant to Section 76b(1) of the CC, the statute of limitation for extended confiscation and independent confiscation amounts to 30 years. This 30-year period commences at the termination of the unlawful act from (or for) which the subjected person obtained something. However, it should be remembered that the limitation period does not apply to some of the most serious offences, such as the crime of murder and war crimes (Section 76b(2) of the CC; see also Section 5 of the Code of Crimes against International Law 2002 and Section 78(2) of the CC). This can also be seen in the context of the position expressed by the FCC in the case 2 BvL 8/19, that under the reform of 2017, confiscation is not an additional penalty but a *sui generis* legal measure, therefore the principle of guilt is not applied (BVerfG, 2 BvL 8/19, 10 February 2021). Accordingly, the retroactive effect of confiscation is admissible. The FCC held that Section 316h(1) of the Act to reform the system of criminal confiscation (transitional provision) is not to be assessed under Article 103(2) of the German Basic Law. Article 103(2) constitutes the principle *nullum crimen sine lege poenali anteriori* concerning a criminal punishment (see also some concerns regarding this ruling expressed by, e.g., Bülte 2021; Lenk 2021; Bauerkamp 2022). Thus, non-penal confiscation measures can also be applied to confiscate the proceeds of an offence committed before the entry into force of the reform of 2017 (1 July 2017). In view of this ruling, the principle *prioritas legis mitior* does not apply (see Section 2(5) of the CC). The FCC expressed a similar view in the case 2 BvR 2194/21, 7 April 2022, in which they indicated that dishonestly obtained proceeds ('any' proceeds, the type of offence is irrelevant) do not merit protection. And highlighted that the prohibition of 'retroactive effect of legal consequences' is rooted in the principle of protection of legitimate expectations and its limits, thus accordingly, the interests of the common good may prevail (cf. BVerfG, 2 BvR 794/95, in which the FCC challenged the constitutionality of the former Section

43a of the CC – *Vermögensstrafe*, determining a special financial penalty, the amount of which was limited only by the value of the assets of the perpetrator, in the context of Article 103(2) of German Basic Law).

When answering the question of what guarantees of victims' rights are specifically provided within confiscation settings, it should be noted that changing the position of victims in a positive direction was one of the pivotal elements of the reform of 2017. One of the amendments provided for the deletion of Section 73(1) Sentence 2 of the CC, which precluded ordering forfeiture (*Verfall*) to the extent that the unlawful act has given cause to victims' claims, the fulfilment of which would deprive the perpetrator or participant of the value of what has been gained from the act. This regulation was called in the German legal doctrine as the 'gravedigger of forfeiture' (e.g., Meyer 2015; Burchard 2019). Thus, before the reform of 2017, victims' claims were perceived in German law as a negative prerequisite for the imposition of forfeiture. The former legal *status quo* required the victims themselves to engage in civil law enforcement of their claims, and difficulties were identified when they did not act in this respect. The procedure of the 'substitute acquisition' of the seized assets by the State to prevent the perpetrator from retaining the proceeds of crime, as determined in the former Section 111i of the CCP, was perceived as complicated and long-lasting, as follows from the Explanatory Memorandum of the Draft of the Act to reform the system of criminal confiscation (2016, German Bundestag Document No 18/9525). The idea was to satisfy victims' claims in criminal execution proceedings under a simpler principle. Firstly, an object should be confiscated and after that returned to a victim (if the actual object is not available, 'value confiscation' should be applied). According to the Explanatory Memorandum in question, the assets secured for the purpose of enforcement of value confiscation should be sold and the profits should be paid out to the victim. If the recovered assets are less than the claims, the victims should be compensated *via* the appropriate insolvency procedure (*Insolvenzordnung* 1994, Federal Law Gazette 1994, I, 2866, as amended), (Explanatory Memorandum, 2). Importantly, the statutory provisions secure the right of victims to information. Pursuant to Section 459i of the CCP, the injured party should be informed without delay about the entry into force of confiscation orders, and notification must be served (see also Section 111l (4) of the CC). As far as confiscation of the object is concerned, the notification should be accompanied by a reference to the claim pursuant to Section 459h(1) and to the procedure determined in Section 459j of the CCP. In case of value confiscation, it should be accompanied by a reference to the claim pursuant to Section 459h(2) and to the procedure determined in Sections 459k to 459m of the CCP.

However, the Explanatory Memorandum in question did not refer to EU law in the context of changing the position of victims in national confiscation settings. It should be recalled that EU law lacks clear provisions on the victim's position in confiscation settings (Article 8(10) of Directive 2014/42/EU, cf. Article 18 of the Directive 2024/1260 representing a more advanced approach in this respect, see more Chapter 4). Accordingly, the discretion of MS in this respect is quite broad, i.e. these rights may be perceived from the positive or negative side as in Directive

2014/42/EU, under which the confiscation measure should not prevent victims from seeking compensation for their claims (Article 8(10)). Given the above, it should be recognised that resolving the problem of victims' claims in the framework of confiscation settings (at the enforcement stage) was a genuine idea from the German legislators, which could be a worthwhile legislative option for the EU and EU jurisdictions to follow. Ultimately, this concept strengthens the position of victims in confiscation mechanisms, giving them greater rights to previously confiscated assets during the enforcement proceedings (see Section 459h and Section 459g of the CCP; Burchard 2019).

Moving on to the next point of consideration, i.e., whether the comparator jurisdiction established a specialised and central system for the redistribution of confiscated assets for non-State purposes (to public interest and social purposes), it has to be noted that, to date, such a system has not been effectively introduced. Baruzzo, Giannone, and Pasinato (2021) indicated that Germany 'did not assimilate' Article 10(3) of Directive 2014/42/EU which pertains to considering 'taking measures allowing confiscated property to be used for public interest or social purposes' (35).

Similar to the Polish legal solutions, the State is the main beneficiary of confiscated assets. Notably, when preparing the reform of 2017, the expected increase in asset confiscation measures was seen also through the prism of a positive effect on 'public budgets' (Explanatory Memorandum, 4). The main rule is the transition of ownership of the object or right to the State when a decision on confiscation becomes final (Section 75(1) of the CC, see also Section 76a(4) of the CC). In addition, the provisions of Criminal Enforcement Regulations (CER) (*Strafvollstreckungsordnung* 2011, last amended on 8 August 2024) specify that ownership of the object or the right is transferred to the State, namely the Judicial Treasury whose court ordered confiscation in the first instance, also when exercising federal jurisdiction (Section 60(1)). However, the Federal Republic of Germany (Judicial Treasury, *Justizfiskus*) becomes the owner when the court has ordered confiscation to the federal government. In principle, the rights of third parties are retained, though some exceptions concern dangerous objects, when the court orders the expiration of rights. A similar type of court decision on expiration may be issued towards third parties who contributed, at least recklessly, to the use of the object for criminal purposes, or obtained the right to the object with knowledge of the circumstances justifying confiscation (Section 75(2) of the CC, see also Section 60(6) of the CER).

It should be noted, however, that the provisions of the CER provide for some solutions enabling the transfer of assets to non-State purposes. For instance, in the case of post-confiscation sale of everyday objects, charitable organisations and persons in need have priority (Section 64(4) of the CER). There are also specific provisions on the use of the objects confiscated in proceedings related to offences against intellectual property determined in several detailed off-code acts (Section 67a of the CER). Such objects if suitable for use in charitable or humanitarian purposes should be offered to appropriate associations or institutions free of charge, provided it does not involve disproportionate costs. If the objects are of significant value, the approval of the General Public Prosecutor is required. Another route of disposal concerns objects serving as fishing equipment or its part, having cultural or historical value which can become museum pieces. They can also be used for the administration of justice, forensic examinations, or teaching purposes (Section 71(4) of the CER). In addition, confiscated objects may be offered to federal or state authorities for conducting their official activities or transferred to them (at their request) if they are of importance for research, teaching, training, or education (on a loan basis with an obligation to return on demand for important reasons). Moreover, the confiscated objects, if suitable, may be used for the purposes of the administration of justice, the post-conviction penal system and services, and the police (Section 66 of the CER). If the objects are of significant value, the approval of the General Public Prosecutor is additionally required (Section 67 of the CER).

Notably, the provisions of the CER prevent the re-acquisition of confiscated objects by offenders (such provisions are lacking in EU law). When a public auction or sale is carried out by a bailiff (appointed by the enforcement authority), the order must be placed in writing and indicate the persons to whom sale is excluded (Section 64(1) of the CER). It should be noted that the function of the enforcement authority is performed by the public prosecutor's office (Section 451 StPO; Böse and Weyer 2019). The perpetrators or participants can reacquire such objects only in exceptional situations, under the approval of the highest judicial authority or other assigned body (in the case of a public sale through the use of an internet platform, consent is generally deemed, Section 64(5) of the CER). Judges, public prosecutors, other judicial officials (also from the prison system), investigators from the public prosecutor's office, and police employees cannot be party to the transaction of private sale (Section 64(6) of the CER).

Comments on the German model

Similarly to Polish forfeiture law, German confiscation law partly reflects the shortcomings previously identified at the EU law level. Notably, in the area of the scope of triggering offences relevant to ordering extended confiscation, the German legislators have significantly exceeded the minimum threshold of harmonisation by introducing an unlimited scope of triggering offences. Accordingly, under German law, extended confiscation can also be applied in cases concerning offences of minor and medium gravity, i.e., across the spectrum of offences. For comparison, Polish law limits the applicable scope to offences of at least medium gravity. In addition, there is the possibility to order extended confiscation against a low-profile or first-time offender without any ties to organised crime or other criminal conduct. Thus, extended confiscation in the form applied in the examined jurisdiction can no longer be considered a measure of special reaction to serious crime, especially in an organised form. This further increases the risk of judicial error inherent in extended confiscation settings. This should also be seen in the context of the lack of clear and statutory guidance on which a court should base its conviction about the criminal origin of assets, which may put the subjected person in a situation of legal uncertainty about the minimum evidence required to challenge the court's reasoning ('hard' *v* 'probability' counter-evidence). Nevertheless, the issue of the court's 'conviction' has been resolved by doctrine through reference to the former Section 73d of the CC on extended forfeiture (prior to the reform of 2017), and Section 437 of the CCP pertaining to NCBC determined in Section 76a(4) of the CC. Compared to Polish criminal law, the 'gross' principle is determined by the statutory provisions, and after the reform of 2017, its extent has been rationalised; thus, the margin of the court's discretion in this field has been reduced. In contrast, there are no statutory provisions in this regard in Polish criminal law, and this issue has so far been resolved in the case-law of the criminal courts, especially in cases concerning drug offences. The retroactive effect of confiscation under German law is even greater than under Polish law, which can make exercising the right of defence impossible in practice, contrary to the standard of a fair trial (from the 'procedural justice' viewpoint, not entering here into the penal or non-penal nature of confiscation and the application of the principles *lex retro non agit* and *prioritas legis mitior*).

Although some possibilities exist to transfer assets to non-State entities, including charitable organisations, in principle, German law, like Polish law, represents the traditional approach where the State is the main beneficiary of confiscated assets. A complex and centralised system of redistributing confiscated assets to public interest and social purposes has so far not been established at the normative and institutional levels. Nevertheless, it should be recognised that the German legislators resolved the issue of embedding victims' rights directly in the confiscation mechanism in a manner which can be a legislative option for both the EU and other EU jurisdictions to follow. After the reform of 2017, victims' claims are no longer treated as a 'negative prerequisite' to the ordering of confiscation and can be satisfied at the enforcement stage of confiscation proceedings.

France

The core substantive rules on criminal confiscation are contained in Article 131-21 et seq. of the French CC (*Code pénal*, 1994).[22] Confiscation constitutes, in principle, an additional penalty (*la peine complémentaire de confiscation*). However, it may also be ordered as a 'primary' penalty substituting for imprisonment or other additional penalties, and in some cases, it may also perform the function of a 'security measure', for instance, when it concerns objects recognised as dangerous, harmful, or illegally possessed (see, e.g., Giudicelli-Delage et al. 2019; Article 131-6, Article 131-11, and Article 131-21(8) of the CC). Pradel (2019) indicated that there is no single response to the question about the juridical nature of confiscation, especially when it concerns third parties or is adjudicated under special provisions, for instance for security reasons (611–613).

From the perspective of the influence of EU law, it should be pointed out that FD 2005/212/JHA was of crucial importance for French substantive criminal law concerning confiscation. Secondly, Directive 2014/42/EU influenced, i.a., the possibility of ordering confiscation independent from conviction, and asset freezing. The next observation is that the provisions of the French CC are not an exact reflection of the concepts adopted in EU instruments and follow them less closely than the provisions of the Polish or German CCs. However, this does not mean that they are incompatible with EU law but that the French legislators prefer adhering to well-established domestic solutions, which are then 'tuned' to EU law, sometimes in a manner that may seem complicated to foreign lawyers, as in the case of aligning national law to EU law provisions on non-conviction-based confiscation. In 2007, French law was aligned to FD 2005/212/JHA by the Act on the prevention of delinquency 2007 (*Loi n° 2007-297 du 5 mars 2007 relative à la prévention de la délinquance*). The justification of Amendment No. 238 concerning Article 131-21 of the CC explicitly referred to FD 2005/212/JHA. The idea was to allow for ordering confiscation in cases of offences punishable by imprisonment with a lower limit exceeding 1 year (except press offences, however, there are some possibilities of ordering confiscation under Article 61 of the Act on freedom of the press 1881, *Loi du 29 juillet 1881 sur la liberté de la presse*). Secondly, to allow for ordering extended confiscation of assets of unjustified origin in cases of offences (felonies and misdemeanours, *crimes* and *délits*) punishable by imprisonment with a lower limit of at least 5 years (*Assemblée Nationale*, *Prévention de la délinquance*, 16 November 2006, No. 3338). Thus, similarly to Polish forfeiture law, extended confiscation can be applied also to offences of medium gravity, whereas German law, as indicated in the previous subsection, went even further by opening up the possibility of ordering extended confiscation across the spectrum of offences.

Among the various amendments introduced to confiscation law, special attention should be paid to the Programming Act related to the execution of penalties 2012 (*Loi n° 2012-409 du 27 mars 2012 de programmation relative à l'exécution des peines*) which allowed for ordering confiscation of assets being at the free disposal (*libre disposition*) of the convicted person (Article 16) and broadened the application of value confiscation (Article 17). The latter change was aimed at guaranteeing the enforcement of confiscation from available assets even in cases when they had not previously been seized, or when they were acquired after a judgment, to the extent corresponding to the proceeds of an offence (see *Circulaire du 14 mai 2012 présentant les dispositions de droit pénal et de procédure pénale de la loi n° 2012-409 du 27 mars 2012 de programmation relative à l'exécution des peines*, NOR: JUSD1222695C, Bulletin Officiel du Ministère de la Justice, No. 2012-05). Other important amendments concerned the establishment of AGRASC and its mandate. However, given that AGRASC was established in 2010, the French solutions adopted in the area of the management and disposal of frozen or confiscated assets should be considered to be a genuine national concept, the origins of which were not influenced by EU law[23] (cf. Thony and Camous 2013, 214–215). Quite the contrary, the French solutions in this field represent a more advanced approach than current EU law and may serve as inspiration for the EU and other EU jurisdictions in developing rules on managing and disposing of assets captured in criminal proceedings. However, it should be noted that some of the advances introduced in this area over time were to some extent inspired by the Italian model, for instance as regards direct social reuse of assets (on the Italian model, see Vettori and Di Nicola 2017, 329; Vettori 2018, 719; Diamanti et al. 2019; Mosca 2020).

Accordingly, thus far EU law cannot be considered to be a crucial factor influencing French national legislation in this field.

As far as the scope of triggering offences is concerned, this depends on the type of confiscation. The legal construct of regular confiscation uses two alternative methods to determine scope, 'catalogue offences', and the 'severity of criminal threat'. Accordingly, regular confiscation is applied in cases provided for by the statutory or regulation provisions, including cases of petty offences. In addition, it is applied 'automatically' (*de plein droit*, Mayaud and Gayet 2020, 296), in respect of felonies and misdemeanours punishable by imprisonment with a lower limit established as at least 1 year, with the exception of press offences (Article 131-21(1) of the CC). More stringent rules apply to extended confiscation. In this type of confiscation, the scope of triggering offences is limited to felonies and misdemeanours, punishable by at least 5 years of imprisonment, which have provided a direct or indirect profit (Article 131-21(6) of the CC). As a rule, confiscation measures are not mandatory; however, confiscation is obligatory when security reasons are at stake, as in the case of objects recognised as dangerous, harmful, or prohibited (Article 131-21(8) of the CC). In addition, the court shall order confiscation of seized property considered an instrumentality, object, or product of crime. Nevertheless, the court may depart from ordering confiscation in view of the circumstances of the concrete offence and the personality of the perpetrator (Article 131-21(4) of the CC).

It should be pointed out that French law also operates with its own categorisation of confiscation measures, which does not follow that adopted in EU law. In addition, it distinguishes the variety of extended confiscation in more extensive form, having a general character, the so-called 'confiscation of patrimony' (Giudicelli-Delage et al. 2019, 180; Pradel 2019, 606). It concerns all or part of the property (*tout ou partie des biens*), belonging or being at the free disposal of the convicted person, with respect for the rights of *bona fide* owners (Article 131-21(7) of the CC). Thus, there are two varieties of extended confiscation: one of general character, as determined in Article 131-21(7) of the CC, and one of special character, extended confiscation of assets of unjustified origin, as determined in Article 131-21(6) of the CC. The legal construct of extended confiscation in its more extensive form (Article 131-21(7) of the CC) is based on 'catalogue offences'; thus, it is only applied when prescribed by statutory provisions regarding felonies or misdemeanours. This catalogue covers some serious offences, for instance, offences against humanity (Article 213-1(4) of the CC) or the human species (Article 215-1(4) of the CC), drug trafficking (Article 222-49 of the CC), arms trafficking (Article 222-66(2) of the CC), exposure of someone to conditions violating human dignity (Article 225-26 of the CC), sexual offences against minors (Article 227-33 of the CC), possession of assets of unjustified origin (Article 321-10-1 of the CC), money laundering (Article 324-7(12) of the CC), acts of terrorism (Article 422-6), organised crime (Article 450-5 of the CC), and war crimes (Article 462-6 of the CC).

Notably, when it comes to confiscation from a third party, French law does not reflect the terminology applied in EU harmonising rules and does not separate this type of confiscation in the systematics of Article 131-21 of the CC. According to Article 131-21(2) of the CC, confiscation covers assets owned or being at the free disposal of the convicted person, and therefore, it may concern assets to which other persons have a legal title (except for *bona fide* persons). Extended confiscation of assets of unjustified origin may be addressed not only to the convicted person but also to the third parties, because it similarly concerns the assets belonging to or being at the free disposal of the convicted person. It is applied when the convicted person or the owner (any other person than the convicted person) has not explained the origin of the assets despite having such opportunity (Article 131-21(6) of the CC). Accordingly, the burden of proof is reversed. In case of extended confiscation targeted at third parties, the scope of triggering offences is the same (offences with a minimum threshold of five years of imprisonment which have brought a direct or indirect profit). Third parties are also included in the legal construct of general confiscation provided for in Article 131-21(7) of the CC. Mandatory confiscation determined in Article 131-21(8) of the CC covers dangerous, harmful, or prohibited objects, including cases when they do not constitute the property of the convicted person (see also special mandatory confiscation relating to the instrumentalities and products of drug trafficking offences provided for in Article 222-49 of the CC, which is addressed to the 'owner' conscious of their origin or usage). Pursuant to Article 131-21(13) of the CC, confiscation may be ordered only when the procedural right to be heard attributed to the owner of property was respected, i.e., when a third party with title to the assets, which is known or claimed in the course of the proceedings, had the opportunity to present their own stand on the confiscation measure, especially to assert their rights or good faith (Article 131-21(13) of the CC, except in the case provided for in Article 131-21(8) of the CC).

In this context, it should be noted that the right of third parties to be heard has been addressed in the decisions of the French Constitutional Council, *Conseil constitutionnel* (see Decision No. 2021-932 QPC, 23 September 23, 2021, and Decision No. 2021-949/950 QPC, 24 November 2021). The Constitutional Council challenged the conformity of the provisions concerning confiscation targeted at third parties with Article 16 of the Declaration of the Rights of Man and Citizen (1789). Accordingly, Article 131-21 of the CC on confiscation has been supplemented with a new sentence securing the right of the third parties to present their views on the confiscation measure (see Article 131-21(13) of the CC). The amendment in this respect was introduced by the Act No. 2021-1729 of 22 December 2021 for the confidence in the judiciary institution (*Loi n° 2021-1729 du 22 décembre 2021 pour la confiance dans l'institution judiciaire*, Article 51).

When it comes to non-conviction-based confiscation, the French CC does not contain substantive legal solutions in this respect. Instead, in 2016, procedural provisions similar in effect to NCBC were introduced to the CCP (*Code de procédure pénale* 1958) by the Act reinforcing the fight against organised crime, terrorism, and their financing and improving the efficiency and guarantees of criminal procedure (*Loi n° 2016-731 du 3 juin 2016 renforçant la lutte contre le crime organisé, le terrorisme et leur financement, et améliorant l'efficacité et les garanties de la procédure pénale*). One of the reasons behind these changes was the transposition of Directive 2014/42/EU containing the rules on NCBC. The function of the new Article 493-1 of the CCP concerning the execution of confiscation imposed by default was to ensure that a convicted person will not be able to require the restitution of the confiscated assets after the period of limitation *(Assemblée Nationale, Rapport*, 2016, No. 3515, 339).[24] Under French law, proceeding *in absentia* is admissible; therefore, illness or flight are not negative conditions against ordering confiscation (Giudicelli-Delage et al. 2019, 183–184). Property confiscated *in absentia* becomes the property of the State after the period of limitation of the penalty (Article 493-1 of the CCP). It is worth referring to one of the responses given by the French Ministry of Justice (2023), in which the mechanism of non-return of instrumentalities and proceeds (in the form introduced in 2016 under the influence of Directive 2014/42/EU) was considered to be similar in effect to confiscation without criminal conviction (see also Latimier 2017, 346).[25] Pursuant to Article 41-4 of the CCP, there is no need for restitution if it may create a danger to persons or property, when the property which has been seized in the course of proceedings constitutes an instrumentality or product of an offence (direct or indirect) or when under a specific provision objects placed in the court's custody are subjected to destruction (see also Article 41-5 of the CCP). The decision of the public prosecutor or the General Prosecutor on 'non-restitution' may be submitted by the interested person to the first president of the court of appeal or to the counsellor designated by him, with suspensory effect. When the decision on non-restitution can no longer be challenged, or the judgment on non-restitution has become final, objects whose restitution may create a danger to persons or property become the property of the State (subject to the rights of third parties). The 'decision on non-restitution' lies also in the competence of the investigating judge and certain courts (Article 99, 373, 481, and 512 of the CCP, see also Ministère de la Justice, 'Guide for the recovery of criminal assets in France', 2022).[26]

It should also be noted that the French CC determines an offence of unjustified resources (Article 321-6(1) of the CC). The constitutive elements of this offence are: the inability to justify resources corresponding to lifestyle or the origin of the asset, habitual relations with person(s) who committed a profitable offence punishable by at least 5 years of imprisonment or being the victims of such offences. The offence of unjustified resources is punishable by 3 years of imprisonment and a fine in the amount of 75,000 EUR. The same criminal threat is envisaged for facilitating the explanation of fictitious resources for persons involved in profitable offences punishable by at least 5 years of imprisonment (Article 321-6(2) of the CC). The criminal threat is aggravated when the related offences are committed by a minor subordinated to a person who is not able to prove the licit origin of resources or are 'catalogue offences' (e.g., human trafficking, organised crime, offences related to weapons or explosive products, drug trafficking, including in the case of habitual relations with drug users, Article 321-6-1 of the CC). Notably, an additional penalty of general (extended) confiscation, provided for in Article 131-21(7) of the CC, may also be ordered (Article 321-10-1 of the CC).

As far as the subject of confiscation is concerned, the legal solutions vary by the type of confiscation. As a rule, confiscation measures concern natural and legal persons.[27] Similarly to Polish and German law, French law allows for imposing extended confiscation also on a first-time offender without any criminal record or ties to organised crime. To limit its use, the severity of criminal threat and the profitability of an offence are relevant, not the conditions relating to the perpetrator. When it comes to general confiscation, the CC uses the method of 'catalogue offences' (applicable in cases provided for by law). Nevertheless, it should be remembered that the constitutive elements of the offence of unexplained resources refer to habitual relations with a person (or persons) who committed a profitable offence punishable by at least 5 years of imprisonment (Article 321-6 of the CC).

Confiscation can be ordered *in specie* or in value. Value confiscation concerns an amount of money equivalent to the value of a confiscated object (Pradel 2019, 610). It may be executed on all assets belonging to or being at the free disposal of the convicted person, with respect to the rights of the *bona fide* owners (Article 131-21(10) of the CC). Obligatory confiscation of certain objects (dangerous, harmful, or prohibited) is ordered regardless of their ownership. Accordingly, this concerns third parties as well (Article 131-21(8) of the CC). In any other case, the rights of the *bona fide* owners must be respected (Article 131-21(13) of the CC).

Confiscation covers any movables or immovables, tangible and intangible (including rights), if used to or intended to commit an offence (instrumentalities), owned or being at the free disposal of the convicted person (Article 131-21(2) of the CC).[28] In addition, it covers various assets determined by numerous statutory and regulations provisions relating to penalties for offences (Article 131-21(5) of the CC). One example of this is the provisions on money laundering, which allow for the confiscation of a vehicle belonging to the convicted person and a weapon owned by or being at the free disposal of the convicted person (Article 324-7(6) of the CC). In case of offences committed with the use of online public communication service, confiscation may also cover the instrumentality which served to access such service (Article 131-21(2) of the CC). The latter possibility was introduced in 2022 by the Act No. 2022-299 of 2 March 2022 aimed to combat school harassment (*Loi n° 2022-299 du 2 mars 2022 visant à combattre le harcèlement scolaire*).

In addition, confiscation covers all assets constituting the objects, direct and indirect products of an offence (proceeds), unless they are liable to be returned to the victim, and with respect for the rights of *bona fide* third parties (Article 131-21(3) and (13) of the CC). If the criminal proceeds have been mixed with the assets of licit origin for acquiring one or more of the assets, confiscation should not exceed the estimated value of these proceeds (Article 131-21(3) of the CC). Compulsory confiscation concerns property seized in the course of proceedings if have been used to or intended to commit an offence, or constitutes an object or product of an offence (direct or indirect) (Article 131-21(4) of the CC). General confiscation ('confiscation of patrimony') concerns all or part of the property belonging to or being at the free disposal of the convicted person, subject to the rights of the *bona fide* owners (Article 131-21(7) of the CC).

In view of the positions formulated in the doctrine and case-law of domestic courts, the concept of 'free disposal' (*libre disposition*) refers to the 'economic' power of the convicted person over the assets, despite not having a legal title to them. This concept was introduced in 2012 and developed in the case-law of domestic courts. Importantly, it involves protecting the rights of *bona fide* third parties (see, e.g., Ascensi 2021, 109–110; Matsopoulou 2021, 116; Dechenaud 2019, 144; and the rulings of the Court of Cassation, Criminal Chamber: No. 13-80.062, 29 January 2014; No. 13-80.063, 29 January 2014; No. 13-81874, 15 January 2014; No. 13-88.331, 19 November 2014; No. 13-85.150, 9 December 2014; No. 14-87.754, 3 February 2016; No. 17-82.632, 8 November 2017; No. 19-86.979, 25 November 2020).

The French CC does not explicitly indicate the method of calculation of the proceeds from an offence. However, this issue has been recognised by the doctrine as being important to the determination of the proceeds (*producta/fructa sceleris*). For instance, Acensi (2021, 95) posed the question of whether economic advantage should be considered as a 'net' or 'gross' gain, accompanied by the comment that the possibility of deducting expenditures incurred to commit an offence seems legally and morally doubtful (see also Segonds 2020). In this context, Ascensi (2021, 95) referenced the Explanatory Report to the Strasbourg Convention (1990), pointing to the different national solutions which exist in this field, and rather a common approach towards applying the broad meaning of 'proceeds' in cases of drug offences. In the latter type of cases, the French Court of Cassation, Criminal Chamber has displayed a similar approach (e.g., rulings No. 99-84.559, 27 April 2000; No. 19-87.809, 6 January 2021; Ascensi 2021, 95). However, a narrower approach has also been presented by this Court, such that the proceeds of an offence should not be confused with the 'turnover including tax' generated by suspicious contracts (Court of Cassation, Criminal Chamber, No. 20-84117, 10 March 2021; see also ruling No. 19-86.199, 6 January 2021). Given the above, a view has been presented that the issue of the proceeds of crime should be further clarified in the judicature (Hy 2021). In this context, it should also be noted that confiscation of assets of unjustified origin may be subject to proportionality control (Court of Cassation, Criminal Chamber, No. 18-83.396, 12 June 2019; cf. the rulings No. 17-82.098, 3 May 2018, and No. 16-87.009, 27 June 2018).

As far as procedural facilitations for proving a link between assets and criminal conduct are concerned, the legal construct of extended confiscation adopted in French law involves a statutory presumption of the criminal origins of assets and a reversal of the burden of proof. As indicated previously, the scope of confiscation is extended to any property belonging to or being at the free disposal of the convicted person, with respect for the rights of the *bona fide* owners, if the convicted person or the owner, despite having an opportunity to provide explanations about the property likely to be confiscated, has not been able to justify its origin (Article 131-21(6) of the CC). Under this concept of extended confiscation, establishing a link between the assets and criminal conduct, in principle, does not depend on the court's discretion; however, the court has to take into account all the facts and circumstances of the case when deciding on extended confiscation, in particular, when assessing the evidence submitted by the subjected persons in order to rebut the legal presumption on the criminal origin of the assets. Notably, the current version of the statutory provisions on extended confiscation was put in place as a consequence of aligning French law to EU law. As indicated above, extended confiscation was introduced in 2007 with the view of transposing FD 2005/212/JHA. Then, under the influence of Directive 2014/42/EU, its legal construct was amended in order to allow confiscation of assets being 'at the free disposal' of the convicted person. The statutory presumption about the illegal origin of property is mandatory, and its rebuttal burdens the subjected person. Importantly, third parties should be given an opportunity to present their views on the planned confiscation measure (Article 131-21(13) of the CC). The position of third parties was strengthened in confiscation settings as a result of the previously mentioned amendment of 2021. However, similarly to Polish and German confiscation law, the statutory provisions do not clarify whether proof beyond a reasonable doubt is required to rebut the assumption on the criminal origin of assets, or if the standard of proof may be lessened. This aspect is also important from the perspective of the possible retroactive effect of extended confiscation. It should be remembered that the date of acquisition of assets considered to have an unjustified origin is irrelevant in legal appraisals (Ascensi 2021, 102; the Court Cassation, Criminal Chamber, No. 16-87.296, 21 March 2018).

Moving on to the next point of consideration, i.e., the guarantees of victims' rights provided within confiscation settings, pursuant to Article 131-21(3) of the CC, assets constituting an object or product of an offence are excluded from confiscation if they are liable to be returned to the victim. Restitution may also be carried out in the pre-judgement phase, if the assets were captured in the course of proceedings (Articles 41-4 and 99 of the CCP concern the objects placed under judicial control; on procedural aspects in this respect, see more Giudicelli-Delage et al. 2019, 217). What distinguishes the French confiscation mechanism from the Polish version is that it allows victims' claims to be satisfied from the confiscated assets (cf. Articles 44(5) and 45(1) of the Polish CC). In this respect, AGRASC plays a crucial role in the French system. This Agency was established in 2010 and has been active since 2011. It was inaugurated by Act No. 2010-768 aimed at facilitating seizure and confiscation in criminal matters (*Loi n° 2010-768 du 9 juillet 2010 visant à faciliter la saisie et la confiscation en matière pénale*) and (executive) Decree No. 2011-134 on the Agency for the management and recovery of seized and confiscated asset (*Décret n° 2011-134 du 1er février 2011 relatif à l'Agence de gestion et de recouvrement des avoirs saisis et confisqués*). Its mission and structure were determined in the constituent act (No. 2010-768), which introduced the new Title XXX to the CCP. According to Article 706-159 of the CCP, AGRASC is a public State institution of administrative character, jointly supervised by the Minister of Justice and the Minister responsible for the budget. AGRASC operates on several levels – central, regional (*via* the regional branches), and international (it is engaged in various international initiatives focused on tackling criminal assets, including the ARO network and CARIN).[29]

AGRASC is administered by the board of directors, chaired by a judicial magistrate appointed by the decree (Article 706-162, Article R.54-1 of the CCP). It is composed of seven representatives of the State: the director of criminal affairs and pardons, the director of the budget or his/her representative, the secretary general of the Ministry of Justice, and the directors general of: public finances, customs and indirect taxes, the national police, the national gendarmerie. In addition, three persons appointed by the Minister of Justice qualified in contract law, corporate law, property management, and public procurement (for a three-year term of office, renewable). Moreover, two representatives of AGRASC (for a three-year term of office, renewable). However, the chairman may invite at the meetings any person in an advisory capacity (Article R.54-2 of the CCP).

Among the competences of AGRASC are, i.a., managing assets seized, confiscated, or covered by a precautionary measure in criminal proceedings entrusted to it and requiring administrative acts and centralised management of all sums seized in criminal proceedings.[30] It should be added that movable property, the ownership of which has passed to the State may be allocated free of charge to various services, institutions, foundations, associations of public utility, etc., under the General Code of Public Property (*Code général de la propriété des personnes publiques*). According to Article L.2222-9 of this Code, movable property obtained by the State under a final decision issued in criminal proceedings may be assigned, free of charge, to various services (judicial, police, prison, customs, or the French Biodiversity Office), in addition, to gendarmerie units, and public entities supervised by the Ministry of Justice. If the movable property is not allocated to the above-mentioned entities, it may be assigned to the administrative units of a national park or a syndicate for developing and managing a regional natural park, as well as foundations or associations of public utility or sports federations.

AGRASC has also been empowered to make immovable property under its management available to certain associations of general interest (philanthropic, educational, scientific, etc., as mentioned in Article 200(1)(b) of the General Tax Code (*Code général des impôts*), foundations of public utility, local authorities, and certain organisations (managing projects concerning social housing or accommodation), where appropriate, free of charge (Article 706-160(9) of the CCP).[31] The possibility of social usage of immovable property was introduced in 2021 by the Act No. 2021-401 of 8 April 2021 improving the efficiency of local justice and the criminal response (*Loi n° 2021-401 du 8 avril 2021 améliorant l'efficacité de la justice de proximité et de la réponse pénale*). The procedural issues, including contracts on the provision of immovable properties, were specified at the end of 2021, in the Decree for the application of the ninth paragraph of article 706-160 of the CCP relating to the social allocation of confiscated immovables (*Décret n° 2021-1428 du 2 novembre 2021 pris pour l'application du neuvième alinéa de l'article 706-160 du code de procédure pénale relatif à l'affectation sociale des biens immobiliers confisqués*). However, this Decree relates to immovable properties being under the management of AGRASC after a final confiscation decision, but not those seized in criminal proceedings (see Article 706-1609(1) and (9) of the CCP). Hence, the legislative scheme has raised some doubts in the subject literature about the real intentions of the legislators (see Ascensi 2021, 195).

In the context of EU law, the introduction of the possibility of social reuse of confiscated immovables in 2021 should be seen more as the next step towards developing an original French system of managing and disposing of seized and confiscated assets, than a response to EU law recommendations in this respect. Indeed, during legislative works, reference was made to the 'authorisation' of the States by EU law for the reuse of confiscated assets for public or social interest (*Sénat, Rapport No. 352, Session ordinaire de 2020–2021*, 22);[32] however, this reference should be considered to be secondary reasoning. The allusion to EU law was made *en passant*, without wider reflections referring to concrete EU instruments. Conversely, in this respect EU law lags behind the solutions found in French law. Accordingly, the recommendation of EU law to take measures 'allowing confiscated property to be used for public interest or social purposes' (Article 10(3) of Directive 2014/42/EU) cannot be considered as the vehicle for these changes in French law.

The annual reports for the last two years (the procedures for the social reuse of immovable assets were determined at the end of 2021 in the aforementioned Decree No. 2021-1428 of 2 November 2021) show the activity of AGRASC in this area. The AGRASC activity report for 2022 states that the new legislation offered an alternative solution to the sale of confiscated immovable properties and transferring the proceeds to the State Treasury. Instead, as indicated in this report, 'ill-gotten assets' can be returned to the 'population' in a direct and visible manner (3). According to this report, in 2022, social allocations covered three immovables (2, 24).[33] As far as victims, acting as civil parties, are concerned, in 2022, the total sum allocated to civil parties amounted to 16.8 million EUR, in 236 cases (137, 140). The AGRASC report for 2023 indicates that five social allocations of buildings were carried out, and an additional five were in process (3). The total sum allocated to civil parties amounted to 97.8 million EUR, in 247 cases (48, 99). However, the report in question noted that of this total, 79 million EUR was allocated as the result of one case.[34]

In addition, AGRASC provides guidance and assistance to the authorities competent for criminal matters (judicial and prosecutorial) in the area of planned seizures and confiscations, and managing the captured assets. The Agency also arranges training activities and promotes good practices for seizures and confiscations (Article 706-161 of the CCP). The mission of AGRASC includes also paying contributions to the State aimed at financing the fight against delinquency and crime, as well as the prevention of prostitution and various forms of support of prostituted persons (Article 706-161(3) of the CCP). Notably, the resources at the disposition of AGRASC also come from various subventions and contributions from the State, the EU, public institutions and other public and private entities, donations and legacies, certain tax revenues, and other revenues (see Article 706-163 of the CCP).

It should be noted that a special competition fund operates in the French system, the replenishment of which also remains within the Agency's competences. This fund collects revenues from confiscation of assets imposed in drug trafficking cases. As a general rule, the ownership of the confiscated object is transferred to the State, unless special provisions provide for its destruction or allocation (Article 131-21(11) of the CC). The Decree of 17 March 1995, No. 95-332, enabled assimilation of the revenues from confiscations ordered in drug trafficking cases by the competition fund intended for expenditures in the public interest (*Décret n° 95-322 du 17 mars 1995 autorisant le rattachement par voie de fonds de concours du produit de cession des biens confisqués dans le cadre de la lutte contre les produits stupéfiants*). Such proceeds are allocated through the competition fund to the budget for social affairs, health and the city, namely, to the section devoted to 'inter-ministerial activities to combat drug addiction', and 'social affairs and health'.[35] Assets are allocated to this fund during the calendar year, and the interministerial initiative 'Interministerial mission to combat drugs and addictive behaviours' (*Mission interministérielle de lutte contre les drogues et les conduites addictives* – MILDEC) is responsible for the execution of the credits transferred to various institutions. The funds are allocated according to the following scheme: Police (35%); Gendarmerie (25%), Customs (10%), Justice (20%), and importantly, prevention actions (10%).[36] These prevention actions are undertaken under the aegis of MILDEC, and this way of disposing of confiscated assets can be considered as (indirect) social reuse (see Vettori and Di Nicola, 2017). The other credits, allocated to Police, Gendarmerie, and Customs, can be considered in terms of incentivisation scheme. MILDEC engages the funds in various prevention projects. Notably, these projects are conducted by the municipalities or intercommunal structures following calls for national projects. They may concern education, creating supportive and protective environments, organisation of local festivities (regular and occasional), coordination of health centres, supporting local actions preventing the participation of youth in drug trafficking, or direct support for people in need, like vulnerable drug users. The idea is to undertake the actions close to the people. In addition, in view of the consumption of psychoactive substances by persons placed under the supervision of the justice system, the Ministry of Justice is responsible for supporting preventive actions in this respect.

Importantly, the French model of disposal of confiscated assets also serves to compensate the victims of offences. There is some synergy between confiscation and compensation mechanisms, accordingly, confiscation began to be regarded in French doctrine, also as a 'reparation measure' (e.g., Dezeue and Horion, 2018).

According to Article 706-164 of the CCP, a person having the status of a civil party, who has benefited from a final decision awarding compensation or reparation and costs, may obtain payment from the confiscated assets. Firstly, it concerns the persons who have not obtained compensation or reparation from the offender (Article 706-15-2), or from the resources of the Victims Guarantee Fund through the Commission for Compensation of Victims of Offences (*Commission d'indemnisation des victimes d'infractions* – CIVI). Such commissions operate within the jurisdiction of each court (Article 706-4 of the CCP; Pereira 2023, 558). Secondly, it concerns the persons who have not obtained assistance with recovery through the Recovery Assistance Service for Victims of Offences (*Service d'aide au recouvrement des victimes d'infraction* – SARVI; see Title XIV bis of the CCP). The solutions in this respect were introduced in 2008 by the Act of 1 July 2008 creating new rights for victims and improving the execution of penalties (*Loi n° 2008-644 du 1er juillet 2008 créant de nouveaux droits pour les victimes et améliorant l'exécution des peines*). In such cases civil parties may ultimately obtain payment from AGRASC (see also Ascensi 2021, 191).[37] However, AGRASC must be the custodian of confiscated assets to use them for this purpose (see the Court of Cassation, Civil Chamber, No. 18-20.973, 16 January 2020). The payment is made by deduction from the funds at the disposition of AGRASC or from the liquidation value of the assets of the debtor subjected to a decision on confiscation or non-restitution, including when assets have become the State's property under Article 41-4 of the CCP (Article 706-164 of the CCP). The consequence of such payment is that the State enters into the rights of the victim against the perpetrator. However, from the procedural viewpoint, the path of obtaining the payment from the confiscated assets *via* AGRASC is currently perceived as an additional route (see, e.g., Hilger 2016; Pereira 2023, 560; Ambroise-Castérot et al. 2020, 1342; Court of Cassation, Civil Chamber 2, 20 October 2016, No. 15-22.789).

It should also be noted that AGRASC may inform victims and competent services, *ex officio* or upon request, about assets to be returned on the basis of judicial decisions, with a view to ensuring the payments of debts, such as tax, customs, etc. (Article 706-161(4) of the CCP). In addition, the public has the opportunity to learn about the activities of the Agency. Firstly, AGRASC has been authorised to conduct information actions aimed at presenting its operational activities to the public, and to promote good practices for seizures and confiscations (Article 706-161(2) of the CCP). Moreover, it has been obliged to prepare annual reports, including not only statistical data but also reflections and proposals, with a view to improving the normative framework and practices of seizures and confiscations (Article 706-161(7) of the CCP). These competences should be seen in the context of enabling public discussion and social control over the national mechanism of the management and the disposal of the seized and confiscated assets.

Comments on the French model

Comparing the French model of confiscation with the German and Polish models, attention should be paid to the following aspects. Similar to the Polish and German confiscation laws, French confiscation law partly reflects the shortcomings previously identified at the EU law level. Firstly, the scope of triggering offences adopted in the legal construct of extended confiscation opens it up to application against offences of at least medium gravity (as in the Polish model, in the German model extended confiscation can be applied across the full spectrum of offences). Combining this possibility with the lack of requirements as regards the subject of extended confiscation, which can even be a first-time offender or a third party without any ties to organised crime or with a clean criminal record, and a lessened standard of proof enabling the assumption that assets of unjustified origin have a criminal origin – the conclusion is justified that the risk of judicial error inherent in this type of confiscation is not mitigated by statutory provisions but is further increased. However, on the formal side, all the solutions adopted in this respect by comparator jurisdictions, Poland, Germany, and France, are in line with EU law, which itself lacks any hard or soft law solutions aimed at mitigating such risk. Accordingly, similarly to Polish and German models, under the French model, extended confiscation can no longer be considered to be a measure of special reaction to serious crime, especially in its organised form. Notwithstanding its roots being deeply linked with the fight against such types of crime posing clear challenges when proving a real link between suspicious assets and a concrete offence under a criminal standard of proof (for instance asset sources concealed by the use of fictitious entities or complex transactions). Under all three models, extended confiscation may be imposed not only in cases of serious offences committed in an organised form, posing, in principle, obvious evidentiary difficulties, but also in cases of offences of medium gravity (or minor gravity in the German model), the proving of which, in principle, should not pose such an extraordinary challenge for public authorities so as to justify searching for solutions in the area of a lowered standard of proof. Therefore, the procedural facilitations lessening the criminal standard of proof, if used in cases of medium or even minor gravity, may be questioned in terms of their 'necessity' and 'proportionality', relevant in assessing the admissibility of interference with the right to property (Article 1 of the first Protocol to the ECHR; Article 17 of the Charter).

Another point is that challenging the scope of a confiscation order may be difficult in practice, as it can be equated with a requirement to rebut the legal presumption about the criminal origin of the targeted assets. Extended confiscation is only possible when the subjected persons, having been given the opportunity to provide explanations, were unable to justify the licit origin of the assets (a reversal of the burden of proof). However, similarly to Polish and German law, there are no clear statutory provisions determining the minimum evidence required to effectively challenge an extended confiscation order ('hard' v 'probability' evidence justifying the licit origin of the assets). This should also be seen in the context of the possible retrospective effect of extended confiscation, as French provisions, similarly to the German model, do not limit the period of the acquisition of the confiscable assets. In Poland, the mandatory presumption of the criminal origin of forfeitable property extends the scope of confiscation to property obtained by the perpetrator within the period of 5 years prior to committing an offence (until the moment of issuing even a non-final sentence, cf. Article 45(2) of the Polish CC). Given the retroactive effect of extended confiscation permitted by French law, the ability to justify the licit origin of assets may be difficult in practice, which raises questions about the real possibility of exercising the right of defence (unless such a situation is treated as the subjected person having been given insufficient possibility to justify the origin of the assets due to the passage of time, e.g., after the expiry of the statutory periods for retaining tax, accounting, or banking documentation, cf. Article 131-21(6) of the French CC *in fine*).

Similarly to Polish law, and differently from German law, the French CC does not determine the method of calculation for assets which may be covered by the confiscation order, with no guidance on whether the 'gross' or the 'net' principle should be applied. This issue has been explored in the case-law of the Court of Cassation, Criminal Chamber, where it was argued that certain expenditures should not be deductible, especially in cases concerning drug offences. Nevertheless, the opinion that this issue needs further clarification can be observed in the doctrine.

Unlike in the Polish and German models, under the French model, the State, in principle, is not necessarily the 'ultimate' beneficiary of confiscated assets. It should be underlined here that the key point is not the formal transfer of the property rights to the State but the method of the ultimate disposal of the confiscated assets. Since 2011, when AGRASC began its activities, the issues of managing and disposing of seized and confiscated assets are handled together by a single State agency at the central level (including its regional branches). Furthermore, it should be highlighted that the French model recognises the synergy between the confiscation and compensation mechanisms, which means that victims' claims can also be satisfied from the confiscated assets, not only *via* the traditional compensation mechanisms (from the offender or the State). Simply put, civil parties disposing of a final compensation decision may obtain their payments directly from AGRASC (through the deduction from the funds or the liquidation value of the assets of their debtor subjected to confiscation or non-restitution decisions). This is an auxiliary solution for obtaining compensation, separate from the typical pathways serving the civil parties in the pursuit of their claims. Finally, in 2021, AGRASC gained the new competence for direct social reuse of confiscated immovable properties, inspired by the Italian solutions existing in this respect. The first social allocations were recorded in the AGRASC annual activity reports for the years 2022 and 2023.

Nonetheless, when we examine the development of the most important innovations in the area of interconnecting the confiscation and compensation schemes, introducing a central mechanism of the management and disposal of seized and confiscated assets, or the possibility of the direct social reuse of confiscated immovable properties, we can conclude that their introduction in the French context did not result from the direct impact of EU law. From the very beginning, AGRASC's creation in 2010, and the very concept of its mandate, were truly innovative when seen against the background of other EU jurisdictions and the EU *acquis*. However, on a global scale they are less revolutionary. For example, when discussing the solutions introduced in France, Thony and Camous (2013, 213) recalled the example of Colombia, as one of the countries in which the management of assets from illicit activities had been entrusted to a separate body (Society for Special Assets, *Sociedad de Activos Especiales*).[38] At most, referencing EU law in the legislative processes was a secondary justification for national legislators when developing genuine concepts in those areas.

Conversely, EU law lacks advanced legal solutions in the area of social reuse of confiscated assets or embedding victims' rights into the confiscation mechanism, compared with those provided for in the French model. Accordingly, in these areas, EU law cannot be regarded as a factor which effectively contributed to reforming the national confiscation mechanism. Considering the French example, one might conclude that so far, EU law has offered very little added value to the national legislation during the development of solutions for the social reuse of confiscated assets, nor when strengthening the position of victims within the confiscation mechanism.

Broadening the view: the approach to confiscation of the proceeds of crime in England and Wales

While a member of the EU, the UK applied the opt-clause against Directive 2014/42/EU, a key harmonising instrument in the area of confiscation. In the opinion of Jenney (2016), 'the special opt-out status of the UK already provided a prelude to its complete departure from the AFSJ' (138). However, the non-participation in that directive should also be seen in the context of an already well-developed domestic confiscation scheme. Thus, EU harmonising rules could not be considered as a potential agent of change at that time. Conversely, the confiscation mechanism adopted in the UK was considered one of the maximum policy options in the legislative procedure preceding the adoption of Directive 2014/42/EU, so one might say that the direction of influence was quite the opposite – more advanced national confiscation solutions were taken as inspiration by the EU legislators to formulate policy options when shaping common rules on confiscation.[39] In addition, before Brexit (2020), the UK notified its wish to participate in the mechanism of mutual recognition of confiscation orders laid down by Regulation 2018/1805 (Recital 55 of the Preamble), which notably provides for a broader scope of recognition of confiscation orders than the minimum level of harmonisation set by Directive 2014/42/EU.

Currently, the UK participates in legal exchange in the area of confiscation with the EU MS under the EU–UK Trade and Cooperation Agreement (2021) – TCA.[40] However, despite not involving the mutual recognition mechanism, the provisions of the TCA reflect the UK's willingness to maintain broad cooperation with the EU MS in the area of freezing and confiscation. Ramos and Pons (2021) noted that the provisions of Title XI of the TCA – Freezing and Confiscation correspond to the Warsaw Convention (2005) and Strasburg Convention (1990), and to some extent to FD 2003/577/JHA and FD 2006/783/JHA. It should be added that, to enable broad cooperation, the provisions of the TCA on freezing and confiscation to some extent resemble the solutions contained in Regulation 2018/1805, and partly, those in Directive 2014/42/EU.[41] Nevertheless, EU confiscation law has been strongly influenced by the Strasbourg Convention and the Warsaw Convention, and one can say that these two CoE conventions helped the EU and the UK to find solutions for broad cooperation in the area of freezing and confiscation of assets after the UK's exit from the EU. Before moving to the main considerations concerning the alternative model of post-conviction confiscation adopted in England and Wales, and its possible usefulness when shaping common rules on confiscation, it is worth pointing out the similarities between the EU instruments concerning confiscation and the TCA, which allow the legal possibility of broad cooperation with EU MS in this area, despite the UK having the status of a non-EU state and using its own specific confiscation mechanisms.

Similarities can already be discovered at the definitional level, for instance between the legal definition of 'confiscation' contained in Article 657(a) of the TCA, and the definition of 'confiscation order' contained in Article 2(2) of Regulation 2018/1805. According to Article 657(a) of the TCA, 'confiscation' means a 'penalty or a measure ordered by a court following proceedings in relation to a criminal offence or criminal offences, resulting in the final deprivation of property' (cf. Article 1(d) of the Strasbourg Convention, and Article 1(d) of the Warsaw Convention). Bearing in mind the distinctions of legal terms in national legislation, the TCA defines the terms 'freezing' or 'seizure' (Article 657(b) of the TCA), which in fact, correspond with the definition of 'freezing' adopted in Article 2(5) of Directive 2014/42/EU (cf. Article 1(g) of the Warsaw Convention). The TCA also includes the broader term of 'provisional measures' (covering 'freezing' and 'seizing', see Article 663). In addition, the definition of 'property' is similar in both of these acts; however, for obvious reasons, the TCA does not directly reference Directive 2014/42/EU in this respect (cf. Article 2(3)(c) of Regulation 2018/1805 and Article 657(f) of the TCA). Another example is the similar definitions of 'instrumentalities' adopted in the TCA (Article 657(c)), and in Regulation 2018/1805 (Article 2(5); cf. Article 1(c) of the Strasbourg Convention, and Article 1(d) of the Warsaw Convention). Similarities can also be found in the definitions of 'proceeds' (cf. Article 657(e) of the TCA and Article 2(4) of Regulation 2018/1805, cf. Article 1(a) of the Strasbourg Convention, and Article 1(a) of the Warsaw Convention). However, the definition of 'judicial authority' in the TCA (Article 657(d)) differs from the definition of 'issuing authority' in Regulation 2018/1805 (Article 2(8)), but in fact, its scope is similar, as it encompasses a judge, a court, or a public prosecutor. In addition, the TCA provides for a similar way of sharing confiscated assets between States. Notably, the highest priority should be consideration of 'returning the confiscated property to the requesting State so that it can give compensation to the victims of the crime or return such property to their legitimate owners' (cf. Article 667(2) of the TCA, and Article 30 of Regulation 2018/1805).

The provisions of the TCA concerning confiscation reflect a mutual willingness for wide cooperation, albeit on a different basis of cooperation than Regulation 2018/1805. The latter deals with the recognition and execution of confiscation orders (Articles 18, and 20-21), whereas the TCA deals with the 'obligation to confiscate' (Article 665). This may also be decoded as an 'obligation to cooperate' in the area of confiscation, for instance, Ramos and Pons (2021) pointed to a 'duty to cooperate'. If a request concerns the execution of measures 'equivalent to confiscation of property', including 'by means of applications to civil courts' (Article 665(6) of the TCA), a State 'shall cooperate to the widest extent possible under its domestic law'. However, such obligation is limited to situations when such measures have been ordered by a 'judicial authority of the requesting State in relation to a criminal offence', and 'provided that it has been established that the property constitutes proceeds', or other property or income specified in Article 665(5) of the TCA. Schomburg and Oehmichen (2021) and Ramos and Pons (2021) indicated the departure from a formal inclusion of the *ordre public* clause in refusal grounds, as provided for in the CoE system (see Article 28 of the Warsaw Convention, and Article 18 of the Strasbourg Convention). However, apart from the typical grounds, based on the principle of *ne bis in idem*, double criminality, and others, special attention should be paid to Article 670(5)(d) of the TCA, which states that cooperation may also be refused if 'the request does not relate to a previous conviction, or a decision of a judicial nature or a statement in such a decision that an offence or several offences have been committed, on the basis of which the confiscation has been ordered or is sought' (without prejudice to Article 665(5) and (6) of the TCA). In this context, it is also worth quoting the Explanatory Notes related to the European Union (Future Relationship) Bill, as introduced in the House of Commons on 30 December 2020 (Bill 236).[42] The Explanatory Notes indicated that the Agreement 'provides for more limited grounds for refusal of a request allowing for the broadest cooperation possible' (para. 33).[43]

The rules on post-conviction confiscation applied in England and Wales equate the consequences of confiscation to a 'debt to be paid'. Such an approach is markedly different from that adopted in the examined civil EU jurisdictions, even if they recognise in value confiscation as distinct from confiscation *in specie*. However, the type of value-based confiscation (Alldridge 2011) adopted in England and Wales represents an example of an alternative model of confiscation. The intention of including this example is not to make comparisons but to broaden the research perspective. Accordingly, the following considerations are not structured in the same way as previous subsections dealing with the research questions concerning the confiscation models adopted in Poland, Germany, and France. To offer a broader look at possible designs for confiscation (in the criminal realm) and its potential shortcomings when orienting a confiscation mechanism primarily towards the effectiveness of repayment of debt, the further considerations are focused on the position of two actors in post-conviction confiscation settings, the defendant and the victim. Both roles are important in a more restorative approach to justice. Indeed, from the perspective of EU law, which in many respects represents a rather cautious approach to confiscation, and sometimes does not even realise the assumed policy objectives, the solutions of POCA may be regarded as more advanced and far-reaching. However, when considering their possible implantation in EU law to be followed by the EU MS, attention should be paid to some serious concerns regarding procedural justice and human rights protections, which have also been expressed in domestic literature on the topic, pointing out some deficiencies of the post-conviction scheme, especially in respect of the weakened position of the defendant. These observations may be valuable for both the EU and national legislatures, especially when resolving the difficulties which occur in 'border-line' legal situations, for instance when confiscation goes beyond restoring the status *quo ante* and enters into the area of criminal punishment. It should be remembered that such 'legal trespassing' may be enabled at the law level even if it is contrary to the policy underpinning confiscation. As with the observations made on the background of the confiscation models adopted in the comparator jurisdictions, analysis of the solutions adopted in POCA confirms that the method of calculation of the confiscable assets is conclusive in identifying the point at which confiscation starts to carry the element of 'hardship' characteristic of criminal punishment. Confiscation may of course merge various functions, from compensatory to punitive, but when the latter is at stake, this book suggests adopting the approach that the guarantees of criminal process remain relevant. In addition, the appropriate choice of the type of procedure under which a confiscation measure is adjudicated, especially correctly matching the standard of proof to the intended objective of a measure, may be seen as one of the basic manifestations of procedural justice. All of these aspects are also important when embracing a minimalist restorative approach to justice, one which pays attention to the position of all the stakeholders, not excluding the defendants.

The post-conviction confiscation procedure takes place before the Crown Court (Part 2, Section 6 et seq. of POCA). As a rule, its initiation depends on the 'conviction of the defendant for an acquisitive crime' (Williams, Hopmeier, and Jones 2018, 161). The crucial point in this procedure is the decision by the Crown Court on whether the case concerns 'particular' or 'general' criminal conduct'. According to Section 76(1) of POCA, the criminal conduct relevant in confiscation settings is that which 'constitutes an offence in England and Wales' or 'would constitute such an offence' if it occurred there. Accordingly, 'particular criminal conduct' is understood as all the criminal conduct constituting the offence for which the defendant has been convicted in the same proceedings, or which has been 'taken into consideration by the court in passing sentence' (The Crown Prosecution Service – CPS, Legal Guidance, Proceeds of crime, 2019; Section 76(3) of POCA). Importantly, in the case of 'particular criminal conduct', the benefit obtained must be proved, and assumptions are not applied (Rees, Fisher, and Thomas 2015, 25; Bullock and Lister 2014). Alternatively, 'general criminal conduct' is understood as all the criminal conduct of the defendant (Section 76(2) of POCA). Here, the time when such 'general criminal conduct' occurred is irrelevant, thus, reaching back into the past is admissible, and establishing a link between such conduct and any conviction or prosecution is not required. It is 'immaterial (…) whether conduct occurred before or after the passing of this Act', or 'whether property constituting a benefit from conduct was obtained before or after the passing of this Act' (Section 76(2) of POCA). Importantly, the concept of 'general criminal conduct' is connected with a 'criminal lifestyle', enabling the application of assumptions when determining benefit. According to Section 75(1) and (2) of POCA a 'defendant has a criminal lifestyle' if their offence(s) satisfies any of these conditions:

> (a) it is specified in Schedule 2; (b) it constitutes conduct forming part of a course of criminal activity; (c) it is an offence committed over a period of at least six months and the defendant has benefited from the conduct which constitutes the offence.
>
> (Section 75(2) of POCA)

The catalogue of so-called 'lifestyle offences' (Schedule 2 of POCA) covers: drug trafficking, money laundering, directing terrorism, slavery, servitude and forced or compulsory labour, people trafficking, arms trafficking, counterfeiting, certain offences against intellectual property, prostitution and child sex, blackmail, inchoate offences (attempting, conspiring, or inciting the commission of an offence specified in Schedule 2, and several other inchoate offences). Apart from the first condition pertaining to 'lifestyle offences', the additional requirement of the other two conditions is that the value of a benefit must be at least 5000 GBP (Section 75(4) of POCA). The second condition has been further clarified in Section 75(3) of POCA:

> Conduct forms part of a course of criminal activity if the defendant has benefited from the conduct and — (a) in the proceedings in which he was convicted he was convicted of three or more other offences, each of three or more of them constituting conduct from which he has benefited, or (b) in the period of six years ending with the day when those proceedings were started (or, if there is more than one such day, the earliest day) he was convicted on at least two separate occasions of an offence constituting conduct from which he has benefited.

The procedure runs as follows. The court 'must decide whether the defendant has a criminal lifestyle' (Article 6(4)(a) of POCA). If the court decides that the defendant has a 'criminal lifestyle', it must decide whether he/she has benefited from the 'general criminal conduct' (Article 6(4)(b) of POCA). Similarly, if the court decides that the defendant 'does not have a criminal lifestyle', it must decide whether he/she has benefited from the 'particular criminal conduct' (Article 6(4)(c) of POCA). When the court decides that the defendant has benefited from the conduct (general or particular), it must determine the 'recoverable amount' and 'make an order (a confiscation order)' requiring the defendant to pay that amount, however, 'if, or to the extent that, it would not be disproportionate to require the defendant to pay the recoverable amount' (Section 6(5) of POCA). The 'recoverable amount' is an 'amount equal to the defendant's benefit from the conduct concerned' (Section 7(1) of POCA). However, the defendant may show that the 'available amount' is less than that benefit, in which case the recoverable amount is the 'available amount', or a 'nominal amount, if the available amount is nil' (Section 7(2) of POCA). The 'available amount' is the aggregate of the 'total of the values (at the time the confiscation order is made) of all the free property then held by the defendant minus the total amount payable in pursuance of obligations which then have priority, and (…) the total of the values (at that time) of all tainted gifts' (Section 9(1) of POCA; see also CPS, Legal Guidance, Proceeds of crime 2019; Boucht 2019, 63).[44]

In order to decide whether the defendant benefited from the 'general criminal conduct', four assumptions are applied. Rees, Fisher, and Thomas (2015) indicated that the first three assumptions deal with what the defendant has 'received' (1), 'retained' (2), and 'spent' (3), in addition, the first and third assumptions 'cover the six-year period ending on the day when proceedings were started' (Rees, Fisher, and Thomas 2015, 38). According to the fourth assumption, the property obtained by the defendant is treated as obtained 'free of any other interests in it' (Section 10(5) of POCA). Importantly, the burden is on the defendant (the defence) to prove, on the balance of probabilities, that the mandatory assumption concerning particular property or expenditure is incorrect (Section 10(6) of POCA). Thus, the burden of proof is reversed in this respect (see, e.g., Schunke 2017, 58), However, when it comes to the 'serious risk of injustice', allowing for rebutting such an assumption, the provisions do not explicitly reverse the burden of proof, and accordingly, it is considered that this issue also concerns the judge (Rees, Fisher, and Thomas 2015, 42; *R v Rezvi* [2002] UKHL 1; *R v Benjafield* [2002] UKHL 2). Notably, the 'risk of injustice' clause does not cover the issue of 'hardship'. In this vein, Bullock and Lister (2014) indicated that this risk pertains only to 'injustice' resulting from the method of application of the assumptions, not any 'hardship' resulting from the order, for example the 'sale of the family home' (55). In this context, it is worth referring to the analyses of Fletcher (2019, 2020), showing that sales of family homes were not exceptional results of the confiscation mechanism and were negatively regarded by defendants, as exceeding the scope of their 'ill-gotten gains', primarily affecting their families, and thus hindering the process of their rehabilitation.

To understand the concept of confiscation as a 'debt to be paid', the form of its execution is crucial. A confiscation order is executed like a fine, 'as if the amount ordered to be paid were a fine imposed on the defendant by the court making the confiscation order' (Section 35(2) of POCA).[45] In this regard, under the Sentencing Act (2020), provisions allowing for ordering imprisonment in case of non-payment are applicable (UK Public General Acts 2020, c. 17). Section 129(3) of the Sentencing Act reads:

> The court must make an order (a 'term in default order') fixing a term— (a)of imprisonment, or (b)of detention under section 108 of the Powers of Criminal Courts (Sentencing) Act 2000, which the offender is to undergo if any sum which the offender is liable to pay is not duly paid or recovered.

As a rule, the amount ordered must be paid on the day on which the confiscation order is made. However, if the court is satisfied that the defendant is unable to pay the full amount at that time, it may determine a specified period in which a specified amount must be paid (not exceeding three months, with some possibilities to extend the period of payment, Section 11 of POCA). A confiscation order 'is satisfied when no amount is due under it' (Section 87(1) of POCA). An important aspect of the severity of the confiscation mechanism is the obligation to pay interest on an unpaid sum at a rate of 8% per annum (Section 12(2) of POCA in connection with Section 17 of the Judgments Act (1838), c. 110, concerning 'interest on civil judgment debts').

In view of the above, one can conclude that POCA puts an emphasis on the efficiency of confiscation (Schunke 2017, 67). In other words, the procedural structure is oriented such that the 'debt' must be paid. However, the issue of efficiency, as well as human rights protections has faced criticism in the domestic subject literature. For instance, the analyses of Bullock (2014) and Bullock and Lister (2014) have shown a discrepancy between the 'rhetoric' of post-conviction confiscation (focused on such issues as not profiting from crime, reducing or controlling crime, and inhibiting the 'corrosive effects of "organised crime" on financial systems') and the 'reality' of its operation, for instance, using the mechanism against low-level offenders (Bullock and Lister 2014, 48-49, 60; cf. the critics of the rhetoric of a 'follow-the-money' policy by Naylor, 1999). Bullock and Lister (2014) suggested that:

> the value of the "confiscation" strategy lies more in its communicative properties, by enabling the State to reassert its moral certitude within criminal justice policy, than its instrumental properties as an effective technology of crime control (47).

In addition, the quoted analyses showed some implications arising as consequences of confiscation on the part of the defendants and their families, demonstrating its 'creeping' and 'punitive' character (Bullock and Lister 2014, 55). This situation may be seen as resulting from different factors: the standard of proof (balance of probabilities), the legal construct of the assumptions applied in confiscation proceedings, and the reversal of the burden of proof. Criticism of the confiscation regime was also expressed by Lawrence (2008) in the article under the telling title 'Draconian and manifestly unjust: how the confiscation regime has developed', pointing out that the discretion of the court under POCA 2002 'is practically non-existent' (23). Lawrence also questioned the aspect of proportionality and peaceful enjoyment of a person's possessions, especially when the calculation of benefit substantially exceeds the personal benefit (Lawrence 2008, 23). In a similar tone, Rees, Fisher, and Thomas (2015) argued that the 'scheme of the Act is meant to be severe and unforgiving' (10), in addition:

> defendants are penalized for criminal conduct that is unproven; civil standards and methods of proof apply to most issues; assumptions of fact and reverse burdens of proof punctuate the various stages; hardship is never a consideration. It cannot be fathomed without an appreciation that it is public policy, not procedural fairness, that drives its workings.
>
> (Rees, Fisher, and Thomas 2015, 10)

These observations correspond with the research carried out by Fletcher (2019, 2020), focused on the perception of the post-conviction confiscation mechanism by defendants:

> Some research participants discussed how they had sold their family home and handed the proceeds from the sale over to the court but despite this, because their 'available' amount figure was made up of other assets for which they no longer possessed or had control over, the default prison sentence was still imposed. Such assets, which were often listed as 'hidden assets' or 'tainted gifts' by the financial investigator, are 'impossible' to recover.
>
> (Fletcher 2020, 88)

It should be noted that one of the procedural aspects of the post-conviction confiscation mechanism is a 'statement of information', delivered to the court by the prosecutor (Section 16 of POCA; see also Section 18 on provision of information by defendant and Section 22 on reconsideration of 'available amount'; *R v O'Flaherty*, [2018] EWCA Crim 2828). In practice, the statement of information should include, i.a., the 'extent of any allegation of hidden assets and the basis for such a belief' (CPS, Legal Guidance, Proceeds of crime (2019); Part 33.13 of the

Criminal Procedure Rules 2015, as amended, UK Statutory Instruments 2015, No. 1490, L. 18). As indicated by Wood (2016), it is on the part of the defendant to prove, on the balance of probabilities, that their 'asset base (the available amount) is worth less than the criminal benefit figure' (11), however:

> Where the defendant is either unwilling or unable to demonstrate the availability of assets, the court is bound by law to make an order to the tune of the full recoverable amount, regardless of whether that is realistic or not in terms of enforceability. These orders are called 'hidden assets orders'.
>
> (Wood 2016, 11)

The national confiscation procedures were examined by the ECtHR, which recognised that in principle confiscation constitutes a part of the sentencing process without a connection with any new criminal charge. Accordingly, Article 6(2) of the ECHR does not apply. Therefore, the guarantees of rights may be derived from the civil limb of Article 6 of the ECHR – its para. 1 (see also Schunke 2017, 78–86; Simonato 2017; and the observations of King (2014) in the context of 'civil forfeiture'). In this vein, the ECtHR reasoned in the following cases: *Welch v the UK*, Application no. 17440/90, 09 February 1995 (the procedure under the Drug Trafficking Offences Act 1986); *Phillips v the UK*, Application no. 41087/98, 5 July 2001 (the procedure under the Drug Trafficking Act of 1994); *Butler v the UK*, Application no. 41661/98, 27 June 2002 (the procedure under Drug Trafficking Act 1994); *Grayson and Barnham v the UK*, Applications nos. 19955/05 and 15085/06, 23 September 2008 (the procedure under the Drug Trafficking Act 1994); *Webb v the UK*, Application 56054/00, 10 February 2004, dec. (the procedure under the Drug Trafficking Act 1994); *Walsh v the UK*, Application 43384/05, 21 November 2006 (the procedure under POCA 2002); *Minhas v the UK*, Application no. 7618/07, 10 November 2009 (the procedure under POCA 2002); see also the case in progress: *Bagnall v the UK*, Application no. 54241/12 (the procedure under POCA 2002).

The relevance of the civil limb of Article 6 ECHR has also been considered by domestic courts in the context of the Human Rights Act (1998), 'An Act to give further effect to rights and freedoms guaranteed under the European Convention on Human Rights', UK Public General Acts 1998, c. 42 (see, e.g., *Leonard Lloyd v Bow Street Magistrates Court*, [2003] EWHC 2294 (Admin); *Syed v Westminster Magistrates Court*, [2010] EWHC 1617 (Admin);[46] *R. v Benjafield* [2002] UKHL 2; *R. v Rezvi*, [2002] UKHL 1).

Despite the severity of the confiscation regime, the aspect of proportionality, in principle, has not been challenged by the domestic courts (see, e.g., *R v Carter* [2006] EWCA Crim 416, *R v May* [2008] UKHL 28; both cases concerned the Criminal Justice Act 1988; *R v Mohammed Shabir* [2008] EWCA Crim 1809; concerned POCA 2002). Nonetheless, in *R v. Waya* [2012] UKSC 51, the UK Supreme Court held that the judge should refuse to make a confiscation order if it would be disproportionate (*R v. Waya*, 16; see also *R v Cole* [2018] EWCA Crim 888, and *R v Ahmad* [2014] UKSC 36 referring to *Paulet v the UK*). Two points should, however, be made here. Firstly, the case *R v Waya* concerned 'particular criminal conduct' (the defendant was not considered as having a 'criminal lifestyle'). Secondly, the Supreme Court indicated that the obligation to refuse to make an order due to proportionality issues 'is not the same as the re-creation by another route of the general discretion once available to judges but deliberately removed' (*R v Waya*, 24; see also Williams, Hopmeier, and Jones 2018, 163, 228). In addition, the Supreme Court pointed out that there was 'no need to invoke the concept of abuse of process' (*R v. Waya*, 18; see also *R v Sale*, [2013] EWCA Crim 1306; *R v Neuberg*, [2016] EWCA Crim 1927). The aspect of proportionality was also examined by the Supreme Court in *R v Ahmad* [2014] UKSC 36, concerning jointly obtained benefit. The Supreme Court held that 'it would not serve the legitimate aim of the legislation and would be disproportionate for the state to take the same proceeds twice over' (*R v Ahmad*, 71, 74).

Attention should also be drawn to the position of the ECtHR in *Paulet v the UK* (Application no. 6219/08, 13 May 2014), in which the post-conviction confiscation regime was successfully challenged in respect of Article 1 of the first Protocol to the ECHR. The applicant raised arguments concerning proportionality and the 'public interest', given that the case did not concern serious criminal offences such as drug trafficking or organised crime. The ECtHR examined the proceedings before the domestic courts and found that, indeed, the Court of Appeal 'did ask whether or not the order was in the public interest', but 'they did not go further by exercising their power of review' to determine whether the 'requisite balance' was maintained, i.e., the fair balance between the protection of the right of property and the requirements of the general interest (*Paulet*, 67; see also *Sporrong and Lönnroth v Sweden*, Applications nos. 7151/75; 7152/75, 23 September 1982, 69). Accordingly, the ECtHR concluded that 'the scope of the review carried out by the domestic courts was too narrow to satisfy the requirement of seeking the "fair balance" inherent in the second paragraph of Article 1 of Protocol No. 1' (*Paulet*, 68). The ECtHR took into account the following aspect of domestic proceedings:

> On the contrary, the Court of Appeal made it clear that the abuse of process jurisdiction had to be exercised 'sparingly'. In particular, it noted that 'the responsibility for deciding whether properly to seek a confiscation order is effectively vested in the Crown. When it does so, the court lacks any corresponding discretion to interfere with that decision if it has been made in accordance with the statute'.
>
> (*Paulet*, 67; see also *R v Shabir* [2008] EWCA Crim 1809, 24)

Moving on to the next point, that being the position of victims in confiscation settings, it should be noted that POCA provides for some possibilities to execute 'compensation orders' within the confiscation mechanism. The Law Commission Report (2022) stated: 'there are many instances where confiscation orders and compensation orders intersect', and even if the victims are not involved in confiscation proceedings, 'they might be indirectly affected when a compensation order is made against the defendant in their favour' (Law Commission, Confiscation of the proceeds of crime after conviction, summary of report 2022, 18). Work by the Law Commission of England and Wales on the review of the post-conviction mechanism was started in 2018. Some of their recommendations concern the prioritisation of the payment of compensation to victims of crime. A 'compensation order' is one of the 'priority orders' (Section 13(3A)(a) of POCA).[47] However, the compensation order has priority only in cases when the Crown Court makes both a confiscation order and one or more priority orders (like a compensation order) against the same person in the same proceedings and believes the person will not be able to satisfy all those orders in full, because of insufficient resources (Section 13(5) of POCA):

> In such a case the court must direct that so much of the amount payable under the priority order (or orders) as it specifies is to be paid out of any sums recovered under the confiscation order; and the amount it specifies must be the amount it believes will not be recoverable because of the insufficiency of the person's means.
>
> (Section 13(6) of POCA)

The procedural challenges when both types of order must be paid (compensation and confiscation) have been addressed in both the doctrine and cases brought before domestic courts (see, e.g., Williams, Hopmeier, and Jones 2018, 601). In *R v Davenport* [2015] EWCA Crim 1731, the Supreme Court held that the 'Court is empowered to make both a confiscation order and a compensation order' (75(1)). Nevertheless, the 'court should be alert to any risk of double counting inherent in such a combination of orders and should be alert to the risk of making a confiscation order which is disproportionate' (75(2)).[48] It should be noted that the case *R v Davenport* has been referenced in 'Guidance for prosecutors on the discretion to instigate' (Confiscation Proceedings 2020), which states that:

> In a case involving loss to one or more victims it may be legitimate for the court to make both a compensation order (compensating the victim or victims for the loss) and a confiscation order (requiring payment of the amount of loss to the state). That said, in such a case it is necessary to consider carefully whether it is legitimate to impose both orders. If, approaching the issue practically and realistically, the court thinks that any compensation order is certain to be satisfied, a confiscation order based on the same loss may be disproportionate: *R v Davenport* (…) (para 75 in particular).

Notably, the Law Commission recommended introducing changes aimed at extending prioritisation of the payment of compensation from sums recovered under the confiscation order not only in cases when the defendant does not have the means to pay both orders (a limitation which exists under the current regime). Secondly, they presented the view that compensation payments should also be given priority in cases of multiple confiscation orders (Law Commission, Confiscation of the proceeds of crime after conviction, summary of report 2022, 18). Finally, the Law

Commission recommended empowering the Crown Court 'to adjust the compensation element to be paid out of a confiscation order when the confiscation order is varied either upwards or downwards'. The reasoning behind these recommendations was 'fairness' for victims and for defendants ('preventing the defendant from facing unpayable orders') (18).[49]

The Law Commission report indicated the objectives which have been associated with the confiscation regime 'throughout its evolution', where the compensation of victims was listed as one of them. The report identified four objectives:

- taking away the profits or proceeds of crime,
- punishment,
- deterring and disrupting criminal activity, and
- the compensation of victims (Law Commission, Confiscation of the proceeds of crime after conviction: a final report, 2022, No. 410, 63).

However, the social aspect of confiscation was not identified therein. In the broader perspective, detached from the concrete national confiscation scheme, unleashing the social potential of confiscation, through returning the confiscated assets to the population, could be regarded as the next evolutionary step for confiscation mechanisms. Moreover, the social reuse of confiscated assets may foster public confidence in the criminal justice system and a culture of legality (see also Montaldo 2015; LIBE Report 2013[50]).

One of the provisional proposals made by the Commission concerned expressing the view the statutory purpose of the confiscation regime should include the compensation of victims (Law Commission, Confiscation of the proceeds of crime after conviction consultation paper (2020), No. 249, 86, 532).[51] Nonetheless, in their final report, the Law Commission recommended the narrow objective of Part 2 of POCA be 'placed on a statutory footing':

> The objective should be 'to deprive a defendant of their benefit from criminal conduct, within the limits of their means' and bodies exercising powers under Part 2 of POCA 2002 should pursue this objective. We observe that punishment, compensation, deterrence and disruption may be consequences of the regime but should not be stated aims.
>
> (Law Commission, Confiscation of the proceeds of crime after conviction: a final report, 2022, No. 410, 42)

In addition, although considering that the Criminal Injuries Compensation Authority (CICA) scheme operates as a 'measure of last resort' and in a limited area (compensation for blameless victims of violent crime), and acknowledging that the similar scheme does not serve the victims of economic crime (Consultation Paper, No. 249, 535), the Commission did not endorse the creation of a 'central compensation scheme, funded from sums collected pursuant to confiscation orders' (Confiscation of the proceeds of crime after conviction: a final report (2022), 516).[52] Furthermore, they opined that if such a scheme existed, similarly to CICA, it should operate as a 'measure of last resort' (Consultation Paper, No. 249, 535).

Notably, a majority of the consultation responses shared the opinion that a central compensation scheme financed *via* the confiscation mechanism should not be created (Confiscation of the proceeds of crime after conviction: a final report (2022), 523). However, there were also some responses which presented a different view in this regard. Special attention should be drawn to the response presented by the Garden Court Chambers (a multi-disciplinary set), advocating for transferring confiscated funds primarily to victims, rather than into a 'central pool to support "community projects" (often for police forces) and from which the victims may not benefit' (Garden Court Chambers, Response to Law Commission Consultation on 'Confiscation of the Proceeds of Crime After Conviction' (2020), 91).[53]

Above all, it should be acknowledged that the synergy between the confiscation and compensation mechanisms and the need to intensify this has, to some extent, also been recognised in discussions on shaping the future confiscation mechanism in a jurisdiction traditionally treating these mechanisms as distinct systems (cf., the Hodgson report of 1984, referenced in the Law Commission Consultation Paper, No. 249, 534). Nonetheless, when observing these discussions, one cannot exclude that the sense of the future confiscation mechanism being made more victim-oriented will take on increased significance over time, especially once internal difficulties are surmounted at the organisational or institutional levels.

It should be remembered that, in principle, this sense has not been substantively questioned, but the issues of financial resources and administration have been considered the main obstacles to the creation of a central compensation scheme funded from sums collected within the confiscation mechanism. Already well-established mechanisms, like that operating in France, may serve as a point of reference for other jurisdictions. This also relates to better recognition of the social potential of confiscation mechanisms, and accordingly, to enabling the return of confiscated assets to the population, however not under the aegis of the State but, at least partially, *via* direct transfers of confiscated assets to various social groups affected by or vulnerable to crime in a broad sense, including local communities.

Conclusions

The Polish, French, and German models of confiscation reflect in part the shortcomings previously found in the EU law standards on CPC in the following areas: the scope of triggering offences in the legal construct of extended confiscation, the method of determination for confiscable assets, the position of victims in confiscation schemes, and the social reuse of confiscated assets. All of these elements are important when considering how to make the EU confiscation scheme more restorative, a process which implies creating more inclusive, consultative, and balanced confiscation procedures and giving stakeholders (defendants, victims, communities) the opportunity to play more 'proactive' roles.

The scope of triggering offences in the legal construct of extended confiscation adopted in Polish and French law enables its application in cases of offences of at least medium gravity. However, under the influence of EU law, German law went even further by enabling its application across the whole spectrum of offences, including offences of minor gravity. The inherently risky nature of this measure should incline legislatures towards its restrained use as an extraordinary response to serious and organised crime. The predetermined risk of judicial error inherent in extended confiscation settings (see Boucht 2019) results from: a lessened standard of proof (the balance of probabilities), the mandatory application of legal presumptions on the criminal origin of assets at the expense of limiting the court's discretion, or alternatively, granting courts too broad a discretion in determining the criminal origin of the assets, while not giving them any statutory guidance in this respect. Comparative analysis shows that this risk is not mitigated by national laws but is further increased. Regrettably, however, this comment also concerns EU law. The gateway to overbroad application was opened to national legislatures by EU law itself, as Directive 2014/42/EU was itself a departure from the roots of extended confiscation which lay in the fight against serious organised crime and terrorism (cf. FD 2005/212/JHA). The specific legal construct of extended confiscation evidently grew from these roots, as serious and organised crime poses a clear challenge for public authorities in proving the link between the suspicious assets and the offence, and thus justifies the public interest in lessening the standard of proof in this respect. The same cannot be said about the reasonableness of the departure from a criminal standard of proof when combating crime of minor or medium gravity.

Comparative analysis shows that the national legislatures, under the influence of EU law, have willingly entered into the risky area of extended confiscation, due to it offering their public authorities a wider extent of confiscation through a facilitated procedure. However, the procedural simplifications which do not require establishing a link between confiscable assets and an offence under the criminal standard of proof primarily serve the public authorities, and disadvantage defendants, whose legal situation may be precarious when it comes to rebutting assumptions on the criminal origin of property. Therefore, the right to defence may be significantly impeded in practice, especially when faced with the retroactive effect of confiscation, allowing for exceptions from the *lex retro non agit* and *prioritas legis mitior* principles, with the tenuous justification that confiscation does not constitute a penalty. It should be pointed out that both EU law and the laws of the comparator jurisdictions lack provisions mitigating an excessive retroactive effect of confiscation which may make exercising the right of defence impossible, in particular when the statutory periods for retaining tax, accounting, or banking documentation have expired. In addition, both EU law and the laws of the comparator jurisdictions do not raise any requirements as regards the subject of confiscation, which may even be a person without any ties to organised crime or other criminal conduct, including low-profile and first-time offenders. Accordingly, the examined extended confiscation schemes, similar to EU law on extended confiscation, are not targeted at high-level offenders. When all these aspects are viewed together, the proportionality and public interest in ordering extended confiscation may be called into question in cases of offences of medium gravity (in Polish and French law), and especially those of minor gravity (the example of German law), in view of the conditions which limit admissible interference with the right to property (Article 1 of the first Protocol to the ECHR; Article 17 of the Charter).

The next point is that that EU law does not examine the procedural consequences of the choice of national legislatures between the 'net' and 'gross' principle and offers no rules concerning the method of calculation for confiscable assets. Accordingly, extended confiscation based on the 'gross' principle (even though not determined by statutory provisions), while at the same time departing from the criminal standard of proof, is still formally in compliance with EU law. However, these confiscation settings present an increased risk of judicial miscarriages. Similarly to the situation in EU law, this issue has still not been resolved in Polish or French law. Conversely, the 'gross' principle has been determined in German law, and after the reform of 2017, its extensive form has been rationalised. The case-law of the Polish and French courts ultimately supported the application of the 'gross' principle, especially in cases of drug trafficking offences. However, the question remains open as to whether the same rules of 'extensive counting' should be applied to other types of offences, for instance, economic crime where the value of contracts or taxes may be relevant. Whether the 'net' or 'gross' principle is applied is deeply interconnected with the procedural standards under which confiscation measures should be adjudicated, as depending on the method of calculation of confiscable assets, confiscation may push past the borders of reparation and enter into the area of criminal punishment. EU law should recognise this interconnection and provide the national legislatures with appropriate guidance in this respect.

EU law has so far been indecisive about embedding victims' right to compensation in the confiscation mechanism. Directive 2014/42/EU approaches this right from a negative side, i.e., that confiscation should 'not prevent the victims from seeking compensation for their claims' (Article 8(10)). A more innovative (positive) approach was adopted in the new Directive 2024/1224 (Article 18(1) and (5)). Thus far, in Polish law, victims' rights are treated similarly to the original approach, positioned as a negative premise for imposing confiscation. Furthermore, there are no concrete legal solutions which allow for satisfying victims' claims from confiscated assets. Comparative analysis shows that under Polish law the confiscation and compensation mechanisms are not interconnected. The German legislators, however, resolved this issue on their own, without any guidance from EU law. Victims' rights are embedded directly within the confiscation mechanism in a manner which presents a valid legislative option to follow for both the EU and other EU jurisdictions. After the reform of 2017, victims' claims under German law are no longer treated as a 'negative prerequisite' to the ordering of confiscation and can be satisfied at the enforcement stage of confiscation proceedings. The synergy between the compensation and confiscation mechanisms can also be observed in French law, which, as with German law, developed its own legal solutions in this respect without reference to EU law. Under the French model of confiscation, victims' claims can be satisfied not only *via* the traditional compensation mechanisms (from the offender or the State) but also directly from confiscated assets (civil parties disposing of a final compensation decision may obtain their payments directly from AGRASC). Accordingly, the French doctrine has also started to perceive confiscation as a 'reparation measure' (e.g., Dezeue and Horion 2018).

EU law also offers very little added value for national legislation in the area of social reuse of confiscated assets. As with EU law, the Polish and German confiscation schemes lack comprehensive solutions in this respect. Although some possibilities do exist for the transfer of assets to non-State entities, including charitable organisations, German law and Polish law principally represent the traditional approach, where the State is the main beneficiary of confiscated assets. Both these jurisdictions have so far not established a complex and centralised system for redistributing confiscated assets to public interest and social purposes, neither at the normative nor institutional levels. Conversely, France has been developing innovative solutions in this respect since 2010, starting with the establishment of AGRASC. Issues of managing and disposing of seized and confiscated assets are collectively handled by this State agency. In 2021, AGRASC gained a new competence in the area of direct social reuse of confiscated immovable properties. It should also be noted that under the General Code of Public Property (Article L.2222-9), movable property, the ownership of which has passed to the State, may be allocated free of charge, i.a., to foundations and associations of public utility, and sports federations. However, similar to how the national legislatures resolved the issue of embedding victims' rights to compensation in their national confiscation schemes, the innovations introduced in France in the area of social reuse of confiscated assets were not prompted by EU law. From the very beginning, the creation of AGRASC and the concept of its mandate was ahead of EU law, which, to date, has not offered the EU MS any advanced legal solutions in this respect. Thus, EU law cannot be regarded as a factor which has effectively contributed to strengthening the position of victims in the German and French confiscation schemes, or as having influenced the legal solutions on the disposal of confiscated assets introduced by France, both of which should be regarded rather as original national concepts not influenced by EU law. In light of the above, one might conclude that the EU soft law recommendation encouraging MS to reuse confiscated assets for the public interest and social purposes (Recital 35 and Article 10(3) of Directive 2014/42/EU), has not been effective in influencing the law of the examined EU jurisdictions. Regrettably, however, the new Directive 2024/1260 still pursues the route of a soft law recommendation addressed to MS (Recital 38 and Article 19(1)) and lacks any hard law stipulations in this respect. The official rhetoric around EU confiscation policy has highlighted the importance of two aspects important to the restorative perspective – prioritising victims' rights in the confiscation mechanism and enabling broad social reuse of confiscated assets, though, thus far EU law has not adequately reflected the policy assumptions in this respect, and to date has offered very little added value to national legislation.

However, even in the area of harmonising rules on extended and non-conviction-based confiscation, which reflects the EU policy focus on increasing the effectiveness and the extent of confiscation, the rules adopted in this respect in the comparator jurisdictions do not exactly reflect the solutions presented in EU law. The minimum character of the common rules gives MS some flexibility in their implementation, but some rules are of special importance for the position of subjected persons and should be better reproduced in national legislation. One example of this is guidance for national courts on which basis they should build their conviction about the criminal origin of property: 'the circumstances of the case, including the specific facts and available evidence, such as that the value of the property is disproportionate to the lawful income of the convicted person' (Article 5 of Directive 2014/42/EU; Article 14(2) of Directive 2024/1260). Thus, EU law provides the court with rather broad discretion when determining, on the balance of probabilities, that the assets in question have a criminal origin, whereas Polish and French law involves a legal presumption of the criminal origin of assets, which significantly limits a court's discretion. At the same time, the courts and the subjected persons have not been given sufficient indications of what aspects are relevant to rebut such presumptions, nor what standard of proof is required to rebut the legal presumptions (the balance of probabilities *v* the proof beyond a reasonable doubt). This latter aspect also remains unaddressed by EU law.

Broadening the research perspective to look at the alternative approach to post-conviction confiscation adopted in England and Wales, which equates the consequence of confiscation with a 'debt to be paid', we can observe that putting the emphasis primarily on effectiveness issues is not the way to develop inclusive, consultative, and balanced confiscation procedures, in which all the stakeholders may play more 'proactive' roles (defendants, victims, communities). Special attention should be paid to these observations presented in the domestic subject literature which point out some shortcomings of the national confiscation model, because EU confiscation policy is similarly primarily oriented towards increasing the effectiveness of confiscation. Furthermore, EU legislators considered this model to be a 'reasonable approximation' of one of the far-reaching (maximal) legislative options discussed in the Impact Assessment accompanying the Proposal for a Directive on the freezing and confiscation of proceeds of crime (2012). In view of the above, when reconsidering the EU confiscation scheme, the serious concerns around this model should not be omitted, as they indicate to which elements special attention should be paid by the legislatures, especially given that the post-conviction confiscation regime adopted in England and Wales has often been described as 'draconian'. First of all, a discrepancy has been identified between the official 'rhetoric' of criminal confiscation (focusing i.a. on crime control or organised crime) and the 'reality', including its use against low-level offenders, which poses a question about the 'proportionality of the response' (Bullock and Lister 2014, 67; Bullock 2014). Secondly, the weakened position of the defendants and procedural fairness have both faced criticism (Rees, Fisher, and Thomas 2015; Bullock and Lister 2014). Thirdly, serious concerns were raised regarding interference with the conventional right to property, and the lack of discretion available to the courts (Lawrence 2008). Last but not least from a restorative perspective, the procedural fairness of the post-conviction confiscation scheme has been questioned by defendants, as shown in the analysis of Fletcher (2019, 2020).

Works by the Law Commission of England and Wales reviewing the post-conviction mechanism started in 2018. Importantly, the Law Commission indicated the compensation of victims as among the objectives attributed to the legal institution of confiscation over time, in addition to commonly identified objectives such as 'taking away the profits or proceeds of crime', 'punishment', and 'deterring and disrupting criminal activity' (Law Commission, Confiscation of the proceeds of crime after conviction: a final report, 2022, No. 410, 63). One of the provisional proposals made by the Law Commission was 'that an express statement of statutory purpose of the confiscation regime should include the compensation of victims, where such compensation is to be paid from confiscated funds' (Law Commission, Confiscation of the proceeds of crime after conviction consultation paper (2020), No. 249, 86, 532). Nevertheless, this idea was not continued, and their final recommendation was that the objective of the post-conviction mechanism be focused on depriving a defendant of the benefit from criminal conduct, 'within the limits of their means' (Law Commission, Confiscation of the proceeds of crime after conviction: a final report, 2022, No. 410, 42).

In this context, it is worth recalling that EU law lacks a proper determination of the objective of confiscation, and this shortcoming is rooted in EU law-making policy. This book argues that a proper determination of the actual objective of confiscation at the EU policy level should be the starting point for reforming the EU confiscation scheme and national confiscation schemes towards integrating more restorative aspects of confiscation. Modern confiscation schemes should understand not only the need to involve the interests of victims but also the broader social potential of confiscation which can be realised, i.a., by returning assets to the populations affected by a crime (in a broad context). Enabling the social reuse of confiscated assets may also bolster the traditional objectives of confiscation connected with crime control, which have been highlighted in the rhetoric of EU confiscation policy, though its effectiveness in this respect remains unprovable.

One of the rationales for the social reuse of confiscated assets is a broad definition of crime as a 'wrong against society as well as a violation of the individual rights of victims' (Recital 9 of the Preamble to Directive 2012/29/EU). Accordingly, a broad definition of the victim should cover individual and collective victims, including various social groups and local communities, who should be the main, not marginal beneficiaries of the confiscation mechanism. In State-centred confiscation mechanisms, the State benefits from various transfers of confiscated assets to the State budget, State purpose funds, State institutions, or through incentivisation schemes. Displacing the centre of gravity of such mechanisms from the interests of the State to the interests of victims and communities involves redirecting the inward flow of asset transfers. Accordingly, at least some portion of confiscated assets should be transferred to public interest and social purposes *via* direct transfers, in a transparent manner and under social control. Apart from administrative and financial obstacles that may occur in reforming confiscation mechanisms, ultimately, finding arguments to support the dominant position of the State as the main beneficiary of confiscated assets - except *for assets* derived from fiscal offences detrimental to the State budget - seems more difficult than identifying arguments which justify returning assets to populations affected by crime (in a broad sense) or using assets to compensate the victims of crime.

The main EU legal instruments currently operating in the area of confiscation are: Directive 2014/42/EU (Directive 2024/1260 is to be transposed by MS by 23 November 2026), FD 2005/212/JHA, Regulation 2018/1805, FD 2006/783/JHA, and FD 2003/577/JHA. Their legal force in relation to the national law of MS follows from Article 288 TFEU, Article 4(3) TEU, and in the case of FDs, from *ex* Article 34(2)(b) TEU, as amended by the Treaty of Nice. However, the fact that national confiscation regimes of comparator EU jurisdictions contain some shortcomings should not be perceived as a result of improper transposition of EU harmonising instruments or incorrect application of directly binding EU rules, because the reason for this *status quo* lies in EU law-making policy concerning confiscation. Thus far this policy has not offered the MS a coherent vision of confiscation incorporating its restorative elements, one that could be implemented in EU confiscation law as a means of realisation of this policy, and under its influence, appear in national confiscation laws. Given that EU law-making policy on the CPC is the main determinant of EU law in this field, and under its influence, also national laws, the gaps and shortcomings identified in this policy may still be 'inherited' by EU law, and accordingly, national laws. In view of the above, redirecting EU confiscation law towards a more restorative direction, and a more restorative course for national confiscation laws, is highly dependent on a substantive change of EU law-making policy concerning confiscation, which should start with properly defining the entire array of objectives of confiscation, with particular emphasis on its restorative objectives.

Notes

1 Commission, Commission Staff Working Paper, Accompanying document to the Proposal for a Directive on the freezing and confiscation of proceeds of crime in the EU, Impact Assessment (2012), 12.3.2012, COM(2012) 85 final.
2 Law Commission, 'Confiscation of the proceeds of crime after conviction. A final report' (2022), Law Com No 410.
3 The Act of 6 June 1997 – the Criminal Code, Journal of Laws (1997), item 553, as amended.
4 The Fiscal Criminal Code (1999) contains separate rules on forfeiture (Articles 29–33), Journal of Laws (1999), item 930, as amended. See more Błaszczyk 2016, 235 et seq.
5 See the Act of 23 March 2017 amending the CC and several other acts, Journal of Laws (2017), item 768.
6 See, e.g., the Report of the circuit courts on the persons judged in the first instance for 2023, MS-S6o, Ministry of Justice, 3; the Report of the district courts on the persons judged in the first instance for 2023, MS-S6r, Ministry of Justice, 10. https://isws.ms.gov.pl/pl/baza-statystyczna/opracowania-jednoroczne-w-tym-pliki-dostepne-cyfrowo/rok-2023/download,3858,3.html (26.08.2024).
7 Draft of the Act amending the Criminal Code and several other acts (2016), the Sejm, eighth term of office, print no. 1186.
8 The Act of 10 February 2017 amending the CC and several other acts.
9 See the Explanatory Memorandum of the Draft of the Act amending the CC and several other acts (2014), the Sejm, 7th electoral term, Document No 2393.
10 Supreme Court, V KK 154/15, 22 October 2015.
11 Supreme Court, V KK 515/18, 26 September 2019.
12 Supreme Court, V KK 505/21, 25 May 2022.

13 Supreme Court, KK 189/17, 31 October 2017.
14 See the Explanatory Memorandum of the Draft of the Act amending the CC and several other acts (2016), the Sejm, eighth term of office, print no. 1186.
15 Cf. Article 44(1) of the Act of 6 June 1997 – the CC, Journal of Laws (1997), item 553; and Article 44(5), after the amendments introduced in 2003 under the influence of the OECD Convention on Combating Bribery of Foreign Public Officials in International Business Transactions (1997), the CoE Criminal Law Convention on Corruption (1999), ETS No 173, and Joint Action on corruption in the private sector 98/742/JHA (1998), OJ L 358/2). Poland joined the EU on 1 May 2004.
16 See Article 45(1) of the CC changed by the Act of 9 September 2000 amending the CC, the CCP, the act on combating unfair competition, law on public procurement, and banking law (2000), Journal of Laws (2000), item 1027.
17 The Executive Criminal Code (1997), Journal of Laws (1997), No 90, item 557, as amended.
18 On the purchase price applied in respect of used items or secondary raw material. See also Article 105(2) of the Act of 17 June 1966 on administrative enforcement proceedings.
19 The Criminal Code of 1871 (as revised and amended), the version published on 13 November 1998 (Federal Law Gazette I p. 3322), last amended by Article 2 of the Act of 30 July 2024, Federal Law Gazette (2024) I No 255.
20 See the Explanatory Memorandum of the Draft of the Act to reform criminal asset confiscation (2016), German Bundestag Document No 18/9525, 18th term of office, https://dserver.bundestag.de/btd/18/095/1809525.pdf (27.08.2024).
21 Legal terms translated by the Author. The point of reference was the translation of the German CC by Prof. Dr Michael Bohlander, revised and updated by Ute Reusch, and made available by the Federal Ministry of Justice. https://www.gesetze-im-internet.de/englisch_stgb/ (29.08.2024).
22 Separate regulation of confiscation is provided for in the Customs Code (*Code des douanes*), Article 430.
23 See Article 10(3) of Directive 2014/42/EU.
24 Assemblée Nationale, Rapport (2016), No. 3515, 339. https://www.assemblee-nationale.fr/14/pdf/rapports/r3515.pdf (6.09.2024).
25 *Réponse du Ministère de la justice publiée*, 18 May 2023, Journaux officiels des Questions – Sénat, 3262. https://www.senat.fr/questions/base/2023/qSEQ230305859.html (6.09.2024).
26 Ministère de la Justice, 'Guide for the recovery of criminal assets in France' (2022), https://www.unodc.org/documents/corruption/G20-Anti-Corruption-Resources/G20-Step-by-step-guides-on-nternational-cooperation-and-asset-recovery/Asset-Recovery-Guides/France_-_English.pdf (7.09.2024).
27 See Article 131-39 No. 8 of the CC; in respect of general confiscation, see Article 213-3, Article 215-3 No. 3, Article 225-25, Article 222-49, Article 222-66(2), Article 227-33, Article 324-9(1), Article 422-6, Article 450-5, and Article 462-6 of the CC.
28 Special provisions concern the confiscation of animals, when they have been used (or are likely to be used) in the character of instrumentalities or objects of an offence (Article 131-21-1 of the CC). In addition, there are special provisions on the confiscation of vehicles (e.g., Article 221-8 No. 10 of the CC or Article L. 221-2 No. 1 of the Traffic Code).
29 See AGRASC, 'Un rayonnement international' (2024). https://agrasc.gouv.fr/un-rayonnement-international (11.09.2024).
30 See also UNODC, 'Effective management and disposal of seized and confiscated assets' (2017), 33.
31 See Article L. 365-2 of the Construction and Housing Code (C*ode de la construction et de l'habitation*).

32 *Sénat, Rapport No. 352, Session ordinaire de 2020–2021, 22.* https://www.senat.fr/rap/l20-352/l20-3521.pdf (11.09.2024).

33 AGRASC, Rapprt d'activité (2022). https://agrasc.gouv.fr/sites/default/files/2023-07/ra_2022_a4_v4_interactif.pdf (11.09.2024).

34 AGRASC, Rapprt d'activité (2023). https://agrasc.gouv.fr/sites/default/files/2024-05/ra_2023_a4_v7_interactif-web_0.pdf (11.09.2024).

35 See also Order of 23 August 1995 establishing the conditions for crediting the proceeds from the sale of property confiscated in the fight against drugs to the competition fund (*Arrêté du 23 août 1995 fixant les modalités de rattachement par voie de fonds de concours du produit de cession des biens confisqués dans le cadre de la lutte contre les produits stupéfiants*).

36 See MILDECA, Mission interministérielle de lutte contre les drogues et les conduites addictives, 'Fonds de concours «Drogues»: un cercle vertueux pour lutter contre le trafic de drogues', (2023). https://www.drogues.gouv.fr/fonds-de-concours-drogues-un-cercle-vertueux-pour-lutter-contre-le-trafic-de-drogues (27.09.2024). MILDECA, 'La Mission'. https://www.drogues.gouv.fr/la-mission (27.09.2024).

37 See more, the official site of the French administration: Service-public.fr., 'Aide aux victimes d'infraction pénale pour recouvrer les dommages et intérêts'. https://www.service-public.fr/particuliers/vosdroits/F1744 (10.09.2024). 'Fonds de garantie des victimes'. https://www.fondsdegarantie.fr/victime-dune-infraction-sarvi/ (10.09.2024). A separate aid fund is dedicated to victims of terrorism (*Fonds de garantie des victimes d'actes de terrorisme et d'autres infract*ions – FGTI). https://www.fondsdegarantie.fr/fgti/statuts/ (21.09.2024).

38 See more UNODC, 'Effective management and disposal of seized and confiscated assets' (2017), 19, and the official site of the Society for Special Assets: https://www.saesas.gov.co/nuestra_entidad/quienes_somos (21.09.2024).

39 See Commission, Commission Staff Working Paper, Accompanying document to the Proposal for a Directive on the freezing and confiscation of proceeds of crime in the EU, Impact Assessment (2012), 12.3.2012, COM(2012) 85 final.

40 Trade and Cooperation Agreement between the European Union and the European Atomic Energy Community, of the one part, and the United Kingdom of Great Britain and Northern Ireland, of the other part (2021), OJ L 149/10, as amended.

41 See also Freezing and Confiscation Request Forms, Annex 46 to the TCA.

42 Explanatory Notes, European Union (Future Relationship) Act 2020, Chapter 29. https://www.legislation.gov.uk/ukpga/2020/29/pdfs/ukpgaen_20200029_en.pdf (16.09.2024).

43 See also the observations of Oehmichen and Keith (2021) on the procedural aspects of cooperation.

44 Under Section 78 of POCA, a gift is made to a 'recipient' when the 'defendant transfers property to another person for a consideration whose value is significantly less than the value of the property at the time of the transfer'. The gift is treated as 'tainted' if the conditions set out in Section 77 of POCA are met.

45 According to Section 35(2) of POCA, Sections 129(1) to (3) and (5) and 132(1) to (4) of the Sentencing Act (2000) apply, UK Public General Acts 2020, c. 17.

46 See also ECtHR, *Crowther v the UK*, Application no. 53741/00, 1 February 2005.

47 The 'compensation order' is defined in Section 133 of the Sentencing Act (2020).

48 See also the procedural nuances in the event of the postponement of confiscation proceedings, Sections 14 and 15 of POCA (Williams, Hopmeier, and Jones 2018, 601; Rees, Fisher, and Thomas 2015, 63).

49 See also Law Commission, Confiscation of the proceeds of crime after conviction: a final report (2022), 56.

50 EP, LIBE, Report on the proposal for a directive of the European Parliament and of the Council on the freezing and confiscation of proceeds of crime in the European Union, 20.5.2013, Document A7-0178/2013.

51 See also Home Office, Policy paper, Government response to the Law Commission's review of confiscation (2023), 23. https://www.gov.uk/government/publications/government-response-to-the-law-commissions-review-of-confiscation/705339e1-caee-4954-87a7-48cb145f5d8c (20.09.2024).

52 See more on the eligibility criteria to obtain compensation from the CICA scheme: The UK Rules, 'Compensation for Victims of Violent Crime'. https://www.theukrules.co.uk/rules/legal/compensation/for-victims-of-violent-crime/ (23.09.2024).

53 See also the Asset Recovery Incentivisation Scheme (ARIS). Home Office, 'User guide to Asset recovery statistics' (2024). https://www.gov.uk/government/statistics/asset-recovery-statistics-financial-years-ending-2019-to-2024/user-guide-to-asset-recovery-statistics#asset-recovery-incentivisation-scheme-aris (23.09.2024). The National Audit Office, 'Confiscation orders' (2013), HC 738. https://www.nao.org.uk/wp-content/uploads/2013/12/10318-001-Confiscation-Book.pdf (23.09.2024). The National Audit Office, Confiscation orders: progress review (2016), HC 886, Session 2015–16. https://www.nao.org.uk/wp-content/uploads/2016/03/Confiscation-orders-progress-review.pdf (24.09.2024).

References

Alldridge, Peter. 2011. "The Limits of Confiscation." *Criminal Law Review* 11: 827–843.

Ambroise-Castérot, Coralie, Jean-François Renucci, Jean-Paul Céré, and Maud Léna. 2020. *Code de procédure pénale. Annoté.* Paris: Dalloz.

Ascensi, Lionel. 2021. *Droit et pratique des saisies et confiscations pénales.* Paris: Dalloz.

Bar, Karl Ludwig von. 1916. *A History of Continental Criminal Law.* Translated by Thomas S. Bell et al. (not indicated by name). Originally published: Boston: Little, Brown, and Company (1916), reprinted 1999. Union, NJ: The Lawbook Exchange.

Baruzzo, Giulia, Tatiana Giannone, and Giulia Pasinato. 2021. *The Social Re-use of Confiscated Assets in Europe: A First Mapping.* Translated by Orsetta Spinola and Denise DeVries. Good(s) Monitoring Europe! Accessed August 8, 2024. https://www.confiscatibene.it/sites/default/files/blog-upload/The%20social%20re-use%20of%20confiscated%20assets%20in%20Europe_a%20first%20mapping.pdf.

Bauerkamp, Jan. 2022. "Die rückwirkende Anwendbarkeit der Neuregelung zur strafrechtlichen Vermögensabschöpfung (Art. 316 h EGStGB) ist verfassungsgemäß, da die Vermögensabschöpfung keine Nebenstrafe, sondern Maßnahme eigener Art mit kondiktionsähnlichem Charakter ist: BVerfG 2. Senat, Beschluss vom 10. Februar 2021 – 2 BvL 8/19." *Juristische Rundschau* 2: 89–97. https://doi.org/10.1515/juru-2021-0082.

Bhat, P. Ishwara. 2019. *Idea and Methods of Legal Research.* New Delhi: Oxford University Press.

Błaszczyk, Magdalena. 2016. *Przepadek w polskim prawie karnym skarbowym.* Warszawa: Wolters Kluwer.

Bohlander, Michael. 2009. *Principles of German Criminal Law.* Oxford and Portland, Oregon: Hart Pub.

Böse, Martin, and Wera Weyer. 2019. "Germany." In *Improving Confiscation Procedures in the European Union*, edited by Alessandro Bernardi, coordinated by Francesco Rossi, 249–285. Napoli: Jovene Editore.

Boucht, Johan. 2019. *The Limits of Asset Confiscation: On the Legitimacy of Extended Appropriation of Criminal Proceeds.* Oxford: Hart Pub.

Bullock, Karen. 2014. "Criminal Benefit, the Confiscation Order and the Post-conviction Confiscation Regime." *Crime, Law and Social Change* 62 (1): 45–64. https://doi.org/10.1007/s10611-014-9517-7.

Bullock, Karen, and Stuart Lister. 2014. "Post-Conviction Confiscation of Assets in England and Wales: Rhetoric and Reality." In *Dirty Assets. Emerging Issues in the Regulation of*

Criminal and Terrorist Assets, edited by Colin King and Clive Walker, 47–69. Farnham: Ashgate Pub.

Bülte, Jens. 2021. "Strafrechtliche Vermögensabschöpfung bei bereits vor Inkrafttreten des Reformgesetzes verjährten Erwerbstaten mit dem Grundgesetz vereinbar: Anmerkung zu BVerfG, 10.2.2021 – 2 BvL 8/19." *Neue Zeitschrift für Wirtschafts* 10 (5): 188–208.

Burchard, Christoph. 2019. "Confiscation as Criminal Law (or What)? – On How the ill-Advised Discussion about "the" Legal Nature of Confiscation Obfuscates What Really Needs to Be Discussed." *Latin American Legal Studies* 4: 211–242.

Dechenaud, David. 2019. *Code pénal. Annoté sous la direction de David Dechenaud*. Paris: LexisNexis.

Dezeuze, Éric, and Martin Horion. 2018. "La confiscation comme mesure de réparation." *Gazette du palais*: *Recueil bimestral* 138(6): 3466–3469.

Diamanti, Francesco, Eleonora Anna Alexandra Dei Cas, and Samuel Bolis. 2019. "Italy." In *Improving Confiscation Procedures in the European Union*, edited by Alessandro Bernardi, coordinated by Francesco Rossi, 287–368. Napoli: Jovene Editore.

Dubber, Markus Dirk. 2005. "Theories of Crime and Punishment in German Criminal Law." *The American Journal of Comparative Law* 53 (3): 679–707.

Eser, Albin. 1993. "Neue Wege der Gewinnabschöpfung im Kampf Gegen die organisierte Kriminalität?" In *Beiträge zur Rechtswissenschaft: Festschrift für Walter Stree und Johannes Wessels zum 70. Geburtstag*, edited by Wilfried Küper and Jürgen Welp, 833–853. Heidelberg: C.F. Müller.

Esser, Robert. 2015. "A Civil Recovery Model. The German Perspective and European Human Rights." In *Non Conviction-Based Confiscation in Europe*, edited by Jon Petter Rui and Ulrich Sieber, 69–109. Berlin: Duncker & Humblot.

Fischer, Thomas. 2021. *Strafgesetzbuch mit Nebengesetzen.* München: C.H. Beck.

Fletcher, Craig. 2019. "'Double Punishment' — The Proceeds of Crime Act 2002 (POCA): A Qualitative Examination of the Post-Conviction Confiscation Punishment in England and Wales." Doctoral thesis (PhD), Manchester Metropolitan University. Accessed September 18, 2024. https://e-space.mmu.ac.uk/625283/.

Fletcher, Craig. 2020. "Social Value or Social Harm? The Impact of the Proceeds of Crime Act 2002 Upon the Defendant and Their Families." In *Assets, Crimes, and the State. Innovations in 21st Century Legal Responses*, edited by Katie Benson, Colin King, and Clive Walker, 79–93. Abingdon: Routledge.

Giudicelli-Delage, Genévieve, Olivier Cahn, Juliette Tricot, Iryna Grebenyuk, Nicolas Jeanne, and Marie Nicolas. 2019. "France." In *Improving Confiscation Procedures in the European Union*, edited by Alessandro Bernardi, coordinated by Francesco Rossi, 249–285. Napoli: Jovene Editore.

Heuer, Bastian. 2021. *Einziehung ohne Verurteilung?* Baden-Baden: Tectum.

Hilger, Geoffroy. 2016. "Précisions sur les conditions de saisine de l'AGRASC par les victimes aux fins d'indemnisation." *Gazette du Palais* 22: 28.

Hodgson, Derek. 1984. *Profits of Crime and Their Recovery. Report of a Committee Chaired by Sir Derek Hodgson.* London: Heinemann.

Hoecke, Mark Van. 2015. "Methodology of Comparative Legal Research." *Law and Method* 12. https://doi.org/10.5553/REM/.000010.

Höft, Kersten. 2018. "§ 76a Abs. 4 StGB – Ein neues und verfassungswidriges Instrument im deutschen Vermögensabschöpfungsrecht." *HRRS Onlinezeitschrift für Höchstrichterliche Rechtsprechung zum Strafrecht* 5: 196–204. https://www.hrr-strafrecht.de/hrr/archiv/18-05/hrrs-5-18.pdf. (26.09.2024).

Hy, Matthieu. 2021. "[Focus] Droit des saisies pénales et confiscations: repères jurisprudentiels." *La lettre juridique*, September 2021. https://www.lexbase.fr/article-juridique/72477525-focusdroitdessaisiespenalesetconfiscationsreperesjurisprudentiels (9.09.2024).

Jenney, Petra. 2016. "The European Union's Area of Freedom, Security and Justice without the United Kingdom — Legal and Practical Consequences of Brexit." *Elte Law Journal* 1: 117–139.

Kilchling, Michael. 2004. "Organised Crime Policies in Germany." In *Organised Crime in Europe*, edited by Cyrille Fijnaut and Letizia Paoli, 717–762. Dordrecht: Springer.

King, Colin. 2014. "Civil Forfeiture and Article 6 of the ECHR: Due Process Implications for England & Wales and Ireland." *Legal Studies* 34 (3): 371–394. https://doi.org/10.1111/lest.12018.

Köhler, Marcus. 2017. "Die Reform der strafrechtlichen Vermögensabschöpfung – Teil 1/2. Überblick und Normverständnis für die Rechtspraxis." *Neue Zeitschrift für Strafrecht* 9: 497–512.

Konarska-Wrzosek, Wioletta. 2023. "Komentarz do Artykułu 45." In *Kodeks Karny. Komentarz*, edited by Wioletta Konarska-Wrzosek. Warszawa: Wolters Kluwer.

Latimier, Corentin. 2017. "Le recouvrement des avoirs illicites de la corruption internationale. Évolutions récentes en droit français et recommandations à la lumière de la Convention des Nations Unies contre la corruption." Droit. COMUE Université Côte d'Azur (2015–2019), 2017. Français. NNT: 2017AZUR0036. https://theses.hal.science/tel-01721324/document (6.09.2024).

Lawrence, Ivan. 2008. "Draconian and Manifestly Unjust: How the Confiscation Regime Has Developed." *Amicus Curiae* 76: 22–24.

Maximilian, Lenk. 2021. "Vermögensabschöpfung bei vor Inkrafttreten der Reform verjährten Erwerbstaten: GG Art. 2 I, 14 I, 20 III, 103 II; EMRK Art. 7 I; EGStGB Art. 316 h S.1; StGB §§ 11 I Nr. 8, 76 a II 1, 76 b I, 78 I 1, 2: BVerfG, Beschluss vom 10.2.2021 - 2 BvL 8/19: Anmerkung." *Neue juristische Wochenschrift* 74 (17): 1231–1232.

Masferrer, Aniceto. 2018. "Tradition and Foreign Influences in the 19th Century Codification of Criminal Law: Dispelling the Myth of the Pervasive French Influence in Europe and Latin America." In *The Western Codification of Criminal Law. Studies in the History of Law and Justice*, edited by Aniceto Masferrer, 3–50. Cham: Springer. https://doi.org/10.1007/978-3-319-71912-2_1.

Matsopoulou, Haritini. 2021. "La saisie et la confiscation des biens des tiers. " In *La confiscation des avoirs crminels. Nouveaux enjeux juridique*, edited by Lionel Ascensi, Pascal Beauvais, and Raphaële Parizot, 109–117. Paris: LGDJ, Lextenso.

Mayaud, Yves, and Carole Gayet. 2020. *Code Pénal. Annoté par Yves Mayaud avec le concours de Carole Gayet.* Paris: Dalloz.

Meyer, Frank. 2015. ""Reformiert die Rückgewinnungshilfe! – Denkanstöße für eine Generalüberholung der Vermögensabschöpfung." *Zeitschrift für die gesamte Strafrechtswissenschaft* 127 (2): 241–283. https://doi.org/10.1515/zstw-2015-0010.

Montaldo, Stefano. 2015. "Directive 2014/42/EU and Social Reuse of Confiscated Assets in the EU: Advancing a Culture of Legality." *New Journal of European Criminal Law* 6 (2): 195–212.

Mosca, Michele. 2020. "Policies to Combat Organized Crime in Europe: The Italian Experience." *The Journal of European Economic History* 49 (3): 167–185.

Mueller, O. W. Gerhard, and Fré Le Poole-Griffiths. 1969. *Comparative Criminal Procedure.* New York: New York University Press.

Naylor, R. T. 1999. "Wash-out: A Critique of Follow-the-Money Methods in Crime Control Policy." *Crime, Law and Social Change* 32: 1–58. https://doi.org/10.1023/A:1008386203362.

Ochnio, Ariadna H. 2016. "Implementation of the New EU Directive on Confiscation in Poland: The Challenge of Overcoming the Negative Historical Experiences of Confiscation Orders." *European Journal of Crime, Criminal Law and Criminal Justice* 24 (1): 19–38.

Oehmichen, Anna, and Ben Keith. 2021. "Mutual Legal Assistance under the EU–UK Trade and Cooperation Agreement." *New Journal of European Criminal Law* 12 (2): 222–232. https://doi.org/10.1177/2032284421995938.

Peters, Kai, and Boris Bröckers. 2019. *Vermögensabschöpfung im Strafverfahren.* Heidelberg: C.F. Müller.

Pereira, Cédric Marques Bento. 2023. *Saisies pénales et droits fondamentaux.* Droit. Le Mans Université, Français. NNT: 2023LEMA2001. Accessed September 21, 2024. https://theses.hal.science/tel-04501096v1/preview/2023LEMA2001.pdf#page=2.

Podolsky, Johann, Tobias Brenner, Roland Baier, and Christian Veith. 2019. *Vermögensabschöpfung im Straf- und Ordnungswidrigkeitenverfahren.* Stuttgart: Boorberg.

Pradel, Jean. 2019. *Droit Pénal Général.* Paris: Édition Cujas.

Raglewski, Janusz. 2016. "Komentarz do Artykułu 44." In *Kodeks karny. Część ogólna. Komentarz*, edited by Włodzimierz Wróbel and Andrzej Zoll, Vol. 1. Warszawa: Wolters Kluwer.

Ramos, Vânia C., and Gary Pons. 2021. "Freezing and Confiscation under the EU–UK Trade and Cooperation Agreement." *New Journal of European Criminal Law* 12 (2): 233–245. https://doi.org/10.1177/2032284421995244.

Rees, Edward, Richard Fisher, and Richard Thomas. 2015. *Blackstone Guide to the Proceeds ofn Crime Act 2002.* Oxford: Oxford University Press.

Reitemeier, Wiebke. 2017. "Die Reform der strafrechtlichen Vermögensabschöpfung." *Zeitschrift für Jugendkriminalrecht und Jugendhilfe* 4: 354–364.

Rzeplińska, Irena. 1997. *Konfiskata mienia. Studium z historii polityki kryminalnej.* Warszawa: Instytut Nauk Prawnych PAN.

Schmidt, Wilhelm. 2019. *Vermögensabschöpfung. Handbuch für das Straf- und Ordnungswidrigkeitenverfahren.* München: C.H. Beck.

Schomburg, Wolfgang, and Anna Oehmichen. 2021. "Brexit: First Observations on the EU–UK Trade and Cooperation Agreement in Criminal Law." *New Journal of European Criminal Law* 12 (2): 193–201. https://doi.org/10.1177/2032284421996035.

Schunke, Thunberg Malin. 2017. *Extended Confiscation in Criminal Law: National, European and International Perspectives: Supranational Criminal Law.* Cambridge: Intersentia.

Segonds, Marc. 2020. "A la recherche d'une définition du produit de l'infraction (selon la loi pénale)." *Annales de l'Institut de criminologie et de sciences pénales* 1 (1): 115–131.

Segonds, Marc. 2021. "Les droit des tiers." In *La confiscation des avoirs crminels. Nouveaux enjeux juridique*, edited by Lionel Ascensi, Pascal Beauvais, and Raphaële Parizot, 85–105. Paris: LGDJ, Lextenso.

Simonato, Michele. 2017. "Confiscation and Fundamental Rights Across Criminal and Non-criminal Domains." *ERA Forum* 18: 365–379. https://doi.org/10.1007/s12027-017-0485-0.

Thony, Jean-François, and Éric Camous. 2013. "Gel, saisie et confiscation des avoirs criminels: les nouveaux outils de la loi française." *Revue international de droit pénal* 84: 205–216.

Tokarczyk, Roman. 1989. *Wprowadzenie do komparatystyki prawniczej.* Lublin: Wydawnictwo Lubelskie.

Ullenboom, David. 2019. *Praxisleitfaden Vermögensabschöpfung.* Heidelberg: C.F. Müller.

Vettori, Barbara. 2018. "The Disposal of Confiscated Assets in the EU Member States: What Works, What Does Not Work and What Is Promising." In *The Palgrave Handbook of Criminal and Terrorism Financing Law*, edited by Colin King, Clive Walker, and Jimmy Gurulé, 705–733. Cham: Palgrave Macmillan.

Vettori, Barbara, and Andrea Di Nicola. 2017. "The Social Reuse of Confiscated Assets in EU Member States: From Current Experiences to an EU policy for a 'Powered-by-Citizens' Fight Against Crime." In *Chasing Criminal Money: Challenges and Perspectives on Asset Recovery in the EU*, edited by Katalin Ligeti and Michele Simonato, 321–343. Oxford: Hart Pub.

Williams, Mark Sutherland, Michael Hopmeier, and Rupert Jones. 2018. *The Proceeds of Crime*. Oxford: Oxford University Press.

Wood, Helena. 2016. *Enforcing Criminal Confiscation Orders. From Policy to Practice.* RUSI Occasional Paper, February 2016. London: Royal United Services Institute for Defence and Security Studies.

Zakrzewski, Piotr. 2024. "Komentarz do Artykułu 45." In *Kodeks karny. Komentarz*, edited by Jarosław Majewski. Warszawa: Wolters Kluwer.

6 Changing the approach to confiscation: possible implications for other fields of EU criminal justice policy

EU confiscation policy is strongly interconnected with other specific EU policies concerning criminal justice, especially anti-corruption, anti-fraud, and AML/CFT policies. All of these policies are also relevant to the protection of the licit economy and the Union's financial interests. It should be remembered that confiscation-related issues are a traditional part of the rhetoric behind these EU policies. One might even say that confiscation is a kind of confluence of the anti-corruption, anti-fraud, and AML/CFT EU policies. Thus, confiscation policy is of special importance for shaping the AFSJ. For instance, references to confiscation recently appeared in the new Proposal for a directive on combating corruption (2023), COM (2023) 234 final, which considers corruption in a broad context, as 'a tool for foreign interference in democratic processes'. The corrosive impact of corruption on democracy has been addressed in the Defence of Democracy package,[1] and the Commission Work Programme (2023).[2]

Notably, a similar interaction occurs between national confiscation policies and national anti-corruption, anti-fraud, and AML/CFT policies. This should be seen in the context of 'multi-level' governance, which implies some interconnection of European and national politics (see, e.g., Lenschow 2006, 56). In the bigger picture, the EU confiscation policy is also an important element of the global efforts to combat organised crime, corruption, money laundering, and terrorism, being global phenomena requiring an integrated international community's response. Accordingly, confiscation policies designed at the national, EU, and global levels may be perceived as a system of connected spheres. Therefore, assuming that EU confiscation policy changes course towards becoming minimally more restorative regarding conventional confiscation mechanisms, it can be expected that this change would also have an impact on other interconnected policies. All the more so, given that there is a strategic need for an integrated approach to link all EU-specific policies concerning criminal justice, and more broadly, the entire area of freedom, security, and justice.[3] When we take into account that confiscation-related issues have begun to be linked with international security, introducing changes to confiscation policy may also be relevant for the CFSP, especially in the context of transnational returns to 'victim countries' of assets captured within the confiscation mechanism.

Assuming that EU policy takes a firmer stance on the necessity of enabling the broad social reuse of confiscated assets in national confiscation mechanisms,

DOI: 10.4324/9781003465829-6

and effectively delivers changes in national legislation regarding the division of confiscated assets, i.e., ensuring that at least some portion of confiscated assets be directly returned to the populations affected by or vulnerable to a crime (in a broad sense), it may also indirectly support the Europeanisation of these areas, in which the EU holds supporting competences. The rationale behind the removal of the issue of reuse of confiscated assets from the exclusive remit of States is to enable asset transfers in support of various public and social purposes (*via* direct or indirect transfers, e.g., through the use of specialised aid/competition funds).

Vettori and Di Nicola (2017) aptly noted that the 'citizen', being a 'neglected actor', should be placed at the centre of confiscation policies in the EU (343) and that encouragement by the EU of the reuse of confiscated assets for social purposes across the EU may potentially contribute to a '"powered-by-citizens" fight against crime', one that is 'powered-by-hundreds-of-millions-of-EU-citizens' (321, 343). In this perspective, the social reuse of confiscated assets may also be perceived as being a significant factor in building civil society and the resilience of communities to crime, one of the most important concerns of the EU.

Confiscated assets may support projects aimed at building at the grassroots level the resilience of communities vulnerable to crime (local, school, professional, and national minorities, etc.). For instance, such projects may be aimed at increasing the operational capacities of local educational institutions, organising vocational training, establishing assistance centres, putting in place youth sports infrastructure, or organising events supporting the cultural and festive life of communities. Thus, confiscated assets may be invested to support almost all the areas where the EU has supporting competences. According to Article 6 TFEU, the EU shall have the competence to 'carry out actions to support, coordinate or supplement the actions of the Member States' in the following areas: protection and improvement of human health, industry, culture, tourism, education, vocational training, youth, and sport. Konstadinides (2018) noted that 'there is hardly today an area of regulation in which the EU does not play an active part – from trade and energy to sport and fundamental rights protection' (191). Respectively, one might say that it is hard to find an area of supporting competences of the EU, where confiscation policy is unable to add significant value.

An important element of returning confiscated assets to victims (individual and collective, including communities) is making this process transparent and visible to the public. These two factors, transparency and public visibility, have a role to play in promoting the principle that 'crime does not pay', as well as fostering public confidence in the criminal justice system and a culture of legality (see, e.g., Montaldo 2015; LIBE Report 2013;[4] Bauhr and Carlitz 2021; Bisogno et al. 2024). Notably, Forsaith et al. (2012) indicated the function of the media in coalescing 'local impacts' of 'asset-confiscation work' into 'wider impacts' (22). In view of the above, it should be pointed out that the current EU normative framework lacks comprehensive solutions on interstate cooperation aimed at transnational returns of assets captured within confiscation mechanisms (see, e.g., Brillaud and Manzi 2020; Ochnio 2024). Thus, the possible 'global impact' of the social reuse of confiscated assets requires increased attention in EU policy. All the more so, given that interstate cooperation is another key area where confiscation policy may support the objectives of the CFSP. However, some progress in this regard is visible in the new Directive 2024/1260, which states that MS may use confiscated assets to 'contribute to mechanisms to support third countries affected by situations in response to which Union restrictive measures have been adopted, in particular in cases of war of aggression' and that the Commission 'may provide guidance on the arrangements for such contributions' (Article 19(2)).

In sum, rethinking EU confiscation policy towards a more restorative direction may influence legal integration in the area of shared competences between the EU and MS (the AFSJ). Secondly, given that this reconsideration would involve putting a greater emphasis on the social and public reuse of confiscated assets, EU confiscation policy may influence the Europeanisation of almost all areas in which the EU has supporting competences (protection and improvement of human health, culture, education, vocational training, youth, and sport). Finally, since confiscation-related issues at the EU level are connected with international security issues (combatting terrorism, war crimes, ensuring the effectiveness of Union restrictive measures, and returns of assets to 'victim countries'), changing the course of confiscation policy may also have an impact on the CFSP – the area of special competences of the EU (see, e.g., Cremona 2018).

Ultimately, it is worth noting that the minimalist restorative approach taken in this book as regards conventional confiscation mechanisms is characterised by a certain versatility; thus, it may also be applied to other fields of EU policy concerning conventional criminal justice. Accordingly, answering the questions of how restorative a concrete EU policy is, and how its restorativeness can be increased, may lead to substantial changes at the level of its objectives and means of implementation.

To this end, a simple test may be employed to build up a picture of who is actually at the centre of the examined policy (victims and communities or States) and whose interests are primarily recognised:

1) Does the examined policy determine restorative objectives, such as restoration of the status *quo ante* (before a crime) and reparation of the harm caused by a crime?
2) Does it prioritise the position of victims (in a broad sense) and communities over the position of the State?
3) Does it identify the interests of all stakeholders in criminal cases (victims, communities, defendants, third parties)?
4) Does it protect the rights of these stakeholders (the human rights protection perspective)?
5) Going beyond the human rights protection perspective, does it offer stakeholders an opportunity to play more 'proactive' roles in delivering justice?
6) And finally, does the implementation of its officially declared objectives involve restorative actions taking place close to the people affected by or vulnerable to a crime, thus, giving them the chance to support the policy at the grassroots level (the local justice perspective)?

Answering these questions also presents the opportunity to identify the shortcomings of the examined policy, and if appropriate, to reorient it along a more restorative course. As a further step, these questions may also be applied to examine the EU normative framework aimed at implementing the objectives of the examined policy. Such examination may reveal discrepancies between the concrete legal solutions presented and the officially declared policy objectives.

Conclusions

EU confiscation policy is strongly intertwined with other EU policies, such as the anti-corruption, anti-fraud, and AML/CFT policies, all important for the EU's financial interests and the protection of the licit economy. In addition, confiscation-related issues have also begun to be considered in terms of securing the effectiveness of Union restrictive measures, and thus the link between EU confiscation policy and the objectives of the CFSP, already supported by the use of confiscation to combat terrorist-related offences, has been strengthened. Accordingly, with the strategic importance given to the CPC at the EU level, changing the course of EU confiscation policy towards a more restorative path may have implications for other areas covered by these interconnected EU policies. Firstly, a reconsideration of EU confiscation policy may influence legal integration in the area of shared competences between the EU and MS (the AFSJ). Secondly, it may influence the Europeanisation of almost all areas in which the EU has supporting competences (protection and improvement of human health, culture, education, vocational training, youth, and sport), due to the opportunity to redirect confiscated assets to support these areas at the grassroots level. In the long term, this could translate into strengthening civil society and increasing the resilience of communities to crime, both values promoted by the EU, important to its interests, and determining its policy in many areas. Finally, changing the course of EU confiscation policy may have an impact on the area of special competences of the EU (the CFSP), especially in the context of enhancing interstate cooperation in returning confiscated assets to 'victim countries', e.g., touched by corruption or war crimes. The minimalist restorative approach adopted in this book relates to the conventional criminal confiscation mechanisms; however, due to its versatility, it may also be applied to examine the minimal restorative aspect of other EU policies concerning conventional criminal justice.

Notes

1 Commission, Communication on Defence of Democracy (2023), COM(2023) 630 final.
2 Commission Work Programme (2023), COM(2022) 548 final. See also Commission, Joint Communication of the EP, the Council and the EESC on the fight against corruption (2023), JOIN(2023) 12 final.
3 Cf. Council, A new Strategic Agenda 2019–2024. https://www.consilium.europa.eu/media/39914/a-new-strategic-agenda-2019-2024.pdf (3.10.2024). Commission, Strategic Plan 2020–2024, Publications Office of the EU. https://commission.europa.eu/system/files/2020-10/op_sp_2020_2024_en.pdf (3.10.2024).

4 EP, LIBE, Report on the proposal for a directive of the EP and of the Council on the freezing and confiscation of proceeds of crime in the EU, 20.5.2013, Document A7-0178/2013.

References

Bauhr, Monika, and Ruth Carlitz. 2021. "When Does Transparency Improve Public Services? Street-level Discretion, Information, and Targeting." *Public Administration* 99 (3): 500–516. https://doi.org/10.1111/padm.12693.

Bisogno, Marco, Beatriz Cuadrado-Ballesteros, Francesca Citro, and Giovanni Vaia. 2024. "Transparency in the Use of Assets Confiscated from Mafia Organizations." *International Review of Administrative Sciences* 90 (3): 701–720. https://doi.org/10.1177/00208523231219495.

Brillaud, Laure, and Matilde Manzi. 2020. *Stop Kleptocrats. The EU Must Not Be a Vault for the World's Stolen Assets*. Transparency International EU. Accessed October 3, 2024. https://transparency.eu/wp-content/uploads/2024/07/Asset-Recovery_Policy_Report_2020.pdf.

Cremona, Marise. 2018. "The Position of CFSP/CSDP in the EU's Constitutional Architecture." In *Research Handbook on the EU's Common Foreign and Security Policy*, edited by Steven Blockmans and Panos Koutrakos, 5–21. Cheltenham: Edward Elgar Pub.

Forsaith, James, Barrie Irving, Eva Nanopoulos, and Mihaly Fazekas. 2012. *Study for an Impact Assessment on a Proposal for a New Legal Framework on the Confiscation and Recovery of Criminal Assets*. RAND Europe, EU. Accessed July 4, 2024. https://home-affairs.ec.europa.eu/system/files/2020-09/external_study_used_as_a_basis_for_the_commission_ia_october_2012_en.pdf.

Konstadinides, Theodore. 2018. "The Competences of the Union." In *Oxford Principles Of European Union Law: The European Union Legal Order: Volume I*, edited by Robert Schütze and Takis Tridimas, 191–220. Oxford: Oxford University Press.

Lenschow, Andrea. 2006. "Europeanisation of Public Policy." In *European Union. Power and Policy-making*, edited by Jeremy Richardson, 56–71. Abingdon, Oxon: Routledge.

Montaldo, Stefano. 2015. "Directive 2014/42/EU and Social Reuse of Confiscated Assets in the EU: Advancing a Culture of Legality." *New Journal of European Criminal Law* 6 (2): 195–212.

Ochnio, Ariadna H. 2024. "Recent Developments in EU Anti-corruption Strategy: The Missing Element of the Return of Corrupt Assets to "Victim Countries." *Journal of Money Laundering Control* 27 (7): 1–12. https://doi.org/10.1108/JMLC-11-2023-0176.

Vettori, Barbara, and Andrea Di Nicola. 2017. "The Social Reuse of Confiscated Assets in EU Member States: From Current Experiences to an EU policy for a 'Powered-by-Citizens' Fight Against Crime." In *Chasing Criminal Money. Challenges and Perspectives on Asset Recovery in the EU*, edited by Katalin Ligeti and Michele Simonato, 321–343. Oxford: Hart Pub.

7 How to increase the restorativeness of EU law-making policy on the confiscation of the proceeds of crime?

Adopting at least a minimalist restorative approach in EU confiscation policy may lead to significant changes in the EU confiscation scheme, influential on the development of national confiscation schemes, *hic et nunc* (here and now), without substantial reforms of the existing conventional confiscation mechanisms. This approach implies identification of the interests of all stakeholders (victims, communities, defendants, third parties) and better protection for their interests. In addition, it promotes the prioritisation of the position of victims (in a broad sense) and communities over the position of the State. Importantly, it may inspire the legislatures to go further than the human rights protection perspective, i.e., encouraging them to search for more inclusive, consultative, and balanced confiscation procedures, allowing the stakeholders to play more 'proactive' roles.

Analysis of the evolution of EU confiscation policy over time shows that it already recognises some restorative aspects of confiscation, but in principle, it is still programmed to achieve traditional objectives attributed to confiscation, centred around the idea of preventing profit from crime, along with crime control. However, care should be taken to avoid overemphasising these objectives of confiscation, especially in view of the known problems with estimating the scale of 'criminal profits', or confirming the effectiveness of confiscation in crime control (see, e.g., Reuter 1984; Naylor 1999; Forsaith et al. 2012; Bullock and Lister 2014; Levi 2015; Europol 2023).[1]

The rhetoric of EU confiscation policy is consistently underpinned by the phrase 'crime does not pay'. It is worth remembering that this phrase was initially related to a certain moral attitude. For instance, in the article 'Reformation of Adults' published in *The Law Magazine and Law Review, Or Quarterly Journal of Jurisprudence* (1860), 8(15), the author pondered on the reflections of convicted serving a prison sentence in isolation from other fellow-prisoners and supposed that the earliest thought of such a person 'will probably be that crime does not pay' (89), and in a broader perspective, that '[a]mongst the men, it will be a sense of self-interest — a feeling that crime does not pay, and that honesty is the best policy' (94). One might wonder whether the incorporation of this catchphrase in the underpinnings of public policies concerning confiscation has in fact limited recognition of the complex objective of confiscation.

The Law Commission of England and Wales began work on a review of the post-conviction mechanism in 2018 and in its final report (2022) identified the

DOI: 10.4324/9781003465829-7

range of possible objectives that may be associated with confiscation, from taking away the profits of crime, through punishing, deterring and disrupting criminal activity, and ending with compensating the victims.[2] Nonetheless, the spectrum of the possible objectives of confiscation, with which it may be tasked at the policy level, is broader than indicated in that description, especially considering its social potential. This book firstly argues that any comprehensive discussion of the CPC should begin with properly identifying its complex objectives, and secondly, that EU confiscation policy shows that due consideration has not yet been given to this fundamental question.

The possible objectives of confiscation can be grouped as follows:

(1) restoring the status *quo ante* (before a crime), not profiting from crime,
(2) punishment,
(3) controlling crime,
(4) compensating the victims of crime,
(5) returning confiscated assets to the populations affected by or vulnerable to a crime,
(6) strengthening civil society,
(7) fostering public confidence in the criminal justice system,[3]
(8) and contributing to a culture of legality.[4]

One might argue that some of these objectives are results of confiscation rather than its objectives, but how they are approached only depends on the perspective adopted. All of the possible objectives of confiscation indicated may be incorporated within policy questions and goals. Given the wide range of objectives which may be attributed to confiscation, one might also conclude that EU policy does yet not sufficiently promote the wider modern concept of confiscation.

Before answering the question of the possibilities of increasing the restorativeness of EU law-making policy on the CPC, its present development should be considered. Adopting the perspective that this policy is a dynamic, still-evolving process, it becomes clear that over time it has incorporated many elements included in the minimalist restorative approach. Especially in the post-Lisbon period, when it started explicitly referring to ‘restorative justice’. However, these references were made in a general manner, without delving into the concrete definition of ‘restorative justice’, or exploring its various concepts.[5] For instance, the protection of the rights of defendants and third parties in the EU confiscation scheme has been strengthened over time, and endeavours have been taken to improve the position of victims. Nevertheless, despite being emphasised in the rhetoric of EU policy, the latter issue has not fully translated into concrete solutions in EU law, which was initially silent about the position of victims in confiscation settings, and then only approached victims’ claims from the negative side, i.e., that a confiscation measure should not prevent the victims from seeking compensation (Article 8(10) of Directive 2014/42/EU). The perception of confiscation is constantly evolving in EU policy, as reflected by the recent mutual recognition and harmonising instruments – Regulation 2018/1805 and Directive 2024/1260 – both of which better recognise the possibilities of using the confiscation mechanism to compensate victims of crime, and even further, try to prioritise the interests of victims over the interests of the State. For the first time in EU confiscation law, Directive 2024/1260 encourages MS to use confiscated assets to 'contribute to mechanisms to support third countries' affected by situations addressed in Union restrictive measures (Article 19(2) of Directive 2024/1260). However, there is still much to be done in this field.

In addition, a new approach to victims' rights emerged in Directive 2024/1260, which affirms that victims' claims should be embedded into and satisfied directly within the confiscation mechanism. Nevertheless, the wording of Article 18(1–4) of Directive 2024/1260 could be clearer for the legislatures, as it still leaves room for differing interpretations, especially in the context of Article 18(5) of that Directive still approaching the victims' rights from a negative side. In view of the above, requiring MS to enable the possibility of satisfying victims' rights directly from confiscated assets, in a manner that leaves no room for doubt, and requiring that victims must be informed about their rights in this respect, seems to be a convincing option for effectively connecting confiscation and compensation schemes in national legal orders.

Analysing EU confiscation policy from the angle of a minimalist restorative approach to justice reveals that it does not exploit the full social potential of confiscation. This potential may be effectively unleashed, for example, by introducing an obligation (rather than optional suggestions, as at present) requiring MS to enable the broad reuse of confiscated assets for public interest and social purposes. Another aspect is the possibility of using confiscation to foster public confidence in the criminal justice system and promote a culture of legality, especially by introducing a rule that confirms confiscated assets are to be returned to the populations affected by or vulnerable to crime in a transparent and publicly visible manner (see, e.g., Forsaith et al. 2012; Montaldo 2015). This would require centring the EU confiscation scheme more around the interests of victims and communities, shifting away from the existing State-centric models. Additional benefits from redirecting EU confiscation policy in this way may include the reinvestment of confiscated assets into these areas in which the EU has supporting competences (protection and improvement of human health, culture, education, vocational training, youth, and sport). In the long term, this may translate into strengthening civil society and increasing the resilience of communities against crime, two constant concerns of the EU and vitally important to its interests and the effectiveness of its policy in many areas.

It should not be forgotten that EU policy is under a certain amount of positive pressure to effectively influence domestic legal orders in a more restorative direction, for instance by enabling support for grassroots initiatives aimed at strengthening the resilience of communities to crime, and thus bolstering achievement of objectives traditionally attributed to confiscation (crime control, not profiting from crime, etc.). Persuasive arguments in this respect have already been delivered to the EU lawmaker by various actors supporting confiscation-related legislative procedures (e.g., LIBE;[6] Basel Institute on Governance;[7] EESC[8]). The 'double constructiveness' of confiscation has already been observed by the EP, which stated in the Resolution of 2011 that the social reuse of confiscated assets 'both helps to prevent organised crime and has the effect of boosting economic and social development' (8).[9] This aspect has also been addressed in the subject literature. As indicated by Vettori and Di Nicola (2017), the reuse of confiscated assets for social purposes across the EU may contribute to a '"powered-by-citizens" fight against crime' (321).

A comparative analysis of Polish, German, and French law has shown that these national confiscation schemes reflect many of the gaps previously identified in EU law standards of confiscation, and these schemes may be seen as an extension of EU confiscation policy. The main observation is that EU law has offered national legislatures very little added value in the area of using confiscation mechanisms to compensate the victims of crime or support communities affected by or vulnerable to crime. It also does not promote playing proactive roles in confiscation procedures for victims, communities, and defendants, for instance by encouraging MS to search for innovative legal solutions enabling communication between these stakeholders on possible ways of restoring the *status quo* before a crime and repairing harm. Making a confiscation scheme more restorative does not end with strengthening human rights protections, all the more so given that the contents of these rights are often arbitrarily addressed by public authorities, along with determining the best way of protecting them.

It should be also remembered that the position of defendants in the EU confiscation scheme still needs to be improved, especially by mitigating the procedural risk and excessive legislative reach inherent in the legal construct of extended confiscation promoted in EU law, which, starting from Directive 2014/42/EU, is no longer only targeted at the most serious and organised crime, and accordingly, at high-profile offenders. This construct has willingly been implemented by MS, because it extends the powers of their public authorities to capture assets deemed as illicit, under the lessened standard of proof. In addition, EU confiscation policy does not recognise the relationship between the method of calculation of assets to be applied in confiscation settings and the appropriate choice of criminal or civil routes by national legislatures. This issue should be detailed in policy questions and solutions, because whether extended confiscation is based on the 'gross' (profit) principle or the 'net' principle may be critical in determining its legal nature, i.e., whether it amounts to a criminal penalty (because of the surplus element of 'hardship') for which the standards of criminal procedure apply, or whether its function is intended to restoring the previous financial condition (the status before a crime) justifying the use of civil route (see more in Vogel 2015).

In sum, the EU should put greater legal pressure on effectively reorienting national confiscation schemes towards a more restorative direction. Accordingly, EU law should take advantage of its full capabilities to help national legislatures reconsider the dominant position of the State in domestic confiscation mechanisms, moving to favour victims and communities. Nonetheless, for public authorities, redirecting of asset flows means that confiscated assets will not be primarily assigned to the State budget or national incentivisation schemes but returned to the populations. Thus, it would be difficult for the EU to use soft law means to reinforce changes which would prevent public authorities from benefiting from confiscation mechanisms. This should be seen also in light of the comparative analysis results, which showed that EU law had not effectively influenced national legislation to enable broad social reuse of confiscated assets. National developments in this area instead represented genuine nationally originated and varied concepts, without drawing inspiration from EU law. Regrettably, the new Directive 2024/1260 still pursues the path of soft law recommendations and introduces no strict legal obligations for the MS in this respect.

Rethinking EU law-making policy on the CPC towards a more restorative direction should also involve a reconsideration of the narrow concept of 'victim' adopted in Directive 2012/29/EU (Article 2(1)(a)), especially in view of the broad concept of 'crime' which is presented therein (Recital 9 of the Preamble). Resolving this matter would be relevant for the position of victims not only in EU confiscation law but also for the entire framework of EU law addressing victims' interests. Finally, redefining the objectives of confiscation and the concept of a 'victim' (encompassing its societal dimensions) at the EU policy level could drive further changes in standards for confiscation presented by other standard setters, as ongoing dialogue between all parties motivates mutual development.

Taking all this into consideration, the restorativeness of EU law-making policy on the CPC may be enhanced by aligning its questions and goals with the needs and interests of people – primarily the EU's citizens and residents, but also populations from third countries victimised by a profitable crime, the proceeds of which are situated within the EU territory. From this perspective, MS play the role of the local intermediaries of this policy and not its main addressees. The integration of the three strengths of the minimalist restorative approach may help deliver desirable policy changes. Firstly, by critically rethinking the very objective attributed to confiscation at the EU policy level, and tasking confiscation with the restorative objectives of restoring the status *quo ante* (before a crime) and repairing the harm caused by a crime (in a broad sense, encompassing individual and societal dimensions). Secondly, by reconsidering the position of the State as the main beneficiary of traditional confiscation mechanisms, and instead centring these mechanisms around the interests of victims and communities. Thirdly, through better safeguarding of the interests of all stakeholders (victims, communities, defendants, third parties). The interests of defendants and third parties especially should not be overlooked. This group of stakeholders, as the addressees of confiscation decisions, should have the possibility of recognition of the harm done by a crime and dialogue with other stakeholders (harmed by a crime) about the possibilities of repairing 'conscious harm'.

'Law' and 'policy' are intertwined and autonomous at the same time. In principle, however, the content of 'law', considered as an 'object' and an 'agent' of integration (Azoulai 2016), is decided at the 'law-making policy' level. Accordingly, when contemplating how to increase the restorativeness of this policy, the sophisticated juridical nature of confiscation escaping the civil-criminal dichotomy, and the difficulties identified in the area of human rights protection when departing from the criminal standard of proof in confiscation settings, should all be taken into account. From this perspective, adopting a twofold approach seems the most sustainable option for the legislatures, including the EU, involving the interests of all stakeholders in a 'confiscation case' (victims, communities, defendants, third parties) and also the interest of the States. The proposed approach is focused, on the one hand, on developing policy questions and goals consistent with the restorative approach to justice, and on the other, on the appropriate choice of criminal or civil routes for confiscation (see also Vogel 2015). This choice is determined by the inextricably linked issues of 'law-making policy' (the objectives of confiscation determined by the legislature) and 'law' (the legal construct of confiscation).

Notes

1 Europol, 'The Other Side of the Coin', European Financial and Economic Crime Threat Assessment (2023). https://www.europol.europa.eu/cms/sites/default/files/documents/The%20Other%20Side%20of%20the%20Coin%20-%20Analysis%20of%20Financial%20and%20Economic%20Crime%20%28EN%29.pdf (9.10.2024).

2 Law Commission, Confiscation of the proceeds of crime after conviction: a final report, 2022, No. 410, 63.

3 See Forsaith et al. 2012, 19–22.

4 See Montaldo 2015.

5 However, cf. definition of restorative justice adopted for the purposes of Directive 2012/29/EU (Article 2(1)(d)).

6 EP, LIBE, Report on the proposal for a directive of the European Parliament and of the Council on the freezing and confiscation of proceeds of crime in the European Union, 20.5.2013, Document A7-0178/2013.

7 Basel Institute on Governance, Note requested by the LIBE, 'The need for new EU legislation allowing the assets confiscated from criminal organisations to be used for civil society and in particular for social purposes', (2012), http://www.europarl.europa.eu/RegData/etudes/note/join/2012/462437/IPOL-LIBE_NT(2012)462437_EN.pdf (3.07.2024).

8 EESC, Opinion: Asset recovery and confiscation, SOC/738, 14.12.2022. https://dm-publicapi.eesc.europa.eu/v1/documents/P6FJPSUHKDC2-1050578159-9846/download (12.07.2024).

9 EP, Resolution of 25 October 2011 on organised crime in the European Union (2010/2309(INI)), P7_TA(2011)0459. See also EP, Report on organised crime in the European Union, 25.11.2010, Document A7-0333/2011. https://www.europarl.europa.eu/doceo/document/A-7-2011-0333_EN.html (28.06.2024).

References

Azoulai, Loïc. 2016. ""Integration Through Law" and Us." *ICON* 14 (2): 449–463. https://doi.org/10.1093/icon/mow024.

Bullock, Karen, and Stuart Lister. 2014. "Post-Conviction Confiscation of Assets in England and Wales: Rhetoric and Reality." In *Dirty Assets. Emerging Issues in the Regulation of Criminal and Terrorist Assets*, edited by Colin King and Clive Walker, 47–69. Farnham: Ashgate Pub.

Forsaith, James, Barrie Irving, Eva Nanopoulos, and Mihaly Fazekas. 2012. *Study for an Impact Assessment on a Proposal for a New Legal Framework on the Confiscation and Recovery of Criminal Assets*. RAND Europe, EU. Accessed July 4, 2024. https://home-affairs.ec.europa.eu/system/files/2020-09/external_study_used_as_a_basis_for_the_commission_ia_october_2012_en.pdf.

Levi, Michael. 2015. "The Impacts of Organised Crime in the EU: Some Preliminary Thoughts on Measurement Difficulties." *Contemporary Social Science* 11 (4): 392–402.
Montaldo, Stefano. 2015. "Directive 2014/42/EU and Social Reuse of Confiscated Assets in the EU: Advancing a Culture of Legality." *New Journal of European Criminal Law* 6 (2): 195–212.
Naylor, R. T. 1999. "Wash-out: A Critique of Follow-the-money Methods in Crime Control Policy." *Crime, Law and Social Change* 32: 1–58. https://doi.org/10.1023/A:1008386203362.
Reuter, Peter. 1984. "The (Continued) Vitality of Mythical Numbers." *The Public Interest* 75: 135–147.
Vettori, Barbara, and Andrea Di Nicola. 2017. "The Social Reuse of Confiscated Assets in EU Member States: From Current Experiences to an EU policy for a 'Powered-by-Citizens' Fight Against Crime." In *Chasing Criminal Money: Challenges and Perspectives on Asset Recovery in the EU*, edited by Katalin Ligeti and Michele Simonato, 321–343. Oxford: Hart Pub.
Vogel, Joachim. 2015. "The Legal Construction that Property Can Do Harm." In *Non Conviction-Based Confiscation in Europe*, edited by Jon Petter Rui and Ulrich Sieber, 225–243. Berlin: Duncker & Humblot.

Index

Note: Page reference followed by 'n' indicate note numbers.

Papier | Fördert gute Waldnutzung
FSC® C083411

Kolibri 360 GmbH
Ferdinand-Jühlke-Straße 7
99095 Erfurt, Deutschland
produktsicherheit@kolibri360.de